PEOPLE AND POWER IN SCOTLAND

Prof. T. C. Smout, MA, PhD, FRSE, FBA.

PEOPLE AND POWER IN SCOTLAND

ESSAYS IN HONOUR OF
T.C. SMOUT

edited by
Roger Mason and Norman Macdougall

With many thanks for
many things !

Christopher .

JOHN DONALD PUBLISHERS LTD
EDINBURGH

ISBN 0 85976 392 7

British Library Cataloguing in Publication Data
A catalogue record for this book is available from the
British Library.

Typeset by ROM Data Corporation Ltd, Falmouth, Cornwall

Printed and bound by J.W. Arrowsmith Ltd, Bristol

Contents

Acknowledgements

The editors would like to thank the contributors for their enthusiasm and
punctuality, and Mrs. Margaret Richards for her invaluable assistance in
preparing some of the material for publication. Above all, we are grateful to
Dr. Alexander Grant Gordon of William Grant and Sons Ltd. for a most
generous contribution towards the costs of producing this volume.

St. Andrews, 1992
Roger Mason
Norman Macdougall

Professor T.C. Smout: An Appreciation

In the early summer of 1979, after more than five-and-a-half centuries of existence, Scotland's oldest university finally committed itself to the creation of a department of Scottish History. That it did so at all was due in no small measure to the remarkable individual appointed as professor of Scottish History in that year. The choice was in itself unusual, for Christopher Smout was not, in Pitscottie's famous phrase about one of his Lindsay ancestors, 'ane man of the auld world', but a distinguished social historian of early modern and modern Scotland who had held a personal chair in Economic History at Edinburgh University for some nine years. Cynics were quick to prophesy that he would not stay long at St. Andrews, and various academic institutions in Britain and the United States were cited as his inevitable destination in a matter of months at most. Twelve years later Christopher Smout *is* leaving St. Andrews, but to retire, having tripled the number of staff in the department which he created — and that in a period of harsh university cutbacks — having introduced single honours degrees in Scottish History and Economic and Social History, taken a major role in the establishment of the Scottish Institute of Maritime Studies, and — perhaps most important of all — having consistently encouraged and stimulated historians working in areas of the subject which were not primarily his own.

Christopher Smout's enthusiasm for Scottish History goes back more than thirty years to his student days at Clare College, Cambridge. Having graduated MA (1st class) in both parts of the tripos in 1956, he looked for an original research area and found it in a study of Scottish trade in the late seventeenth century. For this he received the degree of PhD in 1959, and in the same year was appointed assistant lecturer at Edinburgh University, the beginning of an association with Edinburgh which was to last for twenty years. A spate of publications on Scottish social and economic history –including a lively book, *Scottish Trade on the Eve of Union 1660–1707* – throughout the 1960s paralleled rapid promotion at Edinburgh – to lecturer in 1962, reader in 1966, and professor, with a personal chair in Economic History, in 1970.

In 1969 he produced the book with which, perhaps more than any other, his name is still associated – *A History of the Scottish People, 1560–1830* –

one of the very few scholarly works to commend itself to a vast popular audience, awarded a Scottish Arts Council prize, and rightly described by one reviewer as 'an unrivalled introduction to the life of the people of Scotland from the formation of the nation to the great flowering of Scottish intellect and technology in the decades around Waterloo'. The same writer, it is true, went on to complain that there was not enough in the book about prices, wages and the cost of living; yet it was perhaps the absence of endless forbidding tables and graphs which made *A History of the Scottish People* an immediately accessible and attractive book to so many people. Above all, it was, and is, a very good read. Those teaching or studying Scottish history in 1970, having been subjected to a decade during which economic and social historians vied with one another in their efforts to be dull or obscure, or both, fell upon Smout's book with a mixture of gratitude, enthusiasm and excitement. Suddenly, the social history of Scotland seemed to make a new kind of sense.

A steady flow of articles – and five edited or co-edited books – appeared in the 1970s, during which time Christopher Smout also held ESRC research grants for demographic and poor law history; and in 1978 he was made a Fellow of the Royal Society of Edinburgh. Then in 1979, the vacancy in the chair of Scottish History at St. Andrews, created by the appointment of Geoffrey Barrow to Edinburgh, offered him the chance to move to Fife. The job at St. Andrews was no safe haven, but rather a considerable challenge; for in 1979, although there were a number of scholars in the university with research interests in Scottish History, and a general goodwill towards the subject, there was no Scottish History department, and therefore no budget, no departmental library of any consequence, and of course no single honours degree. Before accepting the post, Christopher Smout insisted on the appointment of one other full-time lecturer in Scottish History; and William Grant & Sons Ltd., who two years before had endowed the Glenfiddich Research Fellowship in Scottish History at St. Andrews, generously renewed it for a further three years (and have indeed continued to do so ever since). So the department in 1979–80 numbered three – the new professor, a lecturer, and a research fellow. St. Andrews is a relatively small place; but even within it the fledgling Scottish History department had no geographical coherence, with the professor in one room close to St. Salvator's Tower, the lecturer and research fellow in the Psychology department building on the other side of town, and the departmental secretary – without a phone – in the attic of the printing department in North Street.

Faced with these problems, a more cautious individual might have opted for a narrow coverage of parts of the subject, with a concentration on the period he knew best. From the start, however, Christopher Smout chose a bold course – the department would teach Scottish History from Roman times, through the medieval and early modern period, to the present day, and would offer as many honours courses in the subject as possible with a view to being able to introduce a single honours degree at the earliest possible opportunity. He pursued this aim with missionary zeal, forging alliances with other St. Andrews history departments, offering them service teaching and acquiring it in return, building a close relationship with the economic and social historians (and eventually producing the brainwave of a joint second year course which would make single honours degrees in both Scottish History and Economic and Social History possible), bringing into the department Dr. Colin Martin, a first-rate maritime archaeologist (with whom, together with Dr. Robert Prescott of the Psychology department, he would found the Scottish Institute of Maritime Studies at St. Andrews), and constantly haranguing the Faculty on its duty to support Scottish History in Scotland's oldest university.

Underpinning this crusade was Chris Smout's popularity with students, both undergraduates and postgraduates. His enthusiasm for his subject was infectious, and was reflected in the growing numbers of students who flocked to his classes as the department gained strength. Unlike some academics, who seem to believe that by some mysterious alchemy they confer lustre on the university which employs them by being there as seldom as possible, Chris Smout has been throughout a hard-working teacher who combined a hectic schedule of research, lectures in the USA, Canada and Europe, with teaching hours in St. Andrews which on their own would have exhausted many younger men. In lectures, tutorials and seminars, he preferred to dress casually, often in a tee-shirt and jeans, a habit which earned him the affectionate student nickname of 'the Oxfam professor'. To his colleagues in Scottish History he was invariably 'the Boss', to those in other departments 'the Hustler'.

Throughout his twelve years at St. Andrews, Chris Smout has been the ideal departmental head, leading from the front and trusting his staff to follow, supporting and encouraging, but not interfering with, their work. The result of this leadership has been the early attraction to the department of a third member of staff under the UGC's 'new blood' scheme, a string of important publications, the largest research income of any department in the Faculty of Arts, lively programmes of research seminars, workshops and conferences, and the emergence of St. Andrews as an important centre – at least comparable with the other ancient Scottish universities – for academic Scottish History. The fact that all this has been achieved against a background of ever-deepening cuts in university funding since 1981 is a remarkable tribute to his qualities of leadership; indeed, he even turned the continuing crisis to St. Andrews' advantage by securing the transfer of two more staff from Dundee and Heriot-Watt universities in 1988, and a third from Aberdeen in 1989. Thus the department of Scottish History at St. Andrews enters the 1990s immeasurably stronger than at the start of the 1980s.

Together with these successes within St. Andrews itself, Christopher Smout has further enhanced his reputation throughout the 1980s with many external achievements. His most important recent publication, the keenly awaited sequel to his 1969 *History of the Scottish People*, appeared in 1986. Entitled *A Century of the Scottish People 1830–1950*, it combines the same qualities of scholarship, clarity and readability, easily crossing the narrow frontiers of academia to embrace a wide reading public, and it was duly awarded the Agnes Mure MacKenzie Prize for Scottish Historical scholarship by the Saltire Society. Recognition of his growing reputation, in and out of Scotland, continued; he served as president of the Scottish History Society between 1984 and 1988, as chairman of the Scottish Economic and Social History Society from 1988; and in 1988 he was made a Fellow of the British Academy.

Chris Smout's principal interest, apart from his family and his work, is bird-watching, which he pursues with a single-minded passion, and which probably explains his allegiance to Anstruther as a home throughout his years at St. Andrews. It is an interest happily shared by his wife, Anne-Marie, who has published a book on the birds of Fife. Both Smouts have taken part enthusiastically in Fife competitions to identify as many different species as possible in a single day, winning on at least one occasion with a total of 108; and the entire Scottish History department is unlikely to forget the occasion when, having for years searched in vain to identify a waxwing in Fife, Chris brought a departmental meeting to an abrupt end, rushed to his car, and disappeared, when a First Arts student reported sighting hundreds of wax-wings at Guardbridge. His priorities were undoubtedly correct; anyway, no-one can now remember what was on the agenda of the meeting.

Even given much more space than is available to us, it would be difficult to do proper justice to Christopher Smout's scholarly achievements; however, the imposing list of his publications provides more eloquent testimony to these than mere words of praise. And the recipient of this *festschrift* would be – justifiably – indignant if we were to imply that retiral meant an end of historical writing or lecturing. Both show every sign of continuing apace; a book is expected this year on the history of prices, wages, food and living standards in Scotland 1580–1780, following years of work on the subject by Chris and his research assistant, Alexander Gibson; and the history of the Scottish environment since 1600, and of environmentalism in Scotland since 1750, already themes of his Raleigh Lectures in Glasgow and London in 1990, occupy more and more of his time. Since 1985, in fact, he has been a member of the Committee for Scotland of the Nature Conservancy Council, a post to which he was reappointed by the secretary of state in 1989.

In retirement, Chris Smout will never be idle, even though he may feel the occasional twinge of regret at having just missed the pleasures of academic audit. We are delighted that he will maintain his connection with St. Andrews as an honorary professor, and also, for the next few years, as director of St. John's House, the university's Centre for Advanced Historical Studies, his 'contact with reality', as he describes it himself. This volume is a modest tribute to the man, and to a part – we like to think an important part – of his career. We hope that it reflects at least some of his interests, and that it is also representative of the wide range of historical themes which he stimulated and supported throughout his years at St. Andrews.

T.C. SMOUT: A List of Publications

A Books

1. *Scottish Trade on the Eve of Union 1660–1707* (Edinburgh and London, 1963).
2. *A History of the Scottish People, 1560–1830* (London and New York, 1969; 2nd edn 1971; paperback edn 1972).
3. *A Century of the Scottish People, 1830–1950* (London, 1986; paperback edn 1987).
4. (with Sydney Wood) *Scottish Voices, 1745–1960* (London, 1990).
5. (with M. Flinn, J. Gillespie, N. Hill, A. Maxwell & R. Mitchison), *Scottish Population History from the 17th Century to the 1930s* (Cambridge, 1977).
6. (with Ian Levitt), *The State of the Scottish Working Class in 1843: A Statistical and Spatial Inquiry based on Data from the Poor Law Commission Report of 1844* (Edinburgh, 1979).

B Edited volumes

7. (with M.W. Flinn), *Essays in Social History* (Oxford, 1974).
8. (with L.M. Cullen), *Comparative Aspects of Scottish and Irish Economic and Social History 1600–1900* (Edinburgh, 1977).
9. *The Search for Wealth and Stability: Essays in Economic and Social History Presented to M.W. Flinn* (London, 1979).
10. *Scotland and Europe, 1200–1850* (Edinburgh, 1986).
11. (with Antoni Maczak), *Gründung und Bedeutung kleinerer Städte im nördlichen Europa der frühen Neuzeit*, Wolfenbütteler Forschungen, Band 47 (Wiesbaden, 1991).

C Edited sources and archival lists

12. 'Letters from Dumfries to a Scottish Factor at Rotterdam, 1676–1683', *Transactions of the Dumfriesshire and Galloway Natural History and Antiquarian Society*, 3rd series 38 (1960), 157–167.
13. 'Report on the Lead-mining Papers at Hopetoun House, West Lothian, 1625–1799', cyclostyled and deposited in National Library of Scotland, 1962.
14. 'Sir John Clerk's Observations on the Present Circumstances of Scotland, 1730', *Scottish History Society Miscellany X* (Scottish History Society, 1965), 175–212.
15. 'Customhouse Letters to the Officers at Dunbar, 1765', *Transactions of the East Lothian Antiquarians and Field Naturalists' Society*, 11 (1968), 17–36.
16. *The Statistical Account of Scotland 1791–1799*, ed. D.J. Withrington *et al.*, vol. ii, *The Lothians* (Edinburgh, 1975).

17. 'Journal of Henry Kalmeter's Travels in Scotland, 1719–1720', *Scottish Industrial History: A Miscellany* (Scottish History Society, 1978), 1–52.

18. 'US Consular Reports: A Source for Scottish Economic Historians', *Scottish Historical Review*, 58 (1979), 179–185.

19. 'American Consular Reports on Scotland', *Business History*, 23 (1982), 304–8.

20. Edwin Muir, *Scottish Journey*, ed. with an introduction (Edinburgh, 1979; paperback edn., London, 1985).

D Papers in books and periodicals

21. 'Scottish Commercial Factors in the Baltic at the End of the 17th Century', *Scottish Historical Review*, 39 (1960), 122–128.

22. 'Some Problems of Timber Supply in later 17th-Century Scotland', *Scottish Forestry*, 14 (1960), 3–13.

23. 'The Development and Enterprise of Glasgow, 1556–1707', *Scottish Journal of Political Economy*, 7 (1960), 194–212.

24. 'The Overseas Trade of Ayrshire, 1660–1707', *Ayrshire Archaeological and Natural History Collections*, 6 (1958–60), 56–80.

25. 'The Early Scottish Sugar Houses, 1660–1720', *Economic History Review*, 2nd series 14 (1961), 240–253.

26. 'The Lead Mines at Wanlockhead', *Transactions of the Dumfriesshire and Galloway Natural History and Antiquarian Society*, 3rd series 39 (1962), 144–58.

27. 'The Trade of East Lothian at the End of the 17th Century', *Transactions of the East Lothian Antiquarian and Field Naturalists' Society*, 9 (1963), 67–78.

28. 'The Erskines of Mar and the Development of Alloa, 1689–1825', *Scottish Studies*, 7 (1963), 57–74.

29. 'Scottish Landowners and Economic Growth, 1650–1850', *Scottish Journal of Political Economy*, 11 (1964), 218–34.

30. 'The Anglo-Scottish Union of 1707: 1. The Economic Background', *Economic History Review*, 2nd series 16 (1964), 455–467.

31. (with Alexander Fenton), 'Scottish Agriculture Before the Improvers – An Exploration', *Agricultural History Review*, 13 (1965), 73–93.

32. 'Lead Mining in Scotland, 1650–1850', in P.L. Payne (ed.), *Studies in Scottish Business History* (London, 1967), 103–35.

33. 'The Glasgow Merchant Community in the 17th Century', *Scottish Historical Review*, 47 (1968), 53–71.

34. 'The Road to Union', in G. Holmes (ed.), *Britain after the Glorious Revolution* (London, 1969), 176–96.

35. 'The Landowner and the Planned Village in Scotland, 1730–1830', in N.T. Phillipson and R. Mitchison (ed.), *Scotland in the Age of Improvement* (Edinburgh, 1970), 73–106.

36. 'Union of the Parliaments', in G. Menzies (ed.), *The Scottish Nation* (London, 1972), 147–59.

37. 'An Ideological Struggle: The Highland Clearances', *Scottish International* (February, 1972), 13–16.

38. 'The Lessons of Norwegian Agrarian History: A Review Article', *Scottish Historical Review*, 53 (1974), 69–76.

39. 'Rural Life and Famous Men', in R. Prentice (ed.), *The National Trust for Scotland Guide* (London, 1976), 225–232.

40. 'Aspects of Sexual Behaviour in 19th-Century Scotland', in A.A. MacLaren (ed.), *Social Class in Scotland: Past and Present* (Edinburgh, 1976), 55–85; reprinted in P. Laslett, K. Oosterveen and R.M. Smith (ed.), *Bastardy in its Comparative History* (London 1980), 192–216.

41. 'Famine and Famine-Relief in Scotland', in Cullen and Smout (ed.), *Comparative Aspects* (item 8 above), 21–31.

42. 'The Scottish Identity', in R. Underwood (ed.), *The Future of Scotland* (London, 1977), 11–21.

43. 'Illegitimacy – A Reply', *Scottish Journal of Sociology*, 2 (1977), 97–104.

44. (with Ian Levitt), 'Some Weights and Measures in Scotland, 1843', *Scottish Historical Review*, 56 (1977), 146–52.

45. 'Provost Drummond', University of Edinburgh, Extra Mural Department Pamphlet, 1978.

46. 'Problems of Modernisation: Non-Economic Factors in 18th-Century Scotland', in H. Van der Wee *et al.* (ed.), *Proceedings of the Fifth International Conference of Economic History, Leningrad 1970* (The Hague, 1978), vii, 73–88.

47. 'Coping with Plague in 16th and 17th Century Scotland', *Scotia*, 2 (1978), 19–33.

48. 'Scotland and England, 16th-18th Centuries: Is Dependency a Symptom or a Cause of Under-Development?', *Review*, 3 (1980), 601–630.

49. 'The Strange Intervention of Edward Twistleton: Paisley in Depression, 1841–43', in Smout (ed.), *The Search for Wealth and Stability* (item 9 above), 218–42.

50. 'Scotland in the 17th and 18th Centuries: A Satellite Economy?', in S. Dyrvik, K. Mykland & J. Oldervoel (ed.), *The Satellite State in the 17th and 18th Centuries* (Bergen, 1979), 9–35.

51. 'Centre and Periphery – Some Thoughts on Scotland as a Case Study', *Journal of Common Market Studies*, 18 (1980), 256–271.

52. 'Lifestyles in the Lowlands of Scotland: 17th to 19th Centuries', and 'Lifestyles in the Scottish Highlands: 17th to 19th Centuries', *World Conference on Records: Preserving Our Heritage* (Salt Lake City, 1980), no. 426, 1–13, and no. 428, 1–14.

53. 'The Social Condition of Scotland in the 1840s', Dow Lecture, University of Dundee, 1981.

54. 'Scottish Marriage, Regular and Irregular, 1500–1940', in R.B. Outhwaite (ed.), *Marriage and Society: Studies in the Social History of Marriage* (London, 1981), 204–36.

55. 'Born again at Cambuslang: New Evidence on Popular Religion and Literacy in 18th-Century Scotland', *Past and Present*, 97 (1982), 114–127.

56. 'Tours in the Scottish Highlands from the 18th to the 20th Centuries', *Northern Scotland*, 5 (1983), 99–121.

57. 'Where had the Scottish Economy got to by the third quarter of the 18th Century?', in I. Hont & M. Ignatieff (ed.), *Wealth and Virtue: The Shaping of Political Economy in the Scottish Enlightenment* (Cambridge, 1983), 45–72.

58. (with I.Levitt), 'Farm Workers' Incomes in 1843', in T.M.Devine (ed.), *Farm Servants and Labour in Lowland Scotland, 1770–1914* (Edinburgh, 1984), 156–87.

59. 'Landowners in Scotland, Ireland and Denmark in the Age of Improvement', *Scandinavian Journal of History*, 12 (1987), 79–97.

60. 'Peasant and Lord: The Institutions Controlling Scottish Rural Society, 1500–1800', *Recueil de la Societé Jean Bodin*, 44 (1987), 499–524.

61. 'The Burgh of Montrose and the Union of 1707 – a Document', *Scottish Historical Review*, 66 (1987), 183–4.

62. (with A. Gibson), 'Food and Hierarchy in Scotland, 1550–1650', in L. Leneman (ed.), *Perspectives in Scottish Social History: Essays in Honour of Rosalind Mitchison* (Aberdeen, 1988), 33–52.

63. (with A. Gibson and L.M. Cullen), 'Wages and Comparative Development in Ireland and Scotland, 1565–1780', in R. Mitchison and P. Roebuck (ed.), *Economy and Society in Scotland and Ireland 1500–1939* (Edinburgh 1988), 105–116.

64. (with A. Gibson), 'Scottish Food and Scottish History, 1500–1800', in R. Houston and I.D. Whyte (ed.), *Scottish Society 1500–1800* (Cambridge, 1989), 59–84.

65. 'Problems of Nationalism, Identity and Improvement in Later 18th-Century Scotland', in T.M. Devine (ed.), *Improvement and Enlightenment* (Edinburgh, 1989), 1–21.

66. 'Scotland, 1850–1950', in F.M.L. Thompson (ed.), *Cambridge Social History of Britain* (Cambridge, 1990), i, 209–280.

1

The Man who would be King:
The Lieutenancy and Death of David,
Duke of Rothesay, 1378-1402

STEPHEN BOARDMAN

The death in 1402 of David, duke of Rothesay, the eldest son, heir and lieutenant of Robert III, has remained a rather mysterious episode despite a detailed account of Rothesay's "arrest" by the reliable contemporary chronicler Walter Bower, abbot of Inchcolm. Bower, revealing his clerical prejudices, judged that Rothesay's death came about as the result of the young duke's own moral failings, his dissolute, immoral and headstrong lifestyle.[1] The political objectives of the chief protagonists in the events of 1402, Rothesay and his uncle Robert, duke of Albany, and Rothesay's brother-in-law Archibald, 4th earl of Douglas, remain largely unexplored and unexplained.

Bower's description of Rothesay's arrest and death is a well-known and simple narrative. According to Bower, Rothesay was travelling to St. Andrews in order to occupy the episcopal castle when he was treacherously captured by members of his own retinue, namely Sir John Ramornie and Sir William Lindsay of Rossie, at Strathtyrum just outside St. Andrews city walls.[2] After his arrest Rothesay was imprisoned for a short period in the episcopal castle while his uncle Robert, duke of Albany, and Archibald, 4th earl of Douglas, held a council at Culross to decide what should be done with the young heir to the throne. After their deliberations Rothesay was moved from St. Andrews, heavily disguised, to Albany's own castle of Falkland where, on 25 or 26 March 1402, the young duke died of dysentery or starvation.[3] The dramatic events in and around St. Andrews in early 1402 were, to some extent, a reflection of long-term political tensions between Rothesay and his uncle which can only be fully explained by an examination of the origins of Rothesay's three year lieutenancy.

Rothesay's lieutenancy began in January 1399, in the wake of a disastrous royal siege of Dumbarton Castle in the autumn of 1398. The aim of the siege had been to remove Walter Danielston, the militant and secularised cleric who had seized control of the royal castle in 1397/8.[4] Walter Danielston was the younger brother of two prominent Renfrewshire lairds, Sir Robert and Sir William Danielston.[5] Sir Robert Danielston had been the custodian of Dumbarton Castle and sheriff of Dumbarton/Lennox, dying on some date between 26 April 1396 and 8 May 1397.[6] Sir Robert had succeeded his father Sir John Danielston as both sheriff of Dumbarton and custodian of the castle,[7] so that by 1397 the Danielston family had occupied these offices for at least thirty-seven years and probably considered that they were heritable. After Sir Robert's death Walter Danielston had forcibly occupied the royal castle in defence of his family's heritage. Walter, as a cleric, had no heirs of his own; however, Sir Robert had died leaving two daughters, one married to Sir William Cunningham of Kilmaurs, and the other to Sir Robert Maxwell, who was associated with Walter Danielston in an indenture of 18 December 1400 issued at Dumbarton.[8] In addition, Walter had a nephew, Patrick, who seems to have been a son of Sir William Danielston.[9] The reaction of the royal government to Danielston's occupation of Dumbarton had been to organise a huge siege of the fortress in 1398. For at least three months between early August and the end of October 1398, Robert III was at Dumbarton with a considerable army[10] which required substantial supplies of iron, wood (presumably for siege operations) and foodstuffs.[11] The intensity of the siege is shown by the fact that there was a three year hiatus in the rendering of accounts by the bailies of the burgh of Dumbarton between May 1397 and 13 May 1400,[12] on which later date the burgh was allowed to give in a reduced burghal ferm because of "guerre de uno anno dictorum trium annorum".

The ultimate failure of the royal siege to remove Danielston from Dumbarton seems to have seriously weakened the prestige of Robert III's government in general, and Robert, duke of Albany, in particular. Wyntoun, commenting on Danielston's occupation of Dumbarton, remarks that "Lithcow menyt in Louthiane, And syndry athir landis sare, Menyt, that evyr he gat in thare".[13] Linlithgow's displeasure would seem to have been based on the fact that the keeper of Dumbarton Castle was due an eighty merk pension from the burghal fermes, although there is no evidence to suggest that Danielston ever received this payment.[14] The discontent engendered by the collapse of the Dumbarton siege would seem to be reflected in the general council of January 1399, held in Perth, which appointed David, duke of Rothesay, as the king's lieutenant.[15] The council complained that "the mysgovernance of the reaulme and the defaut of the kepyng of the common law salde be imput to the kyng and his officeris", and decided that the king, because of his personal infirmity, was incapable of governing the realm or restraining transgressors and rebels. Walter Danielston's successful resistance to royal forces in late 1398 would have been uppermost in many men's minds as an example of royal ineffectiveness in January 1399. Rothesay's appointment as lieutenant may also have reflected a change in political influence within the government as a result of the confrontation with Danielston.

The political impetus behind the siege of Dumbarton came from the king's brother Robert, duke of Albany, who had a considerable interest in the fate of Dumbarton Castle and the sheriffship of Lennox after the death of Sir Robert Danielston. By the terms of an indenture of February 1392[16] between Robert, then earl of Fife, and Duncan, earl of Lennox, Robert's eldest son, Murdoch, was to marry Lennox's eldest daughter, to whom the right to the entire earldom of Lennox was to descend. By the same agreement Robert's son Murdoch and Lennox's daughter were to be given the lands and barony of Redhall, in Lothian, in conjunctfeftment. On 8 November 1392[17] Robert III gave his consent to the entailing of the earldom of Lennox to Murdoch Stewart and his heirs. From 1392 onwards, then, Robert, earl of Fife (later Albany), had a vested interest in augmenting the territorial and jurisdictional power of the earl of Lennox in the expectation that the ultimate beneficiary of his patronage would be his own son Murdoch.

In the marriage contract of February 1392[18] Robert, earl of Fife, who at that stage was guardian of the kingdom, transferred half of the revenues produced by the justiciary courts of Dumbarton and Stirling from lands within the earldom of Lennox to Duncan, and in a charter which is probably misdated 6 March 1401[19] Robert granted Duncan and his heirs under the terms of the 1392 entail the office of coroner of all the earldom of Lennox. The most important royal officer operating within the bounds of the earldom of Lennox was the sheriff of Dumbarton or Lennox, who also acted as custodian of the royal castle of Dumbarton. Duncan, earl of Lennox, and his father, Walter of Faslane, had already restricted the sheriff's influence within the earldom by obtaining formal royal grants of the 'wapinschawings' or 'weaponshowings' of the earldom, specifically exempting the earl, his men, tenants and vassals from the sheriff's authority in this respect.[20] Robert Danielston's death in 1396-7 raised the possibility that the sheriffship of Dumbarton and the custody of the castle could also be transferred to the earl of Lennox or one of his vassals and thus, in the long term, to the control of Murdoch Stewart. On 8 December 1396,[21] at Stirling, Robert III confirmed a resignation of the lands and barony of Redhall by his nephew Murdoch Stewart in favour of Sir William Cunningham, the younger, of Kilmaurs. Murdoch's resignation and the regrant to Sir William Cunningham may well have been part of a deal over the sheriffship of Lennox and the keepership of Dumbarton between Cunningham, who was married to Sir Robert Danielston's eldest daughter and heiress, and the earls of Fife and Lennox in the wake of Robert Danielston's death in the winter of 1396. Redhall was the barony which had been given to Murdoch Stewart and the earl of Lennox's daughter in conjunct fee by the indenture of February 1392, so that Duncan, earl of Lennox, must have given his approval to Murdoch's resignation. The duke of Albany's plans for Dumbarton Castle in 1397/8 can probably be discerned from the way in which he settled the Dumbarton issue after Rothesay's death in 1402. Firstly, Albany immediately attempted to remove Danielston from Dumbarton by transferring the belligerent cleric to the bishopric of St. Andrews which had been vacant since Walter Trail's death on some date between 5 March and 1 July 1401.[22] Walter Danielston died around Christmas 1402[23] and by 15 May 1403[24] the keepership of Dumbarton Castle and the sheriffship of Lennox were given to Walter Buchanan of that ilk as the result of an agreement between Walter and Duncan, earl of Lennox. The Lennox/Buchanan settlement appears to have been made with little or no reference to Robert III's right to appoint the constable of the royal castle and the sheriff, with the king, at Dumbarton, simply confirming arrangements already made between Lennox and Buchanan and "reservande till us and till our ayris sic as pertenys til our ryal Majeste". By 2 February 1404[25] Buchanan was styled "our" sheriff of Dumbarton in a charter by Robert III granting him the ward of Adam Gordon's lands and heirs. Walter Buchanan was a major tenant of the earls of Lennox and a frequent witness to Earl Duncan's charters,[26] and in 1392 had twice been associated with Robert, earl of Fife, and his son Murdoch, in charters issued at Stirling, the royal castle of which Fife was custodian.[27] The exact text of the agreement between Lennox and Buchanan is unrecorded, but we can assume that the earl and his heir, Murdoch Stewart, would have ensured that the earls of Lennox would maintain a high degree of control over the actions of the new sheriff and constable. In any case, the absorption of Dumbarton Castle and its associated sheriffdom into the Lennox interest would be guaranteed by the tenurial and personal relationships between the Buchanans and Murdoch Stewart, as heir to the earldom of Lennox. Walter Buchanan seems to have taken part in the Humbleton campaign of September 1402, probably in the service of Murdoch Stewart, and to have been captured with Murdoch by the English on 14 September 1402.[28] In addition, Buchanan's son, also Walter, married Murdoch Stewart's daughter Isobel.[29]

The extension of Lennox control in Dumbarton would thus seem to have been Robert, earl of Fife's objective in 1396-7, an aim thwarted by the sudden seizure of the royal fortress by Walter Danielston. The collapse of the Albany-inspired siege of Dumbarton seems to have precipitated the transfer of royal authority to the duke of Rothesay in January 1399. Rothesay's attitude towards Danielston's occupation of Dumbarton appears to have been less hostile; certainly no new attempt was made during the three years of Rothesay's lieutenancy to remove Danielston from the fortress.

Rothesay's growing political influence in late 1398 was reflected in a charter of 6 September 1398,[30] issued at Dumbarton during the siege of the castle, by which Robert III granted Rothesay the lands of the earldom of

Atholl. Rothesay's acquisition of a considerable territorial interest in northern Perthshire was not designed to improve the relationship between the young heir to the throne and his uncle. In the years after 1388, Albany had carved out a considerable territorial and jurisdictional power base in northern Perthshire at the expense of his brother Alexander Stewart, earl of Buchan, lord of Badenoch and Ross (better known as the Wolf of Badenoch).

During his period as guardian of the kingdom after December 1388,[31] Robert, then earl of Fife, launched a comprehensive attack on the position of Alexander Stewart as a major landowner and the chief representative of royal power in northern Perthshire and the central Highlands. Firstly, Alexander was replaced by Albany's son, Murdoch, as justiciar north of Forth.[32] In addition, Murdoch began to use the title lord of the Appin of Dull.[33] The Appin of Dull covered much of the western half of the earldom of Atholl and encompassed Strath Tay, Fortingall and Glen Lyon. Murdoch's use of the title coincided with the resignation by Isabella, countess of Fife, of her claims to Loch Tay, the Isle of Loch Tay, Strath Tay, Strathbraan and the barony of Strathord in favour of Murdoch's father Robert, earl of Fife, on 12 August 1389.[34] At around the same time Fife was given possession of another element of the Appin of Dull with a grant of the lands and barony of Fortingall.[35] Isabella's resignation and the grant of Fortingall meant that the earl of Fife and his son now sought to exercise control over a block of territory in Atholl and northern Perthshire stretching north and east from the barony of Glen Dochart which Fife had had in his possession since 1375.[36] After Fife's agreement with Duncan, earl of Lennox, in February 1392, the likelihood was that Robert's heir, Murdoch, would personally control a huge unified territorial lordship embracing the earldoms of Lennox and Menteith, Glen Dochart, Glen Lyon, Loch Tay, Fortingall, Strath Tay, Strathbraan and Strathord.

The co-ordinated territorial and jurisdictional expansion made into the Appin of Dull by the Albany Stewarts in 1389 directly supplanted Alexander Stewart. In 1372[37] Alexander had been styled lord of Badenoch and royal justiciar in the "Abthania" of Dull when he held a justiciar court at Dull, and in 1374 Stewart was said to be intromitting with the rents due to the crown from the Appin of Dull.[38] In addition, Alexander Stewart had received possession of lands in Rannoch and Fortingall in October 1379.[39]

The earl of Fife's assault on Alexander Stewart in 1389 may well have been complicated by the death, sometime in that year, of their younger brother David Stewart, earl of Strathearn and Caithness. David's death left his young daughter, Euphemia, as heiress to the earldoms of Strathearn and Caithness and the barony and castle of Urquhart on the western shore of Loch Ness. On 19 June 1371[40] Robert II had granted David, earl of Strathearn, the barony of Urquhart with an entail, on the failure of David's heirs, in favour of David's elder brother Alexander, lord of Badenoch.

Alexander's position as heir by entail to the barony of Urquhart and his established powerbase in Badenoch no doubt explain why he was given an assedation of Urquhart by his younger brother. By the time of a general council of June 1385,[41] however, the arrangement had broken down and David, earl of Strathearn, presented a complaint against Alexander, narrating that his brother was withholding the fermes of the barony and illegally occupying the lands and castle. The case was given over to the arbitration of Alexander and David's brothers in the hope of finding an amicable settlement.

After David Stewart's death the position of his daughter Euphemia as heiress to Urquhart must have been vulnerable to disruption by her uncle, Alexander Stewart, who was the heir by entail and probably in actual possession of the barony. From 1389 to 1392, however, Alexander Stewart's hold on all his Highland territories was undermined by a series of campaigns led by Fife and his son Murdoch, in which men committed to the defence of the heritage of Euphemia Stewart played a prominent part. For example, Walter Stewart of Brechin (later earl of Atholl and Caithness), David's younger brother, received payments for his expenses in remote parts in the exchequer sessions of March 1392 and February 1393.[42] In addition, Walter collected the sums owed to his cousin Sir Walter Stewart of Railston, who was similarly employed in remote parts in 1391-3.[43] Walter Stewart of Brechin, who was described as justiciar general in 1391,[44] had been appointed as one of the tutors of his niece, Euphemia Stewart, countess of Strathearn, before 5 March 1390,[45] while Sir Walter Stewart of Railston had been a feed retainer of David, earl of Strathearn, during the 1380s,[46] and both men were identified as members of Earl David's council in 1381,[47] along with Robert, earl of Fife. David Lindsay, lord of Glenesk (the future earl of Crawford), was a brother-in-law of David, earl of Strathearn, and also became a tutor of Euphemia Stewart after Earl David's death. It was no doubt these men who had supported David Stewart's earlier complaint against Alexander Stewart's occupation of Urquhart in 1385.

One of the targets of the campaigns in which Walter Stewart of Brechin and Sir Walter Stewart of Railston were involved is indicated by a payment, in the same section of the accounts, to Thomas Chisholm for four months' custody and provisioning of the castle of Urquhart at a rate "pro mensem quator decim libriis de voluntate Regis".[48] This was obviously an emergency rate which would have resulted in a huge annual payment of £168, more than four times the pension given to Robert Chisholm for the keepership of Urquhart in the 1360s.[49] Although Thomas Chisholm had some connections with Alexander Stewart,[50] he was obviously regarded as a dependable custodian by 12 October 1391,[51] when he was given possession of Urquhart.

The garrisoning of Urquhart was just one part of the wider military and political campaign unleashed by Fife against Alexander Stewart. In early

1392, two of Alexander's sons, Duncan and Robert, and some of their beleaguered adherents from Atholl, Badenoch and Wester Ross launched a counter-attack into south-eastern Perthshire and Angus which resulted in a pitched battle at Glen Brerachan[52] or Glasclune[53] in which David Lindsay of Glenesk was wounded and Sir Walter Ogilvie, sheriff of Angus, killed. The Atholl kindreds involved in the foray, most notably the Clan Donnachaidh or Robertsons under Robert of Atholl and Patrick and Thomas Duncanson, were probably directly threatened by the earl of Fife's encroachment into the Appin of Dull, Strathbraan and Loch Tay in 1389, as well as having their own territorial dispute with David Lindsay over the lands of Glenesk. Duncan Andrewson, head of the Clan Donnachaidh in the 1340s, was to be found concluding indentures at Dull in 1347[54] and acting as the chief forester of Braan in 1345.[55] In 1358, Duncan Andrewson's son, Robert, was identified as occupying various lands in Atholl and Fortingall.[56] The wide geographical distribution of those accused of being involved in the death of Walter Ogilvie[57] indicates that the expedition of 1392 was far more than a large scale cattle raid, rather it was a co-ordinated politico-military response to the earl of Fife's attack on Alexander Stewart and kindreds associated with him in Atholl, Badenoch, Wester Ross and elsewhere.

Control of northern Perthshire and the defence of his recent territorial acquisitions in the Appin of Dull must have remained a vital consideration for the earl of Fife through the 1390s. Fife's interests in territorial and jurisdictional terms were indicated by his creation as duke of Albany on 28 April 1398,[58] a title which suggested and, indeed, reflected a dominant role in the Scottish kingdom north of the Forth. The Albany Stewarts' control of crown resources and royal policy in the north was, however, increasingly threatened during the 1390s by David, earl of Carrick (the future Rothesay), who began to participate in campaigns in the Highlands from 1395-6 onwards.[59] The Atholl grant of 6 September 1398 gave the young and vigorous heir to the throne a territorial foothold in a highly sensitive area. While the grant, in itself, was not necessarily a disturbing development for Albany, Rothesay seems to have made his uncle Alexander Stewart, lord of Badenoch, Albany's arch-rival in northern Perthshire, bailie of the earldom at some point before the Martinmas term of 1401.[60] Furthermore, in the general council of January 1399 which created Rothesay the king's lieutenant, it was stipulated that the three sons of Sir Alexander Stewart "the qwylkis ar now in prison in the castle of Stryvelyng" should be handed over to the new lieutenant and that "he be obligitt to gerr thaim be kepit fermly and nocht be deliverit but consail general or parlement".[61] Alexander Stewart's imprisoned sons (probably including Duncan and Robert Stewart who had been involved in the great raid of 1392), who had led the Atholl kindreds in resisting Albany's occupation of the Appin of Dull in the early 1390s, were thus to be taken out of the custody of Albany, who was keeper of Stirling

Castle, and handed over to Rothesay. Rothesay may already have indicated his own less hostile attitude towards Alexander Stewart by making him bailie of Atholl, and in these circumstances it was probably Albany and his Perthshire allies who insisted that Rothesay should be sworn not to release Alexander's sons without the express consent of a general council or parliament.

By 1398/9 there were good strategic reasons for a revival in Alexander Stewart's political fortunes, because the duke of Albany's Highland policy had been reduced to tatters by Donald, lord of the Isles, and his brother Alexander, lord of Lochaber. Albany's assault on Alexander Stewart's personal lordship in 1389 had opened up areas which had previously been defended by the lord of Badenoch to encroachment by the MacDonalds and their client kindreds, who at that stage were probably regarded by Albany as useful allies in the attack on Alexander Stewart. From his stronghold in Lochaber, Alexander of the Isles pushed north and east into the Great Glen. By an indenture of 25 September 1394[62] Thomas, earl of Moray, and Alexander of the Isles agreed that the latter would defend the lands of the regality of Moray for a period of seven years. Alexander was to support the earl of Moray against all men except the king, the earl of Fife, and the lord of the Isles. In return for Alexander's "protection", the earl was to give Alexander eighty merks annually, sixty merks of which were to be raised from the lands of Bona (which had been held by Alexander Stewart since 1386) and Essich at the northern end of Loch Ness, with a further twenty merk payment to be arranged "cum consilio domini comitis de Fyffe". Alexander of the Isles had thus gained control of the northern end of Loch Ness and the vital approaches to Inverness and the Moray coastal plain. The castle of Urquhart, on the western shore of Loch Ness, which Alexander Stewart had occupied and defended in the 1370s and 1380s seems to have fallen to Alexander of the Isles between 1395,[63] when Thomas Chisholm received his last payment as custodian, and April 1398,[64] when a parliament largely concerned with co-ordinating an expedition against Alexander of the Isles discussed the need to place a trustworthy constable in Urquhart until the kingdom was pacified. Traditional accounts of the Clan Maclean suggest that it was in the last decade of the fourteenth century that Charles Maclean, a younger son of the Duart family, followed Alexander's advance into the Great Glen and established a cadet branch of the Macleans, known as the Clan Tearlach, in Urquhart and Glenmoriston, where they acted as hereditary custodians of Urquhart and Bona Castles, both formerly held by Alexander Stewart, for the MacDonalds.[65] Certainly by 2 June 1440[66] Charles' son Hector "Tarlackson" was described as "senescallum de Urchard". In addition to these advances in the Great Glen, Donald of the Isles' elder half-brother, Godfrey, is reputed to have launched a huge sea-borne campaign against Skye during the 1390s which was beaten off by the Clan Macleod.[67] The lordship of Skye was held by the earls of Ross, and had been given over to Alexander Stewart on his marriage to Euphemia Stewart, countess of Ross, in 1382.[68] Robert, earl of Fife, seems to have encouraged Euphemia's divorce from Alexander Stewart in the period 1389-92,[69] a policy which served Fife's purpose of weakening Alexander Stewart's position, but left Skye and Wester Ross vulnerable to incursions from the MacDonald lordship. The collapse of Albany's Highland policy and of co-operation with Donald, lord of the Isles, was probably another element behind the complaints of January 1399 which justified the transfer of effective royal power to the duke of Rothesay.

In a sense, Albany's success in the Lennox and Perthshire during the period 1389-1398 illustrates why political tension between Albany and Rothesay was inevitable. Albany's territorial expansion had been built on his ability to control crown resources and patronage. In the Lennox in particular, Albany had used the gift of royal offices to augment, or attempt to augment, the inheritance of his own son, Murdoch Stewart. In order to preserve or build on these territorial gains, Albany needed to maintain a high degree of control over royal policies, a position which was increasingly threatened by Rothesay, the vigorous and assertive heir to the throne. At the outset of Rothesay's lieutenancy, Albany's position and interests were safeguarded, to some extent, by the special council assigned to govern and advise the lieutenant, a council which included several men, such as Thomas Dunbar, earl of Moray, and Alexander Leslie, earl of Ross (Albany's son-in-law), who were closely associated with, and beneficiaries of, Albany's policies in the early 1390s. In the autumn of 1401, shortly before his "arrest", Rothesay seems to have rejected this Albany-dominated council.[70]

The seizure of Rothesay, undated in Bower's account, must have occurred between 22 February and 18 March 1402 if Bower's incidental observation that the duke was at liberty in Edinburgh when a strange and striking comet appeared, and that he had been made captive by the time the comet faded, is correct.[71] The exact duration of the comet's appearance in 1402 can be gleaned from highly accurate Chinese, Japanese and Korean observations, which show that the comet became visible in the far east on 20 February 1402 and faded from sight on 19 or 20 March.[72] Given Scotland's northerly latitude the comet probably became visible there a day or two later, and disappeared a day or two earlier, than in Japan and Korea. If we accept these terminal dates for Rothesay's arrest, then Bower's assertion that the duke was on his way to the castle of St. Andrews (which, in Bower's phrase, was ready to surrender to him) becomes rather curious. The bishopric had been technically vacant since the death of Bishop Walter Trail before 1 July 1401.[72] Bower suggests that Rothesay's counsellors, including Sir John Ramornie and Sir William Lindsay of Rossie, had encouraged the duke to occupy the bishop's castle on the king's behalf until a new bishop was formally entered. This would leave an unexplained gap of at least eight months between Bishop Trail's death and Rothesay's attempt to occupy the episcopal castle in late February or early March 1402. Rothesay had, however, been active in the area around St. Andrews in the period between Trail's death and his own arrest. At some point between 10 June 1401 and 20 February 1402 the duke had been involved in a siege of Reres Castle in Kilconquhar parish near Elie.[74] The owner of the recently constructed castle was Sir John Wemyss of Reres.[75] Aside from the attack on his castle, Sir John Wemyss' lands were taken into royal control towards the end of the Martinmas term of 1401.[76] Sir John Wemyss' forfeiture and the besieging of his castle by Rothesay may have been related to the duke's attempt to occupy St. Andrews, since Sir John had served as the constable of the episcopal castle from 18 June 1383[77] to 6 July 1400,[78] when he granted his second son, Alexander, the lands of Kilmany, Lathocker, Muirston and others near St. Andrews, together with the constableship of the castle. That there had been some resistance to Rothesay is implied in Bower's comment that the castle was ready to surrender to the duke in February/March 1402. As the siege machines which were eventually employed against Reres were actually constructed in St. Andrews, it is possible that the episcopal castle itself was under some form of siege in early 1402.[79] Rothesay's disagreement with Wemyss of Reres may well have increased the tension between the lieutenant and his uncle Robert, duke of Albany, during the winter of 1401-2. Albany, as royal chamberlain, ordered the payments for the siege of Reres and for Rothesay's expenses in these operations,[80] but his own relationship with Sir John Wemyss was far from hostile. As earl of Fife, Albany was Wemyss' feudal superior (although in June 1400[81] this tenurial relationship had given rise to a serious disagreement between Albany and Wemyss), and in November 1399[82] Albany had acted as a surety for Wemyss' future good behaviour towards Walter Lindsay, with whom Wemyss was in dispute, during a parliamentary lawsuit between Lindsay and Wemyss. Sir John was an occasional witness to charters issued by Albany,[83] and the duke had witnessed the arrangements for the marriage of Sir John's eldest son, Duncan, to a daughter of Sir Thomas Erskine.[84] Moreover, Sir John Wemyss was speedily rehabilitated in the months after Rothesay's death. By 24 May 1402[85] Sir John's lands had been restored to him, and it seems likely that this arrangement was made in the general council of 16-20 May 1402, which confirmed the political ascendancy of Albany and the earl of Douglas after Rothesay's death.

On 8 November 1402[86] Sir John Wemyss witnessed a great seal charter issued by Robert III at Southannan in northern Ayrshire, in favour of John Berclay of Kippo, the son of another prominent Albany adherent from the earldom of Fife.[87] Sir John Wemyss' appearance in Ayrshire confirmed not only his own remarkable political revival during 1402 but also the dominance established by the duke of Albany after Rothesay's death. It seems probable that it was Sir John Wemyss or his son, Alexander, who had had custody of Rothesay for the few days that the duke was kept in St. Andrews Castle before his transfer to Falkland. The rather sudden change by which the constable of St. Andrews offered to surrender the castle to Rothesay in February/March 1402, and then became his gaoler after the duke had been captured on his way to St. Andrews, might suggest that Rothesay was the victim of a carefully co-ordinated trap in which most of the chief actors were strongly linked to Albany.

Rothesay's determination to take control of the bishopric of St. Andrews seems to have been prompted by two issues. The first of these was what may have been a developing power struggle over who should succeed Walter Trail as bishop. Thomas Stewart, a half-brother of Robert III, was elected by the St. Andrews chapter as Trail's successor on 1 July 1401,[88] but papal confirmation of Stewart's position was delayed by problems at the papal court. By early 1402, Robert, duke of Albany, may have been pressing the claims of Walter Danielston. Shortly after Rothesay's death Albany met his half brother Thomas, the bishop elect, at Abernethy and persuaded him to resign his claims to the bishopric in favour of Danielston.[89] Albany's aim in obtaining the bishopric for Danielston was, of course, the removal of the troublesome cleric from Dumbarton Castle. Danielston's insertion into St. Andrews was, we are told,

> Agane conscience of mony men: Bot like it wes to
> stanch then, Wykkit dedis, mony and fell, Be the stuff
> oysit off that Castell [Dumbarton].[90]

When Danielston died around Christmas 1402 it was claimed that he had held the bishopric for little over half a year.[91] This would suggest that Thomas Stewart's resignation and Danielston's disputed promotion to St. Andrews both occurred in May or June 1402, shortly after Rothesay's death. Albany's initial approach to Danielston with the offer of the bishopric may, however, have been made in February or March 1402 at a time when Rothesay's relations with both Albany and Robert III were strained.[92] If Albany was close to achieving a settlement favourable to his own interests in the Lennox, an issue which had been of great importance at the start of Rothesay's lieutenancy, then the young heir to the throne's attempt to secure control of the bishop's castle would be an understandable response.

A second consideration which may have spurred Rothesay into action was the collection of the episcopal revenues during the vacancy of the see. St. Andrews was the richest bishopric in the kingdom with an annual income estimated, for taxation purposes, at £3,507 in 1366.[93] The vacancy should have provided a huge fiscal windfall for the crown, and an attempt by Rothesay to occupy the bishop's castle by force and personally supervise the episcopal finances would fit in well with the increasingly aggressive and independent position taken up by the young duke in the late autumn of 1401. Any such move would also have brought Rothesay into direct conflict with the crown's principal financial officer Robert, duke of Albany, the chamberlain. Albany's control of royal finances would also seem to have been threatened in late 1401 by Rothesay's increased use of the right to uplift royal customs revenue directly, a power which had been granted to him as part of his commission of lieutenancy in January 1399.[94] In the months after May-June 1401 Rothesay visited a number of east coast burghs - Edinburgh, Dundee, Montrose and Aberdeen - to take money directly from their custumars.[95] In Montrose and Dundee the custumars had to be persuaded to hand over their money through the application of physical violence by Rothesay and his adherents. In Montrose, the custumar John Tyndale was abducted and imprisoned by Rothesay until he handed over twenty-four pounds, regardless of the fact that Tyndale and his fellow custumar Andrew Panter had already given over all the customs revenues they had received to Albany's deputy chamberlain, Walter Tulloch.[96]

Rothesay's increased assertiveness in late 1401 is presented by Walter Bower, who is highly sympathetic to Albany, in terms of the young duke's return to unruly and frivolous behaviour after the death of his mother, Queen Annabella Drummond, in August/September 1401.[97] Stripped of its anti-Rothesay bias, Bower's account is a simple description of the rejection by Rothesay of the Albany dominated "special council" which had been appointed to supervise and regulate his lieutenancy in January 1399.[98] Rothesay seems to have had little or no contact with his father's court in the second half of 1401[99] and ceased to witness royal charters issued after 12 May 1401.[100] Bower's description of Rothesay's behaviour shortly before his arrest as unruly and intemperate probably reflects the propaganda position established by Albany and Douglas in 1402 in order to justify Rothesay's imprisonment and death. That this view of Rothesay was widely circulated is suggested by the fact that the contemporary English chronicler, John Shirley (1366-1456), who does not appear to have had access to Bower's work, follows a strikingly similar line, talking of the "vicious living of that saide Duke of Rothsay ... " and how the nobles of Scotland were

" ... soare dreiding
if he hadde reynede afther hys fader that many ...
misfortunes and vengeances might have followyd and
fallen uppon al that region by cause of his lyff soo
openly knowen vicious".[101]

The notion underlying Shirley's account, that the arrest and death of the twenty-four year old heir to the throne was a form of pre-emptive strike on the part of Albany, is perhaps given greater weight by Bower's suggestion that Rothesay's councillors were already encouraging the young duke to arrest his uncle.

The Bower/Shirley view of Rothesay's intemperance was not, however, the only historical interpretation of the duke's life. By the early sixteenth century there was, clearly, a distinct tradition which depicted Rothesay as a royal saint whose tomb at Lindores Abbey was the scene of miracles. William Stewart's metrical version of Boece's *History of Scotland* illustrated the clash between these two traditions. Although Stewart basically follows Boece and the narrative of Bower's *Scotichronicon* in the discussion of Rothesay's death, he self-consciously breaks away from Bower's account to try to reconcile Bower's critical description of Rothesay with an obviously widely-held belief that the duke was a saint.[102] Especially significant is the assertion that Rothesay's tomb at Lindores ceased to perform miracles after Rothesay's younger brother James I had avenged his treasonable death.

An interesting feature of Bower's account of Rothesay's arrest is the prominence given to the actions of the two members of Rothesay's retinue who actually seized the duke. One of the men, Sir John Ramornie, had acted as Rothesay's chamberlain and received a retaining fee for his loyalty and service to the king and the duke of Rothesay.[103] At the same time, however, Ramornie had been named as a member of the earl of Fife's council in 1389[104] and acted as a financial receiver for Murdoch Stewart, Albany's son, in his capacity as justiciar north of Forth.[105] Ramornie was thus ideally qualified to play the role of double agent assigned to him by Bower. Sir William Lindsay of Rossie, on the other hand, was said to have developed a grudge against Rothesay because the duke had been betrothed to Sir William's sister, Euphemia, but had rejected her in order to marry Elizabeth Dunbar, a daughter of the earl of March.[106] This would place Rothesay's liaison with Euphemia Lindsay before 28 August 1395,[107] when David, then earl of Carrick, received a papal dispensation to marry Elizabeth Dunbar with whom he had contracted marriage "per verba de futuro".

That David, earl of Carrick, was closely involved with the Lindsay family before August 1395 is undoubted. On 27 December 1394,[108] David, styled earl of Carrick and lord of Nithsdale, confirmed a charter involving lands in Dumfries. The charter was witnessed by Sir James Lindsay, lord of Buchan, Sir David Lindsay (the future earl of Crawford), and Sir William Lindsay (of Rossie), respectively the cousin and brothers of Euphemia Lindsay. David and William Lindsay were to be found in Carrick's household again, this time in company with John Ramornie, as witnesses to a charter dated 17 December 1400 in a great seal confirmation of 3 August 1450,[109] although the titles given to Carrick and David Lindsay would suggest that the original charter was issued before April 1398. If, as seems likely, Euphemia Lindsay was Carrick's mistress or fiancee in the early 1390s then the earl's proposed marriage to Elizabeth Dunbar in 1395 would undoubtedly have upset Sir William and his brother. The Dunbar marriage certainly offended Robert III, who in the autumn of 1396[110] descended on the burgh of Haddington with a large army of "genitibus suis" with the intention of besieging the castle of Dunbar, the earl of March's chief stronghold, because of the irregular marriage of the king's son, Carrick, with Elizabeth Dunbar. Robert III's stance was supported by Walter Trail, bishop of St. Andrews, who sought to have the marriage annulled on the grounds that Carrick and Elizabeth Dunbar had failed to wait for the papal dispensation of August 1395 before consummating the marriage.[111] By 10 March 1397[112] the opposition of Robert III and, presumably, the Lindsays had been overcome as the pope issued a further dispensation clearing away the ecclesiastical impediment to the Carrick/Dunbar marriage at the behest of petitioners who included Gilbert Greenlaw, bishop of Aberdeen (who was to become chancellor of the kingdom between 14 January and 5 June 1397[113]), and the dean of Dunbar. The political changes of early 1397, including Greenlaw's promotion to the chancellorship, and the regular appearance of David, earl of Carrick, as a witness to royal charters were probably related to the issue of Carrick's marriage.

Despite Rothesay's rejection of Euphemia Lindsay, Sir William Lindsay of Rossie and David, earl of Crawford, remained as members of the duke's retinue. In late 1401 or early 1402,[114] for example, William Lindsay, Crawford and John Ramornie were witnesses to a charter issued by Rothesay in favour of Richard Spalding involving lands which had belonged to Queen Annabella. Of more political importance in terms of the success or failure of Albany's arrest of Rothesay in 1402 was the attitude of Sir William's eldest brother David, earl of Crawford. As we have seen, Crawford was a member of Carrick's household throughout the 1390s and received a retaining fee of forty merks for his services to the king and David, duke of Rothesay, from 1390 onwards.[115] Rothesay must have viewed Crawford as a close ally in 1402, despite the fact that the earl had strong links with Albany, probably derived from their mutual campaigning in the north during the 1390s.[116] It seems likely, in fact, that Crawford played no active role in the events of 1402 on either side because, on 1 January 1402,[117] he entered into a bond by which he agreed to serve the duke of Orleans and, by 8 May 1402,[118] was on board a French fleet stationed in Corunna Bay.

This left Sir William Lindsay of Rossie as the chief representative of the Lindsay family in Scotland during early 1402. Sir William's lands of Rossie lay in the sheriffdom of Fife,[119] and in 1398-1402[120] Sir William had witnessed the duke of Albany's confirmation, issued at Falkland (in the presence of Murdoch Stewart, Albany's son and heir and John Stewart of Lorn, whose son Robert was married to Albany's daughter Johanna), of an entail agreement between Thomas Ramsay and Sir John Ramornie, Sir William's co-conspirator in 1402.

Sir William Lindsay and his brother may well have been pleased with Albany's reversal of Rothesay's support for the burgh of Perth in the long-running dispute between Perth and Dundee over where ships entering the Tay could unload their cargoes. Rothesay, at the very start of his lieutenancy, had supported Perth's monopoly of Tay trade at the expense of Dundee,[121] while on 19th May 1402,[122] during the general council which followed Rothesay's death, Albany and his chamberlain's court overturned this position and found in favour of Dundee.

Crawford's departure from Scotland in early 1402 would seem to have left Rothesay with few natural political allies. Rothesay himself controlled the earldoms of Carrick and Atholl and the Stewartry, and could count on more or less committed support from these areas. In addition, in any prolonged political struggle with Albany, Rothesay could probably rely on two of his uncles, Alexander Stewart, earl of Buchan, and Queen Annabella's brother Malcolm Drummond, lord of Mar. Drummond's fate in 1402 was remarkably similar to Rothesay's. Wyntoun informs us that he

> ... wes wyth slycht
> Supprisit and takyn: baith day and nycht
> Kepit in till strait tenouns
> Quhill he deit in hard penawns.[123]

When or where Drummond was captured and imprisoned is unrecorded, but it is not inconceivable that it coincided with Rothesay's arrest. Drummond's death has been blamed on Alexander Stewart, the illegitimate son of Alexander Stewart, earl of Buchan, on the basis that the younger Alexander married Drummond's widow, Isabella Douglas, countess of Mar, in August 1404, some two years after Malcolm Drummond's demise.[124] In fact, on 8 November 1402[125] Isabella, countess of Mar, issued a charter, in her widowhood, at Kildrummy witnessed not by Alexander Stewart and his caterans, but by Gilbert Greenlaw, bishop of Aberdeen and chancellor of the kingdom, William Keith, the marischal, and Keith's son, Alexander. Alexander Keith was Albany's brother-in-law and both he and his father seem to have had a good relationship with the royal duke.[126] Gilbert Greenlaw has traditionally been seen as a man with strong links with Albany. On 18 March 1403[128] Isabella issued another charter from Kildrummy, this time in favour of Gilbert Greenlaw, bishop of Aberdeen, on the advice of Robert, duke of Albany, and David, earl of Crawford, who were part of the countess' "consilio nostro speciali". The presence of the earl of Crawford is interesting, since on 20 November 1400[129] Crawford had bound himself to support the claims of Thomas Erskine and his son Robert to the earldoms of Mar and Garioch after the death of Isabella Douglas. In 1403 Crawford and Albany were clearly looking to protect the Erskine's interests in the Mar and Garioch inheritance (both Thomas and Robert Erskine having been captured by the English at Humbleton in September 1402), interests which would best be served by Isabella Douglas remaining unmarried until her death. It was thus Albany and his associates who obtained control of Kildrummy and the earldom of Mar after Malcolm Drummond's death, and it was the Keiths, Lindsays, the bishop of Aberdeen and Albany himself who were the immediate beneficiaries of Isabella's patronage.[130] Albany's close involvement in Mar in 1402 and 1403 would strongly support the view that Drummond was eliminated as part of a general attack on Rothesay's affinity in 1402.

The most important of Rothesay's potential supporters, however, was his brother-in-law Archibald, 4th earl of Douglas. The real mystery of 1402 is what political advantage Archibald Douglas saw in the removal of Rothesay. The Douglases were undoubtedly the most powerful territorial magnates south of the Forth, and Rothesay's marriage to Mary Douglas c. February 1400[131] would at first sight seem to have secured formidable political allies for the new lieutenant in the shape of Mary's father, Archibald the Grim, 3rd earl of Douglas, and her brother, also Archibald, the future 4th earl. One of the results of the Rothesay/Douglas marriage was the well documented defection of George, earl of March, to Henry IV. Both Bower and Wyntoun suggest that March was pushed into full scale rebellion by the actions of Archibald, master of Douglas, who occupied March's castle of Dunbar with the active assistance or frightened acquiescence of the custodian, Sir Robert Maitland, March's nephew, while the earl was in England negotiating with Henry IV.[132] Archibald's seizure of Dunbar probably occurred in late June or early July 1400,[133] and certainly after 8 May.[134] Archibald the Grim died around Christmas 1400,[135] and certainly before 9 February 1401.[136] The new earl had thus been personally committed to the defence of Dunbar Castle and the earldom of March since the summer of 1400, and in this he was associated with a number of ex-March adherents who had suffered considerable losses in the English-supported raids launched by George Dunbar on Lothian and Berwickshire. Sir Patrick Hepburn of Hailes, for example, a former March adherent,[137] witnessed charters issued by the 4th earl in the castle of Dunbar during 1401.[138] Hepburn's lands of Hailes, Traprain and Markle had been harried, and his castle of Hailes twice attacked during a raid by the earl of March and Henry Percy, son of the earl of Northumberland, which Bower places in early February 1401.[139] The Dunbar/Percy expedition which was probably supported by many Berwickshire families who remained loyal to the exiled earl of March,[140] was eventually defeated near Cockburnspath by a force commanded by Archibald Douglas.

From 1400 onwards, the 4th earl of Douglas had two inter-related aims. Firstly, the consolidation of his tenuous hold on the lordship of Dunbar, and secondly the pursuit of his cross border feud with the earl of March. Parliamentary legislation of 21 February 1401[141] reflected the demands of the new earl of Douglas and his adherents in the earldom of March. One item asserted that where a baron was infeft in a barony by the king within an earldom or other lordship while the earldom was in royal hands, then when the earldom or lordship was regranted by charter with the service of tenants and tenandries, this should not affect the position of the barony, which should still be held directly of the crown. The legislation, which can only be related to the situation in March, clearly envisaged the break-up of the earldom as a unified territorial unit. Although George Dunbar had probably been physically excluded from much of his earldom since July/August 1400, the parliament of February 1401 was the first occasion on which a formal process of forfeiture could be carried through. The legislation would thus seem to anticipate the forfeiture of the earl in the same parliament, and the breaking up of the earldom into a number of lordships to be held directly of the crown. Given forty days' notice for the summoning of a parliament, the decision formally to forfeit George Dunbar must have been taken in early January 1401, just after Archibald the Grim's death and the succession of Archibald Douglas as 4th earl to the earldom of Douglas. George Dunbar's raid into March in February 1401 may thus have been a direct response to the news that his earldom was to be formally forfeited to the Scottish crown at the behest of the man who had been occupying Dunbar Castle since the summer of 1400. Former tenants of George Dunbar who had fought against him during 1400 and early 1401 would, of course, have required the type of tenurial protection offered by the parliamentary legislation of February 1401, if and when Dunbar was restored to the earldom. Douglas' fears on this issue may have been sharpened by Anglo-Scottish negotiations for a truce or peace treaty, which appear to have been planned for March or April 1401.[142] A truce or peace treaty would have had to deal with the position of the exiled earl of March, and Douglas was not keen to have this issued discussed. In March 1401[143] Rothesay wrote to Henry IV asking that a meeting of commissioners proposed by the English king for Carlisle should be transferred to Melrose, partly because the latter offered better provisions but also because the earl of Douglas, who dominated the Scottish western march, was opposed to the negotiations. Rothesay claimed that he and Albany were, in contrast, keen to conclude an agreement.

The parliamentary legislation of February 1401 would also have affected any grant of the earldom of March to another magnate after George Dunbar's forfeiture. In this respect it is interesting to note an entry in the exchequer rolls of 1455 which claimed that David, duke of Rothesay, had died vest and seised in the earldom of March.[144] If this isolated piece of evidence is accurate, then it would mean that Rothesay had at least a short term interest in preserving March as an effective earldom, and that the legislation of February

1401 was not aimed against George Dunbar alone. It may be significant that grants to former March tenants giving them their lands to be held directly of the crown did not begin in earnest until the late autumn of 1401,[145] after Rothesay had rejected the council assigned to him in 1399, and in charters which were not witnessed by the young duke.

Throughout 1401 and 1402 Archibald Douglas displayed a consistently hostile attitude towards any negotiations which might have dealt with the position of the exiled earl of March. On 16 May 1401,[146] the earl of Douglas arranged a temporary truce with the earl of Northumberland which was to last until Martinmas 1401. A meeting was to be held at Kirk Yetholm in October 1401 in order to reach a more permanent arrangement. It seems clear, given Henry IV's instructions to his commissioners in October 1401, that George Dunbar and his allies had been excluded from the truce of May-November 1401 negotiated by Douglas. The talks of 17-20 October were conducted by Scottish commissioners headed by the earls of Douglas and Angus, while most of the other Scots commissioners were firmly attached to the Douglas interest. Six days before the meeting with the English Commission, on 11 October 1401,[147] at Renfrew, Robert III issued a charter to Sir Robert Maitland of the lands of Tibbers in the earldom of March, which were in the king's hands by reason of the forfeiture of the earl of March, the lands to be held directly of the king. On the same day the king confirmed a charter of 28 April 1401 issued at the castle of Dunbar by Archibald Douglas in favour of Sir Robert Maitland.[148] The grants not only rewarded the man who had handed over Dunbar Castle to Douglas in 1400, but their timing suggests that Douglas was seeking to guarantee the position of his supporters within March before the meeting with the English commission, who were under strict instructions to have George Dunbar included in any truce.[149] As it was, the negotiations broke up in acrimonious fashion on 20 October, whereupon Douglas rode north from the Tweed to the castle of Dunbar where, later the same day, he issued charters of lands in his lordship of Dunbar and of Cranshaws near Haddington in favour of Sir John Swinton, one of his fellow commissioners, in the presence of, amongst others, Sir Patrick Hepburn, the most committed of the anti-Dunbar landholders in March.[150] Henry IV later blamed Douglas personally for the break-up of the October meeting with not even an unconditional truce established.[151] Shortly after the inconclusive meeting at Kirk Yetholm, Douglas and his men swept into Northumberland and attacked and burnt the town of Bamburgh. On 1 February 1402[152] Douglas, styling himself lord of Galloway and Dunbar, wrote a defensive letter to Henry IV requesting renewed negotiations and protesting that he was not to blame for the outbreak of cross-border hostilities. By the time Henry IV's reply of 27 February 1402,[153] offering only a low-level commission to treat with the Scots at Kelso on 10 April 1402, reached Scotland, the political situation had been transformed by the arrest of Rothesay.

It seems probable that the earl of Douglas was not actually involved in the initial arrest and imprisonment of Rothesay in St. Andrews. If the move against the heir to the throne had been pre-planned by Albany and Douglas, then there would have been little need for the council held between the two men at Culross a few days after Rothesay's arrest. The use of Culross in the west of Fife, and Rothesay's temporary imprisonment in St. Andrews, indicate that Albany and Douglas met as the latter moved north towards St. Andrews, probably on receiving the news of Rothesay's capture, either to support his brother-in-law or to strike a deal with Albany. Albany would seem to have taken a calculated political gamble in seizing his nephew, knowing that he would have to reach some form of agreement with Douglas if his coup was to be successful. The council at Culross thus took shape as a meeting between the two most powerful magnates in the kingdom, discussing the future of the heir to the throne. In return for Douglas' support, Albany seems to have offered the earl substantial and unrestrained support for Douglas interests and policies in the east march and more aggressive campaigning against the exiled earl of March and his English backers. The policy represented something of a volte-face on the part of Albany, whom Wyntoun identifies as having been opposed to March's exile in 1400 and who was named by Rothesay in March 1401[154] as being in favour of negotiations for a permanent peace between the two kingdoms.

How then did Douglas and Albany decide to deal with Rothesay? During their meeting at Culross, Albany and Douglas agreed to move Rothesay from St. Andrews to Albany's own castle of Falkland. The arrangement seems rather ominous, especially given the fact that the young duke was forced to wear russet robes and to ride on a mule, indicating either that Douglas and Albany hoped to hide the duke's whereabouts from his adherents by disguising him as a cleric, or that they were engaging in a deliberate act of humiliation.[155] Neither interpretation would suggest that a rapid or reasonable political compromise was likely. The options for Albany and Douglas were, in fact, rather limited. As long as Rothesay remained alive he would continue to act as a focus for opposition to Albany and would add the desire for revenge to the other grievances he held against his uncle. If, as seemed likely, Rothesay outlived his ailing sixty-five year old father and succeeded to the throne as David III it would be difficult, if not impossible, for Albany and Douglas to hold the new king to any "constitutional" restraints they managed to place on him in 1402. In any case, there is no indication that Albany and Douglas intended to force through a formal transfer of power in a parliament or general council while Rothesay remained capable of political action. Rothesay's incarceration in Falkland was obviously intended to be a prolonged imprisonment, and there were no moves to hold a general council or parliament until after the young duke was dead. The general council of 16-20 May 1402[156] was the first recorded piece of royal business for close on six months, and it was probably not until c.18 May 1402[157] that Albany received a commission of lieutenancy in succession to Rothesay. It seems likely, then, that there had been no formal appointment of a lieutenant or governor of the kingdom and no defined political settlement between Rothesay's arrest on some date before 20 March 1402 and the general council of 16-20 May, and that Albany's appointment was only made after a debate on Rothesay's death had concluded that the heir to the throne had died of natural causes and that Douglas and Albany were not to face charges of treason. There seems little doubt that Rothesay's death was, in the end, a political assassination. The terms of the indemnity given to Albany and Douglas in May 1402 suggest that many of their contemporaries were directly accusing the two men of Rothesay's murder. Rothesay's younger brother, the future James I, certainly wreaked vengeance on the men who had been personally involved in keeping Rothesay in Falkland Castle,[158] while the English chronicler John Shirley uses the Rothesay episode, which he describes straightforwardly as an assassination, as an introduction to, and an explanation of, James I's attack on the Albany Stewarts in 1424-25.[159]

After the general council of May 1402 royal charters once again started to be issued. Political opposition was either bought off[160] or, like Malcolm Drummond, eliminated. As we have seen, the duke of Albany, the new lieutenant, settled the Dumbarton issue in his own favour very quickly after Rothesay's death. Indeed, royal patronage of Duncan, earl of Lennox, and Murdoch Stewart, his heir by entail, resumed normal service after the interruption of the Rothesay lieutenancy. On 4 February 1403,[161] at Dumbarton (shortly after Walter Danielston's death), Robert III granted Duncan McDowell various lands in the lordship of Glendaruel, part of the barony of Cowal which was, in itself, part of the wider Stewartry lands which had reverted to Robert III's control after Rothesay's death. The charter specified that on the failure of Duncan's heirs, the lands were to go to Duncan, earl of Lennox, and his heirs. Robert, duke of Albany, was the only significant witness to the charter apart from various clerics who were part of Robert III's household. On 3 September 1403[162] Albany's control of Perthshire was further enhanced by a charter of the earldom of Atholl in free regality to last for Robert III's lifetime. As Albany also looked set to dominate the destination of the earldoms of Strathearn, Ross and Mar to kinsmen or close allies, the lieutenant's control of the future territorial and political shape of the kingdom looked assured.

In the months after May 1402, the Albany/Douglas regime also embarked on its new policy of aggression towards England. Even before the general council of May 1402 the English were aware of a change in the Scottish outlook. By April 1402[163] rumours were spreading through the English shires north of London that Richard II was alive in Scotland and would invade England at midsummer. By 9 May[164] royal officials in Northumberland,

Cumberland and Westmoreland were ordered to arrest anyone who claimed that Richard II was still alive. The aggressive use of the Richard II impostor as a dynastic threat to Henry IV went hand-in-hand with an increase in cross-border raiding co-ordinated by Archibald, earl of Douglas.[165] One of these raids, led by Patrick Hepburn of Hailes, met with disaster on Nisbet Moor on 22 June 1402[166] when Hepburn's force was overcome by a mixed force of March's adherents from Berwickshire and men of the earl of Northumberland. The response of Albany and Douglas was to send a combined army, based largely on their own affinities, into northern England in September 1402, where it was cut to pieces at Humbleton on 14 September with huge losses through death or capture, the captives including the earl of Douglas himself and Murdoch Stewart, Albany's son and heir.[167]

After Rothesay's death, Robert III continued in his semi-retirement on his ancestral Stewart estates, apparently wielding little real influence outside this area up to his death in 1406.

In a sense, Albany's jurisdictional and territorial power was so closely bound up with his ability to control or influence crown policy that any indication given by Rothesay that he was indifferent or openly hostile towards Albany's regional interests must have been highly alarming. The justiciarship north of Forth, control of the Appin of Dull, the entailing of the earldom of Lennox, the descent of Ross, Strathearn and Mar, the custody of Stirling Castle, the office of chamberlain, and numerous pensions and annuities were all guaranteed by Albany's good relations with, or ability to control, his father Robert II and his brother Robert III. For the ageing Albany, who had worked capably for four decades in building up a formidable territorial inheritance for his family and allies, the prospect of his twenty-four year old nephew, who had already deliberately estranged himself from his uncle's council, becoming king must have been appalling. It was in pursuit and defence of these interests that Albany planned and carried out the arrest and assassination of the duke of Rothesay, the man who would be king.

NOTES

1. Walter Bower, *Scotichronicon*, ed. D. E. R. Watt *et al.* (Aberdeen, 1987-), viii, 39.
2. *Ibid.*
3. *Ibid.*
4. F. J. Amours (ed.), *The Oryginale Chronicle of Andrew of Wyntoun* (Scottish Text Society, 1903-14), vi, 391.
5. T. F. Donald, "The Dennistouns of Dennistoun", *Scottish Historical Review*, 15 (1917-18), 241.
6. C. Innes (ed.), *Registrum Episcopatus Glasguensis* (Maitland Club, 1843), i, 289; J. Stuart *et al.* (ed.), *Exchequer Rolls*[ER] (Edinburgh, 1878-1908), iii, *ad indicem* (for custody of castle and sheriffship); *ER*, iii, 422, 425 (for date of death).
7. *ER*, i, 572, 574, 582; *Cartularium Comitatus de Levenax* (Maitland Club, 1833), 58-9. John Danielston as sheriff of Dumbarton in August 1373.
8. W. Fraser, *Memoirs of the Maxwells of Pollock* (Edinburgh, 1863) i, 139-142.
9. Patrick is mentioned in a document of 29 October 1398 relating to Robert III's attempts to negotiate Walter Danielston's surrender of Dumbarton. One of the men involved in the negotiations was Sir James Stewart of Kilbride who had been given the ward of Sir William Danielston's heirs. Scottish Record Office [SRO], Mar and Kellie, GD 124/1/422; *ER*, iii, 350-1, 384-5, 439, 465-6, 499.
10. National Library of Scotland [NLS], Fleming of Wigtown, Ch. no. 15730 (4 August 1398); *Historical Manuscripts Commission* [HMC] *Reports*, XV, viii, 51 (10 August 1398). A resignation by Duncan Kirkpatrick at Dumbarton in the presence of most of the leading men and important nobles in the kingdom; SRO, Mar and Kellie, GD 124/1/525 (11 August 1398); British Museum [BM], Harleian MSS, no. 4694, f. 13r-v (9 September 1398); SRO, Mar and Kellie, GD 124/1/422 (29 October 1398).
11. *ER*, iii, 465-6, 490.
12. *Ibid.*, iii, 502.
13. *Wyntoun*, vi, 391; cf. Walter Bower, *Scotichronicon*, (ed. W. Goodall, Edinburgh, 1747-59), i, 365.
14. *ER*, iii, *ad indicem*; NLS, Adv. MSS, 34.3.25, p. 63
15. T. Thomson and C. Innes (ed.), *The Acts of the Parliaments of Scotland* [APS] (Edinburgh, 1814-75), i, 572.
16. W. Fraser, *The Lennox* (Edinburgh, 1874), ii, 53-5.
17. *Ibid.*, ii, 49-51.
18. *Ibid.*, ii, 43-5.
19. *Cartularium comitatus de Levenax* (Maitland Club, 1833), 95. Robert Stewart is styled earl of Fife and Menteith rather than duke of Albany which suggests that the charter was issued before April 1398.
20. *Ibid.*, 4, 8.
21. SRO, Glencairn Muniments, GD 39/1/no. 13.
22. *Wyntoun*, vi, 391, 395; D. E. R. Watt (ed.), *Biographical Dictionary of Scottish Graduates to 1410* (Oxford, 1977), 542.
23. *Wyntoun*, vi, 399.
24. NLS, Adv. MSS, 34.3.25, p. 63.
25. BM, Harleian MSS, no. 4693, f. 9v.
26. Fraser, *Lennox*, ii, 37-9; *Lennox Cart.*, 58, 59, 64, 72, 73.
27. Fraser, *Lennox*, ii, 45; NLS, Fleming of Wigtown, Ch. no. 15821.
28. *HMC Report*, X, App. vi, 78.

29. W. Fraser (ed.), *The Red Book of Menteith* (Edinburgh, 1880), i, 280.
30. BM, Harleian MSS, no. 4694, f. 13r-v.
31. *APS*, i, 555-6.
32. *Ibid.*, i, 556 (11 December 1388 - Alexander dismissed); *ibid.*, i, 557 (2 April 1389 - Murdoch appointed).
33. National Register of Archives: Scotland [NRAS], 0925, earl of Erroll, no. 42; John Stuart (ed.), "The Errol Papers", in *Spalding Club Miscellany II* (Spalding Club, 1842), 319 (19 January 1390 - also styled justiciar north of Forth); W. Fraser, *History of the Carnegies, Earls of Southesk, and of their Kindred* (Edinburgh, 1867), ii, 498-9 (5 November 1390).
34. SRO, Register House Charters, RH6/no. 196. The grant reflected not only Fife's ambitions in Perthshire, but also the eclipse of the claims of Sir Malcolm Drummond to the barony of Strathord.
35. J. M. Thomson *et al.* (ed.), *Registrum Magni Sigilii Regum Scotorum* [RMS] (Edinburgh, 1882-1914), i, App. 2, no. 1744. Although undated, the charter is on a roll recording charters of 1395-6. It appears, however, that this charter confirmed an earlier grant.
36. *RMS*, i, no. 562; SRO, Breadalbane Collection, GD 112/1/no. 4; GD 112/2/34/1.
37. SRO, Register House Transcripts, RH 1/2/134.
38. *ER*, ii, 425.
39. *RMS*, i, no. 676.
40. *Ibid.*, i, no. 389.
41. *APS*, i, 553.
42. *ER*, iii, 274, 310.
43. *Ibid.*, 274, 290.
44. SRO, Abercairny Muniments, GD 24/5/17.
45. Duke of Atholl's Muniments, Blair Castle, Blair Atholl, Box 2/Parcel 1.
46. *ER*, iii, 37.
47. BM, Campbell Charters, xxx, no. 19.
48. *ER*, iii, 274.
49. *Ibid.*, ii, 143, 187.
50. C. Innes (ed.), *Registrum Episcopatus Moraviensis* (Bannatyne Club, 1837), 353-4.
51. *ER*, iii, 277.
52. Bower, *Scotichronicon* ed. Watt, viii, 7.
53. *Wyntoun*, vi, 371-4.
54. Atholl Muniments, Bound Volume, no. 8.
55. SRO, Murthly Castle Muniments, GD 121/Box 4/Bundle 10/no. 3; W. Fraser (ed.), *The Red Book of Grandtully* (Edinburgh, 1868), i, 3. In addition, Duncan Andrewson seems to have been given a grant of the lands to the north and south of Loch Tay in the reign of David II; *RMS*, i, App. 2, no. 1396.
56. *ER*, i, 555, 558.
57. *APS*, i, 579. Some of the names suggest that a Wester Ross or Caithness contingent was present.
58. Sir J. Balfour Paul (ed.), *The Scots Peerage* [SP] (Edinburgh, 1904-14), i, 147.
59. *ER*, iii, 402.
60. W. Fraser (ed.), *Memorials of the Family of Wemyss of Wemyss* (Edinburgh, 1888), iii, 44.
61. *APS*, i, 572.
62. *Moray Reg.*, 354-5. The terms of the indenture indicate that Alexander of the Isles had directly supplanted Alexander Stewart's position in the Great Glen. On 1 October 1386 Alexander Stewart had received a royal confirmation of his custody

of the lands and castle of Bona on the resignation of John, earl of Moray; SRO, Register House Charters, RH 6/no. 184.

63. *ER*, iii, 376.

64. *APS*, i, 570.

65. A. M. Sinclair, *The Clan Gillean* (Charlottetown, 1899), 276-280.

66. SRO, Rose of Kilravock, GD 125/Box 14; C. Innes (ed.), *A Genealogical Deduction of the Family of Rose of Kilravock* (Spalding Club, 1898), 131.

67. I.F. Grant, *The MacLeods: The History of a Clan 1200-1956* (London, 1959), 45-6.

68. *RMS*, i, no. 742.

69. Euphemia's attempts to gain a divorce from Alexander coincided with Albany's assault on the lord of Badenoch in 1389-92. Euphemia and her son Alexander Leslie, the heir to the earldom of Ross, were closely associated with Albany during the early 1390s. On 1 October 1392, for example, Euphemia issued a charter in Albany's castle of Stirling which was witnessed by Murdoch Stewart, Albany's son and heir, and to which Alexander Leslie gave his consent using the seal of Robert, earl of Fife and Menteith, guardian of the kingdom. NLS, Fleming of Wigtown, Ch. no. 15821. Shortly before Euphemia's charter was issued, on 9 June 1392, the bishops of St. Andrews, Glasgow and Aberdeen had been given a papal mandate to investigate Alexander, earl of Buchan's marriage to Euphemia, countess of Ross, which it was claimed had given rise to "wars, plundering, arson, murders and many other damages and scandals". It seems likely that Robert, earl of Fife, was involved in obtaining the commission because, on the same date, the pope granted a dispensation for the marriage of Robert's son Murdoch to the earl of Lennox's daughter. Charles Burns (ed.), *Calendar of Papal Letters to Scotland of Clement VII of Avignon 1378-1394* (Scottish History Society, 1976), 174. Euphemia submitted a further petition to the pope before 5 December 1392 (probably while she was with the earl of Fife in Stirling) on which date Clement VII gave permission for her separation from Alexander and for the restoration of her goods and property. *Ibid.*, 181. Alexander Leslie married Albany's daughter Isobel on some date before 1398 (*SP*, i, 149), and it seems likely that Albany arranged the marriage of Alexander's sister, Mary Leslie, to Donald, lord of the Isles, in the early 1390s in order to hold together the coalition of forces he had brought to bear against Alexander Stewart.

70. Bower, *Scotichronicon*, ed. Watt, viii, 39.

71. *Ibid.*, viii, 41.

72. Ho Peng Yoke, "Ancient and Mediaeval Observations of Comets and Novae in Chinese sources", *Vistas in Astronomy*, 5 (1962), 200. I should like to thank Dr. F. R. Stephenson, Department of Physics, University of Durham, for this reference.

73. Watt, *Dictionary*, 542.

74. *ER*, iii, 559-60.

75. *RMS*, i, No. 53.

76. Fraser, *Wemyss*, ii, 44.

77. Robert Douglas, *Baronage of Scotland* (Edinburgh, 1798), 553.

78. SRO, Paterson of Denmuir Writs, GD 1/34/1. The office of constabulary of an unspecified "castal" is added as an interlineation to this charter. The castle referred to was probably the episcopal castle since in August 1440 Alexander's son, John, received a charter of the same lands which included a grant of the constabulary of the episcopal castle; *RMS*, ii, no. 244.

79. *ER*, iii, 552, 559.

80. *Ibid.*

81. Fraser, *Wemyss*, ii, 38-42.

82. *APS*, i, 574-5.

83. W. Fraser (ed.), *The Douglas Book* (Edinburgh, 1885), iii, 31-2; W. Fraser (ed.), *The Stirlings of Keir* (Edinburgh, 1858), 207.

84. SRO, Mar and Kellie, GD 124/1/1055. Undated charter but *c.* April 1398 x July 1401.

85. Fraser, *Wemyss*, ii, 44

86. SRO, Register House Transcripts, RH 1/1/2. Original in earl of Mansfield's Muniments, Scone Palace.

87. SRO, Yule Collection, GD 90/1/29. A letter of 1 May 1380 from Falkland, by Robert earl of Fife and Menteith to "oure lufit squier hiwchon [Hugh] the Berclay, Lord of Kyppow".

88. *Wyntoun*, vi, 395-6.

89. *Ibid.*, vi, 398-401.

90. *Ibid.*

91. *Ibid.*, vi, 399.

92. Bower, *Scotichronicon*, ed. Watt, viii, 39.

93. *APS*, i, 498-501.

94. *Ibid.*, i, 572-3.

95. *ER*, iii, 546 (Edinburgh), 549 (Montrose), 552 (Dundee), 559 (Aberdeen).

96. *Ibid.*, iii, 549-50. Rothesay would also seem to have been attempting to gain control of the annual rents and lands which had previously been held by Queen Isabella (*RMS*, ii, no. 181).

97. Bower, *Scotichronicon*, ed. Watt, viii, 39.

98. *Ibid.*

99. SRO, Stair Muniments, GD 135/no. 375 (17 September 1401 - Isle of Cumbrae); HMC *Report*, XV, App. viii, 33 (11 October 1401 - Renfrew); NLS, Fleming of Wigtown, Ch. no. 15821 (1 December 1401 - Rutherglen). The disappearance of Rothesay as a royal charter witness means that it is not inconceivable that his arrest and imprisonment took place earlier than the February/March 1402 dates suggested by Bower's astronomical observations.

100. SRO, Court of Session Records (ADC), CS 5/xviii/Part ii/f. 90r.

101. BM, Additional MSS, no. 38,690, f. 9.

102. William Stewart, *The Buik of the Croniclis of Scotland*, ed. W. B. Turnbull (Rolls Series, 1858), iii, 473-8.

103. *ER*, iii, 363, 391, 415, 445, 474, 487, 492, 494, 496-8, 503, 524, 551, 571.

104. *Moray Reg.*, 197-201.

105. *ER*, iii, 266.

106. Bower, *Scotichronicon*, ed. Watt, viii, 41.

107. Francis McGurk (ed.), *Calendar of Papal Letters to Scotland, Benedict XII of Avignon 1394-1419* (Scottish History Society, 1976), 45.

108. John Stuart (ed.), *Spalding Club Miscellany V* (Spalding Club, 1852), 230.

109. *RMS*, ii, no. 380.

110. *ER*, iii, 406, 428; Bower, *Scotichronicon*, ed. Watt, viii, 5.

111. *Papal Letters, Benedict XII*, 70.

112. *Ibid.*

113. SRO, Register House Charters, RH 6/no. 205 (Duncan Petyt as chancellor); J. Anderson (ed.), *Calendar of the Laing Charters 854-1837* (Edinburgh, 1899), no. 83, 5 June 1397. (Greenlaw as chancellor).

114. *RMS*, ii, no. 181.

115. *ER*, iii, 251 - *ad indicem*.

116. *Moray Reg.*, 197-201. David Lindsay named as a member of Robert earl of Fife's council in 1389 in an arbitration at Inverness between the bishop and earl of Moray.

117. *NLS*, Crawford and Balcarres Collection (Personal Papers 75/1/1-4).
118. Alexander Lindsay, Lord Lindsay, *Lives of the Lindsays; or a Memoir of the Houses of Crawford and Balcarres* (London, 1849), i, 99.
119. *RMS*, i, no. 938.
120. SRO, Maitland-Thompson Notebooks, GD 212/Box 1/Book 6/p. 178.
121. SRO, Perth Burgh Records (Inventory), B 59/23/8 & 9. Originals in Sandeman Library, Perth.
122. SRO, Register House Transcripts, RH 2/2/13, no. 52. Sir James Scrymgeour, the constable of Dundee, appears to have been a member of Crawford's affinity. D. Macpherson *et al.* (ed.), *Rotuli Scotiae in Turri Londinensi et in Domo Capitulari Westmonasteriensi Asservati* (Edinburgh, 1814-19), ii, 136.
123. *Wyntoun*, vi, 404.
124. *ER*, iii, p. lxxix; *RMS*, ii, no. 1239.
125. SRO, Register House Charters, RH 6/no. 211.
126. *SP*, iv, 37.
127. Watt, *Dictionary*, 238-9; Greenlaw was certainly a member of the duke's chamberlain court on 19 May 1402. SRO, Register House Transcripts, RH 2/2/13, no. 52.
128. C. Innes (ed.), *Registrum Episcopatus Aberdonensis* (Spalding Club, 1845), 207.
129. SRO, Mar and Kellie, GD 124/7/3. Robert, duke of Albany, also gave committed support to the Erskine claim to Mar during the 1390s when there appears to have been an attempt by Sir Malcolm Drummond to obtain a male entail of the earldom. SRO, Mar and Kellie, GD 124/1/118 and 119.
130. Eg, J. Robertson and G. Grut (ed.), *Illustrations of the Topography and Antiquities of Aberdeen and Banff* (Spalding Club, 1847-69), ii, 372. A charter of 3 November 1402 by Isabella to Sir Alexander Keith of the lands of Glendowachy and Doun; *Maitland Club Miscellany I* (Maitland Club, 1834), part ii, 358, 8 April 1403. A charter of Melginch and Clova in favour of David, earl of Crawford.
131. BM, Cotton MSS, Vespasian Fvii, no. 18. The earl of March's letter of 18 February 1400 to Henry IV in which he complains that Rothesay has greatly wronged his daughter by marrying another "as it ys said", a phrase which suggests that March did not yet know for certain that the Rothesay/Douglas marriage had taken place.
132. *Wyntoun*, vi, 393-4; Bower, *Scotichronicon*, ed. Watt, viii, 33.
133. Bower, *Scotichronicon*, ed. Watt, viii, 162 (notes).
134. *Liber Sancte Marie de Melros* (Bannatyne Club, 1837), ii, 490-1. A charter of that date issued by George, earl of March, at Dunbar witnessed by, amongst others, Sir Robert Maitland and Sir Patrick Hepburn. On 17 May Dunbar's heritable pension from the burgh of Dunbar was allowed at the exchequer session. *ER* iii, 499.
135. *Wyntoun*, vi, 392-3.
136. SRO, Swinton Charters, GD 12/nos. 14 & 15.
137. Eg, *Melrose Liber*, ii, 490-1; *Laing Charters*, no. 81.
138. SRO, Swinton Charters, GD 12/no. 16.
139. Bower, *Scotichronicon*, ed. Watt, viii, 33.
140. *Ibid.*
141. *APS*, i, 575-6.
142. *Rot. Scot.*, ii, 157.
143. H. Nicolas (ed.), *Proceedings and Ordinances of the Privy Council of England* (London, 1834), i, 127.
144. *ER*, vi, 55.
145. *HMC Report*, XV, App. viii, 33. 11 October 1401. Tibbers to Sir Robert Maitland; *RMS*, i, App. 2, no. 1769, *c.* 1401-2. Gordon and Fogo to Adam Gordon.

146. F. C. Hingeston (ed.), *Royal and Historical Letters during the Reign of Henry the Fourth* (London, 1860), i, 52-56.
147. *HMC Report*, XV, App. viii, 33.
148. *APS*, vii, 159.
149. E. L. G. Stones (ed.), *Anglo-Scottish Relations 1174-1328: Some Selected Documents* (Oxford, 1965), 173-182.
150. SRO, Swinton Charters, GD 12/no. 16; Register House Charters RH 6/no. 210.
151. Hingeston, *Letters, Henry IV*, i, 58-65.
152. *Ibid.*, i, 52-56.
153. *Ibid.*, i, 58-65.
154. Nicolas, *Privy Council*, i, 127.
155. Bower, *Scotichronicon*, ed. Watt, viii, 39; *APS*, i, 582-3.
156. *APS*, i, 582-3.
157. A.A.M. Duncan, "Councils General 1404-1423", *Scottish Historical Review*, 35 (1956), 136. From an examination of the general council of April 1404, Duncan suggests that Albany received a two-year lieutenancy in mid-May 1402.
158. M. Brown, "Crown Magnate Relations in the Personal Rule of James I of Scotland (1424-1437)" (Unpublished PhD Thesis, University of St. Andrews, 1991), 139.
159. BM, Additional MSS, no. 38,690, f. 9-11.
160. C. Innes (ed.), *Registrum Honoris de Morton* (Bannatyne Club, 1853), ii, 202-3. On 30 May 1402 James Douglas, son and heir of James Douglas of Dalkeith, had the forty pound pension due to him for his special retinue service to Rothesay continued by a grant made by Robert III at Dalkeith.
161. SRO, Bruce and Kerr WS, Box 9/Bundle 1.
162. BM, Harleian MSS, no. 4694, f. 15v-16v.
163. H. C. Maxwell-Lyte (ed.), *Calendar of Patent Rolls Henry IV 1401-5* (London, 1905), 99-100.
164. *Ibid.*, 125.
165. Bower, *Scotichronicon*, ed. Watt, viii, 43.
166. *Ibid.*
167. *Ibid.*, viii, 43-49; *HMC Report*, X, App. vi, pp. 77-8.

2

"It is I, the Earle of Mar": In Search of Thomas Cochrane

NORMAN MACDOUGALL

There are surely few historical figures about whom so much has been written, and yet so little is really known, as Thomas Cochrane, the notorious familiar of King James III. In sixteenth-century chronicles he appears enjoying a brief career as the king's evil genius until his well-merited demise, hanged over Lauder Bridge in 1482 by an incensed Scottish nobility[1]; by the early eighteenth century his supposed career as 'Prime Minister' of James III produced a short pamphlet war in London, conducted by individuals seeking to defend or attack the ministry of Sir Robert Walpole[2]; and in the nineteenth and twentieth centuries Cochrane has to some extent been rehabilitated by historians who view him as a court architect of some importance, patronised by an unjustly maligned Renaissance monarch.[3] All this on the strength of two – possibly three – isolated references in contemporary official records,[4] a name on a notarial instrument,[5] and – by far the most influential sources – the stories of chroniclers who with one exception are not contemporaries of the events which they describe.

In recent years there has been something of a reaction against the ever-growing Cochrane legend, and a tendency to play down his roles both as architect and as the malign counsellor who almost cost James III his throne in 1482. The king, it is argued, created his own problems through his inept diplomacy and his failure to govern effectively. Cochrane cannot be shown to be a maker of policy, but may more realistically be identified as a minor household servant who had the misfortune to be present at Lauder and was hanged, together with a few other individuals of little political importance, possibly following a struggle to prevent the seizure of the king. It was only much later, the argument continues, that chroniclers shifted the emphasis of the Lauder crisis from the main event – the arrest of the king by members of his nobility – to the sideshow, the hanging of Cochrane and other familiars.[6] And although Pitscottie, writing of course in the late sixteenth century, credits Cochrane with the skills of a mason who 'bigit money stain house witht his hand into the realme of Scottland',[7] it is possible, as we shall see, to identify only one building which is very probably his work. Yet the legend of Cochrane the architect, and still more that of Cochrane the evil royal adviser, persists in both popular and scholarly literature[8]; and so the time may be ripe to reconsider the evidence in an effort to find the man.

It should be admitted at the outset that any estimate of Cochrane's career can only be a tentative one at best, for we lack the source which would almost certainly have given us a clear answer as to his status and influence at court (or lack of both) – the treasurer's accounts, that mine of information on the disbursement of the casual income of the crown, in which we might have expected to find royal pensions granted to Cochrane and other household men, and probably also the purpose of the grants, during the years associated with the familiars, 1479 to 1482. Sadly, the accounts survive only for some sixteen months of 1473–4. We also suffer from a huge gap in the records of the lords of council in civil causes, the judicial wing of the royal council, a register of whose business begins in 1478. While one would hardly have expected to find Cochrane sitting as a royal judge, his meteoric rise in royal service, if it remotely resembled the descriptions lavished on it by later chroniclers, would have been likely to provoke acrimonious and prolonged litigation. But only the merest hint of this survives, perhaps because there are no recorded sittings of the lords of council between 2 October 1480 and 23 April 1483.

Faced with an unpromising lack of official evidence, the student of Cochranology is more or less forced to begin with chronicle sources. The obvious starting point is a short chronicle – a mere ten folios – which describes the history of Scotland from its mythological beginnings down to 1482. This anonymous work is entitled 'Heir is assignt the cause quhy oure natioun was callyt fyrst the Scottys', and is appended to one of the early manuscripts of Andrew Wyntoun's 'Orygynale Cronykyl of Scotland'.[9] It may have been written around 1530 as one of many sixteenth-century attempts to provide a continuation of Hector Boece's *Scotorum Historiae*; but it is equally likely that it was composed earlier, perhaps in the 1480s, as it provides us with a detailed account of the events of 1479–82, breaking off following the arrest and imprisonment of King James in the latter year.[10] Although Cochrane is not mentioned by name, the writer suggests sinister court forces at work in 1479. 'That zere', he says, 'was mony weches and warlois [witches and warlocks] brint on crag gayt and Jhone the erle of mar the kingis brothir was slayne becaus thai said he faworyt the weches and warlois'. 'Thai' are not named, but there follows immediately a description of the war with England, the consequent high price of meal, and the striking of 'black money' by James III. As a result of all this, 'mony pure folk deit of hunger'. Then in July 1482, 'the king of Scotland purposyt till haif passyt in Ingland with the power of

Scotland' – perhaps a reference to James III's determination to defend or relieve Berwick – 'and passyt on gaitwart to lawdyr and thar the lordis of Scotland held thair counsaill in the kirk of lauder and cryit downe the blak silver and thai slew ane part of the kingis housald and other part thai banysyt'. Thereafter the magnates involved in the seizure of the king put him in Edinburgh Castle 'in firm kepyng', their justification being that James 'wrocht mair the consaell of his housald at [that] war bot sympill [ie, low-born] na he did of thame that was lordis'. The political crisis over, the writer records the ensuing economic improvement, with the price of the boll of meal dropping dramatically.[11]

It is clear from this account of 1479–82 that the chronicler associates the royal familiars – James's 'sympill' counsellors – with the ills of the period, though he stops short of naming them or directly attributing to them any of the crown's policies, for which he criticises the king himself. However, contemporary awareness of the influence of the royal familiars on the king's actions is to be found elsewhere, in the anonymous poem 'The Thre Prestis of Peblis', dating from the 1480s or early 1490s; the poet strongly – if conventionally – criticises the Scottish king – presumably James III – for failing to administer firm justice throughout the land, and explains that 'he luifit ouer weil yong counsel', who encouraged him to waste his time.[12] And the near-contemporary biography of James III's queen, Margaret of Denmark, by the Bolognese writer, Giovanni Sabadino degli Arienti, roundly condemns the king for allowing the affairs of the kingdom to go from bad to worse, and claims that Queen Margaret possessed more aptitude than James for ruling Scotland. The same writer, probably basing his work on information supplied to him by an expatriate Scot in 1487, identifies the king's misgovernance as the principal reason for the crisis of 1482. Sabadino describes this as a seizure of James III by his people, with the consent of his brother (Albany) and the queen, and his subsequent lodging in Edinburgh Castle to rid himself of the bad qualities imputed to him.[13] The Lauder executions and the familiars are absent from Sabadino's work, and the events of 1482 are seen purely in terms of a domestic crisis of dramatic proportions.

Within James III's lifetime and shortly thereafter, therefore, criticisms of the king's style of government prior to 1482 were already widespread, and were associated with the malign influence of his 'yong' or 'sympill' – and as yet unnamed – counsellors. Yet one name at least appears to have been known. In a remarkable aside, noted many years ago by James Burns,[14] John Mair describes a duel or single combat between Robert Cochrane and William Tor, which he says took place in the reign of James III and which was much talked about at the time. This statement appears not, as one might expect, in Mair's *History* of 1521, but in the first edition of his commentary on Book IV of Peter Lombard's *Sentences*, published in Paris in 1509, under the heading *An duellum sit licitum*. Robert Cochrane was the victor in the combat which Mair describes; and he goes on to remark that it was widely said at the time that this was either because Tor's horse had stumbled or because Cochrane had employed witchcraft, concluding that this was also his opinion as a young man at home.[15]

There can be no doubt that the Robert Cochrane of Mair's story is James III's notorious familiar. Mair himself, as Burns reminds us, is an excellent authority for what was being said in James III's Scotland.[16] Born in 1467, he began his education in Haddington, and while still at home on the farm of Gleghornie near North Berwick, he heard James III's cannon pounding Albany's castle of Dunbar, eight miles away, in May 1479.[17] Late in 1489 or early in 1490, Mair left Scotland and, with the exception of one brief visit, did not return until 1518.[18] In short, Mair's youth and early manhood were spent in a politically sensitive area of Scotland in the reign of James III, and the Scotland to which he refers in the *Quartus Sententiarum* of 1509 is the country of his youth, the Scottish south-east of the late 1470s and 1480s.

In addition to Mair's impressive qualifications as a contemporary authority, we may note that the story which he tells about the Cochrane/Tor duel, and which he claims was widely known in his youth, is designed to portray Cochrane in an unfavourable light; and the reference to his winning through use of witchcraft provides a fascinating link with the Royal MS chronicle, mentioned above, which states that the earl of Mar was slain because 'thai said' he favoured witches and warlocks.[19] It may be added that Cochrane's opponent, William Tor, cannot firmly be identified. Possibly, as Burns has suggested, he is the 'umquhile' William Tor of that ilk who appears fleetingly in official records from 1494. If so, he was probably a Fife laird, dead before 15 December 1494, whose lands were subsequently the source of a protracted legal dispute before the lords of council.[20] If Tor's duel with Cochrane took place in the presence of James III, Fife or Lothian – areas where, as parliament was later to declare, the king had 'maist residence'[21] – would be the most likely venues.

Thus the popular contemporary view of Cochrane, first enshrined in Mair's *Quartus Sententiarum* of 1509, was of a victor in a combat, probably before the king, who had achieved his success either through his opponent's misfortune or through use of witchcraft. When Cochrane next appears (that is outwith later editions of Mair's *Quartus Sententiarum*, in which the story of the Cochrane/Tor combat is repeated without Cochrane being named), it is in the chronicle of John Law, a canon of St. Andrews, completed 1521–4; and the notorious familiar has undergone a remarkable sea-change. His Christian name, in Law's account, is Thomas, he is credited with the coining of the royal black money, and his death at Lauder is described as a hanging. Thus Law has absorbed the theme of the unpopularity of the debased coinage, already present in the Royal MS chronicle, linked it directly to Thomas Cochrane, and made the coining of the black money the crime for which

Cochrane was hanged. As we shall see, he appears to have acquired the correct Christian name for Cochrane; but the context in which he places the royal familiar's activities is hopelessly confused. Cochrane appears immediately after Law's description of the fall of the Livingstons (dated 1469!), and it precedes Albany's arrest and escape from Edinburgh Castle and the readeption of Henry VI of England in 1470.[22] All this appears surprising confusion for a man who had sat at the feet of John Mair in the arts faculty of the German nation at Paris in 1508–9;[23] and we must conclude that if the two men ever talked about the recent past in Scotland, the career of Cochrane was not one of the subjects under discussion.

A rather more substantial, not to say more convincing, contribution to Cochranology was made by Sir David Lindsay of the Mount in his long vernacular poem, 'The Testament and Complaynt of Our Soverane Lordis Papyngo', which he completed in 1530.[24] This is of course almost half-a-century after Lauder Bridge; but Lindsay should be taken seriously as a source for earlier events. His first known employment at court was in October 1511 when, though still a young man, he clearly held a position of some importance in the household of James IV, for he received an annual pension of £40 for his services. On the birth of the future James V in April 1512, Lindsay was at once appointed as usher or chief page to the infant heir to the throne.[25] He was thus in an excellent position to learn what was said, not simply in the country at large, but at court, about James IV's predecessor, and to transmit it in writing some twenty years later as a cautionary political tale for his youthful charge, James V.

In Lindsay's long poem (1190 lines), James III takes his place in a chronological sequence of thumbnail sketches of the Stewart kings, being allotted six stanzas, each of seven lines – that is, one stanza more than Lindsay devotes to his illustrious successor and first employer, James IV. Significantly, more than half the section on James III is devoted to the favourites, described by Lindsay as 'Cochrane, with his catyve companye'. Cochrane is given no Christian name, and in Lindsay's account he acts throughout with his 'companye' of familiars, whose rise at court seems to occur at the same time. Their crimes include the fairly conventional complaint of acquiring the ear of the king to the exclusion of all other counsellors, and of advising him badly:

> Allace! that Prince, be thair abusion
> Was fynalie brocht to confusion.

The familiars are not, however, accused by Lindsay of witchcraft or the coining of the black money; but he does indict them of a charge at least as serious, that of sowing discord between James III and his brothers, the duke of Albany and the earl of Mar:

> Thay [the familiars] clam so heych, and gat sic audience,
> And with thair Prince grew so familiar,
> His germane brother muycht get no presence;

The Duke of Albanie, nor the Erle of Mar,
Lyke baneist men, was haldin at the bar,
Tyll in the Kyng thare grew sic mortall feid,
He flemit the Duke, and patt the Erle to dede.

There follows a brief description of the Lauder Bridge hangings as an appropriate end for individuals who 'that tyme in courte clam so presumpteouslye', and a brief reference to the imprisonment of the king.

In "The Testament of the Papyngo", then, Lindsay not only draws on already existing tales of bad counsel, but suggests that it went much further than simply inducing the king to neglect his duties. For the first time, Cochrane and the other royal familiars are held responsible for an active role in James III's break with his brothers, unquestionably the most crucial political events of the period 1479–82. The hints about the death of Mar in the Royal MS chronicler, and Sabadino's claim that the people led by Albany and the queen arrested the king for his misgovernance, are now replaced by Lindsay with specific charges which bring Cochrane and the rest to the very centre of the Scottish political stage.

They remain there in 'The Roit and Quheill of Tyme', a short history of Scotland from its legendary beginnings down to 1537, the work of Adam Abell, a friar of the Observant Franciscan house at Jedburgh.[26] Not surprisingly, Abell's history draws heavily on that of Hector Boece; but for those parts of it closest to his own time, including the section on James III, Abell appears to have relied largely on oral transmission, stories about Scottish rulers circulating in his own neighbourhood.[27] His thumbnail sketch of James III is little more than a eulogy of Alexander, duke of Albany, without whose support the king is lost. King James is portrayed sympathetically by Abell as a devout man, "but gretumlie gevin to carnale pleseure by his halie quene and privat consall of sympill men be the quhilk consall he destroeit his awne bredir maist necessair to him. For the herll of Mar wes slane be consall of ane trucur callit cochrene".[28] A 'trucur' is a rascal or scoundrel; in Scottish historical literature, Cochrane has as yet no trade or profession.

The flight of Albany in 1479 is described by Abell as banishment: 'Alexander the Duke of Albany', he tells us, 'wes banest diverss tymis the yere of god 1480 or thare about', though he does not seem to hold Cochrane responsible, either directly or indirectly, for the duke's fall from grace. However, Abell is in no doubt that 'be the consall of forsaid cochron wes cunyet the blak copir quhar throw raiss gret darth and mortalite in the realm'. This passage is very similar to that in the Royal MS chronicle, reiterating the point that the black money caused hardship and underpinning this by claiming that Cochrane was the man responsible for counselling the king to strike a debased coinage. In this way, some of the blame for the crisis is shifted from James III to Cochrane, who is duly despatched at 'the raid of lawdir quhar the king wes tane be the lordis and put in the castell of edinburgh als cochren and the laif of his priwat consall wes tane and justifiit to be hangit'.[29]

By the 1530s, then, popular oral tradition and historical literature had combined for half-a-century to establish a view of Cochrane as the low-born familiar of James III whose crimes, varying from the assault on the royal brothers and the counselling of Mar's death to the coining of the black money, were the principal cause of the crisis of 1482. John Lesley, bishop of Ross, writing a vernacular history of Scotland covering 1437–1561, which he presented to Mary Queen of Scots in 1570, not only confirms the evil reputation of Cochrane established by the pre-Reformation writers, but adds to it, and for the first time introduces names for the other royal familiars. In Lesley's account, the king "uset young consall of unworthye vyle persouns, sic as Thomas Cochrain, quhome of ane maisone he had maid Erle of Mar, quha causit strik ane cunye of copper unmeit to have course or passage in ony realme'; in addition, King James rejected the counsel of his nobility and 'keipit him self quietlie, leveing voluptuouslie, and had lychtlyit his awin nobill Quene, and intertanit ane howir callit the Daesie, in her place; and siclyk had causit slay his awin brodir, the Erle of Mar, and banisd his uther brodir the Duik of Albany furth of the realme, quhilk all wes done be his said wicked counsell'.[30]

The outraged magnates, according to Lesley, held a council at the muster of the Scottish host at Lauder, seized the royal familiars, who are named as 'Thomas Cochran Erle of Mar, William Roger, and James Hommyll tailyeour, with certane uthers', and at once hanged them over the bridge, sparing only the eighteen-year-old John Ramsay, who begged the king to save his life. Thereafter they placed James III in Edinburgh Castle under the keepership of the earl of Atholl.[31]

Lesley's contribution to Cochranology, then, is to find an occupation for Cochrane – mason – and to declare not only that he was responsible for the death of the earl of Mar, but also that the king *made* him earl of Mar. This statement, if true, enormously increases both the extent of Cochrane's rise and the offence which it is likely to have caused. Lesley also supplies three further names, perhaps to give his account a firmer basis in fact, but none of them need detain us long as offensive royal favourites whom the nobility felt an urgent need to remove. William Roger may perhaps be identified with the clerk of the chapel royal who was in receipt of a pension of £20 from the Haddington customs in 1467.[32] Thereafter, if indeed the records refer to the same man, he did well in the 1470s, being described as the king's familiar squire and receiving the considerable windfall of the lands of Traquair in Peeblesshire, forfeited by the Boyds in 1469. However, some time after the royal revocation of 1476, Roger resigned the Traquair lands to the crown. He did not receive them back; instead they went to the king's devious and ambitious half-uncle, James Stewart, earl of Buchan.[38] And for the period of the supposed crimes of the familiars, 1479–82, Roger is not to be found in the records at all. The Piedmontese chronicler, Giovanni Ferrerio, who came to Scotland in 1528 and spent some years at Kinloss in the 1530s, remarked that Roger was the founder of a school of musicians who remembered him as late as 1529, and claimed that he was innocent of any crimes when seized at Lauder.[34] If William Roger died with the rest at Lauder, then, his crime may have been that he failed to get out of the way in time, and his presence in a royal household which also contained Cochrane cost him his life.

Lesley's other two named familiars, however, survived Lauder Bridge. In the case of John Ramsay, he went on to become Lord Bothwell and a prime target for the rebel nobility in 1488;[35] and James Hommyl, the royal tailor who received an annual pension of £20 for life for the first time in 1478, can be shown to have performed a diplomatic errand for James III in his hour of need in 1488,[36] but can hardly be seen as a malign influence on crown policy before 1482. He might well have been the sort of individual who encouraged the king, not in the pursuit of unpopular policies, but in the neglect of his duties, as in the bringing to court of the whore Daisy; but of this we have no evidence at all.[37]

Lesley confidently throws light on one other obscure area, namely the identities of those magnates who seized Cochrane and the rest at Lauder. They are named as Archibald, earl of Angus, George, earl of Huntly, John, earl of Lennox (that is, John Stewart, Lord Darnley, claimant to the Lennox), James, earl of Buchan, Andrew Lord Gray, Robert Lord Lyle, 'and diveris utheris".[38] This list is not a confused gather-up of virtually every prominent Scottish magnate, such as we find in Pitscottie's later account of Lauder,[39] but rather an interesting combination of individuals who could be seen as having a variety of very real grievances against the government of James III. Inevitably such convincing detail enhances our respect for Lesley as a source for 1482; and it may be that his position at court in the reign of Queen Mary, his task as co-editor of the first edition of Scottish parliamentary acts in 1566, and his claim to have consulted Scottish public archives and monastic chroniclers,[40] all combine to make his vernacular *History* the most convincing post-Reformation account of James III's reign. The same work's glaring errors could be explained in terms of his remoteness from his sources; for when he wrote in 1568–70, he was already a Marian exile in England. The Latin *History*, published a decade later in Rome, adds nothing further to our knowledge of the reign, nor to the career of Thomas Cochrane.

The case of Giovanni Ferrerio, who added an appendix covering the reign of James III to the second edition of Hector Boece's *Scotorum Historiae*, published at Paris in 1574, is rather different.[41] For much of his account, Ferrerio follows Lesley, sometimes word for word; clearly he had seen a manuscript copy of the latter's vernacular history. Certainly the two men were in Paris at the same time during Lesley's exile,[42] and they may have met there in the early 1570s. Yet the variations from Lesley in Ferrerio's text are also significant, and some of them concern Cochrane and the royal familiars. Ferrerio is the first writer to praise two of the king's friends. We have already noted his claim that William Roger, the English musician who was remembered as the founder of a school, was innocent of all crimes when hanged at Lauder; earlier in his account he mentions Roger together with Dr. John Ireland, in the context of James III's enthusiasm for scholarship and the arts.[43]

Ferrerio's sympathetic view of King James extends to his description of the Lauder hangings; not only does he provide the longest list of named familiars of all sixteenth-century accounts, but he also distinguishes between the guilty and the innocent amongst those hanged. Into the former category fall Robert Cochrane (a departure from Lesley's 'Thomas'), a mason greatly valued by the king, whom James had made earl of Mar; William Torphichen, 'in armis vir perstrenuus'; James Hommyl, tailor; and Lonnard (perhaps Leonard), a highly skilled artisan. The innocents, according to Ferrerio, are Thomas Preston, 'nobilis insignis', and William Roger; and he repeats the tale of the sparing of John Ramsay.[44]

If we except John Ireland, whom Ferrerio does not associate with the Lauder Bridge debacle and whose career is in any case well attested in public and private records,[45] there are three new names here – those of Lonnard, Preston, and Torphichen. Nothing can be said with any certainty about Lonnard; but Thomas Preston, the individual of noble birth who would subsequently appear as Cochrane's father-in-law in George Buchanan's *History*, may perhaps be identified with the individual who held the lands of Middle Pitcairn in Perthshire of the crown, who was paid £90 – probably during the Anglo-Scottish war of 1480–82 – for the bringing from Orkney of a captured English ship with a cargo of wine, and who was dead and forfeited before Christmas 1482.[46] Finally, William Torphichen, the familiar skilled in the use of arms, is surely William Tor, Robert Cochrane's opponent in single combat in Mair's *Quartus Sententiarum* of 1509, the name garbled in transmission to, or rationalised by, Ferrerio.

These details, together with Ferrerio's sympathetic treatment of the king and his familiars, indicate that he relied on sources other than Lesley. We know this to be the case; Ferrerio was, after all, no stranger to Scotland, having come there first in 1528, when he spent some time at court, subsequently being employed as a teacher of the monks at Kinloss Abbey between 1531 and 1537. As a result of the persuasions of Robert Reid, abbot of Kinloss while Ferrerio was there, and promoted to bishop of Orkney in 1540, Ferrerio returned to Scotland from Piedmont for a second period at Kinloss, lasting from 1540 until about 1544.[47] Thereafter, although he stayed abroad, he maintained links with Scotland, and in 1555 wrote from Paris to Bishop Reid, requesting his former patron to obtain for him George

Buchanan's Scottish history "for the work on which I am now engaged".[48] Ferrerio's *Appendix to Boece*, as we have seen, was not published till 1574, Buchanan's *History* even later, in 1582. Clearly, however, both men were working on their respective histories in the pre-Reformation period. Thus Ferrerio, in spite of his heavy reliance on Lesley, seems also to have made use of Mair or a source derived from Mair, and to have sought – and perhaps obtained – information from Buchanan, quite apart from having access to Scottish court sources at the end of the 1520s. In the matter of the familiars, he would appear to be influenced by Mair or Mair's source, which would explain both the Christian name Robert for Cochrane and the inclusion of William Torphichen/Tor. Perhaps significantly, Buchanan would also refer to Robert rather than Thomas Cochrane, and introduce Thomas Preston as the first of the royal familiars; but Ferrerio is unique in viewing them sympathetically, and in *praising* James III as an artistic monarch.

It comes almost as a relief to turn from the problems raised by the cosmopolitan Ferrerio to a local man who had no doubts about Cochrane and the rest – Robert Lindsay of Pitscottie, in whose *Historie*, completed around 1579, the royal familiar is accorded fuller treatment than in any earlier chronicle.[49] In Pitscottie's narrative, Cochrane stands alone, without the benefit of any named supporters or, indeed, any Christian name; and his influence on James III is wholly malign. He appears first immediately following Pitscottie's unfavourable comparison between King James and his brothers, Alexander, duke of Albany and John, earl of Mar. As earl of March, Albany was at loggerheads with the Humes and their allies the Hepburns, who challenged him over his right to the March rents and mails. Finding Albany too strong for them, the Humes and Hepburns sought the means to turn the King against his brother, and found the answer in 'ane new courteour ... callit Couchren', who had swiftly acquired pre-eminence at court through his influence with King James. In return for large sums of money, Cochrane promised the Humes and Hepburns that he would find the means to turn the king against his brothers, claiming that he himself stood in equal fear of them. The device employed was a witch whom Cochrane used to predict to James III that 'he sould be suddenlie slaine witht ane of the neirest of his kin.' The credulous king, who had hitherto loved his brothers, became suspicious, his fears and suspicions were fuelled by Cochrane, and finally 'in his awin heart condemnit them baitht to deith, and that be persuation of this fals flatterar Couchrin'. Then follows Pitscottie's description of the death of Mar, who came "obedientlie into his brother the kingis grace not dreadand nor suspecand na malice in the kingis heart", was arrested and quickly murdered in the Canongate of Edinburgh 'in ane baith fatt' – a brewer's or dyer's vat – though Pitscottie admits that he does not know who was responsible. Meanwhile Albany fled from his castle of Dunbar to Berwick;

James III sent 'certane nobell men' to Dunbar, which according to Pitscottie was obediently surrendered.[50]

With the removal of Albany and Mar, the last checks on Cochrane's rise had apparently gone, and he became an enormously powerful 'middle man' at court, without whose influence no-one might transact any business with James III. He charged heavily for his services, and recognising that the king was extremely covetous, paid him large sums to obtain the earldom of Mar. Subsequently, according to Pitscottie, King James gave Cochrane the right to strike his own currency 'as he had ben ane prince'. This coinage, consisting of 'Cochrane placks', is nowhere described as debased by Pitscottie; however, when 'the wyffis' refused the 'Cochrane plack' on the ground that it would soon be 'cryit doun' or demonetised, Cochrane replied that on the day that his currency was cried down, he would be hanged.[51]

The inevitable sequel in Pitscottie's *Historie* is, of course, the Lauder Bridge crisis and the hanging of Cochrane and the other familiars. Pitscottie adds some details about the royal expedition to the muster-point at Lauder, the king setting out from the burgh muir of Edinburgh, having brought artillery out of the castle and placed Cochrane 'earle of Mare' in charge of the guns. The journey south was by Soutra, where there was an overnight stop, and on the following day the royal army camped at Lauder. The 'haill lordis of Scotland' met in the kirk, and agreed to choose twenty-four of their number to deal with the grievances of all of them – the main complaint being the banishing of Albany and slaying of Mar, after which James III 'had maid Cowchrane that was bot ane maissone to fullfill his [Mar's] rowme quhairof they could not be contentit'. The unremarkable conclusion reached was that the king should be taken to Edinburgh Castle 'and in the meane tyme to tak Couchrane the earle of Mar and all the laif of the kingis familiearis and immediatlie hang thame ower the breig of Lawder'. At this point Cochrane himself arrived at the kirk door, dressed in a riding coat of black velvet, with a hunting horn at his belt, a gold chain valued at five hundred crowns round his neck, and accompanied by three hundred liveried men-at-arms who seem to have played a singularly ineffective role in the events which followed. Cochrane in his pride 'raschit rudlie' at the kirk door, and Sir Robert Douglas of Lochleven, who had been stationed there to keep guard, inquired who it was who knocked so rudely. 'Couchrane ansuerit, "It is I the Earle of Mar"', and was at once admitted and seized. Pitscottie names the earl of Angus and Douglas of Lochleven as the chief actors in Cochrane's arrest; his pleas to have his hands tied with silk from one of his tents rather than hemp were ignored, the king was seized, the magnates "hangit all his servandis ower the bredg of Lawder befoir his eine", and Cochrane was hanged 'abone the laif of his compleces'. After the hangings, the nobles issued a proclamation 'crying down' Cochrane's currency, so fulfilling his own prophecy.[52]

Pitscottie concludes with a brief obituary of the royal familiar. In origin, he says, Cochrane was only a mason's apprentice, but because of his skill – he 'bigit money stain house witht his hand' – he was soon made a master mason, and continued to rise until his fall from Lauder Bridge, which Pitscottie describes as a correction and punishment, an example to other low-born persons 'nocht to climb so hie and proceid in so great thingis in ane realm as he did.'[53] Thus in Pitscottie's *Historie*, the career of Cochrane is treated as a moral tale, a greatly expanded version of that contained in Lindsay's 'Testament of the Papyngo'. Together with a number of other Fife men, Pitscottie cites both Lindsay and Mair as sources for his *Historie*.[54] He could have met both men in their old age in north-east Fife, but it seems more likely that he assimilated information, much of it oral, which was circulating locally in their last years, the period of Pitscottie's youth and early manhood.

One writer whose contribution to Cochranology seems to have owed more to John Mair than Pitscottie was George Buchanan, whose *Rerum Scoticarum Historia* was published in 1582.[55] Although Buchanan tells a familiar tale – the favourites are named as Preston, Cochrane, and Roger, they are held responsible for counselling the death of Mar and arrest of Albany, and Cochrane himself for the coining of the black money, the acquisition of the earldom of Mar, and the alienation of James III from his magnates – his thumbnail sketch of Cochrane differs from that contained in other sixteenth-century sources. Having described Thomas Preston as a man descended from a noble family – a statement recalling Ferrerio's account – Buchanan continues by referring to 'Robert Cochrane, a man of great bodily strength with boldness to match it. He was brought to the king's notice by reason of a certain single combat, was at once raised from being an architect to courtiership and encouraged to hope for a more ample way of life'.[56] The single combat which introduced Cochrane to James III in Buchanan's account at once recalls the Cochrane-Tor duel in Mair's *Quartus Sententiarum*; and Mair, like Buchanan, gives Cochrane the Christian name of Robert.

Buchanan's *Rerum Scoticarum Historia* effectively brings to an end additions to the Cochrane saga in Scottish chronicles and histories. In the seventeenth century, Hume of Godscroft[57] and Drummond of Hawthornden[58] would simply repeat the established tales, with Cochrane firmly established as 'Robert' in the Mair- Ferrerio-Buchanan tradition; and Pinkerton[59] at the end of the eighteenth century and Scott[60] in the early nineteenth continue to follow this well-trodden path. In short, by the end of the sixteenth century the story of Cochrane seems to be complete. In spite of its tortuous meanderings, inconsistencies, and blatant exaggerations, the tale has some substance. First, the asides of Mair and the information acquired at court and elsewhere by Sir David Lindsay take us right back into the Scotland of James III and James IV, when it was clearly widely held that the courtier Cochrane had an evil reputation; this contemporary and sub-contemporary comment is reinforced by John Law, writing in the early 1520s, and by Ferrerio, who first came to court in 1528. So the weight of evidence would suggest that it is not possible simply to regard Cochrane as an unfortunate minor household servant who happened to get in the way at Lauder.[61] Secondly, Cochrane is the only royal familiar of any significance in the sixteenth-century chronicle accounts. He is the first to appear; his career is gradually developed; and the others – Roger, Preston, Hommyl and the rest – are peripheral figures, introduced perhaps to give some colour to James III's 'catyve companye', but hardly convincing criminal types. Indeed, Ferrerio, as we have seen, suggests that Preston and Roger were innocent men, and we know that Hommyl survived Lauder Bridge. The evil genius at court is invariably Cochrane; and given the powerful indictment against him in the chronicles, we should expect to find solid contemporary evidence of at least one great crime, directly attributable to him.

At first sight, the meagre contemporary records would appear to dash such hopes. In the period which the chroniclers associate with Cochrane, 1479–82, there are only three references to a Thomas Cochrane, and while it is probable that these all refer to the same man, it is impossible to be certain. Chronologically, the first reference comes in the records of the lords of council for 22 January 1479–80. On that date the lords ordered Hugh Rose of Kilravock, William Thane of Cawdor, Thomas Cumming and Alexander Cumming to pay a total of £60 Scots to Thomas Cochrane. They were to make this payment because they had earlier promised the same sum to the deceased Sir John Colquhoun of that ilk, 'vschare ... of our sowerane lordis chawmer durre', and the king had reassigned the £60 to Cochrane.[62] This is a significant payment, indicating that Cochrane's status was that of a royal household servant and familiar, in this instance paid, for example, three times more than the annual provision for the royal tailor James Hommyl. The date of the grant may also provide an indication of the time at which Cochrane first came to James III's attention; for Sir John Colquhoun of Luss had been killed at the royal siege of Albany's castle of Dunbar some time between 18 April and 24 May 1479,[63] dying, according to Bishop Lesley, as one of three knights on the royal side slain 'with the schot of ane gun'.[64] There is a temptation to associate Cochrane with the siege of Dunbar, perhaps even coming to James III's attention in his single combat with William Tor in the royal camp during the siege, and thereafter an obvious candidate for the dead Colquhoun's pension. However that may be, Cochrane did not take on Colquhoun's mantle; for the knight of Luss had been a prominent crown official and frequent royal charter witness since 1474, with spells as comptroller and chamberlain in the 1460s and 1470s respectively.[65] By contrast, Cochrane enjoyed no known office in state or household, and his name never appears in royal charter witness lists, although no less than sixty-eight such lists are to be found in the register of the great seal between May 1479 and the Lauder Bridge crisis.[66] It follows from this that Cochrane's not inconsiderable royal pension was to be paid for services to the king which remain mysterious, but which at the time provoked sufficient opposition, or at least delay, amongst those who were required to pay the £60 that the matter had to be settled before the lords of council.

Chronologically, the second contemporary record to refer to Cochrane suggests that the royal familiar's status and income had increased significantly by 1482. In an otherwise unremarkable notarial instrument certifying the appointment of procurators in a transfer of Invernessshire lands, and dated 20 May 1482, one of those named as a procurator is Thomas Cochrane, constable of the castle of Kildrummy.[67] There can be little doubt that this is the same Cochrane, for the surname, though common enough in Renfrewshire and the Lothians, is startlingly unfamiliar in Aberdeenshire. The annual fee for the keepership of Kildrummy was £26 13s4d. in 1471,[68] and was probably the same a decade later; but far more significant is the wealth which Cochrane's status as the castle's keeper may have brought him. Kildrummy was the chief castle in the earldom of Mar, and the revenues of Mar do not appear in crown exchequer accounts between the forfeiture of John, earl of Mar, in 1479–80 and Martinmas 1483.[69] If Cochrane had been assigned all or part of the Mar revenues some time between 1479 and 1482, then he was gaining access to crown lands worth £371 6s8d, or £505 13s5d if we include Garioch which the late earl had also held.[70] The conferring of such wealth, or potential wealth, on a familiar of only a few months' standing would explain both the later chroniclers' belief that Cochrane was made earl of Mar – or that he bought the earldom from the king – and also the claim that he had advised James III to remove his brother.

It may, however, be argued that this is carrying the evidence of a single reference to Cochrane as custodian of Kildrummy much too far; but there exists a tradition, not to be found in any of the chroniclers, which suggests that Cochrane was not simply a royal favourite enjoying a pension drawn from the revenues of Mar at a safe distance, but was personally active in the area. In his *History of Scots Affairs, 1637–41*, probably written in the 1670s, James Gordon, parson of Rothiemay, describes the marquis of Huntly's determination to take the part of King Charles I in the struggle against the covenanting party, led in the north-east by James Graham, marquis of Montrose. Gordon comments that Huntly, casting around for strongpoints, considered 'one castell, seven myles west from Strabogye, near Balveny, callit Achindowne castell (built, as is affirmed, by Cochrain, who was minion to King James the Third)'.[71] Auchindoun Castle is an imposing fifteenth-century tower, standing on a commanding promontory overlooking the river Fiddich, less than three miles south-east of the older Balvenie Castle and some fourteen miles west of Huntly.[72] Parson Gordon's belief that Cochrane was Auchindoun's builder is clearly based on local Gordon tradition and must be taken seriously; for the parson includes his comment on Cochrane simply as an aside, he stands quite outwith the mainstream chronicle tradition which by the seventeenth century had created a formidable – and rather different – legend for the royal familiar, and he associates Cochrane with the building of Auchindoun, a north-eastern castle little more than twenty miles from Kildrummy, where record evidence firmly places him in 1482. Thus Cochrane's stone-masonry and his control of the earldom of Mar are convincingly linked.

Cochrane's final appearance in contemporary records – if it is indeed he – comes almost as an anti-climax. In an action before the lords of council on 2 May 1483, £20 worth of the lands of Cousland near Dalkeith are described as having pertained to 'umquhile thomas of cochran'; a dispute over tenancy on these lands had occurred 'eftir the dede and forfature of the said thomas'.[73] The Cochrane described here is likely to be our man. The timing is right, allowing for the dislocation of government business following the Lauder crisis in July 1482, and Cochrane is described as dead before forfeiture, an order of events which would fit the Lauder hangings. In any event, this final reference adds some £20 worth of Lothian land to Cochrane's income, and emphasises his southern origins; he may indeed have been a kinsman of the Renfrewshire Cochranes, three of whom are to be found in Lord Darnley's garrison of Edinburgh Castle in the autumn of 1482.[74]

From all this, it seems clear that Cochrane, a southerner who was employed by James III in the north-east, performed the role which earned him later notoriety in the earldom of Mar. But it would be going too far to associate Cochrane directly with Mar's death, which reads like a much later rationalisation of the fact that he obtained a crown office (and possibly extensive revenues) within Mar. Other apparently promising leads, such as Pitscottie's claims of friction between Alexander, duke of Albany, and the Humes and Hepburns, with Cochrane used by the latter to get rid of the former, do not seem to lead anywhere; and even the theme of witchcraft, which recurs like a leitmotif in the chroniclers from Mair to Buchanan, may be no more than a reflection of hostile public opinion. We have no evidence at all that Cochrane dabbled in the black arts. On the other hand, charges of witchcraft which partially mask indictments for treason are remarkably topical at this time; in 1478, George, duke of Clarence, brother of Edward IV of England, had been executed for conspiracy with necromancers and witches in a fashion which strikingly anticipates later Scottish accounts of Mar's death.[75]

Thus it would be a mistake to believe that during the critical years 1479–82 the government of James III was working to a hidden agenda drawn up by Thomas Cochrane. The policies pursued by king and council – above all consistent adherence to the English alliance – had been followed since the early 1470s, long before Cochrane made his first appearance at court; and even after his arrival, his influence on policy must be doubted. For example, the coining of the black money appears to have been the responsibility of the king – the early Royal MS chronicle says as much[76] – and the coins were presumably struck by the royal moneyer, William Goldsmyth, who may have acquired his later nickname of 'Halfpeny man' from his activities in 1480–82.[77] Nor is there any question that Lauder Bridge, and the 'crying doune' of the black money, put an end to it, for it was still in circulation as late as 1487.[78]

It may be added that Cochrane's activities in royal service do not initially seem to have caused offence. After all, the sum of £60 allotted to him early in 1480 was the result of a decision by the lords of council, who on that occasion included Thomas Spens, bishop of Aberdeen; Andrew Stewart Lord Avandale, the chancellor; Colin Campbell, earl of Argyll, master of the royal household; Archibald Whitelaw, the secretary; Master Alexander Inglis, provost of St. Andrews, clerk register; and John Ross of Montgrenan, the king's advocate.[79] The list includes almost every major officer of state; and it follows that those in charge of the government of James III during the critical years before 1482 initially saw Cochrane as a familiar who could do the king some service and deserved rewards.

If this is so, who then objected so strongly to Cochrane's activities that the muster of the Scottish host at Lauder in July 1482 turned into a lynching party? It may be, as Ranald Nicholson suggests,[80] that the earl of Angus took a major part in arresting and hanging Cochrane because he was incensed at James III's treatment of his Boyd kinsfolk. But such a grievance, while it might prompt Angus to attack and seize the king, does not explain why the earl wished Cochrane dead. There is, however, a fair amount of circumstantial evidence to support the view that those who actively sought Cochrane's death at Lauder were George Gordon, 2nd earl of Huntly, and his kinsman James Ogilvy of Deskford and Findlater.

It seems likely that Cochrane's activities in the north-east – the custodianship of Kildrummy (and likely influence throughout Mar) and the building of Auchindoun – caused considerable offence to these powerful northern magnates. Huntly may indeed be regarded as an earl on the make, prepared to lend active support to the crown in return for a free hand in Gordon expansion in the north. But successive Stewart kings were wary of Gordon ambitions; James II had removed Alexander, 1st earl of Huntly, earl George's father, from the keepership of Kildrummy Castle in 1457,[81] and James III had failed to reward the 2nd earl with the keepership of Dingwall Castle, although Huntly had recovered the castle for the crown from the rebellious earl of Ross.[82] By the late 1470s, then, George, earl of Huntly had both an interest in Mar inherited from his father, and probably also a sense of grievance that he had not been properly rewarded by James III for his military services in Ross. The forfeiture of King James's brother, John, earl of Mar, in 1479–80, must have seemed an opportunity for Huntly to extend his influence into the earldom. The intrusion of a royal familiar of no great standing, and from southern Scotland, into Kildrummy by May 1482, if not before, could be seen as yet another rebuff to a loyal earl from an ungrateful king – and that at a time of crisis, with the problem of Ross largely unresolved and English invasion of south-east Scotland imminent.

Huntly's response was to come south for the Lauder muster. He arrived early, and in strength; on 8 July 1482, a fortnight before the crisis, he was in Edinburgh, accompanied by other northern magnates including William, earl of Erroll, Alexander, master of Crawford, William Lord Forbes, James Innes of that ilk, and James Ogilvy of Findlater.[83] On 21 July, the day before the Lauder crisis broke, Huntly was at Redpath, some seven miles south of Lauder, appointing Sir Alexander Hume of that ilk bailie for life of Huntly's lands of Gordon and Fogo. With him was James Ogilvy of Findlater and two of his Ogilvy kinsmen; indeed, James Ogilvy's seal was impressed on the letter of appointment on behalf of Huntly. Thus it is virtually certain that both men were present at Lauder the following day, when James III was arrested and Cochrane hanged.[84] As we have seen, Huntly had business in the south other than the removal of the royal familiar; but he may have reckoned that a muster of the host – by an unpopular king facing a powerful enemy – was the ideal opportunity to remove the royal keeper of Kildrummy and acquire lasting influence in Mar.

That control of Mar was a factor in Huntly's behaviour at Lauder is strongly suggested by his subsequent actions. On 3 August, less than a fortnight after the crisis, he obtained a remission for all crimes except treason;[85] this might imply that he had been involved in the hangings, but not personally in the seizure of the king. Thereafter Huntly played no part in government until the parliament of December 1482, and the reason may not be far to seek: on 10 October, James III granted the earldoms of Mar and Garioch, with Kildrummy Castle, in regality to Alexander, duke of Albany – possibly under duress, for James had not regained effective power–[86] and Albany, by seeking to have his lieutenant-generalship confirmed in the December parliament, was clearly attempting to deny the king a free hand, possibly permanently.[87] Thus Huntly could best serve his interests by throwing his support behind James III, denying Albany power, and – at last – receiving rewards in Mar from a belatedly grateful monarch. In this he proved successful; by Martinmas 1483 Mar and Garioch had effectively fallen under Gordon control, with Huntly himself becoming lessee of Strathdon and Garioch and his kinsman Gordon of Midmar lessee of Strathdee and Cromar. And by 1486, and probably before, Huntly had replaced the hapless Cochrane – and Albany – as keeper of Kildrummy, at a much higher fee.[88]

Huntly's constant companion at the 1482 muster – at Edinburgh, Redpath, and (presumably) Lauder itself – was, as we have seen, James Ogilvy of Deskford and Findlater. To Ogilvy, Cochrane's crime may well have been the building of Auchindoun Castle, a powerful stronghold which would extend the royal familiar's influence northward beyond his hold on parts of Mar. It also intruded on to lands earmarked by the Ogilvies for themselves, part of the extensive Ogilvy territories, stretching throughout Banffshire and beyond, which would be united into the barony of Ogilvy in 1517. Auchindoun's position above the River Fiddich places the castle only a few miles from the Ogilvy forest of Glenfiddich; and the Ogilvies could count on powerful support in removing the builder of Auchindoun, for James Ogilvy's son and heir was married to one of Huntly's daughters. If Auchindoun provided the motive for Ogilvy of Findlater to travel south to Lauder with Huntly in 1482, then his journey ended in success; for early the following century, if not before, Auchindoun had become part of the barony of Ogilvy.[89]

Thus it is possible, perhaps even probable, that Thomas Cochrane was not a court familiar in the strict sense of being an individual constantly about the king, and therefore credited with unpopular royal policies. His crime, if crime it was, may have lain in his attempt to feather his own nest in the north-east with James III's blessing. Unless further evidence comes to light, we can never be sure; but we might have been saved a great deal of trouble if John Mair, the first exponent of Cochranology, had left his home at Gleghornie, trudged south over the Lammermuirs to Lauder, witnessed the crisis, and then written it all up afterwards.

NOTES

1. As "Cochrane", "Thomas Cochrane" or "Robert Cochrane", he is to be found in the following sixteenth-century sources: *Quartus Sententiarum J. Maioris* (Paris, 1509), f. xcvi^v, col. 1 ('Robert') – a commentary by John Mair on the 4th Book of the *Sentences* of Petrus Lombardus; John Law, 'De Cronicis Scotorum Brevia' (1521–4), Edinburgh University Library, MS Dc. 7. 63, f. 132v ('Thomas'); Sir David Lindsay of the Mount, 'The Testament and Complaynt of our Soverane Lordis Papyngo' (1530), lines 444–471, in David Laing (ed.), *The Poetical Works of Sir David Lyndsay* (Edinburgh, 1879), i, 77–8 (no Christian name); Adam Abell, "The Roit and Quheill of Tyme" (1533–7), National Library of Scotland [NLS], MS 1746, f. 110v (no Christian name); John Lesley, *The History of Scotland from the Death of King James I in the Year 1436 to the year 1561* (Bannatyne Club, 1830), 48–9 ("Thomas"); Giovanni Ferrerio, *Appendix to Hector Boece, Scotorum Historiae* (2nd ed., Paris, 1574), f. 395v ("Robert"); John Lesley, *De Origine, Moribus et Rebus Gestis Scotorum Libri Decem* (1578; Scottish Text Society, 1888), 97–8 (no Christian name); Robert Lindsay of Pitscottie, *The Historie and Cronicles of Scotland* (c. 1579; Scottish Text Society, 1899), i, 165–170, 173–6 (no Christian name); George Buchanan, *Rerum Scoticarum Historia* (Edinburgh, 1582), book xii, f. 138r ('Robert').

2. *The Life of Sir Robert Cochran, Prime Minister to King James III of Scotland* (London, 1734); *A Detection of the Falshood, Abuse, and Misrepresentations in a late Libel, intitled, The Life of Sir Robert Cochran, Prime Minister in Scotland to James the Third* (London, 1735); *A Letter to the Detector of the Pretended Falshoods, etc., in the Life of Sir Robert Cochran* (London, 1735). These pamphlets are in NLS: pamphlets: 3/2367, 1.593/NLS. They are discussed in Norman Macdougall, *James III: A Political Study* (Edinburgh, 1982), 289–291.

3. For example, P. Hume Brown, *History of Scotland* (Cambridge, 1902), i, 269; and even more strikingly, R.L. Mackie, *King James IV of Scotland: A Brief Survey of his Life and Times* (Edinburgh, 1958), 11. The belief that Cochrane was responsible for the building of the Great Hall at Stirling Castle dies hard, though, as Dr. Jenny Wormald has kindly pointed out to me, Taylor, the Water-Poet, attributed the Hall to James IV in 1618: P. Hume Brown, *Early Travellers in Scotland* (Edinburgh, 1891), 118.

4. T. Thomson (ed.), *The Acts of the Lords Auditors of Causes and Complaints [ADA]* (Edinburgh, 1839), 127b; T. Thomson *et al.* (ed.), *The Acts of the Lords of Council in Civil Causes [ACD]* (Edinburgh, 1839), i, 49, 82.

5. Sir William Fraser, *The Chiefs of Grant* (Edinburgh, 1883), iii, 33.

6. Macdougall, *James III*, 140–155 *passim*, 162–5; W.C. Dickinson, *Scotland from the Earliest Times to 1603* (3rd edition, revised and edited by A.A.M. Duncan, Oxford, 1977), 239–240; Jenny Wormald, *Court, Kirk, and Community: Scotland 1470–1625* (London, 1981), 11–12.

7. Pitscottie, *Historie*, i, 176.

8. The most recent – of many – popular views of Cochrane is to be found in Stewart Ross, *Monarchs of Scotland* (Moffat, 1990), 93; while extensive scholarly treatment is accorded Cochrane and other familiars of James III in Ranald Nicholson, *Scotland: the Later Middle Ages* (Edinburgh, 1974), 502–5.

9. British Library [BL], Royal MS 17DXX, ff. 299–308.

10. This chronicle is discussed in Macdougall, *James III*, 275–6, and Appendix A (311–313) where the section relating to the reign of James III is printed in full.

11. BL, Royal MS 17DXX, ff. 307v, 308r.
12. T. Robb (ed.), *The Thre Prestis of Peblis* (Scottish Text Society, 1920), esp. lines 452–462, 567–8.
13. S.B. Chandler, "An Italian Life of Margaret, Queen of James III", *Scottish Historical Review*, 32 (1953), 52–7, at 55.
14. James Burns, "The Scotland of John Major", *Innes Review*, 2 (1951), 65–76, at 75–6. I am extremely grateful to Professor Burns for drawing my attention to this early reference to Cochrane, and for subsequent helpful correspondence on the subject. This article is largely the response to that correspondence, which has convinced me that my views on Cochrane (in my *James III*, 163–4, 278, 280–1, 288-9) require extensive modification.
15. *Quartus Sententiarum* (Paris, 1509), f. xcvi^v col. 1.
16. Burns, "The Scotland of John Major", 76.
17. J.H. Burns, "New Light on John Major", *Innes Review*, 5 (1954), 83–4.
18. *Ibid.*, 85–9.
19. BL, Royal MS 17DXX, f. 307v.
20. *ADA*, 204–5; *ADC*, ii (1496–1501), 341–2.
21. T. Thomson and C. Innes (ed.), *The Acts of the Parliaments of Scotland [APS]* (Edinburgh, 1814–75), ii, 230, clause 2.
22. John Law, "De Cronicis Scotorum Brevia", f. 132v.
23. John Durkan, "St. Andrews in the John Law Chronicle", in David McRoberts (ed.), *The Medieval Church of St. Andrews* (Glasgow, 1976), 137.
24. Printed in full in Lindsay, *Works*, ed. Laing, i, 61–104. The section on James III is on pp. 77–9.
25. *Ibid.*, i, pp. xii–xiii.
26. NLS, MS 1746. The section on James III is on ff. 110v–112r, and is printed in full in Macdougall, *James III*, Appendix B (pp. 314–5).
27. For example, he is convinced that James IV survived Flodden because a relative of his on the friary's farm at Jedburgh told him this: NLS, MS 1746, f. 112r.
28. *Ibid.*, f. 110v.
29. *Ibid.*
30. Lesley, *History*, 48–9.
31. *Ibid.*, 49.
32. George Burnett (ed.), *Exchequer Rolls [ER]* (Edinburgh, 1884), vii, 507, 583, 666.
33. J. Balfour Paul (ed.), *Registrum Magni Sigilii Regum Scotorum [RMS]* (Edinburgh, 1882), ii, no. 1418.
34. Ferrerio, *Appendix to Boece*, f. 391r–v, 395v.
35. For Ramsay's subsequent career, see Macdougall, *James IV* (Edinburgh, 1989), 55–6, 58–9, 62, 88, 127, 128–130, 165, 260, 306.
36. *ER*, ix, 93–4; *APS*, ii, 201, 202.
37. The questions of James III's strained relations with the queen, and his supposed lechery, cannot be dealt with in detail within the scope of this paper. Briefly, although James III has no known illegitimate offspring, there are a number of references to his philandering: Adam Abell opens his description of the king by commenting on the fact that he was "gretumlie gevin to carnale pleseure", but adds "by his halie quene". (NLS, MS 1746, f. 110v.) The author of the contemporary *Thre Prestis of Peblis* (pp. 39–44, lines 815–1004) is probably referring to James III in a story contained within the second tale, which concerns the king's passion for the daughter of a burgess named Innes. Sabadino's biography of Margaret of Denmark suggests that King James caused the queen considerable distress (Chandler, "Italian Life of Margaret", 55); and one might even strain the record evidence

to make something of the following treasurer's account, drawn to my attention many years ago by Kevin Philpott, and relating to Christmas 1473: "Item, gevin to a currour passande to the Lady Glammis, the Lady Edmonstoune, to cum to the Yule, iiii s. Item, to ane vthir passande to Borthwic and to Rosling to caus thai ladis to cum to the Yule, ii s." T. Dickson (ed.), *Accounts of the Lord High Treasurer of Scotland [TA]*, (Edinburgh, 1877), i, 46.

38. Lesley, *History*, 48.
39. Pitscottie, *Historie*, i, 173–177.
40. Lesley, *De Origine*, i, pp. xx–xxi.
41. Ferrerio, *Appendix to Boece*, ff. 384r–402r.
42. William D. Wilson (ed.), *Ferrerii Historia Abbatum de Kynlos* (Bannatyne Club, 1839), p. vi.
43. Ferrerio, *Appendix to Boece*, f. 391r–v.
44. *Ibid.*, f. 395v.
45. For John Ireland, see J.H. Burns, "John Ireland and 'The Meroure of Wyssdome' ", *Innes Review*, 6 (1955), 77–98; and the same author, "John Ireland: Theology and Public Affairs in the Late Fifteenth Century", *Innes Review*, 41 (1990), 151–181.
46. *ER*, ix, 218; *RMS*, ii, no. 1533.
47. Ferrerio, *Kinloss*, p. vi.
48. J.H. Pollen (ed.), *Papal Negotiations with Mary Queen of Scots during her Reign in Scotland 1561–1567* (Scottish History Society, 1901), 416.
49. Pitscottie, *Historie*, i, 165–170, 173–6.
50. *Ibid.*, i, 163–8.
51. *Ibid.*, i, 168–9.
52. *Ibid.*, i, 173–6.
53. *Ibid.*, i, 176.
54. *Ibid.*, i, pp. cxii–cxvii, 2.
55. Buchanan, *Rerum Scoticarum Historia*, book xii, f. 138r.
56. *Ibid.*, f. 138r; and see also Burns, "The Scotland of John Major", 75–6. I have followed Professor Burns' translation of Buchanan's comment on Cochrane.
57. David Hume of Godscroft, *History of the Houses of Douglas and Angus* (Edinburgh, 1644), 226. Godscroft, seeking to praise Archibald, earl of Angus, is the first to introduce the "Bell-the-Cat" story to the episode of Lauder Bridge (see Macdougall, *James III*, 287–8); but this is hardly a contribution to Cochranology.
58. William Drummond of Hawthornden, *History of Scotland from the year 1423 until the year 1542* (London, 1681), 143–4.
59. J. Pinkerton, *The History of Scotland from the Accession of the House of Stuart to that of Mary, with Appendices of Original Papers* (London, 1797), i, 304–8.
60. Sir Walter Scott, *Tales of a Grandfather* (Edinburgh, 1889 edn.), 73–5.
61. As I originally argued in Macdougall, *James III*, 163–4.
62. *ADC*, i, 49.
63. Sir John Colquhoun was alive on 18 April 1479 (*RMS*, ii, no. 1426), and described as killed at the siege of Dunbar Castle on 21 June 1479; W. Fraser, *Colquhoun* (Edinburgh, 1869), ii, 197. The siege was, however, probably over by 24 May, when Albany was summoned for the first time to answer charges of treason which include the defence of Dunbar against James III. (*APS*, ii, 126).
64. Lesley, *History*, 43.
65. For Colquhoun's career, see Macdougall, *James III*, 71, 116, 117–8, 129, 163–4, 184. Sir John's brother was Robert Colquhoun, bishop of Argyll.
66. *RMS*, ii, nos. 1428–1515.
67. Fraser, *Chiefs of Grant*, iii, 33–4.

68. *ER*, viii, 78.
69. *Ibid.*, ix, pp. xliii–xliv.
70. *Ibid.*, viii, 77. The earldom of Mar was divided into Strathdee, Strathdon, and Cromar, which in 1471 were worth respectively £110. 6s8d, £168, and £92 16s.8d, to which must be added the feu-farm on the crofts of Kildrummy, worth 3s 4d. Kildrummy Castle is located in Strathdon.
71. James Gordon, *History of Scots Affairs from 1637 to 1641* (Spalding Club, 1841), ii, 216.
72. See, in general, W. Douglas Simpson, "The Early Castles of Mar", *Proceedings of the Society of Antiquaries of Scotland*, 63 (1928–9), 102–138, esp. 125–7.
73. *ADC*, i, 82.
74. W. Fraser, *Lennox* (Edinburgh, 1874), ii, 122–3.
75. Dominic Mancini, *The Usurpation of Richard III*, ed. C.A.J. Armstrong (Oxford, 1936), 76–7; and see Macdougall, *James III*, 131–2.
76. BL, Royal MS 17DXX, f. 308r.
77. For the black money in general, see Joan Murray, "The Black Money of James III", *British Archaeological Reports*, 45 (1977), 115–130; and Macdougall, *James III*, 158–162.
78. SRO, GD 121/3/19.
79. *ADC*, i, 49.
80. Nicholson, *Later Middle Ages*, 505.
81. For details of James II's attitude to the 1st earl of Huntly, see Christine McGladdery, *James II* (Edinburgh, 1990), 104–5.
82. *Miscellany of the Spalding Club iv* (Spalding Club, 1849), 133.
83. SRO, GD 185/2/1. I am indebted to Dr. Stephen Boardman for drawing this reference to my attention.
84. *Historical Manuscripts Commission Report*, XII, App., part viii, p. 139 (earl of Home MSS). It may be significant that Lesley's short list of magnates present at Lauder, referred to earlier in this article, includes Huntly as one of them: Lesley, *History*, 48.
85. SRO, GD44 13/5/1.
86. SRO, MS RMS, xi, 33; for the details of the 1482–3 crisis, see Macdougall, *James III*, 170–190.
87. Albany is described as lieutenant-general in the royal charter of 10 October 1482, granting him Mar and Garioch: printed in *Illustrations of the Topography and Antiquities of Aberdeen and Banff* (Spalding Club, 1862), iv, 213; for the parliament of December 1482, see *APS*, ii, 143.
88. *ER*, ix, pp. xliii–xliv, 388.
89. J. Balfour Paul (ed.), *Scots Peerage* (Edinburgh, 1904–14), iv, 16–20.

3

Chivalry and Citizenship:
Aspects of National Identity in Renaissance Scotland

ROGER MASON

In a characteristically perceptive article, Christopher Smout recently explored the issue of nationalism in late eighteenth-century Scotland with particular reference to the 'concentric loyalties' which permitted the Scots to retain a powerful sense of their Scottish identity without jeopardising their commitment to the union of Britain.[1] Thought-provoking though his arguments are, it is not the purpose of this paper to engage with them directly. Rather my intention here is to examine the nature of the Scottish identity in a period long before either the union of the parliaments or even the union of the crowns. On the face of it, to focus on the century or so before the Reformation – a century best described in cultural terms as the era of the early Scottish Renaissance – is greatly to simplify the issue.[2] The Scots were still an independent people and, aware though they certainly were of the English threat to their kingdom's autonomy, their sense of collective identity was as yet untroubled by the practical realities of being North British as well as Scottish. Yet the problem remains of defining that identity. What did it actually mean to be a Scot? How was that identity conceived, articulated and sustained? How deeply had it penetrated Scottish society as a whole? Such questions do not admit of easy answers. There are those, indeed, who would deny their validity altogether when asked of 'pre-modern' societies as yet untouched by the nationalist ideologies which swept Europe – though not, as Smout argues, Scotland – in the late eighteenth and nineteenth centuries. Before attempting to answer them, therefore, we must first establish their legitimacy in the context of late medieval and early modern Scotland.

It is certainly true that nationalism in its modern demotic form, founded on a sense of common citizenship and equality before the law, is a product of the political and industrial revolutions which began in Europe in the latter half of the eighteenth century.[3] Yet neither nationalism as an ideology nor nations as a focus of collective identity were created *ex nihilo*. The sociologist

Anthony Smith, from whom the notion of concentric loyalties is also derived, has persuasively argued that the formation of modern nations owed a great deal to pre-existing 'ethnic communities' which, while neither populist nor egalitarian in their social and political structures, possessed many other characteristics which are now seen as the *sine qua non* of nationhood.[4] In his use of the term 'ethnic community' (the closest English equivalent to the Greek *ethnos* and French *ethnie*), Smith is deliberately stressing cultural rather than biological or kin-based unity. The term, he writes, 'unites an emphasis upon cultural differences with the sense of an historical community. It is this sense of history and the perception of cultural uniqueness and individuality which differentiates populations from each other and which endows a given population with a definite identity, both in their own eyes and in those of outsiders'.[5] Essentially, for Smith, the key to ethnic identity lies in a given community's sense of its past: in the existence, that is, of a dynamic and historically-based '*mythomoteur*' capable of explaining the community to itself (and others) by lending meaning and purpose to the particular complex of 'myths, memories, values and symbols' from which it derives its individuality. In short, like most modern nations, pre-modern ethnic communities defined their collective identities very largely through the manipulation of what one might loosely call a 'usable past'.[6]

Smith's work ranges impressively over time and space and Scotland figures only occasionally in his analysis. Yet clearly, in its medieval and early modern guise, Scotland conforms very closely to his model of an ethnic community. It would not be difficult to argue that the six 'dimensions of *ethnie*' which he identifies – a collective name, a common myth of descent, a shared history, a distinctive shared culture, an association with a specific territory and a sense of solidarity – were all present in Scotland in varying degrees from at least the twelfth century onwards.[7] Even if it were thought desirable, however, space does not permit an examination of the Scottish evidence for each and every one of these facets of ethnicity. Instead, at the risk of over-simplifying Smith's arguments, attention will be concentrated here primarily on the uses made of the past in defining and sustaining the Scottish identity and on the development of a Scottish *mythomoteur* – what elsewhere I have called a Scottish national epos[8] – which both explained and legitimised the community's sense of being unique and distinctive. Similarly, and again at the risk of over-simplification, it is not my intention to adhere slavishly to Smith's 'ethnic' terminology. In a context where there is no need to distinguish rigidly between modern and pre-modern communities, it serves no very useful purpose to ban 'nation' and its cognates from the historian's vocabulary. Provided such terminology is used (and understood) in the restricted sense appropriate to medieval and early modern societies, it seems unnecessary to replace it with cumbersome technical jargon. For the purposes of what follows, *ethnie* and nation may be taken as synonymous.

With that in mind, we may return to and rephrase the questions posed at the outset. How did Renaissance Scots define themselves as a nation? And how was that national identity articulated and sustained? At least part of the answer to both these questions was suggested by Abbot Walter Bower when in the 1440s he ended his *Scotichronicon* with the resounding valediction: 'Christ! He is not a Scot who is not pleased with this book'.[9] If this makes clear that Bower himself was supremely confident of his own identity as a Scot, it also signals his belief that the Scottishness of others might be gauged by the degree to which they appreciated his work. It is tempting simply to dismiss the latter suggestion as both self-satisfied and self-serving. Yet there is a sense in which it is perfectly correct. For in writing his chronicle, Bower was intent *inter alia* on revealing the Scots to themselves: on explaining who they were by explaining where they had come from and on differentiating them in the present by establishing the uniqueness of their past. A full evaluation of Bower's personal achievement must await the completion of Donald Watt's splendid new edition of the *Scotichronicon*. But it is already well-established that he added further weight and popularity to an account of the Scottish past which was first given coherent form by John of Fordun in the 1380s and which would be spectacularly reworked and expanded by the humanist historian, Hector Boece, in the 1520s.[10] Rather than construing Bower's words as an overly smug review of his own book, therefore, it is both more charitable and more illuminating to read it in the broader sweep of an historiographical tradition which was of critical significance in shaping the national identity of Renaissance Scots.

To understand its significance, however, we must turn to the wider British context in which it developed. Christopher Smout has noted the apparent inability of eighteenth-century Englishmen to conceive of their loyalties in concentric terms by distinguishing clearly between a 'smaller England' and a 'greater Britain'.[11] The problem was by no means new. Medieval Englishmen were equally prone to equate England with Britain and Britain with England: *natio Anglicana sive Britannica* as the records of the Council of Constance repeatedly describe it in the early fifteenth century.[12] The confusion originates with Roman usage of the term *Britannia* to denote both the British mainland as a whole and that part of it over which the empire had effective control. It was compounded, however, by Anglo-Saxon rulers who, eager to appropriate to themselves the legacy of imperial rule, were increasingly prone to adopt the title *rex* or even *imperator totius Britanniae*.[13] As a result, by the time of the Norman Conquest, the idea of English hegemony over Britain was well-established and William and his successors had no hesitation either in laying claim to the lordship of Britain or in attempting periodically to lend political substance to their imperial pretensions by military force. Their ambitions were further encouraged by the appearance in the 1130s of Geoffrey of Monmouth's extraordinarily influential *History of the Kings of Britain.* For Geoffrey's work served to ensure that the idea of Britain as a single geopolitical entity with a single royal overlord became not just a commonplace, but a commonplace founded on massive historical precedent. Just as Brutus the Trojan had ruled over the whole island of Britain, so too had the illustrious Arthur, and so too did the Norman kings who had fallen heir to the ancient British throne.[14] As far as the Anglo-Norman élite was concerned, it was not simply reasonable to believe that England was Britain and Britain England, it was a matter of proven historical record.

Seen in this light, the emergence of a Scottish kingdom intent on challenging English hegemony was rather more than an inconvenient political irritant. It was a monstrous historical affront. Certainly, that it is how Edward I interpreted it and, well-versed in Galfridian lore, he was able to bring to bear the whole panoply of the so-called British History in support of his claim to lordship. In contemporary terms, it amounted to a formidable body of precedent: the full weight of the British past – of Brutus, Arthur and the many more recent examples of Scottish kings doing homage to their English superiors – told heavily against any claim to Scottish autonomy.[15] Not surprisingly, moreover, the Scots' remarkable success in the ensuing wars made very little difference to English perceptions of what had occurred. So deeply ingrained had the imperial assumptions legitimised by the British History become that, while the Scots might rejoice in the successful vindication of their right to an independent existence, the English continued to deplore their actions as an unlawful rebellion against the rightful overlords of Britain. Taking their cue from Edward I, and building on the work of Geoffrey of Monmouth, the chroniclers of later medieval England were adamant in their insistence on Scotland's vassal status. John Hardyng was perhaps extreme in his obsessive fabrication of the evidence for English feudal superiority.[16] But the hugely popular *Brut* chronicle – published by William Caxton in 1480 as *The Chronicles of England* – was fairly typical both in its Galfridian defence of the English claim and in its denunciation of the Scots in general and Wallace and Bruce in particular as rebels and traitors.[17] For medieval Englishmen, as for so many of their early modern descendants, an independent Scotland was quite simply a political freak which flew in the face of all that was known about the glorious British past.

Given such entrenched assumptions, R.R. Davies is surely right to suggest that modern historians ought 'to express less surprise and rather less moral outrage' when confronted by the British imperialism of English kings like Edward I.[18] They were, in more senses than one, creatures of history. By the same token, however, so too were Scottish kings. Their actions, and those of the Scottish community more generally, were equally informed and legitimised by a sense of the past. When in 1301 Edward I presented his case for British lordship to the papal curia, it did not go unanswered: on the contrary, Master Baldred Bisset assembled an impressive array of historical evidence in support of the claim that the Scottish kingdom was and always had been free and independent.[19] Bisset, needless to say, did not simply invent the past with which he chose to endow the Scots. As we shall see in a moment, there already existed a store of myths and memories – some of them of very remote origin – which had been deliberately fostered by the Canmore dynasty and its clerical allies in the course of the twelfth and thirteenth centuries. If the Scots lacked an historian of Geoffrey of Monmouth's literary gifts, they certainly did not lack the materials from which to construct a coherent version of their own distinctive past. To be sure, the issue was clouded in Scotland by the 'divided loyalties' of Anglo-Norman settlers who owed allegiance to both the king of England and the king of Scots. Nevertheless, it is barely conceivable that a war of independence could have been fought at all had not the Scots already possessed a usable past which differentiated them from other peoples and lent real meaning and purpose to their resistance to Edward I. In short, while the wars with England undoubtedly served to sharpen the Scots' sense of collective identity, they assuredly did not create it. When later in the fourteenth century John of Fordun took issue with what he called 'the foolish babbling of the British people',[20] he did so in the knowledge that, over the centuries, the Scots had developed an understanding of their own unique past which was perfectly capable both of countering the imperial pretensions of the British History and of articulating a powerful sense of their own collective identity.

Stripped to its barest essentials, the account of the Scottish past which Fordun inherited from his largely anonymous predecessors combined a myth of racial origins – the Scots' descent from the Greek Prince Gathelus and the eponymous Scota, daughter of Pharaoh – with the belief that the Scottish kingdom itself was founded by Fergus I in 330 BC and had had a continuous and independent existence under a line of over one hundred kings ever since that date. The sources of this narrative remain obscure, but the tale of the Scots' descent from Scota was of ancient Irish origin and variations on it first began to appear in Scotland itself as early as the tenth century.[21] Its subsequent development as a racial myth which effectively obscured the Scots' disparate ethnic origins and identified Pict, Celt and Anglo-Norman alike with a common 'Scottish' ancestor was almost certainly encouraged by the consolidation of the kingdom which occurred under the Canmore dynasty in the twelfth and thirteenth centuries. As a means of promoting 'regnal solidarity' – of focusing national loyalties on a royal house of venerable antecedents – the uses of such an origins' myth were lost on Scottish kings no more than on those of Europe generally.[22] As is well known, at one point in his chronicle, Fordun described how at the inauguration of Alexander III in 1249 a genealogy of the new king was recited which traced the royal line back through generation after generation to Scota herself, the progenitor of the Scottish race.[23] There is no doubt that this ritual, deeply-rooted in the

Celtic past, was deliberately exploited by the Canmore kings. After all, such a public demonstration of the antiquity of their lineage served not only to confirm the legitimacy of their claim to the throne, but also to reinforce their subjects' sense of identity with a genealogy which was racial as well as royal in scope. It is presumably no accident that, throughout the middle ages and beyond, Scottish monarchs consistently styled themselves *Rex Scottorum* rather than *Rex Scotie*.[24]

While buttressing the authority of the king, then, the genealogy also demonstrated the common, ancient and autonomous origins of all his people. In a context where that people's status as an independent nation was subject to constant questioning, this was clearly of much more than ceremonial significance and it is hardly surprising that such a critical part of the inauguration ritual was retained long after the monarchy was granted in 1329 the coveted rights of ecclesiastical unction and coronation.[25] The royal genealogy – with the reigning monarch as its living embodiment – was the most powerful available symbol of the Scots' claim to an independent existence under a king subject to no higher power but God alone. The monarchy's symbolic role, however, was still further enhanced by the claim that the Scottish kingdom was originally founded as early as the fourth century BC and that a continuous line of over one hundred kings had reigned in the northern realm ever since that date.[26] In reality, of course, the Irish Scots had not begun to colonize the western seaboard of Scotland until the third or fourth century AD and there is little evidence of a settled Scottish kingdom before the year 500. Yet by manipulating the chronological sequence of extant Scottish and Pictish kinglists – in effect placing them sequentially rather than concurrently – it was possible to add seven wholly spurious centuries to the kingdom's existence and virtually to double the number of kings who had reigned over the northern realm.[27] Chroniclers like Fordun and Bower were commendably coy when it came actually to naming the first forty or so monarchs who were said to have occupied the throne in succession to Fergus I. Nevertheless, the long line of Scottish kings, stretching back in unbroken succession to the foundation of the kingdom in 330 BC, played a key role in validating the belief, not only in Scotland's antiquity, but more importantly in its historic and continuing autonomy.[28]

Such, in skeletal outline, was the Scottish *mythomoteur*: the bare bones of a national epos which explained the Scots to themselves and underpinned their collective identity. Of course, the late medieval chroniclers fleshed out the basic narrative in ever more exotic detail. But even without further embellishment, it was sufficient to differentiate the Scots from other peoples and endow them with a sense of their unique individuality. The point is well illustrated by a short vernacular work known as the *Scottis Originale* which was included in the collection of literary fragments compiled by John Asloan in the early years of the sixteenth century. In a few brief sentences, its anonymous author encapsulated the main thrust of the Scottish chronicle tradition and provided in the process a useful insight into what made the Scots feel Scottish:

> And supposs Scotland was langtyme vexit with weire of divers nacionis, that is to say, Romanis, Brettonis, Saxonis, Danys, Pictis and Normanis, nevertheless we Scottis men put thaim ay out throu cruell force and battell ... Sa that we may say this day, be verray suthfastness, thar was never land, nor is no land nor nacioun, so fre bygane of all the warld nor has standing so lang tyme in fredome as we Scottis in Scotland. Ffor we have bene xviij hundreth yeire in conquest nor never was dantit be no nacioun of strange countre or king to this daye, bot evir undere our kingis of richt lyne discendand fra Gathele and Scota, first inhabitaris of this land, and fra Fergus forsaid til our soverane lord that ryngis now present ...[29]

Although impossible to prove, it seems more than probable that the majority of Asloan's contemporaries, if asked to define their identity as Scots, would have begun, as the *Scottis Originale* ends, with a sour and intemperate denunciation of the English as false, treacherous and descended of the devil.[30] To be a Scot was, above all else, not to be English. But if pressed further, if asked what exactly it was that made them different from the English, the chances are that they would have invoked a similar set of crude and selective historical generalisations to those quoted above. Visceral Anglophobia was, as we shall see, a very real and powerful force in Scottish society, but it was founded on the knowledge – however vague and inchoate – that Scotland was an historical community of unrivalled antiquity which had never submitted to foreign lordship. There was, as the *Scottis Originale* proudly boasted, 'no land nor nacioun so fre bygane of all the warld nor has standing so lang tyme in fredome as we Scottis in Scotland'.

As this suggests, the Latin *libertas* and its vernacular equivalents *liberty* and *freedom* were key words in the political vocabulary of late medieval Scots. Memorably invoked in the Declaration of Arbroath and eloquently apostrophised in John Barbour's epic poem *The Bruce*, the idea of freedom was crucial to Scottish self-understanding.[31] Certainly, it was the value of freedom – and freedom as a value – that the Scottish *mythomoteur* served above all else to extol and underwrite. The Scottish chronicle tradition is studded with flights of impassioned rhetoric on the theme of liberty and slavery. To quote but one example, Fordun has the kings of the Scots and Picts defying Roman imperial authority in the following ringing (if somewhat convoluted) terms:

> Think not, O Caesar ... that you can succeed in leading us astray to wander in that most loathsome vale of slavery, along a path impassable, crooked, rough and horrible to every noble-hearted man; leaving the pleasant road of freedom, our birthright, a road wherein our fathers, sustained by help from the gods,

were ever wont to walk straight-forwards, bending neither to the right hand nor to the left ... For the freedom our ancestors have handed down to us, which we must cherish above gold and topaz, and which in our judgement far beyond all comparison transcends all worldly wealth and is infinitely more precious than precious stones; which our high-souled forebears have from the beginning nobly, even to the death, preserved untainted for us, their sons; this freedom, we say, shall we likewise, as not having in our unworthiness degenerated from their nature, but as strenuously imitating their standard, preserve inviolate for our sons after our death and transmit to them unspotted by a single jot of slavishness.[32]

Notably, for Fordun, freedom was not some desirable abstraction to which the Scots might hope to aspire. On the contrary, it was an historical reality intimately related to the moral – or martial – qualities of those Scottish forebears who had realised and maintained it. In his view, those who relinquished freedom – 'the choice garland of our old nobility' – were quite simply 'blasphemers ... of our own race'.[33] The idea of freedom was repeatedly historicised in this way and atavistic appeals to the exemplary heroism of virtuous 'elders' were commonplace in the chronicle tradition. That Scotland had survived as an autonomous nation was invariably credited to the military virtues of succeeding generations of noble ancestors. As this makes clear, however, for Fordun and his contemporaries, history was not simply descriptive, it was also prescriptive: late medieval Scots were constantly being reminded both of the continuity of their struggle to maintain the freedom of their realm and of the martial virtues which were the key to its successful defence. The Scottish *mythomoteur* validated in the present (and for the future) the military values which had guaranteed Scottish freedom in the past.

What emerges from this all too brief analysis is that the constellation of ideas which the Scottish national epos energised – and which the word 'freedom' evoked – was essentially martial and chivalric in character. Indeed, it is worth considering the Scottish *mythomoteur* as a domestic equivalent of the great historical mythologies of chivalry – particularly the matter of Britain and the matter of Rome – which exemplified the values of Europe's militarised élites more generally.[34] The Scots participated fully in this cosmopolitan chivalric culture and had ready access to the literature which shaped it.[35] But the 'matter of Scotland' was altogether more poignant and more pointed than tales of Arthur or Alexander. Its most heroic period was not located in some distant, quasi-fictional, era such as Geoffrey of Monmouth had created. It was set in the comparatively recent past: in the ultimately successful struggle of Wallace and Bruce to defend Scottish freedom from English aggression. It was pre-eminently here, in the glorious martial deeds of this heroic generation of Scots, that the 'elders' assumed real shape and substance. Not surprisingly, therefore, alongside the historical mythology of chivalry developed by the chroniclers, there emerged vernacular epics in the form of Barbour's *Bruce* and Blind Harry's *Wallace* – works specifically focused on the Wars of Independence and overtly intent on the education as well as the entertainment of their audiences. Thus in the episodic structure of Barbour's work, the code of chivalry and the cause of freedom are brought together in a series of *exempla* designed both to instruct and to inspire the 'lordingis' to whom his 'romanys' was addressed.[36] Here, as in the chronicle tradition more generally, the 'elders' exemplified a complex of chivalric values and martial virtues which their descendants were bound to strive to emulate.

Regrettably, although chivalric ideas constituted the dominant secular value system throughout later medieval Europe, their importance in shaping the outlook and aspirations of contemporary Scots has never been explored. Scottish historians have tended simply to dismiss chivalry as so much rarefied idealism with no purchase on social reality.[37] As a result we have yet to discover how the values of the chivalric code operated in Scotland's highly localised and kin-based society. There is good reason to think, however, that the values it prized – nobility, loyalty and courage, for example – readily harmonised with the concerns of a feuding society where honour and lineage were concepts of paramount importance.[38] The households of the Scottish nobility were centres of widely-ramified networks of kin and dependants where fierce lineage loyalties were incubated. We know all too little of the cultural milieu of these households and still less of the 'myths and memories' which sustained the solidarity and corporate identity of individual lineages.[39] Yet we do know that it was the nobility who were the chief patrons and consumers of the substantial quantity of chivalric literature – including the chronicles – produced in late medieval Scotland.[40] It was the noble household, the lord's kin, allies and dependants, which made up the audience for chivalric romance and mythology just as it was the audience for the localised mythologies which it seems safe to assume were generated to sustain the solidarity of individual kingroups. It was a context in which concentric loyalties were the norm: loyalty to local lineages with powerful collective identities contained and controlled – often no doubt with very great difficulty – by loyalty to a royal dynasty which symbolised the freedom and integrity of the nation as a whole.[41] In both such contexts, the martial values of the chivalric code had a lot to offer a highly militarised and honour conscious society.

That said, it is well worth noting here that when in the 1450s Gilbert Haye was commissioned by the earl of Orkney to translate into Scots some of the key texts of chivalric literature, he laid far greater stress than his French sources on the idea of a knight's public responsibilities: 'gude resoun gevis', he declared, 'that all princis, lordis and knychtis specialy suld be mare curious of the commoun prouffit na of thair awin propre gudis'.[42] If this makes clear that Haye was well aware of the need to direct the aggressive militarism of the chivalric code towards public rather than private ends, it also suggests that there existed a vocabulary in terms of which the problem of concentric loyalties – of the relative strength of local and national allegiances – might be formulated by contemporaries. In fact, like the idea of freedom, the idea of the *bonum commune* – the 'common profit' or 'common good' of the realm as a whole – played a highly significant role in contemporary political discourse. Often directly contrasted with the pursuit of 'singular profit' or self-interest, it embodied a perception of Scotland as a community far greater than the sum of its local parts whose common aims and interests necessarily took precedence over those of its individual members. As such, it was an integral part of a political outlook – what elsewhere I have described as an ideology of patriotic conservatism – which not only set a high premium on loyalty to the crown, but viewed the *bonum commune* in essentially Aristotelian terms as the true end of government.[43] To be sure, responsibility for the defence of the realm and the equitable administration of justice within it rested in the first instance on the shoulders of the king. Nevertheless, as Haye makes clear, the aristocracy were also public figures with public duties to perform. Indeed, it was precisely in terms of such 'civic' responsibilities that he attempted to re-interpret the values of the chivalric code. For the true purpose of knighthood was, he insisted, not to aggrandise the individual, but to serve the crown and the 'commoun prouffit'.[44]

Significantly enough, in the first half of the sixteenth century, the idea of 'common profit' was displaced in the Scottish political vocabulary by the idea of the 'commonweal'. This remarkably protean term soon acquired powerful and decidedly patriotic resonances for contemporary Scots and, by the 1530s and 1540s, 'the commonweal and liberty of the realm' – or simply 'the commonweal' *tout court* – had emerged in public discourse as highly effective rhetorical shorthand for both the community's sense of collective identity and the public responsibilities of its members.[45] It is tempting – and probably accurate – to ascribe this change to humanist influences. It is, after all, the humanist educational programme – the classically orientated *studia humanitatis* – which is generally credited with promoting civic ideals among Europe's militarised élites and paving the way for their transformation from knights in the service of Christendom into gentlemen in the service of the crown and the commonwealth.[46] One must beware, however, of overstressing the extent to which the advent of the new learning marked a radical break with the past. It is certainly true that in the course of the sixteenth century the Scottish nobility, like their counterparts elsewhere in Europe, were put under increasing pressure to conform to patterns of behaviour which owed more to classical notions of citizenship than to the medieval code of chivalry.[47] Nevertheless, the pervasive influence of Aristotle had clearly ensured that, even for a pre-humanist like Gilbert Haye, the idea of public service – of duty to the *bonum commune* – was already a highly significant

touchstone of political behaviour. The revival of classical learning undoubtedly served to reinforce the rudimentary civic ethos which the ideology of
patriotic conservatism upheld. In the process, moreover, it generated in the
idea of the 'commonweal' a more succinct and powerful means of articulating
it. Yet, as the writings of Hector Boece bear witness, it did not necessarily
lead its Scottish proponents to turn their backs on the chivalric values and
traditions which had played such a prominent role in sustaining the national
identity of their medieval forebears.

Boece's humanist credentials are unimpeachable. As a student in Paris in
the 1490s he had not only befriended Erasmus but had so distinguished
himself as a Latinist that in 1505 he was chosen by Bishop William
Elphinstone to become principal of his new university foundation at Aberdeen. He was to hold the post until his death in 1536 during which time
King's College established itself as the main Scottish centre for the dissemi-
nation of the new learning.[48] Although Elphinstone died in 1514, his
protegé's *Scotorum Historiae*, published in Paris in 1527, undoubtedly owed
a great deal to the bishop's own intensely patriotic cast of mind. The clergy
had, of course, always played a critical role in developing the myths and
symbols of Scotland's independent identity. Not only were they society's
educated élite, but the predatory ambitions of York and Canterbury had led
them from a very early date to invest heavily in the Scottish *mythomoteur* as
a means of countering English claims to spiritual as well as temporal
overlordship.[49] Elphinstone was, as we shall see, acutely aware of the
importance of Scotland's distinctive ecclesiastical traditions and went to
considerable lengths to revitalise and preserve them. His patriotism, however,
while nourished by his clerical background, appears to have found its
theoretical underpinnings in his training as a civil lawyer and his long
familiarity with the Bartolist doctrine that 'the king is emperor in his own
kingdom'.[50] It is surely no accident that the bell-tower of his new university
chapel was surmounted, in Boece's words, by 'a stone arch in the shape of
an imperial crown'.[51] By the late fifteenth century, the closed imperial crown
had emerged as the most potent available symbol, not only of the kind of
'regnal solidarity' promoted by the Scottish *mythomoteur*, but also of the
complete jurisdictional self-sufficiency – effectively, the independent national
sovereignty – aspired to by the 'new monarchies' of Renaissance Europe.
Interestingly enough, as early as 1469 the Scottish parliament had declared
that James III possessed 'full jurisdiction and free empire within his realm'
and the closed imperial crown was later to feature on the same king's
coinage.[52] Elphinstone was clearly not alone in believing that the Scottish
kingdom was as entitled as any other – and more entitled than most – to lay
claim to imperial status. Possessed of a past of unrivalled antiquity and
uninterrupted continuity, Scotland's right to a place among the 'new
monarchies' of Renaissance Europe was manifest throughout her history.

It is perhaps not surprising, then, that in his *Lives of the Bishops of Aberdeen* Boece paid fulsome tribute to Elphinstone's research into 'the antiquities of the Scottish nation' and claimed that in writing his own chronicle he had drawn extensively on a history of Scotland written by his patron.[53] Whether Elphinstone ever actually composed such a work remains a moot point. But his keen interest in ecclesiastical history, particularly in the lives of Scottish saints, is beyond dispute. As David McRoberts has argued, he was at the forefront of a movement of 'liturgical nationalism' which, culminating in the publication of the *Aberdeen Breviary* in 1510, was aimed at reinvigorating native religious traditions and at lending Scottish public worship a distinctly Scottish accent.[54] Boece interpreted Elphinstone's efforts in characteristically anti-English terms as an attempt to repair the grievous damage inflicted on Scotland by Edward I's alleged campaign to eradicate all vestiges of a separate Scottish identity. The English king, he claimed, 'had burned all the books that gave the history of our famous saints as well as the books of ritual ... so that nothing which was not English might hereafter be found among us held in honour'.[55] It was an accusation which he was to repeat in still more sweeping terms in his *History* where Edward is said to have burned 'all the chronikles of Scotland, with all maner of bukis als weill of devine service as of othir materis' so that 'the memorie of Scottis suld peris'.[56] The accuracy of the charges is much less important than the profound insight which lies behind them. For Boece had clearly recognised that to deprive a people of their past was to deprive them of their identity; that a nation without a history was, in effect, no nation at all. Clearly, both he and Elphinstone were intent on something more than simply chronicling the Scottish past. Their historical research was aimed primarily at affirming – or re-affirming – Scotland's status and identity as a nation.

Seen from this perspective, the problems surrounding Boece's sources, his credulity and inventiveness, are much less significant than the coherence of his narrative and the exuberant self-confidence which informs it.[57] In the hands of the Aberdeen humanist, not only did the Scottish *mythomoteur* attain its most elaborate and exotic form, but in the process Scotland's status among the nations of Europe was asserted more powerfully than ever before. Following the chronology established by Fordun and Bower, though with the addition of an astonishing wealth of circumstantial detail, Boece charted the history of the Scots from their remote origins in Greece and Egypt through the foundation of the kingdom by Fergus I in 330 BC to the subsequent rule of an uninterrupted line of over 100 kings of Fergus's royal stock. Scotland was thus among the most ancient kingdoms of Europe, fit to rank with France and England in terms of antiquity and endurance, and second to none in terms of the continuity of its independent kingship. For, according to Boece, when the rest of Europe succumbed to the might of the Roman legions and groaned under the yoke of imperial tutelage, Scotland alone succeeded in preserving her integrity and, in a long and noble struggle, never once submitted to slavery and subjection. While the kings of the Britons became puppets of the Roman emperors and thereafter fell in rapid succession to the Saxons, the Danes and finally the Normans, the Scots – led by their illustrious race of kings – resisted the Romans, exterminated the Picts, subjected the Britons, repulsed the Danes and for centuries refused to recognise the baseless claims to suzerainty made by a series of arrogant English monarchs. In Boece's expert hands, this is a tale – however fabulous – well and stirringly told which could hardly have failed to appeal to none-too-critical Scotsmen still smarting under the humiliating shadow of Flodden and watching anxiously the ambitious posturing of Henry VIII. Its translation into Scots by John Bellenden and subsequent publication in a magnificent black letter edition in Edinburgh in the late 1530s was a resounding declaration, not only of the Scots' belief in their history, but also of their belief in themselves.[58]

How then did Boece conceive of the Scottish identity? What image of themselves did his countrymen find reflected in the mirror of his history? The short (and not unexpected) answer is that, like his medieval predecessors, Boece saw the Scots as first and foremost a nation-in-arms: a nation distinguished from other peoples, not just by their love of freedom, but by their willingness to fight and die in its defence. In effect, Scotland's history and identity were for Boece compounded of those same martial values and traditions which animated the medieval 'matter of Scotland'. Thus time and again in the pages of his *History*, the warrior kings of the Scots – in this case Eugenius I – are made to address their subjects in the atavistic terms so characteristic of the chivalrous lineage culture evoked by Barbour and Fordun:

> Our eldaris, that began this realm with continewall laubour, and brocht the samin with honour to our days, forcy campionis, commandit thair posterite to defend thair realme and liberte, quhilk is maist dulce and hevinly treasoure in the erd, aganis al invasouris; ...I beseik yow, my good companyeonis, for the unvincibill manheid, faith and virthew of your elderis, and for thair paill goistis, quhilkis defendit this your realme in liberte to thir dayis, to suffir nocht you thair sonnis to be reft and spulyeit of your realme, liberties and gudis; nor yit to be taikin, as cativis, to underly thair tyrannyis.... Knaw youreself dotat with incredibill manheid and virtew; and heritouris, be anciant linnage, als weill to your nobill faderis in wisdome and chevalrie, as in thair lands; nocht gaderit of divers nationis, bot of ane pepill under ane mind; and servandis to the Eternall God that gevis victory to just pepill in reward of thair virtew; and to fals and wrangus pepil schame, discomfiture and slauchter.[59]

But Boece did rather more than simply conjure up the 'pale ghosts' of Scotland's glorious military past. He also presented a minute description of an ancient Scottish discipline which, founded on a regime of Spartan austerity, was in his view the true well-spring of the nation's virtue.[60] Taking his cue from Livy's famous account of how Roman virtue was corrupted when temperance gave way to avarice and voluptuous living, he construed Scottish history in terms of a cycle of decay and regeneration in which the temperate manners of the elders were alternately scorned and embraced: while luxury bred effeminacy and self-indulgence, temperance bred the manly public virtues on which the commonweal and liberty of the realm depended.[61] According to Boece, however, in his own day, the ancient discipline survived only in those areas of Scotland – the Highlands and Islands – which because of their inaccessibility had remained untainted by luxurious living. It was, therefore, on the manners of the Gaels that he exhorted his countrymen to model their conduct.[62] For it was only by emulating the primitive discipline practised in the remoter parts of the kingdom that the public virtue of the elders would be made manifest among their descendants.

It is unlikely that, outside of the Highlands, Boece's readers were particularly impressed by his attempts to glorify the manners and customs of the Gaels. Likewise, his efforts to persuade his countrymen to adopt a lifestyle of Spartan austerity, while not untypical of humanist moralising, were hardly calculated to win universal applause. The appeal of his work lay rather in its ebullient reworking of the Scottish *mythomoteur*: its combination of chivalric and civic idealism together with its emphatic restatement of the historical basis of an autonomous Scottish identity. In this respect, it is well worth noting the immense weight which Bellenden attached to the idea of the 'commonweal' in his version of the chronicles and the highly patriotic resonances which the term had clearly acquired for him.[63] More often than not he used it to mean simply the public welfare or common good of the realm as a whole and references to acts and events which cause 'damage to the commonweal' are legion throughout his work. As this suggests, however, there are also times when the term is employed in much the same way – though with rather greater rhetorical force – as such words as realm, kingdom and nation. Used in this sense, the 'commonweal' implied, like the Latin *res publica* of which it was the nearest vernacular equivalent, not just the welfare of the community, but also the community whose welfare was at stake. Nevertheless, although the term was clearly freighted with classical connotations of civic responsibility, the obligations which citizenship imposed were construed by Bellenden primarily in chivalric terms: in terms, that is, of the martial heroism displayed by the elders in their defence of Scottish freedom.[64] Neither Boece nor Bellenden ever actually quote the Horatian tag *dulce et decorum est pro patria mori*. Their narrative, however, provides ample testimony to their belief that to lay down one's life for the commonweal and liberty of the realm was the greatest honour which could befall a Scot.[65]

There is no reason to doubt that, as Arthur Williamson has observed, the publication of Bellenden's work was 'a major cultural event for contemporaries'.[66] A vernacular account of their national past was at last made available to the increasingly literate lay audience which had been developing in Scotland since the mid-fifteenth century.[67] Nor is it surprising that it should have received full royal backing. In the eyes of James V, the Scottish monarchy, however fortuitous its diplomatic significance in the 1530s, was the equal of any of those European powers which sought to ally with it. The chronicles were admirably suited to the task of underwriting the brash self-confidence of a young king determined to exploit Scotland's unwonted significance on the diplomatic stage. As is well known, James was prepared to go to considerable lengths – and enormous expense – to equip Scotland with the architectural settings and court ceremonial befitting the power and prestige of a Renaissance monarch.[68] Rather less well known, though just as significant, is the fact that it was the same king who finally refashioned the Scottish regalia to reflect the Stewart dynasty's now long-standing claim to the dignity of an imperial crown.[69] The point was apparently not lost on those responsible for the production of the chronicles. The closed imperial crown is prominently featured among the other emblems of Scottish distinctiveness – the thistle, the lion rampant and the St. Andrews cross – in the elaborate version of the royal arms which dominates its titlepage.[70] It was, as Elphinstone and Boece would no doubt have wished, at once an expression of renewed confidence in the Scots' unique history and identity and a statement of the kingdom's parity of status among the imperial monarchies of Renaissance Europe.

With hindsight it is clear that, just as the Scottish *mythomoteur* reached the peak of its development in the 1530s, so too did Scottish national self-confidence. The death of James V in 1542, leaving as his sole legitimate heir the week-old Mary Queen of Scots inaugurated a prolonged period of political, religious and social upheaval which was to test severely the Scottish community's sense of collective identity and to call into question many of the myths and memories enshrined in the 'matter of Scotland'. To be sure, the idea of the Scots as a nation-in-arms still had a very long life ahead of it. As Christopher Smout reminds us, the works of Barbour and Blind Harry were 'still deep in Scottish popular consciousness' in the late eighteenth century when Robert Burns celebrated the mythic heroism of Bruce and Wallace in poems like 'Scots! wha hae wi' Wallace bled'.[71] Nevertheless, even in the sixteenth century, the martial tradition was not without its critics. As early as 1521 the scholastic theologian John Mair had mounted a telling critique of Scotland's chivalrous lineage culture which, paradoxically enough, appears to owe much more to Erasmian humanism than does the idealising atavism so characteristic of Hector Boece. Furthermore, Mair's deep distrust of an over-mighty and irresponsible nobility, allied to a profound dislike of the barbarous customs of the Gaels, had prompted him to develop the first coherent case for Anglo-Scottish union.[72] Mair's evident belief that Scotland's martial past was wholly inadequate as a basis on which to build her future, while cutting little ice at the time, was to fall on increasingly receptive ears as the sixteenth century wore on. It is, however, well beyond the scope of this paper to explore how the Scots set about rewriting their history – and re-inventing themselves – in the light of the momentous changes wrought by the onset of Protestant reform and the prospect of union with England. It is much more appropriate, by way of conclusion, to turn our attention to the full extent and depth of the popular nationalist sentiment out of which a new Scottish identity could be forged. For it is in the course of the 1540s, in the face of intense English pressure, that the sources first begin to reveal just how powerfully a sense of their unique individuality had gripped the Scottish people as a whole.

Not surprisingly, at the roots of this popular feeling lay an unyielding belief in Scotland's freedom from foreign – specifically English – overlordship. In 1542, on the eve of the Solway Moss campaign which was to contribute to James V's early demise, Henry VIII had issued his well-known *Declaration* in which, drawing heavily on the historical lore first systematically exploited by Edward I, he set out in more detail than ever before the case for English suzerainty over Scotland.[73] As a propaganda exercise it backfired badly when, in the following year, the opportunity arose to negotiate a peaceful dynastic union of the two kingdoms through the marriage of Mary Queen of Scots to Henry's own son and heir, Prince Edward. The English king's insistence that Mary should be delivered immediately into his safe-keeping simply confirmed the Scots' profound distrust of his motives and ambitions. As early as March 1543, Henry was warned that the Scots would not countenace such a move until Mary came of age because they believed his intention was not to provide 'for the weill of our soverane ladye' but rather 'to conquiese the realme'.[74] Even those Protestant Anglophiles who favoured the marriage were adamant in their refusal to hand over the child queen. Henry was eventually forced to give way and the Treaties of Greenwich, first drawn up in July 1543, allowed for Mary to remain in Scotland until she had completed her tenth year. Yet this grudging concession neither convinced the Scots of Henry's good-will nor allayed their fears that his ultimate intentions were little different from those of Edward I. In October 1543, his ambassador in Scotland, Ralph Sadler, reported to the English privy council that, regardless of the treaties, 'the whole body of the realm' favoured a French rather than an English marriage because they believed that France would 'continue and maintain the honour and liberty of the realm' whereas England wanted 'nothing else but to bring them in subjection and to have superiority and dominion over them'.[75]

That such antipathy to the prospect of English domination was not confined to the political élite but reached deep into the fabric of Scottish society is repeatedly indicated in Sadler's increasingly paranoid dispatches. Shot at in his garden in Edinburgh, his servant beaten up as an 'English dog'

by an irate Scot and his own life apparently under constant threat from the
enraged burgesses of the capital, the beleaguered English ambassador ought
perhaps to be forgiven his frequent references to the 'malice' of the Scots and
even for concluding that 'under the soonne lyve not more beestely and
unreasonable people than here be of all degrees'.[76] Terrified and deeply
prejudiced though he was, Sadler nonetheless provides insights into Scottish
public opinion which are as invaluable as they are unprecedented. Thus in
August 1543 he assured his superiors in rather bemused terms that the
problem was quite simply 'that this nation is of such malicious nature towards
Englishmen that they cannot abide, nor suffer to hear, that Englishmen
should have any manner of superiority over them'.[77] As Sir George Douglas,
one of the most prominent of the Scottish Anglophiles had made clear to him,
his countrymen would 'dye rather all in a daye then they woolde be made
thrall and subject to England' and, if Henry wanted obedience from the Scots,
he had no alternative 'but to gett it with the swoorde'.[78] It was widely
believed, however, that the use of force would simply stiffen Scottish resistance and make a bad situation still worse. Even the earl of Arran, the Scottish
regent responsible for negotiating the marriage treaty, was moved to warn
Henry that 'the bringing-in of 5000 Englishmen should cause 20000
Scotsmen to forsake them and run to their enemies'.[79] Sir George Douglas
reinforced this view, stating bluntly that any attempt 'to bring the government of this realm to the king of England' by force would meet with
determined resistance: 'there is not so little a boy', he opined, 'but he will
hurl stones against it, and the wives will handle their distaffs, and the
commons universally will rather die in it, yea, and many noblemen and all
the clergy be fully against'.[80]

However exaggerated these reports may be, they clearly indicate that in
the summer of 1543 Henry VIII's dynastic ambitions ran swiftly aground on
a solid bedrock of popular nationalist feeling. Indeed, so powerful were the
emotions unleashed by the marriage negotiations that they not only
jeopardised the imperial designs of the English king, but – rather more
interestingly – they appear also to have threatened the local authority of
those Scottish lords who chose to support him. Sadler reported that the
so-called 'assured lords' – the Scottish nobles who had pledged to further the
English cause in Scotland – had 'almost lost the hearts of the common people'
and that 'such ballads and songs [were] made of them, how the English angels
had corrupted them, as have not been heard'.[81] Not only was Arran being
denounced as 'an heretick' – a jibe often used to insult the schismatic English
– but both he and the earl of Angus were reputed 'good Englishmen' who
had 'sold this realm to the king's majesty'.[82] Still more significant, however,
is Sadler's further comment that, while some of the 'assured lords' might
continue to accept Henry VIII's superiority, 'there is not one of them that
hath two servants or friends that is of the same mind'.[83] It would seem that,

at least under certain circumstances, the Scots' allegiance to their country was ultimately more powerful than their allegiance to their lords. Independently of Sadler, another English informer provided more detailed testimony to the operation of such concentric loyalties within Scottish society. According to his report, Angus's servants and retainers were prepared 'uttirlie [to] relinquishe and forsaik' their master should he and Arran continue to support the English cause: 'Openlie bruting that they bee Scottishemen, and trew Scottes they wolbee in harte and dede against Englande, what covenaunte, pacte or other promyse soever bee made to the contrarie by theire governour and his adherents'.[84]

As this suggests, while fear and hatred of the English certainly ran deep in contemporary Scottish society, so too did a clear awareness of belonging to a distinct community with its own unique values and traditions. There is perhaps no better testimony to this than the great host – one of the largest armies ever mustered by the Scots – which confronted the duke of Somerset's English forces at Pinkie in September 1547.[85] Despite the brutality of Henry VIII's 'Rough Wooing', and despite the pusillanimity of many of their own political leaders, the Scots remained astonishingly united in their resolve to defend the commonweal and liberty of the realm.[86] The abject failure of the national army may well have helped to expose the inadequacy of the martial traditions embodied in the Scottish *mythomoteur*. Nevertheless, while the idea of Scotland as a nation-in-arms was approaching the end of its useful life, it would take more than their defeat in battle to eradicate the sense of nationhood which, in the course of the later middle ages, had penetrated so deeply into Scottish society as a whole. In the 1430s, Aeneas Sylvius Piccolomini (later Pope Pius II) commented that: 'Nothing pleases the Scots more than abuse of the English'.[87] As we have seen, however, while the Scots were always (and understandably) prone to define themselves in terms of what they were not, there was much more to their sense of collective identity than simple Anglophobia. By the early Renaissance period, their long struggle to maintain the kingdom's autonomy had not only generated an historically-based conception of an imperial Scottish monarchy, but had developed in the idea of the commonweal a powerful means of articulating the community's continuing commitment to maintaining an independent Scottish identity. Needless to say, this was a legacy with profound implications for the future of Britain and the place of Scotland within it.

NOTES

I am extremely grateful to Dr. John Robertson for his valuable comments on an earlier draft of this essay. It has also benefited considerably from discussions with Ms. Ellen Colingsworth.

1. T.C. Smout, 'Problems of Nationalism, Identity and Improvement in Later Eighteenth-Century Scotland', in T.M. Devine (ed.), *Improvement and Enlightenment* (Edinburgh, 1989), 1–21.
2. As this paper is confined to the pre-Reformation era (its effective chronological limit is the 1540s), I have not attempted to deal here with the most influential of all the figures of the Scottish Renaissance: George Buchanan. His crucial importance in re-defining the nature of the Scottish identity in the post-Reformation world deserves (and will soon, I hope, receive) separate consideration.
3. Elie Kedourie, *Nationalism* (London, 1960), 1, opens his discussion with the blunt statement: 'Nationalism is a doctrine invented in Europe at the beginning of the nineteenth century'. Cf. Ernest Gellner, *Nations and Nationalism* (Oxford, 1983), for a similar, if more sophisticated, perspective.
4. Most recently, in *National Identity* (Harmondsworth, 1991), but most tellingly in *The Ethnic Origins of Nations* (Oxford, 1986). On 'concentric loyalties', see in particular his *The Ethnic Revival* (London, 1981).
5. Smith, *Ethnic Origins*, 21–22.
6. *Ibid.*, 13–16, 58–68, and *passim*. 'Of course, there is much more to the concept of the 'nation' than myths and memories. But they constitute a *sine qua non*: there can be no identity without memory (albeit selective), no collective purpose without myth, and identity and purpose or destiny are necessary elements of the very concept of a nation. But this is also true of the concept of an ethnic community; it too must be felt to have an identity and destiny, and hence myths and memories'. *Ibid.*, 2.
7. *Ibid.*, 22–30.
8. Roger A. Mason, 'Scotching the Brut: Politics, History and National Myth in 16th Century Britain', in Roger A. Mason (ed.), *Scotland and England 1286–1815* (Edinburgh, 1987), 60–84.
9. Walter Bower, *Scotichronicon*, ed. Donald Watt *et al.* (Aberdeen, 1987–), viii, 340–1.
10. See Marjorie Drexler, 'Fluid Prejudice: Scottish Origin Myths in the Later Middle Ages', in J. Rosenthal and C. Richmond (ed.), *People, Politics and Community in the Later Middle Ages* (Gloucester and New York, 1987), 60–77; and William Matthews, 'The Egyptians in Scotland: The Political History of a Myth', *Viator*, 1 (1970), 289–306.
11. Smout, 'Problems of Nationalism', 7–8
12. Denys Hay, *Europe: The Emergence of an Idea* (2nd edn., Edinburgh, 1968), 137.
13. Eric John, *Orbis Britanniae and Other Studies* (Leicester, 1966), 1–63.
14. Geoffrey of Monmouth, *The History of the Kings of Britain*, ed. and trans. Lewis Thorpe (Harmondsworth, 1966). On Geoffrey's influence, see T.D. Kendrick, *British Antiquity* (London, 1950).
15. For the English claim as set out by Edward I in 1301 in response to the papal bull *Scimus fili*, see E.L.G. Stones (ed.), *Anglo-Scottish Relations 1174–1328: Some Selected Documents* (2nd edn., Oxford, 1970), 192–219.
16. C.L. Kingsford, 'The First Version of Hardyng's Chronicle', *English Historical Review*,

27 (1912), 740–53, discusses the extent and purpose of Hardyng's activities as a forger.

17. See F.W.D. Brie (ed.), *The Brut, or the Chronicles of England* (Early English Text Society, 1906–8), i, 186–211, 254–56.
18. R.R. Davies, 'In Praise of British History', in R.R. Davies (ed.), *The British Isles 1100–1500* (Edinburgh, 1988), 9–26, at 13.
19. See the *Processus Baldredi* in W.F. Skene (ed.), *Chronicles of the Picts, Chronicles of the Scots, and Other Early Memorials of Scottish History* (Edinburgh, 1867), 271–84. Elements drawn from the same body of myths are also to be found in the opening lines of the Declaration of Arbroath and in the Anglo-Scottish peace negotiations of 1321. See James Fergusson (ed.), *The Declaration of Arbroath 1320* (Edinburgh, 1970), 7, and P.A. Linehan, 'A Fourteenth Century History of Anglo-Scottish Relations in a Spanish Manuscript', *Bulletin of the Institute of Historical Research*, 48 (1975), 106–22.
20. John of Fordun, *Chronica Gentis Scotorum*, ed. W.F. Skene and trans. F.J.H. Skene (Edinburgh, 1871–72), ii, 21.
21. The fullest discussion of Fordun's sources remains that of Skene in *ibid.*, ii, pp. xxix–lxxviii. But see also Edward J. Cowan, 'Myth and Identity in Early Medieval Scotland', *Scottish Historical Review*, 63 (1984), 111–135.
22. See Susan Reynolds, 'Medieval *Origines Gentium* and the Community of the Realm', *History*, 68 (1984), 375–90, from where the term 'regnal solidarity' is borrowed.
23. Fordun, *Chronica*, ii, 289–90. See also his genealogy of David I which goes back beyond Gathelus and Scota to Japhet, son of Noah (*ibid.*, ii, 244–46). Logically enough, another genealogy, dating apparently from the accession of William the Lion in 1165, reaches back to 'Adam, son of the living God'. Skene (ed.), *Chronicles of the Picts*, 133–34. For a fuller discussion of the significance of the early inauguration ritual, see John Bannerman, 'The King's Poet and the Inauguration of Alexander III', *Scottish Historical Review*, 68 (1989), 120–49.
24. Most readily illustrated by the plates in Walter de Gray Birch, *History of Scottish Seals. Volume I: The Royal Seals of Scotland* (Stirling and London, 1905). *Rex Scottorum* is almost invariably employed until 1603.
25. R.J. Lyall, 'The Medieval Scottish Coronation Service: Some Seventeenth-Century Evidence', *Innes Review*, 28 (1977), 3–21. In the later ceremony the genealogy was considerably curtailed and was recited by the Lyon King rather than the king's poet.
26. *Declaration of Arbroath*, 7; Fordun, *Chronica*, ii, 78–79.
27. See Skene's discussion of this in Fordun, *Chronica*, ii, pp. lxff, lxxiv–lxxvi. It should be borne in mind that, until the twelfth century, tanistic succession rather than primogeniture prevailed in Scotland. As a result, while they increasingly overlap, the royal genealogies and the kinglists by no means correspond.
28. The problem of Scottish kings doing homage to English superiors was generally sidestepped by claiming that fealty was owed only for the lands they held in England. See, eg, Fordun, *Chronica*, ii, 250, 271, 273, 300.
29. W.A. Craigie (ed.), *The Asloan Manuscript* (Scottish Text Society, 1923–25), i, 185–95, at 193. An earlier version of the same piece is printed in *The Bannatyne Miscellany III* (Bannatyne Club, 1855), 35–43. The editor of the Asloan version believed them to be independent translations of the same Latin original dating from about 1460. *Asloan MS*, i, p. vii.
30. *Ibid.*, i, 194–95.
31. See *Declaration of Arbroath*, 9, for the Sallustian lines: 'It is in truth not for glory, nor riches, nor honours that we are fighting, but for freedom – for that alone which

no honest man gives up but with life itself'. For Barbour's apostrophe – 'A! fredome is a noble thing' – see Matthew P. McDiarmid and James A.C. Stevenson (ed.), *Barbour's Bruce* (Scottish Text Society, 1980–85), ii, 9–10 (Book I, lines 225–36). For more general discussion, see G.W.S. Barrow, 'The Idea of Freedom in Late Medieval Scotland', *Innes Review*, 30 (1979), 16–34.

32. Fordun, *Chronica*, ii, 44–45.
33. *Ibid.*, ii, 45.
34. On these historical mythologies of chivalry, see Maurice Keen, *Chivalry* (New Haven and London, 1984), ch. 6. For introductions to the vast scholarly literature on the British and Roman romance cycles, see R.S. Loomis (ed.), *Arthurian Literature in the Middle Ages: A Collaborative History* (Oxford, 1959), and George Cary, *The Medieval Alexander*, ed. D.J.A. Ross (Cambridge, 1956).
35. For Scottish versions of some of this literature, see R.L.G. Ritchie (ed.), *The Buik of the Most Noble and Valiant Conquerour Alexander the Grit* (Scottish Text Society, 1921–29); M.M. Gray (ed.), *Lancelot of the Laik* (Scottish Text Society, 1912); and F.J. Amours (ed.), *Scottish Alliterative Poems* (Scottish Text Society, 1897). It is worth pointing out that the biblical story of the Maccabees was also construed as an historical mythology of chivalry and it is primarily in this light that one ought to read the Declaration of Arbroath's likening of Robert Bruce to Joshua and Judas Maccabaeus as well as Barbour's identification of the Scots with the Maccabees. It is not necessarily, as is so often suggested, evidence that the Scots thought themselves peculiarly favoured by God. *Declaration of Arbroath*, 9; Barbour, *Bruce*, i, 18 (Book I, lines 464ff.). Further echoes of the books of the Maccabees in contemporary Scottish sources are traced in Barrow, 'Idea of Freedom', 30–32, while the European background is discussed in Keen, *Chivalry*, 119–21.
36. On Barbour's didactic intent, see Lois Ebin, 'John Barbour's *Bruce*: Poetry, History and Propaganda', *Studies in Scottish Literature*, 9 (1972), 218–42.
37. Ranald Nicholson, *Scotland: The Later Middle Ages* (Edinburgh, 1974), invariably treats chivalry dismissively, while Alexander Grant, *Independence and Nationhood: Scotland 1306–1469* (London, 1984), barely mentions it at all.
38. For the general background to what follows, see Jenny Wormald, *Lords and Men in Scotland* (Edinburgh, 1985).
39. Though see David Sellar, 'Highland Family Origins: Pedigree Making and Pedigree Faking', in Loraine MacLean (ed.), *The Middle Ages in the Highlands* (Inverness, 1981), 103–116, which discusses the fabrication of family genealogies in Gaelic society.
40. See John MacQueen, 'The Literature of Fifteenth-Century Scotland', in Jennifer Brown (ed.), *Scottish Society in the Fifteenth Century* (London, 1977), 184–208, esp. 196–199. That most literary patronage stemmed from the aristocracy rather than the court in the fifteenth century is forcefully argued in an as yet unpublished paper by Sally Mapstone presented to the 6th International Conference on Medieval and Renaissance Scottish Language and Literature: 'Was there a Court Literature in Fifteenth-Century Scotland?'. I am grateful to Dr. Mapstone for allowing me to read her article prior to publication. It will appear shortly in an issue of *Studies in Scottish Literature*.
41. Such concentric loyalties are perhaps most obviously expressed in contemporary bonds of manrent which, in binding men to their lords, invariably excepted their allegiance to the king. Wormald, *Lords and Men*, 26–7, 70. Obviously, we are here beginning to engage with the wider historical debate on the nature of crown-magnate relations in late medieval Scotland. The idea of concentric loyalties might well prove useful as a means of conceptualising the kind of relationship between local

and central authority described by 'revisionist' historians like Wormald and Grant. See, eg, Wormald, 'Taming the Magnates?', in Keith Stringer (ed.), *Essays on the Nobility of Medieval Scotland* (Edinburgh, 1985), 270–80, and Grant, *Independence and Nationhood*, chs. 6–7.

42. J.H. Stevenson (ed.), *Gilbert of the Haye's Prose Manuscript* (Scottish Text Society, 1901–14), ii, 65. For a fuller analysis of Haye's sources and how he used them, see Sally Mapstone, 'The Advice to Princes Tradition in Scottish Literature 1450–1500' (Unpublished DPhil Thesis, University of Oxford, 1986), ch. 2.

43. For this and what follows, see my 'Kingship, Tyranny and the Right to Resist in Fifteenth-Century Scotland', *Scottish Historical Review*, 66 (1987), 125–51.

44. *Haye's Prose MS*, ii, 18–34.

45. The change is most readily apparent in parliamentary legislation where before *c.* 1520 the stock formulae employed to denote the public welfare are phrases like 'the common profit of the realm', 'the welfare and public good of the realm', 'the common good of our sovereign lord's realm and lieges', and 'the common profit and universal weal of the realm'. Between 1460 and 1520, in fact, 'the common-weal of the realm' occurs only some 5 times as a convenient shorthand for such clumsy phraseology. In the 1520s and 1530s, however, it is used on more than 20 separate occasions in a variety of types of legislation relating to the economic, social and political welfare of the kingdom. T. Thomson and C. Innes (ed.), *Acts of the Parliaments of Scotland* [*APS*] (Edinburgh, 1814–75), ii, *passim*. For further analysis of the term, see my 'Kingship and Commonweal: Political Thought and Ideology in Reformation Scotland' (Unpublished PhD Thesis, University of Edinburgh, 1983), 67–74.

46. For a survey of the humanist educational programme, see Quentin Skinner, *The Foundations of Modern Political Thought* (Cambridge, 1978), i, 228–43. What follows in this paragraph owes a good deal to Malcolm Vale, *Warfare and Chivalry: Warfare and Aristocratic Culture in England, France and Burgundy at the End of the Middle Ages* (London, 1981), 14–32.

47. Aspects of this as it developed in the later sixteenth century are discussed in Keith Brown, *Bloodfeud in Scotland 1573–1625* (Edinburgh, 1986), and Arthur H. Williamson, *Scottish National Consciousness in the Age of James VI* (Edinburgh, 1979).

48. See John Durkan, 'Early Humanism and King's College', *Aberdeen University Review*, 48 (1980), 259–79, and Leslie J. Macfarlane, *William Elphinstone and the Kingdom of Scotland 1431–1514* (Aberdeen, 1985).

49. This aspect of the *mythomoteur* – not least the legend of St. Andrew himself – and the clergy's role in promoting it deserve much more extensive treatment than it is possible to give them here. But see David McRoberts, 'The Glorious House of St. Andrew', in David McRoberts (ed.), *The Medieval Church of St. Andrews* (Glasgow, 1976), 63–120, for some useful insights.

50. On his French training in civil law and the likely influence of Bartolus, see Macfarlane, *Elphinstone*, 40–47.

51. James Moir (ed.), *Hectoris Boetii Murthlacensium et Aberdonensium Episcoporum Vitae* (New Spalding Club, 1894), 95.

52. *APS*, ii, 95; I.M. Stewart, *The Scottish Coinage* (London, 1965), 65.

53. Boece, *Episcoporum Vitae*, 99.

54. David McRoberts, 'The Scottish Church and Nationalism in the Fifteenth Century', *Innes Review*, 19 (1968), 3–14.

55. Boece, *Episcoporum Vitae*, 99–100.

56. Hector Boece, *The History and Chronicles of Scotland*, trans. John Bellenden and ed. Thomas Maitland (Edinburgh, 1821), ii, 377.

57. For further discussion of Boece's sources, see Marjorie Drexler, 'Attitudes to Nationality in Scottish Historical Writing from Barbour to Boece' (Unpublished PhD Thesis, University of Edinburgh, 1979), ch. 7. The following analysis of Boece's work is based on the much fuller discussion in Mason, 'Kingship and Commonweal', ch. 3.

58. Oddly, for a work of such importance, the precise date of publication is unknown, though the printer, Thomas Davidson, was also responsible for the 1540 edition of the Acts of Parliament. H.G. Aldis, *A List of Books Printed in Scotland before 1700* (2nd. edn., Edinburgh, 1970), 112, notes that the chronicles were printed 'at least as early as 1540, as the copy in Innerpeffray library has an inscription of that year'.

59. Boece, *History and Chronicles*, i, 237–8.

60. This is in evidence throughout the *History*, but is usefully summarised in a preface added by Bellenden to his translation entitled 'Ane prudent doctrine maid be the Auctore concerning the new Maneris and the Auld of Scottis'. See *ibid.*, i, pp. liv–lxii.

61. As a result, for Boece, the domestic history of Scotland consisted of a series of contrasts between virtuous kings who tried to stem the tide of luxury and restore the ancient discipline and vicious tyrants who succumbed to their sensual appetites and were disposed of by those of the nobility who remained uncorrupted. Whether the latter 'depositions' were intended as moral precepts or constitutional principles is still a moot point.

62. *Ibid.*, i, pp. xxvi, li–lii, lxi–lxii.

63. At a minimum count, the term occurs more than 150 times in the course of the *History*. For fuller analysis of its meaning and usage, see my 'Kingship and Commonweal', 72–74.

64. Thus in his verse 'Proheme of the History', Bellenden exhorts his 'martial buke' to 'Schaw now quhat princes bene maist vicius,/ And quhay hes bene of chevelry the rose:/ Quhay did their kingrik in maist honour jois,/ And with thair blud our liberteis hes coft;/ Regarding nocht to de amang thair fois,/ Sa that thay micht in memory be brocht'. Boece, *History and Chronicles*, i, p. cv.

65. There is, however, a distinct echo of Horace in Bellenden's 'Proheme of the History': 'Thairfore he is maist nobyll man thou say/ Of all estatis under reverence,/ That vailyeantly doith close the latter day/ Of natyve cuntre deand in defence'. *Ibid.*, i, p. cvi.

66. Williamson, *Scottish National Consciousness*, 120.

67. On the 'silent revolution in literacy', see Grant G. Simpson, *Scottish Handwriting 1150–1650* (Edinburgh, 1973), 10–14. For some useful comments on its implications, see Jenny Wormald, *Court, Kirk and Community: Scotland 1469–1625* (London, 1981), 68–71.

68. Martin Kemp, 'Humanism in the Visual Arts 1530–1630', in John MacQueen (ed.), *Humanism in Renaissance Scotland* (Edinburgh, 1990), 32–47, esp. 33–35.

69. W. Bell (ed.), *Papers Relative to the Regalia of Scotland* (Bannatyne Club, 1829), 21–2, 30–1. James V also reverted to his grandfather's policy of featuring the imperial crown on his coinage; see Stewart, *Scottish Coinage*, 76–77.

70. For a fuller description, see R. Dickson and J.P. Edmonds, *Annals of Scottish Printing* (Cambridge, 1890), 109. As they point out, the coat of arms 'displays the insignia of the newly-instituted Order of the Thistle: the floral collar surrounding the greater part of the shield, and the jewel bearing the figure of St. Andrew behind his cross, depending from the lower part'. They also make the plausible suggestion that the arms were designed by Sir David Lindsay of the Mount.

71. Smout, 'Problems of Nationalism', 12. In fact, Barbour and Blind Harry went through more editions (the former 6 and the latter a staggering 18) than almost

any other works printed in Scotland before 1700. Apart from the bible, the psalms and the catechism, only the works of Sir David Lindsay (20 editions) were printed more often. See Aldis, *List of Books*, index. The martial heritage was, of course, also a pre-occupation of the Scottish intelligentsia in the eighteenth century; see John Robertson, *The Scottish Enlightenment and the Militia Issue* (Edinburgh, 1985).

72. See my, 'Kingship, Nobility and Anglo-Scottish Union: John Mair's *History of Greater Britain* (1521)', *Innes Review*, 41 (1990), 182–222.

73. Most accessibly reprinted in J.A.H. Murray (ed.), *The Complaynt of Scotlande* (Early English Text Society, 1872), 191–206.

74. Joseph Bain (ed.), *The Hamilton Papers* (Edinburgh, 1890–92), i, no. 337.

75. A. Clifford (ed.), *The State Papers and letters of Sir Ralph Sadler* (Edinburgh, 1809), i, 326–7. Sadler repeated the warning a few days later in a letter to Henry VIII: *Hamilton Papers*, ii, no. 85.

76. *Sadler Papers*, i, 237; *Hamilton Papers*, ii, nos. 2, 14, 27.

77. *Sadler Papers*, i, 259.

78. *Hamilton Papers*, i, no. 350.

79. *Sadler Papers*, i, 255.

80. *Ibid.*, i, 70.

81. *Ibid.*, i, 165–6. Another reference to such 'sclanderous billis, writtingis, ballatis and bukis' occurs in R.K. Hannay (ed.), *Acts of the Lords of Council in Public Affairs 1501–1554* (Edinburgh, 1932), 527–8. Unfortunately, none of this material appears to have survived.

82. *Sadler Papers*, i, 216, 234; *Hamilton Papers*, ii, nos. 99, 120.

83. *Sadler Papers*, i, 326–7.

84. *Hamilton Papers*, i, no. 397.

85. See David H. Caldwell, 'The Battle of Pinkie', in Norman Macdougall (ed.), *Scotland and War AD 79–1918* (Edinburgh, 1991), 61–94.

86. On the continuing importance of this phrase in contemporary political discourse, see my 'Covenant and Commonweal: The Language of Politics in Reformation Scotland', in Norman Macdougall (ed.), *Church, Politics and Society: Scotland 1408–1929* (Edinburgh, 1983), 97–126.

87. P. Hume Brown (ed.), *Early Travellers in Scotland* (Edinburgh, 1891), 27. For similar comments from a Scottish source, see John Mair, *A History of Greater Britain as well England as Scotland*, ed. and trans. A. Constable (Scottish History Society, 1892), 40, 223.

4

The Origins of the 'Road to the Isles': Trade, Communications and Campbell Power in Early Modern Scotland.

JANE E.A. DAWSON

'Sure, by Tummel, an' Loch Rannoch
an' Lochaber I will go'.

This, as the famous song tells us, is the road to the Isles. However, the road with which this paper deals is not the nostalgic one of Kenneth Macleod's song written for 'the lads in France during the Great War'.[1] Rather it is the complex of land routes which in the early modern period for the first time linked the Western Isles with Lowland Scotland. In the medieval period nobody would have approached the Isles except by boat. Even when the kings of Scotland took their armies with them on their expeditions into the west, they travelled by sea. The 'road to the Isles' was not a natural nor a perpetual feature of the communications system within Scotland. It was produced in response to the new set of political and economic conditions which emerged during the early modern period.

The creation of a continuous land route in that period was much more than a simple shift in methods of communication. The new road symbolised a far wider change to the whole economic and political geography of Scotland. It was the visible consequence of a major realignment which permanently and irrevocably attached the Western Highlands and Islands to the rest of the country. The process which transformed the relationship between the Western Isles and the Scottish mainland combined two distinct but related elements. The Isles were joined to the Highlands and they formed the single entity of the Highlands and Islands. The newly unified region also became more closely attached to the Lowlands. These two developments took several centuries to unfold and their progress was slow and uneven. It is sometimes difficult to separate them because they were mutually reinforcing. In the end

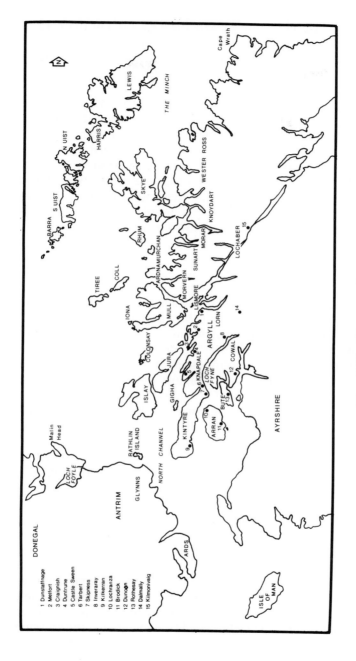

1 Dunstaffnage
2 Melfort
3 Craignish
4 Duntrune
5 Castle Sween
6 Tarbert
7 Skipness
8 Inveraray
9 Kilkerran
10 Lochranza
11 Brodick
12 Dunoon
13 Rothesay
14 Dalmally
15 Kilmonivaig

DONEGAL

Malin
Head

LEWIS

HARRIS

N UIST

S UIST

BARRA

Cape
Wrath

THE MINCH

WESTER ROSS

KNOYDART

LOCHABER

MORAR

SUNART

ARDNAMURCHAN

SKYE

RHUM

COLL

TIREE

MORVERN

LISMORE

MULL

IONA

COLONSAY

ARGYLL

LORN

COWAL

JURA

KNAPDALE

LOCH
FYNE

BUTE

ISLAY

GIGHA

KINTYRE

ARRAN

AYRSHIRE

RATHLIN
ISLAND

ANTRIM

GLYNNS

NORTH CHANNEL

LOCH
FOYLE

ARDS

ISLE
OF
MAN

Map 1 The Western Isles

they were solidified by long-term structural changes in the pattern of trade and by the creation of a network of communications which covered the new region and linked it to the Lowlands. In this latter development the rise of Campbell power and the long-term changes brought by the Reformation were to prove crucial.

The uneasy but unbreakable connection between the new Highlands and Islands region and the rest of the country completed the long process of political integration which by the start of the sixteenth century had produced a unified kingdom of Scotland. The road to the Isles tied the Hebrides first to the Highlands, then to Scotland. Finally, it determined the place which the Highlands and Islands would occupy within the British Isles. Paradoxically, only after the full incorporation of the Isles into Scotland and Britain could the complex geographical, cultural and linguistic differences be reduced to the simplistic concepts of 'Highland' and 'Lowland'.

I

From Viking times the Western Isles had formed a single and coherent entity united by the sea (see Map 1).[2] It encompassed all the islands from Shetland south as far as the Isle of Man and included the mainland coastlines of western Scotland and northern Ireland. The sea defined its bounds and maintained its unity. The significance of its island structure was graphically demonstrated in 1097 by the Norwegian King Magnus Barelegs. He 'sailed' all round Kintyre by standing at the tiller of his ship whilst it was dragged across the portage at Tarbert. Magnus then successfully claimed that as Kintyre was an 'island' it should be part of his territory by the terms of his treaty with Scotland in 1098 which ceded him all the Scottish islands.[3]

In the following century, the great warrior, Somerled, himself of a mixed Norse/Celtic background, led a 'Gaelic revival' through a successful offensive against the Norwegians. By defeating Norway's vassal, the king of Man, in 1156 and 1158 and forcing him to flee to Norway, Somerled was able to set up his own rule in the Western Isles. The three branches of Somerled's descendants dominated the Scottish islands but were no longer able to control the whole of the great spread of territory previously under Norse overlordship. By the fourteenth century Clan Donald had emerged supreme from the struggles with Clan Ruairi and Clan Dougal and ruled over a region from Lewis as far south as Ulster. The lordship of the Isles retained the essential characteristic of a dominion held together by the sea lanes and the galleys which sailed along them. The Macdonald chiefs adopted the appropriate title of 'lord of the Isles', the Latinised version of Somerled's 'Ri Innse Gall', and symbolically placed the lymphad or heraldic galley upon their coat of arms.[4]

The concentration upon islands and the sea meant that the coastline of the Western Highlands formed part of the Isles but the hinterland did not. The influence of the lordship of the Isles declined with distance from the coast. This produced an east-west division within mainland Scotland which split the seaboard from the Highlands. The vague inland boundary was defined by the ease of access from the sea and sea lochs, and so it followed the contours of the land along the ragged coast of western Scotland. In a cultural context the extent of the lordship's influence was apparent in the geographical spread of the magnificent monumental sculpture of the late medieval period. Schools flourished in Iona, Kintyre, Loch Awe, Loch Sween and Oronsay and the carvings were distributed throughout the Isles and by the sea lochs of Argyll. But the cultural influence of the lordship did not penetrate deeply into the mainland. Dalmally was the furthest sculpture site from the sea and Kilmonivaig at the Bridge of Mucomir in the Great Glen, not far from the head of Loch Linnhe, was the most easterly site.[5]

In the late medieval period, the mainland Highlands were largely untouched by the concerns of the lordship of the Isles. The one exception concerned the earldom of Ross which the Macdonalds claimed and actually held at various stages in the fifteenth century. Their pursuit of this title brought them into conflict with the Scottish crown which was willing to tolerate their authority over the Isles but was far more concerned about Macdonald power when it became manifest on the mainland. In their fight to retain Ross the Macdonalds were drawn into political and military adventures as far east as Harlaw in Aberdeenshire, the scene of a famous battle in 1411.[6]

The situation was different in the central Highlands. When royal intervention undermined the local power structure in Rannoch and Breadalbane during the fifteenth century, the Macdonalds were not involved in the subsequent scramble for ascendancy.[7] Similarly, the lords of the Isles took no part in the later succession struggle within Clanranald which sucked in the eastern Highland clans of the Frasers and the Grants as well as the earl of Huntly and culminated in the bloody 'Field of the Shirts' in 1544.[8]

Between the fifteenth and seventeenth centuries the basic east-west divide between the Western Isles and the Highlands disappeared. This was only possible after the dynamic coherence of the lordship of the Isles had been destroyed. The erosion of that unity began during the height of Macdonald power. In the later medieval period a quiet but effective challenge was mounted to the lordship's authority over its mainland frontier. The strip of land running down the western seaboard of the mainland was cut from its ties across the sea to the Isles. From the building of Castle Sween in the thirteenth century to the end of the fifteenth century, the crown, their Stewart kin and the rising force of the Campbells placed a series of castles and fortifications along the Argyll littoral and effectively moved the eastern boundary of the Isles into the sea.

The castles protected the mainland of Argyll and the islands of Arran and Bute from the raids of the Islesmen and drew these areas away from their links to the lordship in the west, bringing them instead into the mainstream of Scottish political life.[9] Dunstaffnage with its excellent harbour was able to control north Lorn, Loch Linnhe and the vital sea lanes around Mull. Melfort and Craignish commanded the sea lochs which led out to the islands of Netherlorn, whilst Duntrune policed the Crinan area. Castle Sween watched the northern end of Jura, and Tarbert from its narrow neck of land looked along both its sea lochs to Jura in the west and Arran in the east. On the north-eastern coast of Kintyre, Skipness complemented Lochranza on Arran and together they kept watch over the Kilbrannan Sound and the southern end of Loch Fyne, while Inveraray guarded the northern reaches of that loch. The southern approaches of the Firth of Clyde were watched by James IV's new castle at Kilkerran (Campbeltown) and Brodick and Dunoon protected Bute and Cowal. This defensive line screened the ancestral lands of the Stewart dynasty as well as the territory of the Campbells who now dominated the area and pushed the boundary with the Isles out into the sea lanes.

The coastline of Ireland to the south was another boundary of the Isles which was subject to long-term erosion. The old seaborne unity was weakened by the gradual removal of the links between northern Ireland and the Isles. New ties had been made between these areas by the Macdonalds when they had acquired territory in Antrim through the Bisset marriage in 1399. The lords of the Isles had expanded their Irish holdings from the original settlement in the Glynns into the Route. By the sixteenth century the southern branch of Clan Donald was as much based in Antrim as on Islay or Kintyre.[10]

However, Tudor policies towards the kingdom of Ireland altered the established relationships across the North Channel. As the English sought to extend their authority throughout Ireland, the Irish Gaelic chiefs, including the Macdonalds, became increasingly preoccupied with domestic concerns. Although this temporarily stimulated the mercenary trade from the Isles, it destroyed any thought of a pan-Gaelic political unity based on the sea routes. The Elizabethan conquest of Ireland, culminating in the Nine Years War (1594–1603) and the final reduction of the Irish Gaelic lordships with the flight of the earls in 1607, transformed Gaelic Ireland. It encouraged the split within the Macdonalds into separate Irish and Scottish branches which had already begun under Sorley Boy's forceful leadership of the Antrim Macdonnells in the second half of the sixteenth century.[11] It destroyed the political and social power of the Gaelic lords and removed their need for Scottish soldiers. The loss of this lucrative mercenary trade was a serious economic blow to the Isles. It was the most tangible consequence of the severance of the links which had bound the Western Isles to the north and the west of Ireland.

Less obvious, but of much greater importance, was the complete reorientation of the British Isles which resulted from the changes within the kingdom of Ireland and the severing of those links across the North Channel. During the reign of James VI and I, the first king of Britain, the plantation of Ulster and its settlement by Lowland Scots inaugurated a new and lasting pattern of relationships between northern Ireland and southern Scotland. Economic, religious and political contacts flowed between Ulster, the Clyde and the south-west of Scotland, relegating the Isles to obscurity.[12] After 1603 the Western Isles were a remote northern periphery of minor importance both to Ireland and to the rest of the British Isles.

The main element of political coherence of the Western Isles was itself dealt a crippling blow by the Scottish crown when it suppressed the lordship in 1493. By removing its central core of leadership, the suppression and the campaigns of the 1490s allowed the longer-term forces of erosion to gather momentum and together bring about the destruction of the political and geographical unity of the Western Isles. In acting against the Macdonalds, James IV and the earl of Angus were seeking to assert full control over the entire kingdom of Scotland. They wanted to put an end to the lordship's independent political role and in particular to prevent any future negotiations between the lords of the Isles and the English.[13] Successful military expeditions against the Macdonalds were one thing, however, making royal authority permanently effective within the Isles was quite another. It proved to be an extremely protracted business which was not completed until after 1745.[14]

In the short term the impact of the suppression of 1493 was negative. It removed the lordship but did not substitute royal authority. This inability to replace Macdonald power with immediate governmental control had far-reaching consequences. A political vacuum was created in the Western Isles which the Scottish crown was unable to fill. It offered instead a golden opportunity for the powerful magnates of the Highland mainland to extend their own authority over the Hebrides. No single clan was able to control the whole area of the lordship so the old unity it had provided was destroyed. The replacement of Macdonald political power was a slow and messy business leading to widescale feuding in the consequent scramble over the pieces of the lordship. In the southern Hebrides the dominance of the Campbells gave a limited new coherence, but in the north and west it was more confused and fragmentary.

The mainland chiefs and their clans were able to use their role as royal agents to help them seize control. They acted in the name of the crown and were permitted a remarkable degree of independence by the Stewart monarchs, but they were not pursuing any consistent royal policy. As a consequence, the limited political unity of the lordship was replaced by a series of local settlements which linked the islands to those parts of the mainland closest to them. The failure to bring the Isles into direct contact with the king and the Lowlands ensured that the remnants of the lordship were combined directly with the Highlands. This new region was fragmented politically but it was united by language, culture and communications to form one single Gaelic area.

II

One of the strongest bonds which cemented together the Highlands and the Isles was the new network of land communications which took shape in the early modern period. For the first time there came into existence continuous routes which traversed the entire region linking the Isles to the Lowlands (see Map 2). This opened up the possibility of regular direct travel across Scotland by road and ferry from Edinburgh and the Lowlands, to the western seaboard, and after a short sea journey to the islands. Though not following the route prescribed by the song, the road to the Isles had been born.

The significance of the new continuous land route lay primarily in its very existence. Hitherto, the sole method of reaching the Isles from the Lowlands had been by travelling entirely by boat, usually from Dumbarton or the other Clyde ports, though occasionally using the northern route from the east coast. Now a choice was available between sea and land. The relative merits of the two methods depended upon a range of variables such as weather, season, safety, urgency and the size and quantity of goods being transported. Sea communications remained essential and the only way to send bulky items to the Isles. On the other hand, the land route had the advantage of immediate access to the central and eastern Lowlands and thence to the capital, Edinburgh, which became an increasingly important destination.[15]

The emergence of this land route both contributed to and resulted from the growing links between the mainland and the Hebrides. It was not a conscious creation nor the result of any technological improvement. The road to the Isles was simply and more accurately a joining together of certain local and regional tracks to make a continuous land route. The communications needs of the Western Highlands and Islands changed in the early modern period and the road to the Isles came into existence to satisfy them.

Two main factors helped to produce a continuous land route to the Lowlands: the development of the livestock trade, and the political and the territorial expansion of Campbell power. For many centuries the products of the pastoral economy of the Western Highlands and Islands had been sent to the Lowlands. Hides, wool, woolfells and skins formed part of the Highland cargoes landed in the Clyde ports before export to the Netherlands and France.[16] Cheese and butter, the least perishable forms of dairy produce, could be stored in the Highlands until such time as a ship arrived to take them

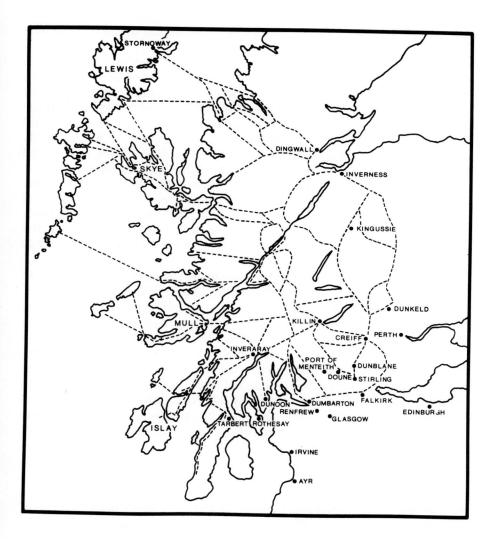

Map 2 Main Drove Routes from the Isles and the Frontier Burghs.

away.[17] Highland timber required water transport close to the felling site to
make its sale profitable outside the immediate locality.[18] Because they were
fast-flowing and full of navigational dangers, Highland rivers were only useful
for moving logs. By contrast the lochs offered easy passage for people and
goods and were used as highways. However, if bulky items were to be sent
any great distance or transported out of the Highlands, access to a sea loch
was needed.

These conditions ensured that while most other Highland exports were
well suited to sea transportation, this was not the case with the livestock
trade. During the sixteenth century there was a marked increase in the
numbers of live cattle and horses sent to the Lowland markets. From the
middle of the century there was also a decline in leather exports from Scotland
which may have reflected the reduction in the number of hides directly
available from the Highlands because the beasts were now being slaughtered
and the leather used to manufacture goods in the Lowland burghs.[19]

The movement of marts and wedders (cattle and sheep ready for slaughter)
and horses from the Highlands to the Lowlands required a continuous land
route. It was considerably cheaper, easier and safer than making a relatively
long sea journey with the livestock. This was obviously the case when the
animals were brought into the central Lowlands, such as the live cattle
making up the crown rents from Kintyre which were delivered to Stirling
Castle in 1541.[20] It was equally true even when the stock were to be sold in
a port, such as the horse fairs at Dumbarton, Perth or Dundee.[21]

The network of drove roads which led from the Isles through the Highlands
was established in the sixteenth century to supply the limited but expanding
domestic market. In addition to the fleshers, the cattle trade provided the raw
materials for a whole range of burgh craftsmen. The tanners, cordwainers,
cobblers, bone workers, ropemakers, horners, gutters, candlemakers and
others all used parts from the slaughtered beasts in their work.[22] After 1603
the trade in beef expanded dramatically with the opportunity to supply the
booming English market.[23] Although smaller than the cattle droves, the horse
trade was still of considerable significance and involved two-way traffic with
stallions for breeding and coursers for fighting being imported into the
Highlands, and mares and their foals being brought out.[24]

Drove routes were also needed by the illegal sector of the livestock trade.
Cattle and sheep rustling within the Highlands and Islands and also into
the Lowlands was a prominent feature of the 'Linn nan Creach' or 'age of
forays' in Highland history. To avoid difficulties with close neighbours, raids
were usually carried out a considerable distance from the home base. Raiding
and its counterpart, blackmail, which offered the 'protection', pursuit and
recovery of stolen cattle, were highly organised. They had evolved their own
codes of practice including legal conventions such as the law of the spoor
trail. This permitted the pursuers to demand restitution from the occupier of

the land which the cattle trail had crossed unless he could prove that the trail continued beyond his settlement. Raiding and its accompanying practices were an extremely important aspect of Highland life. They had deep social and ideological significance as well as their obvious economic advantages.[25]

The establishment of the drove roads only involved minor alterations to the medieval communications system.[26] Tracks such as the String of Lorn or the paths across Rannoch Moor had been used for generations.[27] The important coffin routes, such as those leading over Beinn Resipol to St. Finan's Chapel on Loch Shiel,[28] already provided roads to the traditional clan burial grounds. Wherever possible drove roads followed these pre-existing routes. This was the case with the prehistoric pathway marked by standing stones which ran up the Taynish peninsula[29] or with the pilgrimage tracks to Inishail[30] or the royal burial route to Iona which passed through Lorn via Glen Lonan.[31] During the early modern period these local roads became linked together into continuous land routes which led into the Lowlands. The need to take the livestock to market was a major force for change because it added a new function to those already served by local roads. Droving altered the character of the routes and gave a new purpose and direction to Highland land communications.

These trails were beaten tracks rather than properly constructed roads which were not introduced into the Highlands until the military building programme of the eighteenth century. Instead of constantly repairing or maintaining a route, its line was changed if a landslip, muddy section or seasonal weather made the original track impassable. Although rocky or boggy ground could present problems, gradients seldom did and so the drove roads kept away from the wet valley bottoms preferring high plateaux, like the Leckan Muir running between Loch Awe and Loch Fyne,[32] or they followed the slopes of the glens about a third of the way to the ridge as in Glen Roy. Rather than seeking out the shortest distance, the routes were chosen to provide springs, watering places and grazing areas wherever possible along the way.

Rivers and lochs were crossed by fords and ferries, though in some places it was possible to swim the animals across the water.[33] There were a few wooden bridges in the Highlands, but only where absolutely necessary as in Glen Massan in Cowal or at Ormsary in Knapdale. When bridges were constructed for the military roads in the eighteenth century they were frequently ignored by the Highlanders who believed that they would lose their hardiness if they ceased fording rivers.[34] In the early modern period stone-built bridges were such a rarity that they caused special comment. A striking illustration of this occurred in the covenanting period. By forgetting about the existence of the only stone bridge in Argyll, Alasdair MacColla made a fatal military miscalculation in May 1647. During his retreat through

Knapdale to escape from General Leslie's pursuing army, MacColla consulted his soothsayers about the position of the covenanting army on his heels. On being told that his pursuers were at that moment crossing a stone and lime bridge, MacColla relaxed thinking that they had only reached Dumbarton or Arrochar. In fact, General Leslie and his men were twenty-seven miles further down the road, using the stone bridge near Inveraray at Bridge of Douglas and so were sufficiently close to MacColla to catch and rout his forces before they could take ship from Kintyre.[35]

The drove roads were not simply the best way of getting livestock to the Lowlands, they also provided the only reliable through routes within the Highlands. As these tracks were unsuitable for any form of wheeled transport, carriages and carts were virtually unknown. Travellers went on foot or on horseback and goods were moved by a wide variety of sledges or in panniers carried by horses or people.[36] The drove roads provided an ideal opportunity for the 'cadgers' who carried essential supplies and some luxury items on the backs of their hardy 'garrons'. The developing network of communications made it possible for them to penetrate further into the Highlands.

Apart from these intrepid early salesmen, very few Lowlanders chose to travel beyond the Highland line. None of the foreign or domestic visitors of the medieval and early modern periods who left descriptions of Scotland penetrated into the Highlands.[37] Such reticence was not surprising as there were no inns and travellers had to fend for themselves or accept the legendary but basic hospitality of the ordinary Highlanders to those on the road. Another option, and one taken by the travelling Gaelic bards, was to plan a tour around the residences of the Highland chiefs enjoying – though frequently criticising – the level of provision made for guests.[38] The through routes were primarily used by the Highlanders and Islanders to move themselves and their goods to and from the Lowlands.

III

These improvements in long-distance communications were accompanied by the development of local road networks within the Highlands (see Map 3). This was greatly advanced, in a way not hitherto appreciated, by the changes in religious practices introduced by the reformed kirk in the early modern period. The reformers wanted all the inhabitants of the parish to attend the weekly services which were held in the local kirk every Sunday. In the Highlands the medieval churches had been located on holy sites, particularly those associated with Celtic saints who had preferred inaccessible places.[39] This was true of the churches on Inishail at the top of Loch Awe or St. Finan's on Loch Shiel. A ferry was equally essential to reach the cathedral church of St. Moluag on Lismore which also served Appin across the water. Using a

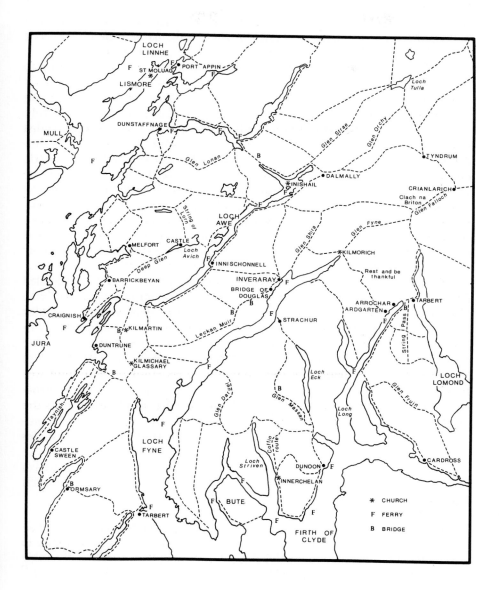

Map 3 Communications in Argyll

ferry to transport large numbers of people who all needed to attend a service at a set time on a particular day put strains upon the capacities of most of the small ferry boats which served the Highlands, as at Innerchaolain. It could also lead to the total disruption of a service if, as at Port Appin in 1643, the ferryman simply refused to transport the minister over from Lismore to the kirk of Appin.[40]

The Highland parishes in any case covered huge areas, sometimes as much as twenty miles across as at Lochaber (Kilmalie) or Knoydart, and the terrain often made travelling extremely difficult. The synod of Argyll recommended that the parish of Kilmichael Glassary be divided because of the 'incommodiousenes of the situation of a good number of the lands thereof, difficulties and distances from Kilmichael, the paroach kirk'.[41] All of these physical barriers and practical impediments to regular church attendance led the synod to consider its parish structure in relation to the region's geographical features and communication problems. After careful consultation, and a special parliamentary commission on the plantation of kirks, they reorganised their parish boundaries and produced a list of preferred sites on which new churches should be built.[42]

Although most of these new kirks were not in fact constructed, the detailed plans provide an interesting insight into the local communications. These recommendations assumed that the main priority was to make regular Sunday attendance a practical possibility for all the parish's inhabitants. In Cowal, for example, the synod of Argyll, 'haveing takine tryall of the difficultie of passage[43] and travelleing of the inhabitants of the lands of Tavnich[43] ... to their own paroach church of Innerchelan by reasone of the farre distance therefrom, being 7 or 8 myles, and of ane interveeneing ferry,[44] wherethrow its impossible for them to keep ilk Sabbath', decided to place them in the parish of Kilmodan in Glendaruel, 'because of the nearnes and commodiousenes unto the kirk of Kilmoden, as being within two or three myles of good way therto'.[45]

Accessibility was to be the main consideration in redrawing parish boundaries, as in Glen Shira which had been part of the parish of Kilmorich and was moved to Inveraray,

> they being some of them eight myles and most of them fyve myles from their own kirk and all of them within three myles, others within halfe a myle to Inneraray [sic]... . seing by this division they may have occasion of weekly preacheing, whereas of before they had but preacheing once in the moneth.[46]

It was proposed that the very complicated parish structure of southern Kintyre be completely reorganised to allow for easy access to local churches. The details of the suggested pattern make clear the communications network of that region.[47]

Ecclesiastical considerations also affected the communications system of the Highlands in other ways. The synod was only too anxious to encourage travel to church but it frowned upon any other journeys on the Sabbath. For example, it requested that the weekly sheriff court at Inveraray be moved from a Friday to a Wednesday in order to avoid forcing people to return home on a Sunday and so profane the Lord's Day. Similarly, the synod decreed that the poor and other travellers who arrived on a Saturday night be entertained until Monday so that they did not travel on the Sabbath. This had the added benefit, at least in the synod's eyes, that the visitors were able 'to repair to the church with these with whom they are lodged'.[48] Their concern suggests that there was a considerable amount of travel through the region but at a slow pace: much of it requiring several days on the road and overnight stops.

The problems of travel determined the patterns of attendance at the synod and was a frequent source of complaints by its members, with the elders observing quite correctly that they were put to much longer and more onerous journeys and greater expenses than any other part of the country.[49] Although usually held at Inveraray, the synod did move its meetings around the region to try to reduce the burdens upon its members. From the outset it was acknowledged that presbytery meetings would be less frequent than elsewhere. The minister coming from the southern Isles was given a special dispensation because having to use 'manifold ferries ... it may fall ofttimes that he be stormstayed both in the coming and returning'.[50]

The long absence from their congregations as well as the distance and difficulty of the journey prompted the synod to excuse all the brethren of the presbytery of Skye from attendance, with the exception of one summer meeting every second year. The very fact that the ministers from the Outer Isles were expected to be part of the synod of Argyll demonstrated that the Isles and the Highlands were already seen as a single region. In 1724 the general assembly finally bowed to the pressure from the presbytery of Skye and created a separate synod of Glenelg. This reduced the strain upon the synod of Argyll but did not alter the underlying assumption that the islands were firmly connected to the nearest section of mainland.[51] Travelling during the winter months was regarded as a major hazard and so only one winter meeting of the Argyll synod was contemplated. It was also decided that 'because the winter quarter is not fitt for travellers to those bounds', the new minister for Lochaber would not be expected to take up his post until the following March.[52]

The synod's records make it plain that within the limitations imposed by weather, season and terrain there was an increasing amount of regional travelling within the West Highlands and Islands by all levels of society. One obvious addition to this local travel was the seasonal migration of the people within the fermtouns to their summer shielings. This large-scale movement required a considerable degree of planning and organisation to transport most of the members of the community and many of its belongings to the shieling huts. The expeditions could take place in two stages and they followed well-defined, traditional routes up the glens, sometimes for a considerable distance if the fermtoun and its mountain pastures were miles apart.[53]

IV

Both these local networks of communications, and the through routes required by the economic need to reach Lowland markets, were reinforced by a political pull towards the royal court and the capital, felt first by the Campbells and through their activities by the rest of the region. During the fourteenth, fifteenth and sixteenth centuries, Clan Campbell had expanded rapidly and over a wide area. To retain its cohesion and to function effectively as a single unit the clan had developed a network which exploited both forms of communication: information and travel. There was a constant transfer of orders and news between the earl of Argyll and the cadet branches of the Campbells. Much of this was in the form of letters, and messengers were continually on the move both between the Highlands and the Lowlands and within "Campbell country" itself.[54] The main seat of the earls at Inveraray became a clearing-house for administrative, judicial, financial and social business and information for the whole of the southern Highlands and Islands serving not just the Campbells but the whole region.

The great internal cohesion displayed by the Campbells was established and maintained by its leading members themselves travelling as well as assiduously circulating information. In the early modern period political authority and leadership were still exercised in person, while ties of loyalty were created and reinforced by frequent individual contacts. The clan chief needed to be present within his territory on a regular basis to ensure the smooth running of his affairs. This involved a great deal of travelling for all the heads of the Campbell branches within their own estates, to Inveraray and elsewhere. From its earliest days Clan Campbell had enthusiastically, and notoriously, adopted certain Lowland practices, such as the use of feudal charters.[55] Many of these required visits to Lowland burghs, thus involving the Campbells in considerable travel to transact financial, legal and political business.

In a similar fashion the extremely close connection which developed between the Campbells and the Scottish crown, together with the clan's deep involvement in national politics, depended upon regular attendance at court. The time spent in Edinburgh or at the other royal residences was a marked feature not only of the itinerary of the earl of Argyll, from whom it would be expected, but also of the heads of the leading cadet families.[56] In addition to their association with the crown, the Campbells were also drawn into the

Lowlands by their close marriage ties with the Lowland aristocracy.[57] The earls spent much of their life on the road and maintained town houses at Perth, Stirling and Edinburgh which they visited frequently in addition to their favourite Lowland residence at Castle Campbell near Dollar. Even within their own "country" of Argyll they were peripatetic. Inveraray, their main residence, was more of an organisational centre than a permanent base.

The nature of Campbell expansion made contacts between the various branches difficult and increased their need for regular and reliable communications. Having secured the west coast with its impressive line of castles, the main thrust of Campbell expansion before the seventeenth century was towards the south and east along the main routes into the Lowlands. There were also important pockets of Campbell Lowland expansion with a distinct group of Campbell families in the south-west and others in Angus, Perthshire, Fife and Clackmannanshire. One consequence of this method of expansion was that it initially left Campbells settled thinly rather than in consolidated blocks. In Knapdale, Cowal and Breadalbane, other clans occupied territory which separated Campbells from each other. In parts of the Lennox and Menteith, the Campbell clan were minority incomers surrounded by other kindreds. Much wider distances divided the territories of the Cawdor branch which retained lands within Argyll even after its move to Cawdor on the Moray Firth.

In such circumstances the Campbell communications network also served a defensive purpose. When a particular Campbell cadet family was threatened or attacked help needed to be able to arrive quickly. On their own the different branches of the Campbells were vulnerable within their localities, but provided they could call upon the assistance of the other members of the clan they could overawe their neighbours. Consequently, the maintenance of good communications was vital to the continuing survival and prosperity of Clan Campbell. Opening and preserving 'supply lines' with the rest of the clan and gathering up-to-date intelligence were part of the formula for the Campbells' spectacular success. Keeping in touch was a practical necessity as well as a social pleasure for the clan.

The care taken to secure their communications can be seen at three different levels of Campbell expansion. In the relatively limited local context the main expansion of the Campbells of Craignish followed a single route. They secured the important road between the castle of Craignish, perched on the west coast directly opposite the northern tip of Jura, up the peninsula to Barrickbeyan, through the Deep Glen to Caisteal na Nighinn Ruaidhe on Loch Avich which gave access to the middle of Loch Awe opposite the earl of Argyll's castle of Innischonnell.[58] The Campbells not only controlled the vital path into the very centre of Argyll but also linked themselves physically to the clan's original and strongest power-base around Loch Awe.

Much farther east and on a larger scale the different holdings of the

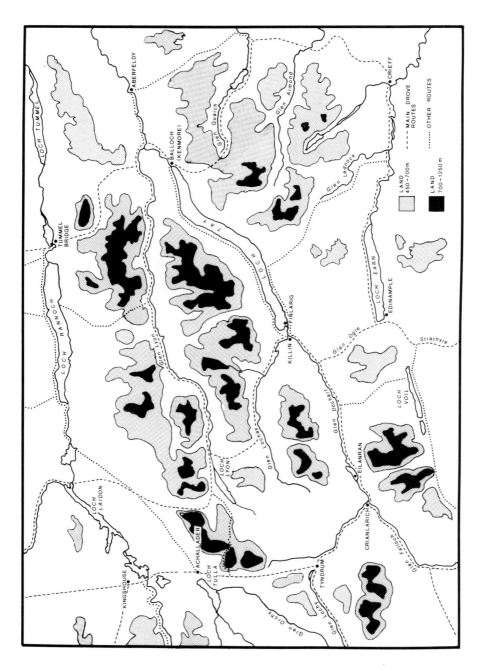

Map 4 Routes through Breadalbane

Campbells of Strachur helped secure the strategic routes leading out of Argyll to the south and east. This branch took its name from the settlement at a ferry point on the south side of Loch Fyne which stood at the head of the route along Loch Eck to Dunoon. They also held lands in the barony of Feorling at Ardgarten which placed them at the top of Loch Long near the Tarbet entrance to Loch Lomond. Together with the Macfarlanes of Arrochar, the Campbells of Strachur controlled the west shore route north from Tarbet up the side of the loch to Glen Falloch and Glen Dochart and the key pass to Crianlarich. The territory of the Strachur Campbells included the great forest of Glen Falloch which contained the very ancient boundary stone at Clach na Briton where Argyll, Perthshire and Dumbartonshire met, a convenient place to maintain a watch on passing traffic.[59]

The largest and best documented Campbell expansion occurred when the Glenorchy branch spread throughout Breadalbane. With their allies the Macgregors, they moved from the top of Glen Orchy and Glen Strae to Loch Tulla.[60] They crossed the Drum Alban range into Glen Meran, Glen Lochay and penetrated the whole length of Glen Lyon, the main route to the east. They also secured the top of Glen Dochart, both ends of Loch Tay, and Lochearnhead by the castles of Eileanran (on Loch Dochart), Finlarig (Killin), Balloch (Kenmore), and Edinample (Loch Earn). By controlling these strategic points, the Campbells of Glenorchy had ensured that they not only had a tight grip over the whole of the Breadalbane area, but also dominated most of the routes which led through Perthshire to the Lowlands (see Map 4).[61]

At all three levels Campbell expansion was dictated by concern to secure territory along key routes. Once possession was gained, the clan's emphasis upon good communications guaranteed that the roads were used more frequently and linked to other tracks in the region. Clan Campbell with its drive towards the south and east sought out the routes into the Lowlands and expanded along them. This in turn increased the strategic importance of these roads and joined them to routes deeper in the Highlands, thus making a wide-ranging system. The network of regional and local communications within the southern Highlands largely grew out of the expansion of Campbell power.

V

Though they always remained a land based clan, the Campbells were certainly aware of the importance of sea communications. During the medieval and early modern periods sea power in the west was based upon galleys, the lineal descendants of the Viking longships.[62] When at the start of the fifteenth century the Campbells of Lochawe, the clan's main branch, moved their principal base away from Innischonnel on Loch Awe, they were careful to site their new castle on a sea loch. Inveraray was chosen for its dominant position on Loch Fyne which gave direct and rapid access to the Firth of Clyde, the North Channel and the western sea lanes of Britain. In a similar way all the Campbell castles on the coast, with the exception of Skipness, had excellent facilities for galleys.[63] To build and repair their fleet the earls of Argyll kept resident families of shipwrights, the MacGille Chonalls on Loch Awe and the MacLucais on Loch Fyne.[64] They also paid particular attention to those clauses in the charters they granted which upheld and enforced the obligations of galley service. Campbell cadets, tenants and allies had to provide and maintain eight and twelve oared galleys and be ready to man them whenever required by the earls.[65] This galley fleet was a devastating weapon both in sea warfare and as a military transport for large numbers of armed men. The galleys were also employed for cattle raiding or in more peaceful times for social visiting and trade.

In their use of galleys and sea power there was little to distinguish between the Macdonalds and the Campbells, but there was a world of difference in their respective outlooks. For the Campbells the sea offered a convenient and speedy means of travel, but it did not provide, as it had earlier for the Macdonalds, the unifying factor which held together their territories. The Macdonalds had been an island power with outposts on the mainland, the Campbells were a mainland force with control over some islands. The difference in attitudes was apparent from the relationship between the earl of Argyll and the Ayrshire Campbells. These 'English' Campbells, were settled just across the Clyde from the Campbell heartland. Economic and communication links were strong between the south-west coast, particularly Ayr and Irvine, and Loch Fyne. The Ayrshire Campbells, whilst acknowledging the earls of Argyll as their chief, always acted as an independent force and were the most detached part of the clan. They were far less controlled from Inveraray than even the Cawdor branch of the Campbells who were situated on the distant Moray Firth. It would seem that the waters of the Clyde divided the earl from his Ayrshire kin. By contrast the southern branch of Clan Donald had used the sea lanes to knit together their scattered lands on Islay, Kintyre and Antrim.

If it did not provide political unity for the Campbells, the Firth of Clyde certainly offered economic opportunity. They were heavily involved in the fish trade which was so important in binding the Highlands to the Lowlands. Barrels of herring and salmon were a major Highland export to domestic and foreign markets.[66] The herring trade was the crucial platform for the initial growth of Glasgow in the late sixteenth century which led to the town's spectacular and better-known rise in the seventeenth and eighteenth centuries.[67] Loch Fyne was the main fishing ground for the herring which were brought into the west coast ports, whilst the fishing burghs of the east coast took their herring from Loch Broom in the north.

As they came to dominate Loch Fyne, the Campbells became closely involved in this commerce. Both the earls of Argyll and the Campbells of Glenorchy received in their rents barrels of herring and salmon from the inland rivers. Loch Fyne herring were judged the best in the country and so some of these rents were reserved for the tables of the earl and Glenorchy, with the rest being sold.[68] The Campbells of Ardkinglas had been granted the extremely lucrative right to collect the crown's duty on herring caught within the Clyde from the end of the freshwater river to the Mull of Kintyre.[69] Sasine of their royal charter granting this assise of herring was appropriately given 'where the sea tide meets the water of Clyde at the Hill of Aderdan' near Cardross.[70] On 18 January 1571 Campbell of Dannye was entrusted by the burgh of Renfrew to be 'saiff admerall and warrands to all their coper bottis', those used by the buyers of herring.[71] Such close relations with the herring trade enabled the 5th earl of Argyll in August 1568 to commandeer two or three hundred herring boats to transport two thousand of his troops to Glasgow to support the queen's party in the civil war.[72]

Herring were an important element in Scotland's exports and so the commerce had to be conducted through the privileged royal burghs. The Clyde ports of Dumbarton, Renfrew and Glasgow and the Ayrshire ones of Ayr and Irvine provided a conduit for the fish and the other raw materials which flowed from the Highlands.[73] Until the seventeenth century Inveraray was the only trading burgh in the whole of the southern Highlands and Islands, though Tarbert (Lochfyne) and Rothesay were royal burghs and administrative centres for their respective sheriffdoms. Even Inveraray did not acquire royal status until the reign of Charles I.[74] It was also primarily an administrative centre with a few craftsmen and a small manufacturing capacity. The same problems beset Stornoway which was the only burgh within the north-western part of the Highlands and Islands.[75] This meant that Highland products were inevitably drawn into the Lowland burghs for processing.[76] The large numbers of craftsmen in Glasgow, Stirling and Perth who worked with foodstuffs or leather were an indication that these burghs were utilising the raw materials produced in the southern Highlands.[77] In return the burghs offered services, luxury goods, wine and meal which was the only basic commodity sent in bulk into the Highlands.[78] The absence of burghs or market centres and the scarcity of regular fairs and markets[79] within the Highlands pushed its products towards the Lowlands and brought the first signs of the penetration of the economic forces which changed Highland society in the seventeenth and eighteenth centuries.[80]

For most of its primary exchanges the Highlands and Islands remained a non-cash economy, but some money did circulate.[81] The mercenary and cattle trades brought cash into the Highlands and with it certain aspects of the market economy. Money was required and could be found at all levels of Highland society. It might be needed by some tenants to pay part of their rents.[82] It was certainly given by Campbell of Glenorchy to his steelbow tenants. In such agreements Glenorchy provided his tenants with all the basic require- ments needed to start farming their land. Money was regarded as an essential prerequisite for a successful tenancy because these agreements included a sum of 'strenthe-silver' along with livestock and agricultural equipment.[83] Money fines were imposed by the barony courts of Breadalbane and they dealt with cases of theft occasionally of quite large sums in coin kept in purses or kists.[84] The ordinary Highlander had to pay for his ale in cash though he had a week's grace to settle his debts and redeem his gage.[85] The chiefs also had to pay for luxuries like wine, fancy foods, weapons and armour in cash, and had to raise more for paying taxes and troops or for building projects.[86]

When extra money was required direct loans or wadsets on land had to be arranged with the merchants of Lowland burghs. The Campbells often had recourse to the commercial communities of Edinburgh or Dumbarton to remedy their cash-flow problems.[87] These financial and economic transac- tions all strengthened the links between the Highlands and the Lowlands, particularly with those burghs which stood on the land borders and whose hinterlands extended into the Highlands. "Frontier" towns such as Dumbarton, Port of Menteith, Stirling, Crieff, Auchterarder, Perth and the ecclesiastical cities of Dunblane, Dunkeld and Brechin, along with Balnakilly and Balnald (now Pitlochry), Rattray, Kingussie, Dingwall, Tain, and Inverness in the north, were well able to supply the limited services needed by the Highlands.[88]

Though such economic dependency was at a low level in the west, it seems to have progressed more rapidly in the central and eastern Highlands. With the decline of its export trade and the stagnation of its manufacturing during the sixteenth century, Perth became more of a consumer society serving a large section of the central Highlands.[89] It sent meal and luxury goods into the Highlands with its packmen, and its merchants, such as Thomas Brown, offered a market for some of the sheep and cattle coming to the Lowlands. During the winter there were comfortable quarters in Perth for Highland lairds and a range of inns, restaurants and brothels for their entertainment. Most of the legal, financial and notarial services required by its Highland hinterland could also be obtained in Perth.[90]

The economic links between the Highlands and Lowlands and the use of land routes affected the "frontier" burghs. Equally they brought into promi- nence the landward boundary areas, in particular the Drum Alban district. Nearly all the drove routes from the west and up to Skye passed through this region on their way to the Lowlands. Even drovers from as far south as Cowal used the route to the head of Loch Fyne through Glen Fyne to Glen Falloch and so to Glen Dochart and Glen Ogle. In 1774 drovers complained bitterly that it took two extra days to reach the Lowland markets when they were forced to go by the theoretically shorter route on the new military road over Rest and Be Thankful to Arrochar and then down Loch Lomond.[91] Cattle from Mull and Lorn came either via Inveraray or through Dalmally to Tyndrum. Further north the routes crossed Rannoch Moor to Tyndrum or through Glen Meran to Glen Lyon or Killin.

It was not surprising that the Campbells of Glenorchy strove hard to achieve control over the whole of Breadalbane which encompassed so many of the main routes. In the 1560s a feud developed between them and their erstwhile allies the Macgregors. One reason why Glenorchy could present the Macgregors as a national and not simply a local nuisance was their threat to so many vital national routes which crossed the Drum Alban area. The Macgregors used the roads for their raids and to dispose of their plunder. Their route to the battle of Glen Fruin in 1603 passed from Rannoch through Glen Meran and across to Glen Dochart, down that glen and Glen Falloch over to Arrochar and along the east side of Loch Long before crossing the hills into Glen Fruin. The geographical spread of the individuals cited in the 1560s for reset, the charge against those who had bought the stolen goods and supplied the Macgregors when they were outlawed, provides evidence of how well the network of Highland communications had developed. The stolen property had been sent to Lorn, Cowal, the Lennox, Atholl and into the Lowlands.[92]

Another pointer towards the central importance of Drum Alban was the large volume of traffic passing through Killin. The barony court ordered that only travellers who had journeyed eight miles or more that day could visit the alehouse. Many long-distance travellers must have used the route because the alehouse continued to flourish. The court also found it worthwhile to distinguish between "country" cadgers and "straingers" when setting the bridge tolls to cross the River Dochart at Killin.[93]

Argyll also became an important through area for trade and travel both from the Isles and as a way into the Highlands.[94] In 1563 the land route through Cowal to Inveraray was considered good enough to use during the royal progress to the west by Mary Queen of Scots. This was the only visit the queen made into the Highlands and Inveraray was the furthest point which she reached.[95] Two years later a royal proclamation in September 1565 prohibited trading with Argyll because the earl was in rebellion against the queen.[96] The autumn and winter of that year witnessed the complete disruption of trade between the Lowlands, Kintyre and the whole of the southern Isles as well as Argyll itself. The subsequent proclamation of 17 July 1566 which lifted the ban decreed that Highlanders should not be prevented from attending Lowland markets because all of the people of Scotland needed the

> interchange of the excrescence and superflew frutis growand in the Laich and Hielandis, swa that necessarlie marcattis mon be kepit, and all men indifferentlie without exceptioun mon repair thairto for selling of thair gudis and bying agane of sic necessar as ar unto thame neidfull and requisite.[97]

A group of cattle traders led by Alan and Thomas Fisher had been seized by Patrick Houston of that ilk when "according to thair accustumat maner thay brocht certane ky furth of Ergyle to be sauld to thair Hienessis liegis in the Lawland" and so had broken the first proclamation. They and their goods were released and they were assured that loyal subjects could bring goods "to be sauld in the Lawland for furnessing and sustenatioun of the cuntre according to use and wont".[98]

VI

The linkage of the Western Isles to the Lowlands through the Highlands had the devastating, if paradoxical, consequence of relegating the Isles to the periphery of Scotland. It gave the borderlands such as Argyll and Drum Alban a new significance and placed the islands at the end of long lines of political and economic communications. The road to the Isles crossed extremely difficult terrain and made the journey long, hard and dangerous. The new land routes had to pass over the natural barriers of the Highlands instead of using the sea to sail around them. For the first time the Isles were placed "beyond" the mountain passes and this isolated them geographically from the Lowlands in a way they had not been before. The Western Isles were marginalised instead of existing as a separate unified area. The land route ensured that they were regarded as more remote from the Lowlands than the distant islands of Orkney and Shetland. The improvement in the land communications led to greater economic and political integration within Scotland but that also brought the domination and subordination of the Isles. The "road" was the symbol of the changing relationships between the component parts of Scotland and the whole of Britain.

In addition to the land route the early modern period saw the emergence of a political road to the Isles. After 1493 royal authority was exercised in the Isles but only at one remove through the use of proxies from among the Highland clans. The Campbells, the Gordons, and the Mackenzies were entrusted with the task of enforcing the crown's will throughout the Highlands and Islands. These clans were all based on the mainland and used their position as royal agents to extend their own influence out over the Isles as well as that of their sovereign. The failure to bring the Isles under direct control from the centre meant that the strongest links would be made within the Highlands and Islands rather than between Edinburgh and the Isles. Government business was channelled through Inveraray for the southern Hebrides and Inverness for the northern islands. This guaranteed that the map of political influence was split along new lines. A north-south divide had replaced the old east-west frontier. The earls of Huntly and Seaforth controlled the Northern Hebrides, while the earl of Argyll's power extended from Skye southwards to Islay and Kintyre. All travellers on the political road to the Isles now had to pass by way of Inverness or Inveraray.

The Campbells were able to exploit that political road most effectively. They dominated the whole of the southern section of the Highlands and Islands and within that area they expanded to fill the vacuum left by the political demise of the Macdonalds. They were not merely passive beneficiaries of this major reorientation within the kingdom of Scotland because they had also contributed to that change. Their own close ties to the ruling Stewart dynasty and their firm commitment to national politics dragged the whole region in the same direction after them. Their participation in the livestock and herring trades, along with the relative security and protection they could offer within Argyll, stimulated economic interchange with the Lowlands. Their firm commitment to the Protestant faith and support for the reformed kirk encouraged the series of changes in local communications brought about by the Reformation. The unusual amount of attention which the Campbells paid to defence and communications opened up the routes within the southern Highlands, particularly in the vital strategic borderlands. The road to the Isles was both a consequence and an agent of Campbell interests.

That road through the Highlands tied the Western Isles to the rest of Scotland. It was only when the new composite region was successfully attached and could be viewed within an exclusively Scottish context that the stark two-fold division of the kingdom into Highland and Lowland could finally emerge. The Highlands and Western Isles shared the Gaelic language and culture which was becoming increasingly distinct from the Scots culture of the Lowlands. The shrinkage of the Gaelic language to the area beyond the Highland fault line encouraged a conscious separation between the two cultures.[99] It permitted the identification of Scottish Gaeldom with a specific geographical area. The firm association of geography and culture created the simplistic division into Highland and Lowland and ensured that previous distinctions between the Western Isles and the Highlands were submerged within a common cultural identity. The new region was regarded as a single entity which was linguistically, socially and culturally distinct from the rest of Scotland. From a Lowland perspective, the Highlands were increasingly regarded as inaccessible, alien and hostile. Such an attitude could only intensify after 1603 when the Scottish monarch moved south. The "Highland problem" had been created.

Thereafter successive Scottish governments sought solutions to the Highland problem all of which were based on securing the road to the Isles. In the first instance the political path of control through the Highland magnates was tried. By the eighteenth century military influence and metalled roads were thought to provide the answer, and General Wade and his successors performed remarkable feats of engineering to open the way for a British army to march directly into the Highlands and Islands. The Highland problem and the road to the Isles were thus inextricably linked. Both originated in the major reorientation of the early modern period which transformed the political, economic and geographical shape of Scotland.

Notes

I am most grateful to Dr. Ronald Cant, Dr. Bruce Lenman and Dr. Graeme Whittington for commenting upon an earlier version of this paper, and to Dr. Anne Johnston who sorted out my rough cartographical jottings and transformed them into maps. I would also like to thank the duke of Argyll for his permission to consult and cite from his papers at Inveraray Castle and for the invaluable assistance of Alastair Campbell of Airds, younger, both with the archives and on all Campbell matters. In addition, I wish to express my gratitude to the many people who made the history and communications of Argyll come alive for me during my visits to their beautiful region, in particular to Marion Campbell of Kilberry, Mrs. Kahane, Colonel Fane-Gladwin, Mr. MacKechnie, Mrs. Rae Macgregor, Mrs. Louise Watson, Murdo Macdonald and all the members of the Inveraray and District Local History Society. Information used to compile the maps has been taken from the following sources which are cited fully in the footnotes below; Steer and Bannerman (n. 4); Haldane, *Drove Roads* (n. 20); Pryde (n. 74); Minutes of the Commission of Supply (n. 91); *Records of Argyll* (n. 27); *Adventures in Legend* (n. 35); Cregeen (n. 32); J.C. Stone, *The Pont Manuscript Maps of Scotland* (1989) and *Illustrated Maps of Scotland (Blaeu's Atlas)* (1991); General Roy's maps (xerox copies in St. Andrews University Library); G. Whittington and A. Gibson, *The Military Survey of Scotland. 1747–1755: A Critique* (Historical Geography Research Series, 18, 1986).

1. *The Road to the Isles* (Edinburgh, 1927), 244.
2. B. Crawford, *Scandinavian Scotland* (Leicester, 1987).
3. *Ibid.*, 24–5.
4. J. and R.W. Munro (ed.), *Acts of the Lords of the Isles* (Scottish History Society, 1986); J. Bannerman, "The Lordship of the Isles", in J. Brown (ed.), *Scottish Society in the Fifteenth Century* (London, 1977), 209–40; and the same author's "The Lordship of the Isles: Historical Background", in K. Steer and J. Bannerman (ed.), *Late Medieval Monumental Sculpture in the Western Highlands* (Royal Commission on the Ancient and Historical Monuments of Scotland [RCAHM], 1977), 201–213.
5. Steer and Bannerman, *Monumental Sculpture*, Fig 1, p.3. The poetry of the Book of the Dean of Lismore suggests that the literary influence of Ireland and the lordship extended as far east as Fortingal in Breadalbane; *ibid.*, 206.
6. A. Grant, "Scotland's 'Celtic Fringe' in the Late Middle Ages: the MacDonald Lords of the Isles and the Kingdom of Scotland", in R.R. Davies (ed.), *The British Isles 1100–1500* (Edinburgh, 1988), 118–41.
7. M. Macgregor, "A Political History of the Macgregors before 1571" (Unpublished PhD Thesis, University of Edinburgh, 1989), ch. 3.
8. D. Gregory, *The History of the Western Highlands and Isles of Scotland* (Edinburgh, 1836), 157–62.
9. *RCAHMS, Argyll*, vols. 1–6. I am grateful to Dr. Stephen Boardman for his discussions with me on this point.

10. G. Hill, *The Macdonalds of Antrim* (Belfast, reprint 1978). For the continuing importance of the Irish sea, see M. McCaughan and J. Appleby (ed.), *The Irish Sea: Aspects of Maritime History* (Belfast, 1989).

11. J. Dawson, 'Two Kingdoms or Three?: Ireland in Anglo-Scottish Relations in the mid-Sixteenth Century', in R.A. Mason (ed.), *Scotland and England, 1286–1815* (Edinburgh, 1987), 113–38; G.A. Hayes-McCoy, *Scots Mercenary Forces in Ireland* (Dublin, 1937).

12. M. Percival-Maxwell, *The Scottish Migration to Ulster in the reign of James I* (London, 1973).

13. N. Macdougall, *James IV* (Edinburgh, 1989), 100–1; J. Munro, 'The Lordship of the Isles', in L. MacLean (ed.), *The Middle Ages in the Highlands* (Inverness Field Club, 1981), 23–37.

14. B.P. Lenman, *The Jacobite Risings in Britain, 1689–1746* (London, 1980), ch. 11.

15. I.D. Whyte, *Agriculture and Society in Seventeenth Century Scotland* (Edinburgh, 1979), ch. 7; the Statutes of Iona required that Highland chiefs report to the privy council in person every year; F. Shaw, *The Northern and Western Islands of Scotland* (Edinburgh, 1980), 183.

16. I.F. Grant, *The Social and Economic Development of Scotland before 1603* (Edinburgh, 1930), ch. 9; S. Lythe, *The Economy of Scotland* (Edinburgh, 1960), ch. 1; M. Lynch *et al.* (ed.), *The Scottish Medieval Town* (Edinburgh, 1988), 279.

17. I.F. Grant, *Highland Folk Ways* (Edinburgh, 1961); A. Fenton, *Country Life in Scotland* (Edinburgh, 1987); A. Fenton, *Scottish Country Life* (Edinburgh, 1976).

18. Grant, *Social and Economic Development*, 500. Even areas close to the sea could have difficulties getting the timber the short distance to the shore, as at the top of Loch Linnhe; A. Mitchell (ed.), *Macfarlane's Geographical Collections* (Scottish History Society, 1906–8), ii, 159, 165.

19. On the increased demand for cattle, see Whyte, *Agriculture*, ch. 9; and for the trends in the export trade, I. Guy, 'The Scottish Export Trade 1460–1599', in T.C. Smout (ed.), *Scotland and Europe* (Edinburgh, 1986), 62–81, at 64.

20. A.B. Haldane, *The Drove Roads of Scotland* (Edinburgh, 1971), 69n.

21. T.C. Smout and A. Gibson, 'Scottish Food and Scottish History, 1500–1800', in R. Houston and I.D. Whyte (ed.), *Scottish Society 1500–1800* (Cambridge, 1989), 59–84; Whyte, *Agriculture*, 81. For the 'haill kye of Argyle' which 'in the auld accustumat way' were used to pass through Dumbarton, see the extract from the burgh records printed in J. Irving, *Dumbartonshire: County and Burgh* (1917–24), i, 119.

22. Lynch (ed.), *Scottish Medieval Town*, 136; it was common to slaughter animals in the streets of a burgh, E.P. Torrie, *Medieval Dundee* (Abertay Historical Society, Dundee, 1990), 45.

23. Haldane, *Drove Roads*; D. Woodward, 'A Comparative Study of the Irish and Scottish Livestock Trades in the Seventeenth Century', in L. Cullen and T.C. Smout (ed.), *Comparative Aspects of Irish Economic and Social History* (Edinburgh, 1977), 147–64, and above n. 19.

24. A.F. Fraser, *The Native Horses of Scotland* (Edinburgh, 1987), ch. 3; and his *The Days of the Garron: The Story of the Highland Pony* (Edinburgh, 1980), ch. 5. The preservation of the horse herd was of major importance and in 1562 the 'wild horses' kept by Patrick Robertson were moved from the muirs of Breadalbane into Argyll to save them from the raids of the earl of Atholl's men; Scottish Record Office [SRO], G.D.112/39/2/6. John Mair also commented upon the horses bred in the Highlands, P. Hume Brown, *Scotland before 1700* (Edinburgh, 1893), 50–1.

25. I.F. Grant and H. Cheape, *Periods of Highland History* (Edinburgh, 1987) ch. 4; R.A. Dodghson, 'West Highland Chiefdoms: A Study of Redistributive Exchange', in R. Mitchison and P. Roebuck (ed.), *Scotland and Ireland* (Edinburgh, 1988), 27–37. For

the law of the spoor trail and other traditional stories concerned with raiding, see J. MacKechnie (ed.), *The Dewar Manuscripts* (Glasgow, 1964), 92–4.

26. G.Stell, 'By Land and Sea in Medieval and Early Modern Scotland', *Review of Scottish Culture*, 4 (1988), 25–43; G. Barrow, 'Land Routes: The Medieval Evidence', and T. Ruddock, 'Bridges and Roads in Scotland, 1400–1750', both in A. Fenton and G. Stell (ed.), *Loads and Roads in Scotland and Beyond* (Edinburgh, 1984), 49–91; A. Ross 'Old Highland Roads', *Transactions of the Gaelic Society of Inverness*, 14 (1887–8), 172–93.

27. The String of Lorn was the site of the battle of Ath-dearg between the Macdougalls and the Campbells in 1294; A. Macdonald, *A History of Argyll* (Edinburgh, 1950), 120; Lord Archibald Campbell, *Records of Argyll* (Edinburgh, 1888), 171–4. The tracks in the north-western Highlands are discussed in detail in D. Ponchin-Mould, *The Roads from the Isles* (Edinburgh, 1950).

28. Grant, *Highland Folk Ways*, 366–70; B. Megaw, 'Funeral Resting Cairns in Scotland', *Scottish Studies*, 5 (1961), 202–6.

29. I am grateful to Marion Campbell of Kilberry for this observation.

30. Campbell, *Records of Argyll*, 75–6.

31. Haldane, *Drove Roads*, 89.

32. E. Cregeen, 'Recollections of an Argyllshire Drover', *Scottish Studies*, 3 (1959), 143–62, for Leckan Muir, see pp. 150–1.

33. M. Weir, *Ferries in Scotland* (Edinburgh, 1988).

34. Ross, 'Old Highland Roads', 181, 185; and above n.26.

35. D. Stevenson, *Alasdair MacColla and the Highland Problem in the Seventeenth Century* (Edinburgh, 1980), 235; for the traditional story, Marquis of Lorne (J.D. Campbell), *Adventures in Legend* (London, 1898), 235–6.

36. Grant, *Highland Folk Ways*, ch. 13.

37. Grant, *Social and Economic Development*, 544; P. Hume Brown, *Early Travellers in Scotland* (Edinburgh, 1891); and his *Scotland before 1700*. The obvious exception was the description of Dean Munro's travels, R.W. Munro (ed.), *Munro's Western Isles of Scotland* (Edinburgh, 1961).

38. D.W. Thomson, 'Gaelic Learned Orders and Literati in Medieval Scotland', *Scottish Studies*, 12 (1968), 57–78; K. Simms, 'Guesting and Feasting in Gaelic Ireland', *Journal of the Royal Society of Antiquaries of Ireland*, 108 (1978), 67–100. The most famous of the travelling bards was Angus of the Satires; W. Matheson, 'Aonghus nan Aoir: A Case of Mistaken Identity', *Scottish Studies*, 21 (1977), 105–8. Lairds and their retinues were often lavishly entertained by the Campbells of Glenorchy, see the household accounts in C. Innes (ed.), *Black Book of Taymouth* [*BBT*] (Bannatyne Club, 1855).

39. C. Innes *et al.* (ed.), *Origines Parochiales Scotiae* (Bannatyne Club, 1850–5), ii, pts. i & ii.

40. D. Mactavish (ed.), *Minutes of the Synod of Argyll 1639–61* (Scottish History Society, 1943–4), i, 83.

41. *Ibid.*, i, 52.

42. The Committee of 1642, *ibid.*, i, 49–59; the Commission of 1651, *ibid.*, App. i, 227–54.

43. Tawnich was a deserted township situated between the head of Lochs Striven and Riddon.

44. Couston ferry across Loch Striven.

45. *Synod of Argyll*, i, 50.

46. *Ibid.*, i, 51.

47. For a detailed discussion of the reorganisation of the Kintyre parishes and its implications, see my forthcoming article on 'Scotland's Other Reformation'.

48. *Synod of Argyll*, i, 191, 200.
49. *Ibid.*, i, 172.
50. *Ibid.*, i, 5.
51. *Ibid.*, i, 73. I am grateful to Dr. Cant for making this point to me.
52. *Ibid.*, i, 42–3.
53. A. Bil, *The Shieling, 1600–1840* (Edinburgh, 1990).
54. This is revealed in the remarkable collection of sixteenth-century letters in the Breadalbane Papers (SRO, GD.112/39 & 40, at present being recatalogued); see my edition on Clan Campbell (Scottish History Society, forthcoming).
55. As Ian Lom bitterly phrased it in the seventeenth century, 'The sharp stroke of short pens protects Argyll', cited in W. Gillies, 'Some Aspects of Campbell History', *Transactions of the Gaelic Society of Inverness*, 50 (1976–8), 267–8.
56. Full details of these itineraries will be published in my forthcoming study, *British Politics and Gaelic Lordship*. The synod of Argyll used the marquis of Argyll's 'post system' to get important papers from Edinburgh to Inveraray; *Synod of Argyll*, i, 192.
57. J. Dawson, 'The Ties that Bind: Marriage and Campbell Expansion', unpublished paper presented to the Conference of Scottish Medievalists, Pitlochry, 1990.
58. H. Campbell (ed.), 'Manuscript History of Craignish', in *Scottish History Society Miscellany IV* (Scottish History Society, 1926), 175–299.
59. 'Strachur Writs' in J. Macphail (ed.), *Highland Papers* (Scottish History Society, 1934), iv, 1–55; for the forest of Glenfalloch, Argyll Transcripts made by Duke Niall [AT], vi, 113.
60. For a full discussion of the Breadalbane expansion, see Macgregor, 'Political History of the Macgregors'.
61. *BBT*; W. Gillies, *In Famed Breadalbane* (Perth, reprint 1987).
62. J. Macinnes, 'West Highland Sea Power', *Transactions of the Gaelic Society of Inverness*, 48 (1972–4), 518–56.
63. Stell, 'By Land and Sea', 26–7; for Skipness, see R. Graham and W. Collingwood, 'Skipness Castle', *Proceedings of the Society of Antiquaries of Scotland*, 57 (1922–3), 266–87. I am grateful to Mrs. Kahane for discussions on these points.
64. Macinnes, 'West Highland Sea Power', 527; Lord Archibald Campbell, *Argyllshire Galleys* (London, 1906).
65. I am grateful to Dr. Boardman for information on these clauses of special retinue.
66. Both Beauly and Ardchattan Priories were largely sustained by their teinds of salmon; Grant, *Social and Economic Development*, 115, 312–6, 534f; *Macfarlane's Geographical Collections*, ii, 144–92.
67. Grant, *Social and Economic Development*, 314, 354–5; T.C. Smout, 'The Development and Enterprise of Glasgow, 1556–1707', *Scottish Journal of Political Economy*, 7 (1960), 194–212.
68. Bishop Lesley was of the opinion that Loch Fyne herring were the best, and he thought that Renfrew had as many as 60 fishing boats; Hume Brown, *Scotland before 1700*, 119, 140. The Inverdouglas lands yielded a fish rent to the earls of Argyll; AT, v, 154. According to an act of parliament (1555 c. 28), the fishermen needed some protection against the charges levied by the lairds of Loch Fyne; J.D.Marwick, *The River Clyde and the Clyde Burghs* (Scottish Burgh Records Society, 1909), 23.
69. AT, v, 166; *Historical Manuscript Commission Report*, IV, 481. In 1594 there was a major row between Campbell of Ardkinglas and the burgh of Dumbarton over the herring assise; F. Roberts and I. Macphail (ed.), *Dumbarton Common Good Accounts, 1614–60* (Dumbarton, 1972), 277.
70. 4 December 1564, AT, vi, 56.
71. Argyll MSS (Inveraray), Bundle 34; AT, vi, 155.

72. J. Bain *et al.* (ed.), *Calendar of State Papers Relating to Scotland and Mary Queen of Scots, 1547–1603* (Edinburgh, 1898–1969), ii, 516.

73. Marwick, *River Clyde*, 1–49. In 1565 the proclamation concerning the passage of goods between Argyll and the Lowlands mentioned these burghs along with Perth and Stirling; n. 96 below.

74. Tarbert was made a royal burgh in 1329 and Rothesay in 1401. In 1554 it was intended that Inveraray, a burgh of barony since 1474, should follow suit but it did not get its charter until 1648. Kilmun had been made a burgh of barony by the earl of Argyll in 1490. G. Pryde, *The Burghs of Scotland: A Critical List* (Oxford, 1965), 21–2, 23, 33, 52, 53.

75. Shaw, *Northern and Western Islands*, 159–60.

76. Grant, *Social and Economic Development*, 326; for a general discussion of the products made from rural raw materials, see M. Spearman, 'Workshops, Materials and Debris – Evidence of Early Industries', in Lynch (ed.), *Scottish Medieval Town*, 133–47.

77. J.S. McGrath, 'The Administration of the Burgh of Glasgow, 1574–86' (Unpublished PhD Thesis, University of Glasgow, 1986), i, 430–3; M. Lynch (ed.), *The Early Modern Town in Scotland* (Edinburgh, 1986), 10, 14, 27, 36–52.

78. The household accounts for the Glenorchy Campbells indicate that in 1590 they needed to buy in approximately a third of the meal (roughly 137 bolls out of 363 bolls) they consumed; *BBT*, 305. A considerable amount of wine was also imported and there was a special wine cellar at Finlarig; *ibid.*, 333. In March 1562, £42 was owed to Dumbarton merchants for wine and ale sent to Macdougall of Dunollie; AT, v, 166. For wine sent to the Isles, see Shaw, *Northern and Western Islands*, 161–2.

79. I.D. Whyte, 'The Growth of Periodic Market Centres in Scotland, 1600–1707', *Scottish Geographical Magazine*, 95 (1979), 13–25; A.B. Haldane, 'Old Scottish Fairs and Markets', *Transactions of the Royal Highland and Agricultural Society of Scotland*, 6 (1961), 1–12.

80. A.J. Youngson, *After the '45* (Edinburgh, 1973), ch. 1.

81. When organising a stent upon the clan in August 1569, the Campbells were concerned about a shortage of silver to pay the tax in the brief time available. However, they expected that the major problem was the need to collect the specie so extensively and so quickly within a confined area; AT, vi, 136.

82. The Breadalbane rental of 1594 sometimes listed a payment due to the laird of 40s per stone of cheese, though the majority of the rent was paid in kind and a score stick was used; *BBT*, 276, 284.

83. In the 1594 rental a maximum of £20 was given in 'strenthe silver'; *BBT*, 268–99. For steelbow tenancy, see M.H. Sanderson, *Scottish Rural Society in the Sixteenth Century* (Edinburgh, 1982), 22.

84. *BBT*, 255. In 1621 20s had been stolen from a purse and 10 double gold angels and 40 marks of silver from a kist; *ibid.*, 368, 373.

85. *Ibid.*, 361–2.

86. The armour kept at Balloch was listed along with its origin and its value; *ibid.*, 336–7.

87. For example on 12 October 1564 John Gibson, a merchant of Dumbarton, lent Dougal Campbell of Melfort 140 marks, in the parish kirk of Dumbarton; AT, vi, 52. In December 1570 the 5th earl of Argyll borrowed £606. 13s. 4d. from Gilbert MacMurryche, a burgess of Edinburgh, and repaid him two years later; AT, vi, 143, 194. K. Brown, 'Noble Indebtedness in Scotland between the Reformation and the Revolution', *Historical Research*, 62 (1989), 260–75; and his 'Aristocratic Finances and the Origins of the Scottish Revolution', *English Historical Review*, 104 (1989), 46–87.

88. The hinterlands of these burghs, particularly Perth and Aberdeen, stretched over the

whole of their sheriffdoms and beyond into the Highlands; see Lynch (ed.), *Scottish Medieval Town*, 148–9. Dumbarton's hinterland reached to the head of Loch Fyne; *Dumbarton Common Good Accounts*, p. vi. For the smaller burghs it is difficult to assess how much local trade was practised and their status and privileges were sometimes questioned, as in 1580 when Dingwall and the other northern burghs of Chanonry, Rosemarkie, Cromarty, Dornoch and Wick were declared to be 'na frie burghis' by the convention of royal burghs and not enrolled or asked to pay the stent; Pryde, *Burghs of Scotland*, 18.

89. I am grateful to Dr. Lenman for allowing me to consult and use his unpublished paper 'Fair Maids of Perth', delivered to the Perth Natural History and Antiquarian Society, 1987. For the brewing trade, which was frequently carried out by women, see Lynch (ed.), *Scottish Medieval Town*, 271–2, 278.

90. *BBT*, 295–7; the Chronicle of Fortingall gave the price of meal in Perth and at the Mill of Dunkeld; *ibid.*, pp. x, 132, 136, 138.

91. Minutes of the Commissioners of Supply for Argyll, 1744–74, CO6/1/1/2, 335 for 22 June 1774. I am most grateful to Murdo Macdonald the archivist at Lochgilphead for allowing me to consult his Calendar of the Commission Minutes and for his many helpful comments on the subject.

92. For a full description of this feud, see Macgregor, 'Political History of the Macgregors'. The route to the battle of Glen Fruin is shown in A. Macgregor, *The History of Clan Gregor* (Edinburgh, 1898–1901), map at end of vol i. For those cited for reset, see J.H. Burton *et al.* (ed.), *Register of the Privy Council of Scotland* [RPC] (Edinburgh, 1877–98), i, 255–6.

93. *BBT*, 361. There was also a rule that wives were only permitted to use the alehouse if accompanied by their husbands; *ibid.*, 359. The carriage obligations of the tenants within the extensive Glenorchy estates ensured that there would have been considerable local traffic between Breadalbane and Argyll; *ibid.*, 358. The normal trade between these two areas was specifically prohibited in the winter of 1565 in addition to the general proclamation; see below, n. 96.

94. In September 1609 a complaint reached the privy council which declared that trade between the Isles and Argyll was essential 'the said Yllismen having no utheris meanis nor possibilitie to pay his Majesteis dewyteis bot by the seale of thair mairtis and hors, and the buying of such commodities being in all tymes bigane a free constant and peceable trade to the merchantis alsweill of Ergyll as of the incuntrey'. Cited in Shaw, *Northern and Western Islands*, 154.

95. T. Small, 'Queen Mary in the Counties of Dumbarton and Argyll', *Scottish Historical Review*, 25 (1927–8), 13–19. The route taken by the thane of Cawdor in the autumn of 1591 when visiting Argyll from the Lowlands also indicated that it was normal to travel through Cowal to Inveraray; *Book of the Thanes of Cawdor* (Spalding Club, 1859), 200–8.

96. *RPC*, i, 388–9.

97. *RPC*, i, 470–1.

98. *RPC*, i, 401.

99. C.J. Withers, 'The Highland Parishes in 1698: An Examination of Sources for the Definition of the Gaidhealtachd', *Scottish Studies*, 24 (1980), 63–88; W. Gillies (ed.), *Gaelic and Scotland* (Edinburgh, 1989), chs. 5, 7.

5

The Laird, his Daughter, her Husband and the Minister: Unravelling a Popular Ballad.

KEITH M. BROWN

I

Sae they've ta'en her to the heading hill,
At morn, afore the sun:
And with mournfu' sighs they've ta'en her life,
For the death of Waristoun.[1]

Thus ends one version of the popular ballad 'The Laird of Waristoun' which like many of its genre is strong on sentiment, even pathos. By contrast, that down to earth Edinburgh diarist, Robert Birrel, recorded Jean Livingston's fate more prosaically: 'Sche was tane to the girth-crosse, upon the 5 day of July [1600], and her heid struck fra her bodie, at the Cannangait-fit; quha deit very patiently'.[2] Behind Birrel's terse entry and the romance of the ballad lies a sad little tale of an unhappy marriage, brutal murder, religious conversion, and family honour. Jean Livingston found herself trapped in an unhappy marriage with a husband she did not love and who beat her, she conspired with her servants to murder him, she was arrested, tried and sentenced to death, had a profound religious experience in which she was overwhelmed with remorse, and finally was executed. It is a story with all the dramatic ingredients a ballad maker required: love, violence and a moral lesson. For the historian both the events and what the ballad made of them have value in allowing us an insight into sixteenth-century attitudes towards marriage, women and justice. Besides, Jean Livingston's story is worth telling if for no other reason than the fact that it is a good story, a much under-rated asset within the historical profession.

Jean Livingston herself was a woman of whom we know very little, other than those events which gave her such a transient notoriety. She was born in 1579, at the end of a harsh decade of war, bitter factionalism, religious divisions, steep price rises, and high unemployment. Jean's family did not belong to the first rank of the nobility, the peerage, but she was born into the landed aristocracy. Her father was John Livingston, younger of Dunipace, and her grandfather, John Livingston of Dunipace, was one of the lesser nobility of Stirlingshire. That locality was dominated by three families. John Erskine, 2nd earl of Mar, was the leading magnate in the county, although at the time he was a very young man. William Livingston, 6th Lord Livingston was the principal rival to Erskine power in the locality, and was the laird of Dunipace's chief. Usually allied to him was Robert Elphinstone, 3rd Lord Elphinstone, whose sister, Margaret, had married Dunipace the elder in 1552. Lord Elphinstone's eldest son, Alexander, married the eldest daughter of Lord Livingston, strengthening the Livingston-Elphinstone alliance against the Erskines. John Livingston, younger of Dunipace, married Margaret Colville, about whom we know nothing, but it is likely that she belonged to the Colvilles of neighbouring Clackmannanshire. The Dunipace lands chiefly lay in Stirlingshire, but lands also were acquired in Kincardineshire and Forfarshire and were conferred on Jean's two uncles. The laird of Dunipace's interests in Angus were increased in 1585 with the marriage of his daughter, Elizabeth, to Alexander Stratoun, younger of Eodem. Jean's other aunt, Margaret Livingston, had married a neighbour, James Kincaid of that Ilk, but they had been divorced in 1570. John, younger of Dunipace, had five sons and three or four daughters, and while it is unclear which of them preceded Jean, she was not the eldest daughter. As a younger daughter of a minor noble house, Jean Livingston's prospects certainly were not brilliant, but she was born into the privileged landed élite and was a member of a family with a good estate and powerful patrons.[3]

Over and above the vicissitudes of health, Jean's welfare lay entirely in the hands of the male members of her family: her father, her grandfather and Lord Livingston. The problem the head of any landed house with a large family faced was to preserve the estate, to seek ways to enlarge its property in order to provide for younger sons, and to lay up the cash to provide dowries for daughters' marriages, hopefully to other members of the landed élite. In the 1580s and 1590s, when the laird of Dunipace and his eldest son were struggling to find a place in the world for all their off-spring, circumstances were particularly difficult. The finances of the landed élite were hit badly by the combined effect of rampaging inflation and poor harvests on incomes held down by long leases and static feus. With the additional problem of political instability and widespread feuding many noble houses found themselves heavily mortgaged and facing outright ruin. The struggle for resources, and hence the incidence of bloodfeud, was particularly intense as a result of the high survival rate of younger sons, and the saturation of the land market. The latter arose as noblemen reached the point where they no longer could afford to parcel out their available land to cadet houses as they had in the fifteenth century, and as the windfall provided by the Reformation, former church lands, largely had been snapped up by c. 1580.[4] This was the stuff of local politics, but the web of lordship which bound landed families like that of Dunipace into alliances and feuds also involved them in national politics.[5] Years of careful planning and the cultivating of good will and an honoured reputation in the locality could be thrown away by a single mistake which left a man on the losing side and at the mercy of his rivals.

The most prominent of the Dunipace family to date had been Alexander Livingston of Dunipace, Jean's great-grandfather, who was an extraordinary lord on the court of session during the reign of Queen Mary.[6] His son, John Livingston of Dunipace, was a man of lesser talents. During the civil war of 1567–73 he supported the queen steadfastly, following Lord Livingston, the most devoted of Mary's adherents among the higher nobility, and consequently he found himself on the losing side. However, Dunipace made his peace with the king's party along with his lord, being granted a remission for his actions on the queen's behalf by the Regent Morton on 23 March 1574.[7] Throughout the years of the Morton regency, 1572–8, Lord Livingston was excluded from any real influence, and while he did rejoin the privy council in 1575, effectively he retired from national politics. As a result his dependants could expect little favour. The affairs of the Dunipace family at this time were not helped by the hot-headed behaviour of John Livingston, younger of Dunipace, who was cited to appear before Morton's privy council in 1573 in a case of cattle theft.[8] At this time the younger Dunipace would have been no older than twenty-one, just the sort of age at which young men were most likely to demonstrate their prowess in local feuds. John Livingston raised the level of tension in the Erskine-Livingston rivalry by exchanging challenges and arranging to fight a dependant of Mar's, William Menteith of Kerse, whose lands lay to the north-west of Stirling. On 21 December 1574, John Livingston was ordered to ward in Doune Castle, both he and Kerse were warded again in December 1577, and in the following April they were obliged to sign assurances promising not to harm one another.[9] But by then local affairs had been overtaken by the dramatic coup and counter-coup at Stirling Castle in March and April of 1578 as a result of which Morton lost the regency, but regained control of the king. The latter was achieved when Mar seized control of the castle, thus asserting his authority and making his claim to be the leading figure in the locality. The political instability of 1578–9, during which Chancellor Glamis was shot dead on Stirling High Street, Morton and his rivals almost came to blows outside the town, and the opposing parties finally agreed a compromise and turned on the Hamiltons, was reflected in the laird of Dunipace being ordered to muster in arms three times between April 1578 and September 1579.[10] Throughout all this factional intrigue Lord Livingston sided with the Argyll-Atholl faction against Morton, and while the latter held onto power his monopoly of patronage began to crumble. It is highly likely that it was Lord Livingston who secured for his son, John Livingston, the appointment in 1578 as king's chamberlain in Biggar in upper Clydesdale. However, the incumbent laird of Cumbernauld, a neighbour of Dunipace with lands between Stirling and Glasgow, refused to surrender the office.[11] The arrival in Scotland in 1579 of Esmé Stewart, the king's cousin, strengthened the hand of Morton's rivals, and the creation of a bedchamber provided Esmé, who was created earl of Lennox in 1580, with a power base from which to challenge Morton whose own power was centred in the privy council. One of those invited to become a gentleman of the bedchamber was Alexander Livingston, master of Livingston, whose father, Lord Livingston, had struck up a friendship with Lennox.[12] Favour now began to fall on the Livingstons. In April 1579 the treasurer paid Dunipace £533. 6s.8d., and in September, close to the time when Jean was born, the young king and his entourage dined at Dunipace Castle. On 24 December 1580 Livingston support for the Lennox faction was shored up by a grant to the master of Livingston. Other promises might have been made for on 1 August 1581 John Livingston of Abercorn was appointed master stabler to the king.[13] Seven days after the master of Livingston's grant, Morton was arrested, and his execution followed in June 1581. For the first time in almost twenty-five years the Livingston kindred again was close to the dominant court faction.

On two occasions during his life John Livingston, younger of Dunipace, risked the good fortune of his family over religious principles. The first time was in August 1582 when he joined the earls of Gowrie, Angus and Mar and Thomas Lyon, master of Glamis, in the Ruthven Raid when they seized King James. The intention of the coup was to destroy the influence of Lennox, whose signing of the Negative Confession in 1581 had failed to satisfy many Protestants that he was not a Catholic agent. John Livingston, therefore, identified himself with the most radical form of Protestantism, the political ideas of John Knox and George Buchanan who advocated limitations on royal authority and revolutionary action to oppose tyranny, with the heirs of the old Morton party, and with Mar. It was a total *volte face* from everything for which his family had stood over the previous fifteen years. It was a stance which he took in isolation from the other members of his kindred. Lord Livingston remained staunchly loyal to Lennox, as he had to Queen Mary years before, accompanying him into exile in France and petitioning for his restoration. To the king's great grief Lennox died in Paris, but Alexander, master of Livingston, was among those who went to France and brought his son and heir, Ludovick Stewart, back to Scotland in November 1583.[14] The laird of Dunipace also remained stubbornly loyal to Lennox, was arrested, and placed in custody in Wigton.[15] This division in the family's loyalties was in one sense destructive, but it had the fortuitous effect of ensuring survival whatever happened. John Livingston's new friends in government no doubt had a hand in the granting to him of two escheats in April 1583,[16] but the fall of the regime two months later left him exposed to the anger of the young king and the late Lennox's allies. Fortunately, his relatively minor status and the loyalty of the elder Dunipace and Lord Livingston was sufficient to protect John who received a remission on 3 October.[17] However, the younger Dunipace remained opposed to the government, now headed by James Stewart, earl of Arran, a fierce enemy of the presbyterians. He continued as a client of the exiled Mar, joining him and other members of the Ruthven party in capturing Stirling Castle on 17 April of that year. That same day he was put to the horn for non-appearance before the privy council to answer 'to sic things as sould have bene inquyrit of him at his cuming', but his escheat was delivered into the relatively friendly hands of the master of Livingston who already had been rewarded with some of Mar's lands.[18] However, Arran was determined to exact some form of retribution. The earl of Gowrie was executed after a trial at which Lord Livingston and Alexander, master of Elphinstone, sat on the assize as loyal supporters of the government. On 20 August parliament pronounced sentence of treason against Angus, Mar and a long list of their supporters, including John Livingston. However, on the next day King James himself appeared to request that John Livingston's name should be removed from the list along with those of two of Lord Elphinstone's younger sons.[19] Once again friends at court had shielded the younger Dunipace from the full consequences of his actions.

The fall of the Arran government in November 1585 and the restoration of the earl of Mar worked to the advantage of John Livingston, but his recent experiences appear to have demonstrated the wisdom of remaining loyal to the king rather than of political adventuring, a policy Mar also followed in future. It was the elder Dunipace with his dogged loyalty to the crown who had preserved the family's fortune, not his son. The laird's past good service, including the loan of a sum of money to the king, was recognised on 20 November 1588 when his Forfarshire lands were erected into a free barony.[20] Fortunately, the plots and rebellions of the Catholic lords between 1586–94 made it easier for men like Mar and John Livingston to identify with royal policies. Further parliamentary ratification of the lands and heritages of the laird of Dunipace and his son followed in June 1592 as the king sought to build up support against Francis Stewart, earl of Bothwell, whose unpredictable behaviour threatened to divide the Protestants.[21] In May 1593 John Livingston signed the bond against Bothwell, whose radical Protestant propaganda was designed to appeal to men like the younger Dunipace.[22] In July the latter and Sir George Hume, an increasingly influential bedchamber servant, were entrusted with a role in administering the escheat of a number of the earl of Moray's murderers.[23] Here the younger Dunipace's idealism was being harnessed to crown service. With his unsullied Protestant credentials, he could be trusted to act as a go-between for the king and the militantly

Catholic earl of Errol in August 1594.[24] Following the Catholic defeat in the autumn John Livingston was appointed to the commission to help the young duke of Lennox, a friend of Lord Livingston, to administer the north-east over the winter of 1594–5.[25]

It was in 1594 that John Livingston married his fifteen year old daughter Jean to John Kincaid of Wariston. By this time he had lived down his earlier reputation for brushes with the law and an attraction to radical politics. The younger Dunipace now was a man of about forty, attached to the dominant court party, and was heir to a prosperous estate. However, within the year John Livingston's aggressive temperament again landed him in trouble. In the spring of 1595 a local Stirlingshire feud between Alexander Forrester of Garden, a client of Mar, and Sir Alexander Bruce of Airth was sucked into a struggle at court between the earl of Mar and Chancellor Maitland. John Livingston took the side of the Bruces thus putting him at odds with Mar and forcing him into Maitland's faction at court where very recently he had been tipped as the man 'that could and did most agans' the ageing chancellor. On 24 June the younger Dunipace was involved in a dramatic escalation of the feud when he and a party of Bruces killed David Forrester, a bailie of Stirling and one of Mar's servants. John Livingston was fortunate to have the powerful protection of not only Maitland but Queen Anne, who was jealous of Mar's custody of Prince Henry, and his own kinsmen, Alexander, 7th Lord Livingston (he succeeded his father in 1592) and Lord Elphinstone. Consequently he escaped the wrath of King James and the infuriated Mar, but the younger Dunipace was forced to flee into exile and it was April 1599 before he and Mar were reconciled.[26] For John Livingston this feud proved a near disaster, costing him the king's favour as well as that of his old patron, and he was in exile when his father died in 1598, leaving his family leaderless and his estates exposed.[27] Fortunately, the pacification of the feud allowed the new laird of Dunipace to make his peace with Mar, while his own favour with the queen and the high standing of Lord Livingston ensured a return to court. Lord Livingston was an active privy councillor who was entrusted with the charge of Princess Elizabeth in 1596, in spite of protests over his wife's Catholicism. In February 1599 he was appointed constable and keeper of Blackness Castle, at a 'great feast' at Christmas of that year James created him earl of Linlithgow, and on 25 March 1600 his lands were erected into a free barony.[28] At the same time Dunipace's cousin, Alexander, 4th Lord Elphinstone, had been appointed lord treasurer and an extraordinary lord of the court of session in 1599. Another cousin, Sir James Elphingstone, also was a privy councillor and was an ordinary lord of the court of session before becoming secretary of state in 1598.[29] Dunipace now had very powerful friends and patrons, and in March 1599 he was described as 'a gallant courtier' by one of his servants who was questioned by inquisitive English agents.[30] The king was taking a personal interest in his affairs,[31] and by

January 1599 Dunipace was sufficiently intimate with James to be able to discuss the English succession with him over dinner at Dalkeith, home of the earl of Morton. On that occasion Dunipace told James that the king of Spain would never conquer England for his benefit.[32] This was the old presbyterian sympathiser talking, politely warning the king not to court Spanish aid against England. Here then was a man who had risked royal favour to pursue religious ideals and a private bloodfeud, but had re-established himself close to the centre of court life. Dunipace was not a rich or powerful man, but he stood on fortune's threshold. Then in the summer of 1600 his daughter brought disgrace on her entire family.

II

By the summer of 1600 Jean Livingston was, after six years of marriage and the birth of one son, Patrick, an unhappy wife. We know nothing about her upbringing, and only can assume that Jean received a standard female education in those skills required to run a household as well as reading, writing, possibly music and embroidery.[33] Presumably, had she been in any way exceptional in her education the records would have commented on the fact. The ballad tradition insists that she was something of a beauty, and while this was a required ingredient of the genre, there might have been some truth in it.

> She has twa weel-made feet, I trow;
> Far better is her hand;
> She is as jimp in the middle small
> As ony willow wand.[34]

The ballad also makes the point that Wariston fell in love with Jean Livingston, while she and her father jumped at the opportunity of an easy and relatively rich match. In fact, this is the moral to which the ballad hopes to draw attention. Jean herself is left to confess this to her father:

> For Waristoun married me for love,
> But I wed him for fee;
> And sae broke out the deadly feud,
> That gar'd my deaie dee.[35]

This, the ballad insists, is a recipe for disaster. Yet the implication that Jean was somehow at fault in going through with the arrangement could not have been intended to be serious. Most fathers took their daughter's views into account if they had any sense, but there was no way a fifteen year old girl was at all responsible for her actions. As a minor and as a female under the authority of an ambitious father, Jean would have had little option but to marry Wariston whether she loved him or not.

Like his wife, John Kincaid of Wariston is a figure about whom very little is known, and his family is equally difficult to uncover. A few facts about his father can be pieced together. Margaret Bellenden, presumably a daughter of the neighbouring laird of Broughton, recorded her testament in 1569 and John Kincaid of Wariston is described there as her husband. He then appears to have married Margaret Ramsay, a daughter of the laird of Dalhousie, another of the east Lothian gentry. At least two sons were born, John and Henry. Wariston held lands in feu from Adam Bothwell, commendator of Holyrood Abbey, and he became involved in a quarrel with Chancellor Arran in 1585 when the latter tried to extort money from him in one of his many crooked schemes. The laird of Wariston appears to have died before January 1589 when his testament was recorded at Edinburgh.[36] His son, John Kincaid of Wariston, therefore, could have been a man of around twenty-three or twenty-four when he married Jean Livingston in 1594. Apart from the fact that he owned a house between Edinburgh and Leith, and property in that vicinity, the extent of his wealth can be gauged from his own testament. With assets of a little over £2,000 and debts of almost £700, the laird of Wariston can be described as a man of modest prosperity.[37] The connection between the two families might have its roots in earlier relations between the Livingstons and Kincaids. James Kincaid of that Ilk, the chief of the kindred, was a near neighbour of the Dunipace family. His property lay in Linlithgowshire, in close proximity to Lord Livingston. Until their divorce in 1570 the laird of Kincaid, or his father, had been married to the younger Dunipace's sister.[38] Geographic and familial ties between the two families already were strong, and John Livingston's increasing presence at court in Edinburgh possibly brought him into contact with Wariston. It seems reasonable to conjecture that, love apart, Wariston saw an opportunity to connect himself with an upwardly mobile court family, while his own comfortable standard of living was sufficient to convince the younger Dunipace that this man would make a very satisfactory husband for Jean.

We can only speculate on her marital difficulties, although as far as the ballad is concerned the roots of this unhappy relationship went back six years to the very basis of the marriage. An arranged marriage between an older husband and a very young wife was far from uncommon, but in this case it appears to have caused frustration and bitterness, leading in turn to violence. How often or how badly Wariston abused his wife is unknown, but Jean Livingston's desperate remedy suggests that she had been beaten more than once. In Robert Weir's trial records there is reference to a furious quarrel in June 1600 when Wariston was accused of the 'allegit byting of hir in the arme, and streking hir dyverse tymes'.[39] The ballad evidence also draws attention to Wariston's violence, but in seeking to reinforce male authority it places the blame on a sour faced wife with a sharp tongue. The scene described is an apparently happy domestic one with the laird and his lady sitting down to their meal:

> But Waristoun spake a word in jest;
> Her answer was not good;
> And he has thrown a plate at her,
> Made her mouth gush with bluid.[40]

Here Wariston is seen humouring and then disciplining his wife, although the implication is that his anger, while justified by her sulky tone, is excessive. There is no surviving evidence to suggest that Jean sought a peaceful escape from this wife beating. Her father would have been the most obvious person to tell, especially as she still was a minor, being aged twenty-one. The church too could have intervened. Even the privy council was not uninterested in marital violence, and in 1578 condemned Lord Borthwick for his behaviour towards his wife, ordering him to pay alimony after she fled from him.[41] Possibly Jean Livingston had tried one or all of these courses without any success. In any event she decided to take control of her own life by killing her husband. As for the risk of being discovered, she herself admitted that 'my father's moen [influence] at Court would have saved me'.[42]

Following this latest fight with her husband, Jean sounded out the idea of murder on Janet Murdo, her son's nurse. The latter agreed that murder was the only course of action, and suggested they seek out the services of Robert Weir. In Jean's confession, which appears to have been confirmed by Murdo, the nurse said 'I shall go and seek him; and if I get him not, I shall seek another! And if I get none, I shall do it myself'.[43] Robert Weir is described in the ballad as Dunipace's steward, but both David Calderwood and the contemporary Roger Aston, the king's huntsman, describe him as a 'horse-boy', and this seems the more likely.[44] Presumably Janet Murdo knew Weir well enough to risk approaching him with such an offer. Violent, ruthless men were common enough in Scottish society, and as a family servant he might have been sympathetic to Jean's circumstances. Up until the first week of July the court was in residence at Holyrood Palace, and it was here, towards the end of June, that Janet Murdo found Robert Weir in attendance on Dunipace. On two occasions Weir turned up at Wariston to speak to Jean, but was unable to see her. But on the morning of Tuesday 1 July she again sent Murdo to bring Weir to her and on this occasion they made contact. The king left for Linlithgow Palace on or around 1 July where he engaged in hawking, and Dunipace probably had gone with him, leaving Weir behind.[45] Weir arrived at Wariston House a little after noon, and Jean told him she wanted her husband killed. None of the evidence mentions payment, but it is difficult to believe that terms were not discussed. Weir agreed to do the job that night, and was hidden in the laich or underground cellar. The plan appears to have been that he would murder Wariston in his bed, making it look like the work of a thief. However, everything went dreadfully wrong. According to the ballad, Jean ensured that her husband drank more than usual that evening. Around mid-night she went to the cellar and led Weir up through the house to the hall, and then went to her own room where she sat on the bed. The laird was asleep, but he awoke as Weir entered his chamber. Before Wariston could cry for help or grab a weapon, Weir ran across the room, and leapt on him, bringing his knees crashing down on Wariston's jugular. He then knocked the laird to the floor where he kicked him in the stomach. Hearing the 'pitifull and fearfull cryes which he gave when he was strangled', Jean jumped from her bed in the adjoining chamber, and ran down to the hall where she sat and waited for Weir to finish the job. This he did by garotting Wariston who continued to kick and struggle to the last breath.[46]

The noise Weir and Wariston made in their desperate struggle aroused the other servants and someone raised the alarm. Clearly the murder had been badly botched. A frightened and horrified Jean Livingston begged Weir to take her with him as he prepared to make his escape. He argued with her, saying that 'You shall tarry still; and if this matter come not to light, you shall say, 'He died in the gallery' and I shall return to my Master's service: But if it be known, I shall fly, and take the cryme on me; and none dare pursue me'.[47] Possibly Weir did not expect anyone to believe Jean's story of an intruder, and he might have calculated that he had a better chance on his own. In any event he fled, evaded capture, and escaped abroad. Jean herself later guessed that had she fled she would have ended up as a vagabond and whore. Instead she was left behind with Janet Murdo and at least two other female servants who had been awakened and were ordered to agree with their mistress's account of what had happened.[48] Although the brutality of the murder had shocked Jean, and she later said that her husband's corpse was the first she had seen in her life, she found it impossible to maintain the pretence of a grieving wife. She was not a good actress, and admitted 'that I mycht seem to be innocent, I laboured to counterfeit weeping; but do what I could, I could not find a tear'.[49]

Wariston House lay within the regality court of Sir James Bellenden of Broughton, but the magistrates of Edinburgh often were in dispute with Bellenden over the limits of his authority.[50] However, since the murder had taken place within a mile of the burgh it is not surprising to find that Edinburgh officers were first on the scene to arrest Jean and her three servants, and it was a house in the burgh to which Jean Livingston was taken in the early hours of Wednesday morning to await trial. It is likely that there was a preliminary, informal hearing on Wednesday 2 July, and the evidence suggests that Jean refused to admit to her crime, or at least did not answer.

Janet Murdo was a much tougher woman, and held to her story of an intruder, while the other two servants lied on their mistress's behalf. Jean admitted at a later stage that Janet Murdo 'helped me too well in mine evill purpose', but that the other two had been entirely innocent.[51] However, in a case of this nature, in which the normal social conventions had been turned on their heads, the community required more than a legal judgement. Not only must Jean Livingston be punished, but she must be brought to acknowledge the justice of her punishment. It was important that Jean Livingston recognised both her sin against God and her crime against the social order. This male hierarchy needed a subservient and apologetic victim for the scaffold, not a defiant virago. The popular ballad makes this point. There Jean repeatedly admits her guilt in killing her 'gude lord', and agrees 'It's richt that I now shou'd dee'.[52]

Instead Jean was unrepentant, raging against the circumstances which had brought about her misfortune, and demonstrating a complete disregard for her fate while subconsciously still hoping her father would use his influence to save her. Perplexed by this reaction the Edinburgh magistrates sent for Mr. James Balfour, minister of the north-west quarter of the burgh. Balfour was a younger son of Robert Balfour of Powis, thus sharing a similar social background to Jean Livingston, and was one of those radical presbyterian clergy prepared to express his disagreement with the king when the occasion arose. Over the winter of 1596–7 he had been one of the Edinburgh clergy to be imprisoned by the king for his alleged part in the Protestant riot which gave James his excuse to crack down on the presbyterians.[53] At ten o'clock on the morning of Thursday 3 July, shortly after he had finished preaching, Mr. Balfour was asked to go and visit Jean. He found her pacing up and down in her room in a frantic, almost hysterical rage brought on by a mixture of trauma, fear and anger that events should have worked out so badly. She refused to talk to Balfour and threw his bible against the wall. Undeterred by this shocking behaviour, Balfour warned her of the consequences of God's wrath if she failed to seek forgiveness. From the outset he made no attempt to pretend that as far as her life was concerned the time left to her was short. Jean scoffed at him, 'Trittle. Trattle', she exclaimed bitterly, and when threatened with hell said, 'I regard not ...I will die but once. I care not what be done with me'. In spite of this apparent stoicism, Balfour recorded that she tore out her hair and seemed to be on the edge of an emotional breakdown. He prayed for her, but when Jean continued to be unrepentant and defiant he lost his professional patience, charging her with murder, saying she would change her tune after sentencing, and then left, admitting in his 'Memorial' that he had got nowhere.[54]

The trial took place around midday on Thursday 4 July. No records of it have survived, and in any case it is unlikely to have involved more than an appearance before the burgh magistrates to hear sentence. Jean, Janet Murdo, and the two other female servants who had had the misfortune to be on the scene when the authorities arrived, were taken 'red handed'. In effect this meant that their guilt was sufficiently manifest for them to be put to an assize without the formal proceeding of serving a dittay. Jean was found guilty, and was sentenced to hang, her body then to be consigned to the flames. Death was the least Jean could expect, but the court went further in expressing their disgust at her crime, imposing a manner of death reserved for those of a lesser status while the disposal of her corpse was the same as that used for witches. The three servants all were sentenced to be burned, probably after being strangled, although it is unclear if the sentence was for the more horrible burning alive. There was to be no doubt that Jean Livingston's behaviour was utterly taboo in this male dominated hierarchy. On hearing the sentence she displayed no hint of emotion, a level of self-control which Mr. Balfour thought was explicable only in terms of diabolic influences, a typical response to female behaviour which defied conventions.[55]

A little before one o'clock on Thursday afternoon, shortly after returning from the trial, Jean turned to a friend who was keeping her company and said 'I find ... a spark of grace, and a spark of life beginning in me'. Immediately word of this was sent to Mr. Balfour. After the shock of her husband's murder, the surprise at finding herself under arrest, the universal horror at what she had done, and the finality of the trial, it is hardly surprising that guilt and fear had worked a change in Jean's fiery, defiant temperament. Jean herself later admitted to Balfour that she had hoped that by not admitting her guilt there remained the possibility of holding onto life.[56] However, there is no reason to doubt Balfour's conviction that the change was attributable to the working of the Holy Spirit. There is nothing to indicate that Jean previously was very religious; indeed she confessed to her former neglect of religion and her formal attendance at church services to hear the sermon.[57] Arriving again at the prison, Balfour persuaded Jean to join him and the others in attendance in prayer. She prayed a prayer she would repeat hundreds of times: 'Lord, for mercy and grace at thy hand for thy dear Son, Jesus Christ his sake, to the glory of thy mercy and safety of my silly soul'. There followed some seven hours of prayer, devotions and confession during which Jean attained a level of near spiritual ecstasy. However, Balfour also used this time to write her will. He left at around eight o'clock in the evening, but returned an hour later to find Jean still spiritually excited. They continued to pray until midnight when he persuaded her to take a short sleep. He then left again, promising to return at daybreak as it was expected she would be executed at around nine o'clock on the morning of Friday 4 July.[58]

After Balfour left to get some rest Jean continued with her devotions before finally succumbing to sleep. Balfour awoke early and visited Janet Murdo, one of the other prisoners, but found her a harder character. She was, he thought, 'very evil, and over ready an instrument to her [Jean Livingston] in this horrible fact'. He returned to Jean's room between four and five o'clock on the morning of Friday 4 July, and awoke her at six o'clock. He sent for his colleague, Mr. Robert Bruce, scourge of the aristocracy and the king, and one of the most formidable of all the presbyterian clergy. Bruce arrived to witness this remarkable conversion, and to reinforce Jean in prayer. Balfour also had made arrangements for Jean to see her son, Patrick, after overcoming a feeling of reluctance that the experience would only make his charge cling more fiercely to life. Jean held her son briefly, kissed and blessed him before committing him to the care of Mr. Bruce who then took the infant way. Soon after this sad parting word came from the authorities that Jean's sentence had been altered to an honourable beheading. Also it became clear that the execution would not be until later in the day. The Livingston family clearly had been at work, their pleading helped no doubt by Jean's compliant behaviour. Balfour told her it was a reward from God for her repentance, an encouragement which left Jean apparently radiant with joy. The remainder of the morning and early afternoon were passed in a round of devotions in which Jean's spiritual hyperactivity was punctuated by spells of exhaustion. Balfour repeatedly tried to calm her down, advising her to save her energy, but he knew he was witnessing something outside the normal course of his parish work even in this time of highly-charged spiritual expectation. Genuinely astonished by what Jean was experiencing, Balfour realised he ought to recall and record the words of this 'preacher of mercy and repentance to us all'. It was at this point he began writing his 'Memorial'.[59]

At around four o'clock on Friday afternoon the Maide — Edinburgh's guillotine – was heard being moved into position. Jean expressed relief that the end was near, and repeated again that she deserved nothing less than death. But then word arrived that there had been another postponement. If anything this heightened Jean's spiritual intensity as she saw the temporary reprieve as a period when she could witness more to her repentance and forgiveness. Jean was convinced that she was directly inspired by God:

> It is not myself that speaketh, neither flesh nor blood, but it's the gloriouse Majesty of God who hathe imprinted thir heavenly speches in my heart, with his holy spirit, that I should speak them unto you; and its no wonder I have got grace, for you have never seen the like sin in any sinner that you have seen in me, neither have you seen the like mercy bestowed upon any sinner which is bestowed upon me.[60]

There was, of course, a danger in this egocentric line of thought which did in fact lead Jean to remark that God allowed her to sin in order that he might bring her to this point of repentance and conversion. If Balfour was unhappy with such thinking he gave no indication of it. He continued to reassure Jean of her salvation, and directed her in a mixture of public and private devotions until supper at around eight o'clock on the Friday evening. She ate well and appeared cheerful, saying to her friends 'I sup with you this night, but I will sup with the Lord tomorrow at night'.[61] After supper there were further religious exercises, and an intimate confession with Balfour in which Jean cleared herself of many scandals associated with her house, a possible hint at there being rumour of her involvement in adultery. It was at this time that she spoke openly to Balfour about the murder, revealing how it was planned and executed. Unable to sleep, and unsure of when her own punishment would take place, she spent a second night talking to Balfour, a father figure in whom she had complete and absolute trust.[62]

The stain on the reputation of her family was something which weighed heavily with Jean, but clearly she was hurt by the lack of support her father gave to her. Her earlier hope that Dunipace's influence at court would be used to protect her was disappointed. John Kincaid of Wariston's murder was a sensational affair on three counts: a wife and her servants had conspired to kill their husband and master thus offending against the social order; a man had been slain in his own house, a crime – hamesuckin – which was considered particularly evil; and the cold-blooded planning of the deed and its brutal execution could not have failed to arouse comment. All this in a society where the king very recently had made a great deal of his determination to clean up the appalling level of private and criminal violence, and on the eve of a parliament which would pass legislation designed to curb lawlessness.[63] Whatever the private feelings John Livingston of Dunipace might have felt towards his daughter there could be no question of him defending her. His own part in the killing of David Forrester in a bloodfeud five years earlier was understood, even if an increasing number of people were calling for the end to private war and vengeance. His daughter's crime was unforgivable. According to the ballad, Dunipace, along with other members of the family, visited Jean in prison, but he neither saw her nor interceded for her life. His greatest concern was that he and his family should not suffer disgrace after the only too recent recovery of his own fortune. Therefore his efforts were bent towards damage limitation. Dunipace used his influence at court to ask that the pain and ignominy of a public execution be minimised, and in this he had some success. It appears to have been Dunipace who persuaded the magistrates to alter the form of execution to beheading, and he secured the postponement from the Friday afternoon when a large crowd had gathered to view the grisly business. But he refused to see his daughter and probably remained at Linlithgow. Instead Dunipace sent word to the prison that he was very sorry for her, but rejoiced to hear of her repentance. Jean hid what disappointment she must have felt: 'God comfort my father with his Holy Spirit; and God instruct him, and all that are with him, as he hath done me'. Balfour related that in their conversation Jean repeatedly came back to her father and his attitude towards her, saying that many times she longed for his presence if only so he could witness the great change that had taken place in her. But Dunipace was determined not to allow any of the ignominy associated with his daughter to touch him. Jean forgave him, but the deep hurt she felt comes across in Balfour's account. She also criticised her father's stratagem of trying to ensure that her execution took place at night when no-one would be around to see it. Jean's concern was that such a public show of repentance would be a witness to God's grace. She now was an all too willing player in the piece of street theatre that church and state had arranged.[64] Dunipace saw only the enormous social embarrassment of the occasion, but his efforts to have his daughter quickly and quietly dispatched in relative privacy ran into difficulties. The burgh magistrates denied a request that Jean be put to death at nine o'clock on the Friday evening when it still would be light, but when few people would be around and no-one would expect an execution. Instead the execution would take place on the next morning. Frustrated by this show of civic duty, the Livingstons had the burgh magistrates out of their beds before three o'clock on the Saturday morning, demanding Jean's death before sunrise which would have been between four and five o'clock. The argument put up by the magistrates, Mr. Balfour and Jean herself was that the point of an execution was not only to punish the criminal, but also to instruct the public. Thus they asked:

> Will you deprive God's people of that comfort which they might have, in that poor woman's death? And will you obstruct the honnour of it, by puting her away, before the people rise out of their beds? You do wrong in so doing; for the more publict the death be, the more profitable it shall be to many; and the more gloriouse, in the sight of all who shall see it.[65]

Jean herself asked her kinsmen to allow her to see the sun one last time, and had hoped for a few hours more. A compromise was agreed and the execution was set for sunrise. In contrast to the behaviour of the Livingstons, Jean's brother-in-law, possibly Henry Kincaid, visited her while this argument was going on. He prayed with her, and she asked his forgiveness. She was concerned that her mother-in-law too would forgive her, but there is no record of Margaret Ramsay's attitude.[66]

At around four o'clock on the morning of Saturday 5 July 1600 Jean Livingston was taken from her prison to the girth cross at Holyrood at the bottom of the Canongate. In order to minimise interest in the event the magistrates had agreed to distract attention at the other end of the town where 'the nurse and ane hyred women..were burnt in the Castell Hill'.[67] At the end Janet Murdo confessed to her part in the crime, and the execution of only one of the other servants might indicate a reprieve for the other. According to Mr. Balfour, Jean walked to her place of execution cheerfully 'as if she had been going to her wedding, and not to her death'. The knowledge of sins forgiven and the self-control expected in one of her rank must have relieved any of her family who were in attendance. Jean was frightened a little by the appearance of the Maiden which she was seeing for the first time, but Balfour assured her it was the least of her enemies. Then she mounted the scaffold, spoke briefly with her friends about the disposal of her corpse, and delivered a short confession at each of the four corners. It was a succinct expression of those values expected of a godly wife:

> The occasion of my coming here, is to shew that I am, and I have been a great sinner, and hath offended the Lord's Majesty; especially, of the cruell murdering of mine own husband; which, albeit I did not do with mine own hands, for I never laid mine hands upon him all that he was murdering; yet I was the diviser of it, and so the committer! But my God hath been alwise mercifull to me, and hath given me repentance for my sins; and I hope for mercy at his Majesty's hands, and for his dear son Jesus Christ's sake. And the Lord hath brought me hither to be an example to you, that you may not fall into the like sin as I have done: And I pray God, for his mercy, to keep all his faithfull people from falling into the like inconvenient as I have done! And therefore, I desire you all to pray to God for me, that he would be mercifull to me![68]

Sadly, perhaps, the efforts of her family ensured that scarcely anyone heard what Jean Livingston had to say.

There is no suggestion of Jean Livingston retaining any hope of a last minute reprieve. A friend tied a cloth over her face, and Balfour approached to lead her to the block. It was he now who was the more nervous and fearful, and his words of comfort seem trite by comparison with Jean's faith. Responding to his assurance that soon she would be with God, Jean told him 'I am with the Lord already; for I see no death – I know not where I am, but only that I am with my God'. Filled with a deeper joy than Balfour was able to grasp she pressed for one last favour. Bereft of her father she recalled an earlier promise made during their conversations. 'And now, I desire you to keep your promise; give me to God out of your own hand'. Holding back his own mounting emotion, Balfour conducted Jean to the block where he offered her to God as 'a purifyed sacrifice'. The intensity of the relationship formed between this presbyterian stalwart and the doomed girl during the last forty-two hours reached its height when laughingly Jean took her leave. 'The Lord be with you my heart', and kissing him, 'There is a token that I have the spirit of God in greater measure than ever I had'. Unable to speak, Balfour hurriedly left the scaffold. Kneeling down, Jean placed her neck on the Maiden, moving around until she found the most comfortable position. She tried to remain kneeling as long as possible while the blade was very slowly pulled aloft, and twice the executioner had to straighten her legs out behind in order to lengthen her neck. For what seemed like a very long time Jean continued to pray aloud, and as she said the words 'Into thy hand, Lord ...', the axe fell.[69]

III

For Robert Weir punishment was much more prolonged and agonising. Four years later, in the summer of 1604, he returned to Scotland and was captured. On 26 July Weir appeared in the justice court in Edinburgh before the justice depute. The dittay, containing Jean Livingston's damning confession, was read, leaving the fifteen man assize in no doubt about his guilt. Death was to be expected, but when James Sterling, the dempster of the court, read the sentence it contained a surprise. The court ordered that Weir be taken to Edinburgh cross where a scaffold would be erected, and there 'to be brokin upoune ane Row'. This unique form of punishment was imported from the continent (its origins were Frankish) to underline the terrible nature of Weir's crime. He was tied to a cart wheel and broken, his bones literally being smashed one by one by the hangman 'with ane coultar of ane pleuch'. Between eight or ten blows was common before a *coup de grace* to the head or heart. The pulverised corpse was left there on the wheel for twenty-four hours before being set up 'in ane publict place, betuix the place of Warestoun and the toun of Leyth' where it would remain indefinitely.[70]

The laird of Dunipace survived the scandal brought on his family by Jean's actions. In 1595 the Livingston family acted together to protect Dunipace from the law when he was accused of murder. In 1600 Dunipace and his kinsmen threw his daughter to the legal process, hastening her execution rather than seeking to plead her case. In both instances the welfare of the family was served. Within a month of Jean's death public interest switched to the Gowrie Conspiracy. The king's friends closed ranks around him in the face of criticism over the details of the events in Perth. Dunipace remained at court, and there is no evidence of him sympathising with those presbyterian sceptics led by Robert Bruce who had doubts about the death of their champion, John Ruthven, 2nd earl of Gowrie, son of the man who had led the Ruthven Raid in which Dunipace had participated eighteen years earlier. Mr. James Balfour, however, was reluctant to accept the king's interpretation of events, and it required the intervention of the privy council to force him to submit. In May 1601 he was removed from Edinburgh by a worried general assembly.[71] But Dunipace had not been transformed into a tame courtier. In December 1600, five months after his daughter's death, the privy council ordered him and Alexander Lindsay of Pantoshen on one side, and the Ayrshire noblemen, Andrew Stewart, Lord Ochiltree, Hugh Campbell of Loudon and Gilbert Kennedy of Bargany, to find caution not to attack one another. While Pantoshen's caution was set at only 2,000 merks, Dunipace's was set at the same as the other noblemen, 5,000 merks, an indication that he was now a wealthy man.[72] A year later, in December 1601, James made what might have been his first visit to Dunipace Castle since the year of Jean Livingston's birth.[73] Dunipace did not accompany James to England in 1603, and in January 1606 he parted company with the king whose ecclesiastical policies were now so at odds with his own. Sitting on the assize in the state trials of those presbyterian clergy who had staged an illegal general assembly at Aberdeen in the preceding year, he voted for their acquittal, agreeing with the majority that they were 'honest ministers, faithful servants of Jesus Christ and good subjects of the King'.[74] This was not what James wanted to hear, and he was furious with Dunipace and the other members of the assize who had thwarted him. The assize was dismissed and a new trial held in which the king got his way, convicting the ministers who were banished. A further batch of presbyterian malcontents, including Dr. Andrew Melville and Mr. James Balfour, was summoned south to London later that year. Balfour was detained in England where his health deteriorated, and he only was permitted to return to internal exile in the north of Scotland on condition he did not preach. He died on 1 May 1613.[75] But if the disagreement over the freedom of the clergy marked an end of any close relationship with the king, Dunipace's local stature continued to grow. In 1610 he was appointed a justice of the peace for Kincardine, and in 1612 the now Sir John Livingston of Dunipace sat in parliament as one of the two shire commissioners for Stirling.[76] At a personal level there was further tragedy in the deaths of his two eldest sons. Fortunately they had younger brothers, David who became Dunipace's heir, and James who was provided with an estate at Kirkhill in Kincardineshire.[77] Sir John Livingston of Dunipace died in 1619, honoured by his friends and respected by his rivals.[78]

Yet for all his efforts to suppress the events of July 1600 it was chiefly as the father of Jean Livingston that Dunipace was remembered. What he could not have foreseen was the immortalisation of his daughter's story in a popular song. Having whisked her out of life to preserve his own and the family's honour, Dunipace found his family's shame turned into a form of popular entertainment. Of course, the ballad, which probably was being sung within a year or two of the events described, was entertainment with a point. The ballad writer or writers clearly saw tragedy in Jean Livingston's death, and certainly there was much about it which was tragic. This is not the same as saying she was innocent. Jean Livingston arranged the murder of her husband, and her actions caused the deaths of four, possibly five, other people, including herself. By the standards of the day she was justly treated. The moral the ballad writers wished to get across to their public in no way questioned this justice; in fact they reaffirmed it as emphatically as Mr. Balfour and Jean herself in her scaffold speech. The conclusion offered is almost fatalistic, offering a view of marriage which was romantic and unrealistic, at least for the propertied élite:

> And oh, ye maidens young and fair,
> Take warning now by me,
> And see ye never marry ane
> But wha pleases your e'e.[79]

The solution is, of course, trite. Neither lust nor love guarantees a happy marriage. The real tragedy, perhaps, was that neither Jean nor other women in this society had much control over their lives. Bargained over by an ambitious father, lorded over by an older husband for whom she felt no affection and who treated her cruelly, driven to seek the help of a vicious man-servant, tried and convicted by an all male jury, sentenced by a male judge, confessed by a man, and quietly ushered out of the world by embarrassed kinsmen; only the Maiden itself was given a female character. One cannot avoid the fact of Jean Livingston's guilt, but neither can one avoid sensing that her greatest sin was to challenge male authority. It was not romantic love she and other women in this society needed, it was freedom from the customs and laws of a society in which even women born into the privileges of landed society were little more than the chattels of their fathers and husbands. It is a cliché to say it, but most clichés are true, and for Jean Livingston freedom might only have been possible in death. Yet somehow it would be inappropriate to end with the fact of Jean Livingston's death. It is Balfour's 'Memorial' and not the ballad which relates the liberating experience which preceded her death. Jean herself believed in the forgiveness of her sin, she found peace and reconciliation with God, with the crown, the church and the community – only with her father was there a failure of reconciliation. She welcomed death when it came, looking forward to an after–life immeasurably better than the one she left behind. There is something attractive and dignified in a system of justice which is able to impose punishment of the most severe form, but without vindictiveness, and with the willing consent of the criminal. In her own eyes Jean Livingston's execution was just and right, and was in itself an evangelical action, proclaiming God's sovereign justice and mercy. Instead of ending with her death, it is more fitting to conclude with the first hopeful words of her final prayer in prison before she took those steps on the road to the scaffold: 'Lord, I am a sinfull creature, let thy mercy be above my sin'.[80].

Notes

1. *The Ballad Minstrelsy of Scotland* (Glasgow, 1872), 611. The ballad, 'The Laird of Waristoun', which is found here is a composite based on three different versions.
2. 'The Diary of Robert Birrel', in J.G. Dalyell (ed.), *Fragments of Scottish History* (Edinburgh, 1798), 49.
3. J. Balfour Paul *et al.* (ed.), *Registrum Magni Sigilli Regum Scotorum* [RMS] (Edinburgh, 1882–), v, 837; E.W. Livingston, *The Livingstons of Callendar* (Edinburgh, 1920), 346–9.
4. K.M. Brown, 'Aristocratic Finances and the Origins of the Scottish Revolution',

English Historical Review, 54 (1989), 46–87; K.M. Brown, 'Noble Indebtedness in Scotland between the Reformation and the Revolution', *Historical Journal*, 62 (1989), 260–75.

5. J.M. Wormald, *Lords and Men in Scotland: Bonds of Manrent, 1442–1603* (Edinburgh, 1985); K.M. Brown, *Bloodfeud in Scotland, 1573–1625: Violence, Justice and Politics in an Early Modern Society* (Edinburgh, 1986).

6. Livingston, *Callendar*, 343–5.

7. *Ibid.*, 346; J. Balfour Paul (ed.), *The Scots Peerage* (Edinburgh, 1904–14), v, 439–42.

8. J.H. Burton *et al.* (ed.), *The Register of the Privy Council of Scotland* [RPC] first series (Edinburgh, 1877–98), ii, 250–1.

9. [RPC] ii, 660, 672, 727; T. Dickson *et al.* (ed.), *Accounts of the Lord High Treasurer of Scotland* (Edinburgh, 1877–), xiii, 188, 202; W. Fraser, *The Red Book of Menteith* (Edinburgh, 1880), ii, 411.

10. G. Hewitt, *Scotland under Morton, 1572–80* (Edinburgh, 1982), 48–71; *Treasurer's Accounts*, xiii, 214, 263, 265, 288.

11. Livingston, *Callendar*, 348.

12. *RPC*, iii, 323.

13. *Treasurer's Accounts*, xiii, 394; J. Bain *et al.* (ed.), *Calendar of the State Papers relating to Scotland and Mary, Queen of Scots, 1547–1603* [CSP Scot.] (Edinburgh, 1898–1969), vi, 560, 572, 622; *Scots Peerage*, v, 443–5; M. Livingston *et al.* (ed.), *Registrum Secreti Sigilli Regum Scotorum* [RSSRS] (Edinburgh, 1908–), viii, 432, 1432; Livingston, *Callendar*, 346–9.–9.

14. *Scots Peerage*, v, 443–5.

15. *CSP Scot.*, vi, 560, 572, 622; Livingston, *Callendar*, 346–9.

16. *RSSRS*, vii, 1172; viii, 1281.

17. *Ibid.*, viii, 1527.

18. *Scots Peerage*, v, 444; *RSSRS*, viii, 2012.

19. T. Thomson and C. Innes (ed.), *The Acts of the Parliaments of Scotland* [APS] (Edinburgh, 1814–75), iii, 332, 334. Dunipace kept up his association with Mar, acting as a cautioner for him in August; *RSSRS*, viii, 2281.

20. *RMS*, v, 1595.

21. *APS*, iii, 649.

22. *RPC*, v, 72–3.

23. *APS*, iv, 15. Parliament also ratified infeftment on former church lands with rights of patronage.

24. *Original Letters of Mr John Colville 1582–1603* (Bannatyne Club, 1863), 119, 126, 146.

25. *RPC*, v, 188.

26. Brown, *Bloodfeud*, 130–2.

27. He might have died around January 1598 as there is a settlement at this time on his younger son; *RMS 1593–1608*, 727.

28. *Scots Peerage*, v, 443–5, Brown, *Bloodfeud*, 222–3.

29. Brown, *Bloodfeud*, 223–4.

30. *CSP Scot.*, xiii, I, 423.

31. *RPC*, vi, 47. On 22 November 1599 James set aside a fine of £2,000 incurred as surety Dunipace had put up as caution for a man subsequently charged with non-entry. *CSP Scot.*, xiii, I, 377–8.

32. *RPC*, vii, 151. 'Memorial of the confession of Jean Livingston, Lady Waristoun, with an account of her execution, July 1600', in C.K. Sharpe (ed.), *Lady Margaret Cunninghame. Lady Waristoun* (Edinburgh, 1827), p. ix.

33. R. Marshall, *Virgins and Viragos: A History of Women in Scotland from 1080–1980*

(London, 1983); R.A. Houston, 'Women in the Economy and Society of Scotland, 1500–1800, in R.A. Houston and I.D. Whyte (ed.), *Scottish Society 1500–1800* (Cambridge, 1989), 118–47.

34. *Minstrelsy*, 609.
35. *Ibid.*, 611. Dunipace already had married another daughter, Margaret, to James Arbuthnott, portioner of Arrat, a younger son of the laird of Arbuthnott, in November 1590; *Scots Peerage*, i, 298.
36. *RPC*, iii, 650, 752; iv, 6–13; *RMS*, v, 1980, 1181; *RSSRS*, vii, 1777.
37. *RPC*, iv, 783; Scottish Record Office [SRO], CC8/8/1/352-3; CC8/8/20/1–3b; CC8/8/35.
38. Livingston, *Callendar*, 347.
39. R. Pitcairn (ed.), *Criminal Trials in Scotland from 1488–1624* (Edinburgh, 1833), ii, 449.
40. *Minstrelsy*, 611.
41. *RPC*, iii, 34–5, 54–5, 108–9, 204–5, 251, 328, 402, 467.
42. 'Memorial', p. xxviii.
43. *Ibid.*, p. xxviii. One version of the ballad does have the nurse help Weir strangle Wariston; *Minstrelsy*, 610.
44. *Minstrelsy*, 609; D. Calderwood, *The History of the Kirk of Scotland* (Edinburgh, 1842), v, 262; *CSP Scot.*, xiii, II, 666–7.
45. *CSP Scot.*, xiii, II, 666–7. Roger Aston got the date of the murder wrong, presumably because he did not hear about it until 6 July when he penned his account.
46. 'Memorial', p. xxviii.
47. *Ibid.*, p. xxviii.
48. *Ibid.*, p. xxviii.
49. *Ibid.*, p. xxviii.
50. For example, *RPC*, vi, 322–3.
51. 'Memorial', p. xxviii.
52. *Minstrelsy*, 611.
53. Calderwood, *History*, v, 520, 538, 875; H. Scott (ed.), *Fasti Ecclesiae Scoticanae. Synod of Lothian and Tweedale* (Edinburgh, 1915), i, 53, 63.
54. 'Memorial', pp. ii–iv. Of some use in understanding the following is E. Berggren, *The Psychology of Confession* (Leiden, 1975).
55. 'Memorial', pp. v–vi.
56. *Ibid.*, p. xv.
57. *Ibid.*, p. xxi.
58. *Ibid.*, pp. vii–viii.
59. *Ibid.*, pp. ix–xii.
60. *Ibid.*, pp. xiv–xv.
61. *Ibid.*, pp. xv–xxiii.
62. *Ibid.*, pp. xxiii–xxviii.
63. *APS*, iv, 158–9; Brown, *Bloodfeud*, 240ff.
64. 'Memorial', pp. xxi, xxvi.
65. *Ibid.*, pp. xxx–xxxi.
66. *Ibid.*, pp. xxiii, xxxi.
67. Calderwood, *History*, vi, 27.
68. 'Memorial', pp. xxxii–xxxiv.
69. *Ibid.*, pp. xxiv–xxv; Birrel, 'Diary', 49 Calderwood, *History*, vi, 27.
70. Pitcairn, *Criminal Trials*, ii, 450; P. Spierenburg, *The Spectacle of Suffering and the Evolution of Oppression: From a Preindustrial Metropolis to the European Experience* (Cambridge, 1984), 71–2.

71. *Fasti*, i, 63; Calderwood, *History*, vi, 57, 121.
72. *RPC*, vi, 325.
73. *Ibid.*, vi, 525.
74. Livingston, *Callendar*, 349; Calderwood, *History*, vi, 375–89; Pitcairn, *Criminal Trials*, ii, 502.
75. *Fasti*, i, 63; Calderwood, *History*, vi, 633, 660, 668.
76. *RPC*, ix, 76, 79; *APS*, iv, 446, 468. Dunipace had sat in the 1605 convention of the nobility: *RPC*, vii, 55.
77. Livingston, *Callendar*, 349.
78. SRO, CC21/5/2/252–3, 7 June 1620.
79. *Minstrelsy*, 611.
80. 'Memorial', p. xxxvi.

6

The English Devil of Keeping State:
Élite Manners and the Downfall of Charles I in Scotland

DAVID STEVENSON

> And learn to fly, to shun and hate,
> This English devil of keeping state.[1]

In the late 1640s an elderly Aberdeenshire laird, Patrick Gordon of Ruthven, mused on the causes of the overwhelming disasters which had struck his country in the previous decade. First had come the great rebellion of the covenanters against King Charles I, a disaster in the eyes of the royalist Patrick Gordon because it had been successful. Then had followed the outbreak of civil wars in Ireland and England, civil wars in Scotland in which the royalist cause suffered catastrophic defeat, and great epidemics of plague. How were these great and painful upheavals to be explained?

Gordon's explanation was that they were the work of God, who was reacting to the corruptions of the age. But God was acting not — or not only — to punish a corrupt generation, but to cure its ills. The sufferings which seemed to be tearing Britain, and in particular Scotland, apart were the side effects of supernatural medical intervention. According to the principles of physic, the divine physician was treating the land with blood-letting for the liver, vomiting for the stomach, and purging for the belly. Scotland's nobility and gentry were her liver, and were suffering blood-letting by the sword; the merchants and craftsmen of the towns, the main victims of the plague, were the land's purged belly. If this treatment did not cure the infirmity, famine, analogous to vomiting as it emptied the stomach, was sure to follow. However drastic the successive treatments prescribed might seem, the illness was so serious that they were necessary — and resort to alternative medicine was not an option: the Scots must continue to trust their doctor.[2]

In keeping with his cosmic medical framework of explanation, Gordon entitled his observations on the troubles *Ane Short Abridgement of Britane's Distemper*. A more appropriate title might have been *On some Side-Effects of*

Divine Medical Treatment, since strictly speaking in his analogy the actual events of the decade which he describes were not themselves the distemper, but symptoms produced by the treatment designed to cure it. Gordon himself, however, was distinctly ambiguous on this point, for he also called the momentous events he was living through "this dreadful and never to be matched distemper".

Patrick Gordon was a modest and scholarly man, whose career was of such exemplary obscurity that virtually nothing is known of it. But events had

> found an unwonted motion in my soul to leave a memorial to posterity of such observations as I have noted ... although I cannot but confess my own weakness, there being so many judicious, learned, and able spirits who can and will go in hand with the business. This only shall be my best encouragement, that as I carry spleen nor hatred to no man, so shall my relation go always accompanied with the truth; and therefore, I could wish that it were buried in oblivion till I were in my grave, for well I know that the truth shall never be gracious whilst the actors are on life; and, therefore, true histories are usually written in succeeding ages.[3]

In this Gordon got his way: his history was not published until 1844. Since then it has been widely used by historians of the civil wars for details of campaigns in north-east Scotland, and it has been recognised that it was written partly as an attempt by Patrick Gordon to rescue the name of the head of his own kin, George Gordon, marquis of Huntly, from denigration by supporters of the rival royalist leader, the marquis of Montrose. But the author would have been saddened that later ages have shown virtually no interest in his explanations of the causes of events. Drastic cures by divine doctors are out of fashion as modes of historical explanation, and Gordon's supporting evidence of old prophecies, great comets and threatening conjunctions of the planets have not added to his credibility with modern historians.

Yet there is one sub-theme of *Britane's Distemper*, a specific corruption of the age which Gordon saw as contributing to disaster in Scotland, which deserves serious attention. Indeed, so this essay will argue, it merits wider application than Gordon himself gave it, for whereas he applied it to some members of the Scottish nobility, it applies above all to King Charles I himself. It is hard to believe that Gordon did not realise this. Doubtless he did, but forbore to criticise royalty — while perhaps expecting posterity to read this additional application between the lines.

The sub-theme emerges as Gordon pondered the problem of why his own lord, Huntly, was so uniformly unsuccessful in his efforts to serve the king, arousing very little support or enthusiasm, while Montrose, by contrast, aroused passionate loyalty and dedication from his followers, and won a great reputation as a military leader and cavalier hero in royalist circles. The puzzle was all the greater as Montrose was ultimately defeated conclusively, and had never won united support from Scottish royalists.

Much lay in the general differences of character and ability between the two men, but Gordon focused on one contrast between them: the way they treated their social inferiors. For Gordon, Montrose represented the virtues of traditional Scottish manners, while Huntly displayed the corrupting influences of English manners, alienating those who were his natural followers. Huntly, in terms of property and kinship, was potentially a vastly greater noble than Montrose, but he, like some others amongst the Scottish nobility, suffered the fatal defect of infection by "the English devil of keeping state".

Montrose was a man who by his manner and bearing won the respect due to him from inferiors naturally, without having to ask or demand it. He seemed

> to scorn ostentation and the keeping of state, and therefore he quickly made a conquest of the hearts of all his followers, so as when he list he could have led them in a chain to have followed him with cheerfulness in all his enterprises; and I am certainly persuaded, that this his gracious, humane and courteous freedom of behaviour, being certainly acceptable before God as well as men, was it that won him so much renown, and enabled him chiefly, in the love of his followers, to go through so great enterprises, wherein his equal had failed, although they exceeded him far in power, nor can any other reason be given for it, but only this that followeth.[4]

Gordon then launched into an attack on keeping of state which in its bitterness and sarcasm suggests that he himself had at some point felt personally humiliated by how Huntly, his own lord with new-fangled ways, had treated him:

> For once that English devil, keeping of state, got a haunt amongst our nobility, then began they to keep a distance, as if there were some divinity in them, and gentlemen therefore must put off their shoes, the ground is so holy whereon they tread; but as he is an evil bred gentleman that understands not what distance he should keep with a noble man, so that noble man that claims his due with a high look, as if it did best fit his nobleness to slight his inferiors, may well get the cap and knee, but never gain the heart of a freeborn gentleman.

— or at least not in Scotland, for

> It is true that in England the keeping of state is in some sort tolerable, for that nation (being so often conquered) is become slavish, and takes not evil to be slaves to their superiors.
>
> But our nation, I mean the gentry not the commons, having never been conquered, but always a free-born people, are only won with courtesy, and the humble, mild, cheerful, and affable behaviour of their superiors.... And because

they have never been brought to bow their necks under the yoke of bondage, nor were they ever slaved with the awful tyranny of a conqueror, nor forced to yield respects as the English do, to him that keeps, or rather seeks to keep, great state... , looking for observance so greedily as he cannot stay [stop] till it is given him, but with a lofty look claiming as is due his own awful reverence from all; this I say only, this our Scots nation cannot endure, but are ever found with secret murmurings and private grudges to repine at. And, therefore, although their leader be their chief, their master, of whom they hold their lands or their being, yet was it never found abroad nor at home that a leader of such stately and reserved carriage could, with our nation, perform any great enterprise.[5]

Therefore, Gordon urged, nobles should take heed of the lines of verse about the "English devil" printed at the start of this essay. Montrose was naturally inclined to humility, courtesy and freedom of carriage:

He did not seem to affect state, nor to claim reverence, nor to keep a distance with gentlemen that were not his domestics; but rather in a noble yet courteous way he seemed to slight those vanishing smokes of greatness, affecting rather the real possession of men's hearts than the frothy and outward show of reverence; and therefore was all reverence thrust upon him, because all did love him.[6]

"He that exalteth himself shall be humbled" concluded Gordon piously, and it served them right for failing to make a difference in how they treated free-born gentlemen and servile or base-minded slaves.

In all this adulation of Montrose the contrast was being made with anonymous other nobles. Even the comparison with Huntly was left implicit, perhaps because Gordon at this point was writing before Huntly was executed in 1649. But later in his work, writing after Huntly's death and seeking to explain his abysmal failure in the traditional noble role of war-leader, Gordon was more candid. Self-will, obstinacy, and refusal to take advice contributed to Huntly's failure. So did the fact that, when he experienced difficulties, "Service done... was forgotten, and old servants, for whom there was no use, must be brushed or rubbed off, as spots from clothes". But Gordon remained to the end ambivalent about Huntly, for as the head of the Gordon kin his reputation should be upheld, so he hastily added that this was a truly noble fault, for all nobles were ungrateful! Nonetheless, "the hard construction which was made of this did more harm to himself than to those castaways, for it did, by little and little, insensibly alienate the hearts of his followers". Moreover,

with a certain kind of reserved inclination, he seemed desirous to keep a distance with his inferiors, without distinction of quality; for friends and followers were equalled with domestics ... unless his affairs required it, and then [he] could be both familiar and obsequious. This got him but an outward and constrained obedience.

Consequently, when Huntly planned risings in the king's name, some of his followers simply retired to their homes – and, even more damningly, others went and served Montrose instead. Again ambivalent, Gordon condemned this desertion of Huntly because of his "one fault". Nonetheless, the moral was there to be underlined yet again:

> Thus we may see how far the inward tie of the heart prevaileth against the strong bond of nature, or the duty they owed to their chief, or obedience to their lord and master or superior; and this truly should be a warning to our nobility, letting them see how great an antipathy there is betwixt the genius of our nation and the English keeping of state.

Yet still Gordon tried to excuse his master. His

> keeping of distance, and the proud show of affecting state, was no part of his natural inclination; he was known to be both affable, courteous, and sociable before he was called to court; his breeding in England, the habit and long custom he got there, overcame and wholly changed his natural inclination.[7]

There is a most striking historical irony here. James VI had insisted that the young heir to the Gordon empire in north-east Scotland be brought up in England, with the deliberate intention of cutting him off from his roots, from the Gordon power-base which had enabled his father so frequently to defy the crown. The policy was entirely successful, for when Huntly returned to his estates after his father's death in 1636 he was an Anglicised stranger. But this meant that, though he had been inculcated with loyalty to the crown, he was unable to mobilise Gordon resources to help the king effectively against the covenanting rebels in the years ahead. The great Gordon interest, potentially one of the very greatest in the country, had been successfully tamed by the crown just at the moment when the crown had desperate need of it.

The increasing insistence of the Scots nobility on formality in dealing with inferiors had been lamented long before Patrick Gordon's time. In 1607 James Cleland had advised a degree of humility in dealing with men of all sorts:

> because I see so many of our young nobles deceive themselves herein, thinking that we are bound to respect and honour them in all devotion and service, and that they are not tied to any reciprocal courtesy, as if it were possible that they could stand of themselves, and uphold their imaginary and fantastical greatness without us. For my part I can neither honour nor respect such persons.[8]

In another fine example of historical irony Cleland dedicated one of the books of his work to the future marquis of Huntly – and the whole work to the future Charles I.

* * *

Patrick Gordon ended *Britane's Distemper* with a comparison between Huntly and Charles I, who had been executed just a few weeks before him, pointing out the similarities between them. The comparison was however confined to their merits: no criticism of the "superlative" martyr-king or his "unparalleled" servant was appropriate.[9] But by inference a question lurked beneath the surface: did the two men also share defects which contributed to their downfalls?

The answer is undoubtedly in the affirmative. The manner in which Charles I treated most members of the élites of society of Scotland in the course of personal contacts was frequently regarded as insulting, leading ultimately to alienation and reluctance to support him even by his natural supporters when crisis came — exactly what Huntly experienced in his much smaller sphere. Inferiors were shocked by being treated by superiors in ways which were not traditional and were interpreted as degrading. But the superiors concerned were equally upset: as they interpreted what was happening, it was their inferiors who were behaving with appalling lack of courtesy, failing to behave with the deference necessary to indicate respect and reverence. Social relationships were being destroyed by conflicting codes of manners.

The Scots prided themselves on a degree of robustness and informality in relations between men of different rank. Society might be intensely hierarchical in structure, but nonetheless men of differing rank could indulge in informal interactions, partly indeed because this hierarchy was fairly secure and confident: great emphasis on outward display of differences was unnecessary. As Patrick Gordon indicated, gentlemen knew how to treat a noble with respect, and nobles did not feel that any great show of boot-licking was necessary to re-assure them of their status. The monarchy itself before the union of the crowns in 1603 had frequently been informal in style. James VI might theorise on divine right in grandiose terms but saw no incongruity in addressing a Scots earl as "My little fat pork" or, after 1603, an English earl as "My little beagle".[10]

Such informality might be acceptable in Scotland, but it grated in England, where the trend was towards greater formality of manners, more rigid behaviour, more emphasis on outward show of deference from inferiors, and towards haughty, withdrawn coldness from superiors determined to exact such deference. Tracing this development is not easy — hardly surprisingly, for few contemporaries were likely to comment directly on changing nuances of manners over time, and modern works concerned with the history of manners are usually based largely on published treatises on conduct (often translations of European originals) which tell more about ideals than practical realities. And indeed such treatises generally recommended something like Patrick Gordon's ideal of behaviour towards inferiors rather than "keeping state". A man may "winneth with a look to subdue all the world" and when a noble shows "a gentle and familiar visage" the hearts of lesser men "leapeth for gladness" and they are happy to obey freely.[11]

However, by the later sixteenth century actual English élite manners seem to have come under unusually strong influence from stoic concepts stressing the importance of entirely suppressing strong emotions in outward demeanour,[12] leading to coldness and formality. In addition, insecurity among nobles about their position in society made them touchy and liable to insist on deference, seeing any lack of such formal show of inferiority as threatening to their status. Having lost their role as military leaders, threatened by wealthy gentry, the "most visible feature" of their counter-attack "was an over-weaning arrogance symptomatic of their insecurity" and a withdrawal into inaccessibility.[13]

"Keeping state" was no monopoly of the nobility, however: it was partly copied by them from the crown, and its influence spread quickly down the social ladder. If nobles demanded more explicit deference from lesser men, then they in turn would tend to feel the need to exact it from their inferiors. In 1578 Barnaby Rich lamented that:

> For the most in number of our young country Gentlemen think that the greatest grace of courting [courtesy, manners] consisteth in proud and haughty countenances to such as know them not.

Significantly, Rich linked this to the loss of military power of the nobility, a loss which had led men to seek new ways of bolstering their status: his work was entitled *Alarme to England, for eschewing what perils are procured, where people live without regarde for martiall lawe.*[14]

In some respects the "distancing" effects of keeping state were one aspect of a centuries-long change in life-styles which was transforming élite behaviour in Europe: an emerging emphasis on personal privacy, as monarchs, lords and gentlemen withdrew from the semi-communal life of the great hall to eat, socialise and do business in the privacy of personal or family rooms.[15] In time the domestic servants came to be banished to their own world of servants quarters; and where villages or hamlets of common folk had grown up round castles or country houses, they were banished, pushed out of sight, sound and smell of their betters — or alternatively, the old castle with its distressingly lowly neighbours was abandoned as gentry retreated to splendid isolation on greenfield sites. Thus a "gradual distancing took place between great lords and the social inferiors they dominated".[16] Even when venturing out of their residences, the lords moved towards travelling in increasing privacy, with "the withdrawal on journeys from the equestrian cavalcade to the privacy of the coach or sedan-chair".[17]

In such developments England played a prominent role, and from the late fifteenth century distancing in the interests both of privacy and of enhancing status was given a lead by the example of the crown itself. Monarchs "elevated themselves unapproachably above even the greatest of their lords". Under Henry VII the king withdrew into the privacy of his privy chamber, to which access was strictly regulated.[18] Francis Bacon (writing in 1621) was to identify the key to Henry's style of kingship as being "keeping of distance, which indeed he did towards all".[19] This style, once established, endured as the English court norm until the mid-seventeenth century, though it was modified by the personal character of monarchs.

The greatest shock the style experienced was the arrival of a Scottish king in 1603, inheritor of a very different monarchical tradition. By English standards James VI had remarkably little privacy at his Scottish court, with access to his person being very open — and though restrictions were placed on access to his bedchamber in 1601, it still remained generous. The "English court was designed for the preservation of distance; the Scots for the management of relatively free and open access. Or to put it differently: the English etiquette was English, while the Scottish was French".[20] An English observer in 1601 noted that "anyone may enter the king's Presence while he is at dinner, and as he eats he converses with those about him" in a typically French way.[21]

The clash of these two styles in the years after 1603 was inevitably painful: "no king, I am sure, in Christendom, did observe such state and carried such a distance from the subjects as the kings and queens of England did", whereas "there was no such state observed in Scotland".[22] In terms of institutional structure James was happy to accept the English court model, though with the bedchamber door being the key filter in restricting access to him, rather than the privy chamber, to which access was much more open than in the past. And James's vanity and ideals of kingship made him happy to accept the court ceremonial and excessive (in Scots eyes) deference usual in England: he seemed to the Venetian ambassador to be being corrupted out of his "French familiarity"[23] — a comment echoed by the alleged mutterings of a Scot as the king had travelled south to take up his new inheritance: that the obsequious grovellings with which the English welcomed him would spoil a good king.[24] Much of the personal abuse heaped on James in England reflected, it has been plausibly argued, the depth of anti-Scottish feeling,[25] and one aspect of this was undoubtedly revulsion at aspects of James's manners which were specifically Scottish — especially the familiarity with which he treated his Scots friends. Such informality of kingship was not for the English.

Once one leaves the rarefied circles of the court and delves more generally in society for the influence of the unusual English emphasis on formality, privacy and "distance" emanating from the court, evidence not surprisingly becomes much harder to find. The best witness is the anthropologically-inclined English traveller of the 1590s, Fynes Moryson.[26] The "French use great liberty of conversation and small reverence to superiors" and — like Patrick Gordon — despised English gentlemen for giving so much deference to great lords. In English inns, gentry insisted on eating in rooms shared only with other gentry — or at the very least demanded a separate table for gentry use, whereas in France and Germany it was customary for commoners to sit at the same table — though lower down it. Germans might treat their wives like servants, but they behaved to their servants like companions. Servants served food at table with their hats on, and similarly "continually talk with their masters without any reverence of the cap or like duty". In Scotland in a knight's house Moryson found that the servants served food at their master's table without removing their blue bonnets, "and when the table was served, the servants did sit down with us" — though while the servants ate from "great platters of porridge, each having a little piece of sodden meat", the gentry had "a pullet with some prunes in the broth". Germans did not exact humility or respect from their children, who treated their parents familiarly and talked to them with their hats on. When German children went to bed at night their fathers shook hands with them, a sign of familiarity, whereas English fathers made their children kneel before them to ask a blessing.[27]

These anecdotes from Moryson's vast and rambling work are straws in a wind of cultural change that he, with his interest in comparative codes of manners, was one of the few to comment upon. Another was the abusive anti-Scots English writer, Sir Anthony Weldon, who denounced the Scottish lack of "complimental courtesy", and the fact that that "their followers are their masters, their wives their slaves". Weldon's comments were written in the same year (1617) that Fynes Moryson's work was first published, and his remarks about the relative attitudes of Scotsmen to their servants and wives are so close to what Moryson says about the Germans that there must be a strong suspicion that Weldon was copying Moryson's anecdote. But that he thought it appropriate to apply it to the Scots is significant: as the report of another traveller, in 1629, confirms, one of the things Englishmen felt peculiar enough to be worthy of comment was Scottish servants serving food and dining in presence of their master while wearing their hats.[28]

There is plenty of evidence in writings on the behaviour of individual English nobles at this time of the key importance of the concept of "distance" — the pride they took in preserving distance from men of different status.[29] However, though it is clear that there was a difference between English distance and Scottish familiarity, it is important to stress that such differences were relative, and fluctuated from individual to individual, and circumstance to circumstance. The relative informality of Scots élite manners is clear, and can be linked to their close traditional links with the French court and French culture, and to her nobility enjoying a much greater confidence in their own role and status in society than their English counterparts. Yet a Scots noble could react with the same rage as an English one at what seemed behaviour designed to derogate from his status,[30] and by the late sixteenth century financial problems and changes of perceptions of their role in society, stemming from the teachings of the Reformed Church and the suppression of the honourable violence of the feud, were contributing to producing the first signs of a sense of insecurity in some Scots nobles which paralleled that of the English and elicited the same response — a demand for greater deference.[31] The union of 1603 brought them into much closer contact with English codes of deference just at a time when some at least were likely to find them appropriate to their emerging anxieties.

* * *

England's élites, from the crown downwards, had taken the lead in Europe in the "distancing" inherent in keeping state and demanding greater privacy. King Charles I carried these tendencies to new extremes which even disconcerted many of his English subjects, used as they were to formality. He created the most ceremonially obsessive and ritualistic court etiquette ever seen in Britain, and added to the barriers separating the monarch from the vast majority of members of the court. While maintaining and extending the exclusiveness of the bedchamber, he re-established the exclusiveness of the privy chamber, which had lapsed when James VI had established the former.[32] The court was to be "a shrine of virtue and decorum",[33] with a king at the centre accessible only to a small group of the most privileged. Inter-personal behaviour was to be rigidly formal and deferential.

If the king's extreme ideals of distancing raised English eyebrows, they caused far more shock when they came into contact with traditional Scottish informality. This was demonstrated dramatically when the king came to Edinburgh in 1633 for his coronation. The visit was in many respects a public relations disaster. The king behaved in accordance with his rigidly formal and subtly nuanced codes of manners, whereas some at least of the Scottish nobility blithely sought to relate to him in a friendly informal way that he found deeply offensive. The impression given is that the king returned south convinced that the Scots were boors who did not understand civilised norms of behaviour, and in particular the deference due to a ruler. The Scots were left with bitter confirmation that their native dynasty had "gone native" within a generation of its move to England, and that they were faced by a king who not only was insisting on policies deeply threatening to Scottish noble power, religious traditions and national identity, but who treated them with haughty contempt, expecting them to grovel in a manner which might be acceptable to Englishmen but certainly was not to free-born Scots.

It was an Englishman, Edward Hyde, the later earl of Clarendon, who recorded and analysed this clash of codes of conduct. When the Scottish parliament met, with the king present in person, some nobles dared to speak out against royal policies. Charles took action which he assumed would make clear the extent of his displeasure and break their spirit: he displayed "a little discountenance upon those persons". But unfortunately, continued Hyde, the Scots

> have naturally an admirable dexterity in sheltering themselves from any of those acts of discountenance which they have no mind to own ... when it hath been notoriously visible, as it was then notorious, that many of the persons then, as the earl of Rothes and others, of whom the King had the worst opinions, and from whom he most purposely withheld any grace by never speaking to them or taking notice of them in the Court, when the king was abroad ... when the greatest crowds of people flocked to see him, those men would still be next him, and entertain him with some discourse and pleasant relations, and which made those persons to be generally believed to be most acceptable to his majesty.

The thick-skinned and informal Scots either failed to notice the royal hints that their company was unwelcome, or — in Hyde's opinion — were damned if they were going to admit to noticing them and slink off with tails between their legs like (as Patrick Gordon would have put it) slavish Englishmen. Another Englishman (in spite of his Scottish title) in Scotland with the king, Lord Falkland, commented on his monarch's discomfiture:

> "that keeping of state was like committing adultery, there must go two to it;" for let the proudest or most formal man resolve to keep what distance he will towards others, a bold and confident man instantly demolishes that whole machine, and gets within him, and even obliges him to his own laws of conversation.[34]

As Falkland's seventeenth-century version of "it takes two to tango" stressed, the problem for Charles was that keeping of state rested on mutual observance of a relationship by two parties. As James Cleland had warned a generation before, the imaginary and fantastical greatness of a superior could not be maintained "without us", without the co-operation of inferiors. English subjects would play their part in the game: some Scots at least were determined to show the king that when he was in Scotland they expected him to behave in accordance with their own traditions.

In seeking from the start of his reign to push the show of deference and formality to extremes, Charles I doubtless saw himself as repairing the damage done by his father's often informal style, and by the disorders and scandals at court which had accompanied James's declining years. To attempt to restore the dignity and grandeur of monarchy made sense from the crown's point of view. But the king's motivation (whether he realised it or not) was in some respects highly irrational and potentially damaging to the future of the monarchy, and arose from his personal limitations and weaknesses. His exalted vision of monarchy, his withdrawal into grandiose privacy, his belief in his God-given mission, and his determination to impose his will, were all linked, it seems clear, to fears of inadequacy, perhaps intensified by his smallness of stature, and symptomatised by his stutter and by the inflexibility that sometimes reflected stubborn refusal to face reality rather than confident strength. It has been remarked that "his image-building, unlike that of modern commercial operators, was not based on any consumer research. He neither knew nor cared what prejudices, what traditions, what passions he might antagonise",[35] for the image of remote, indeed almost invisible majesty, distanced even from most of his greatest subjects, resulted largely from his shy and introspective nature. The well-established tradition of keeping of state in England could be seen as combining conveniently with exalted theories of monarchy to justify the creation of protective ramparts around the king to insulate him from stressful contacts with his subjects.

> His deportment was very majestic; for he would not let fall his dignity, no not to the greatest foreigners that came to visit him and his court; for though he was far from pride, yet he was careful of majesty, and would be approached with respect and reverence

testified Sir Philip Warwick.[36]

An article by Judith Richards has illuminated the ways in which Charles's new codes of monarchical behaviour damaged rather than enhanced the prestige of monarchy in England, as they amounted to a remarkably irresponsible abandoning of traditional roles expected of a king.[37] His concern for image was genuine, but the image projected seemed to be intended for consumption largely within the confines of the court. There were deliberate restraints on projecting it more widely, and even within the confines of the court the number of subjects who had an opportunity to experience the image first-hand was limited by policies aimed at the exclusion of members of the public who wanted to petition the king, or even merely to see their sovereign. The latter were informed graciously but bluntly that while their zeal was appreciated, the king wished to dispense with public displays of it. Petitioners would face his majesty's displeasure unless they had matters of great urgency to present. This 1625 proclamation against unnecessary and disorderly resort to court ordered such inconvenient subjects to keep at least twelve miles away. When the king was travelling, the poor were not to flock to him for alms. Instead his almoner would give alms to local overseers of the poor for distribution.[38] Charles's "progresses" were very limited geographically, and anyway were not traditional occasions stage-managed to let subjects see their ruler and observe him at work and recreation. Instead they were often largely private hunting trips, and both on them and on other journeys deliberate attempts were made to discourage people from hastening to see him. On his way to Scotland in 1633 Charles travelled in closed coaches — except when switching to horseback to hunt.[39]

Thus there emerges the seeming paradox of a king at once intent on being treated with great formality and reverence, and on the other going to considerable lengths to prevent most of his subjects from having any opportunity of displaying their awe and loyalty. And if personal feelings of inadequacy and insecurity provide much of the explanation for such strange behaviour, there may also be added laziness. For all his concern to project an exalted concept of kingship, Charles refused to accept that successful authoritarian monarchy required immensely hard work. His tendency to issue orders and assume they would be obeyed automatically reflected naive concepts of what absolute monarchy meant — but it also provided a convenient excuse for not overseeing the nitty-gritty of implementing policies.[40] Theoretical arguments about order were used to justify barring as many subjects as possible from his presence, and this also saved him from a lot of work.

Thus "distancing" was carried so far that the king deliberately remained invisible to as many of his subjects as possible — at which point distancing instead of inspiring reverence was in danger of coming to inspire indifference, or even hostility. Here was a king who evidently did not want the affection of, or personal contact with, his subjects, a king who showed strong distaste for the age-old function of receiving petitions, who sought to depersonalise the royal function of largesse for the poor, who (like the nobility) sought to hide himself from subjects when travelling.

The passion for order and decorum — in part at least pretexts for indulging the royal priority given to privacy — applied within the court itself, with strict regulation of access to the king's presence of members of court as well as exclusion of outsiders, creating the most formal court in Europe. Of all monarchs only Charles kept state to such an extent that those serving his food had to kneel to do so.[41] When the king washed in his private chambers, a groom of the bedchamber had to observe which parts of the royal towel actually touched the royal body, and make sure to carry those parts above the level of his head when he took it away.[42] Thus a fastidious and retiring king, cocooned in self-exalting rituals, gave up or devoted only the minimum time necessary to many of the traditional functions of kingship, and "the result was a personal monarch who for nearly fifteen years [1625–40] withdrew from the vast majority of his subjects to a degree unprecedented for generations".[43] That alienation from Charles's monarchy in Scotland was partly caused by absentee monarchy has long been recognised, but in some respects Charles managed even to create absentee monarchy in England by distancing himself from his subjects, a strange variant of internal exile in which the ruler exiled himself from subjects anxious to display their loyalty.

Significantly, once the Scots had revolted and open dissent became widespread in England, Charles consciously sought to revive in England the traditional and public roles of kingship he had deliberately suppressed, at last taking heed of the expectations of his subjects.[44] North of the border it was too late even to try. But it is worth noting that when in 1638 Charles sent the marquis of Hamilton to Scotland to negotiate with the covenanter rebels, one contemporary remarked that "Truly I have known him keep greater state when he was not the King's Commissioner".[45] Had a deliberate decision been taken that a change in style in dealing with the Scots was expedient, with less keeping of state for fear of antagonising them? Hamilton, like Huntly, was one of the minority of the Scots nobility who were more used to court life than to their native land, and who had fully adopted English state to win acceptance at court. But Hamilton evidently had the flexibility to change his ways when in Rome.

Was Charles I's downfall in Scotland that of the marquis of Huntly writ large? The parallels are most illuminating, demonstrating how loyalty could be eroded by differing codes of manners leading to mutual misunderstanding. Obviously as a cause of the outbreak of rebellion in Scotland, keeping of state was far subordinate to matters of policy and machinery of government. But it was a contributory element, and was inextricably linked with them — not least by Charles's personal traits of stubborn determination and total lack of realisation of how subjects reacted to his actions (or, if he had glimmers of realisation, rejection of this as irrelevant to true monarchy). Moreover, if it was principally the king whose keeping of state offended the Scots, his example, and indeed the general example of English formal state, was inevitably spreading to other Scots under the union of the crowns, as Scots courtiers and officials realised they had to adjust to English norms if their careers at court were to flourish. The English scornfully noted their role in thus "civilising" the barbarous Scots:

> Bonny Scot, we all witness can,
> That England hath made thee a gentleman.[46]

However, though Anglicised court nobles might win favour in the south, the price they had to pay was alienation from their Scottish power-bases. Not only Huntly but others of his ilk found difficulty in rallying their resources to aid the king: there is no direct evidence that their Anglicised manners contributed to this, but this may be suspected. Scottish bishops appointed by

Charles I were said to have increased discontent among parish ministers by "too much slighting of them" and by "carrying themselves so loftily".[47] And, of course, the fact that the formal ceremony of keeping state was the secular counterpart of the widely unpopular reforms in worship that Charles was seeking to impose on the Church of Scotland was so obvious that opposition to the latter was likely to go hand in hand with hostility to the former.

* * *

Matters of precise definition become difficult in discussing manners. Where does offence at generally autocratic attitudes, copied from the king by his servants, shade into offence more specifically at "keeping of state"? Sources are frequently too imprecise to tell us with certainty. The same problem arises with a number or references which occur after the Scottish troubles began to occasions on which contacts between king and subjects became acrimonious not merely about matters of substance, but about manner of address. Edward Hyde recorded that

> The Scots had from the beginning practised a new sturdy style of address, in which, under the licence of accusing the counsel and carriage of others, whom they never named, they bitterly and insolently reproached the most immediate actions and directions of his majesty himself; and then made the greatest professions of duty to his majesty's person that could be invented.[48]

A specific instance concerned the earl of Rothes – the same man Hyde had singled out in 1633 as refusing to play his part in enabling the king to keep state. In 1639 the earl was one of the Scots commissioners who negotiated personally with the king. The meeting got off to a disastrous start when the Scots, in Charles's eyes, insulted him by neglecting to kneel before him. His response was to ignore them, hoping (as in 1633) that such discountenancing would bring the Scots (literally, in this case) to their knees.[49] Not surprisingly the debates which followed were heated. Later Rothes complained about the king's attitude to him:

> I am ... taxed for speaking with less respect to sovereignty than I ought. God bear witness to the true respect of my heart to authority, and of my particular regard to his majesty's sacred person; but his majesty was put on to affront me, calling me twice a liar and twice an equivocator. Those with whom I live know me to be free of both ... The honesty of my heart to speak to my prince that truth which was entrusted to me by so many of his faithful subjects, getting so hard construction made me to exceed, and would have tempted any honest man; but I will not be ashamed to beg his majesty's pardon for any rudeness of my carriage there, and humbly to beseech never to be so used again. [50]

In other words, being a loyal subject did not mean that a free-born Scot had to accept insult from the king: and though Rothes apologised, this was linked with a suggestion that the king mind his mouth in future!

More generally, a covenanting propaganda pamphlet of 1640 replied to complaints from the king of lack of ceremony in his treatment by Scottish commissioners by stating that Charles "knoweth well that the Scottish Nation glorieth more in kindness and realities than in expressions by word or gesture".[51] Part of the Scottish self-perception was of a plain-speaking folk, whose words were more honest and sentiments more sincere for not being wrapped up in courtly coding and the irrelevances of ceremony.

Charles I, by keeping such high state, made a significant contribution to losing his thrones, and appropriately resistance began in Scotland where his imperious manner was seen as much more offensive than in England. In keeping state Charles responded to the dictates of his own personality, but also reacted against his father's laxity of manners. Charles's own son swung the pendulum of formality back the other way — in spite of English courtiers' attempts to prevent this. While the young Prince Charles was in exile in Jersey during the English civil war, Lord Jermyn reported with horror that, in his make-shift court, there was at first "no distance kept, but all suffered to be as familiar with him as if they were his fellows". This was soon rectified and "the English were kept at a great distance". But there remained a problem: in exile Charles spent much time at the French court, or at least closely connected to it, and adopted French standards of taste and conduct. His entourage included many Frenchmen, and while the English distanced themselves from the royal boy they served "the French were as familiar with him as could be imagined".[52] This experience, coupled with a very different personality and, doubtless, realisation of the part excessive keeping of state had played in his father's downfall, persuaded the future Charles II that majesty was compatible with a degree of informality with subjects.

This doubtless worried the duke of Newcastle, who had urged Charles to keep up ceremony, as familiarity bred contempt: "show yourself gloriously, to your people; like a god ... certainly there is nothing keeps up a king, more than ceremony, and order, which makes distance, and this brings respect and duty".[53] That Charles II failed to follow this advice might, from a Scottish point of view, sound like a happy ending, Scots informality triumphing over English state. In fact even after the Restoration of monarchy English élite manners were far from relaxing to correspond to anything like Scottish traditional informality and lack of ceremony. England remained, relatively speaking, a land of keeping state. Before the troubles, most of the Scots nobility had held out against English formality, determined to retain their own identity within Britain's élite. After the Restoration, horrified by the disastrous quarter century which had followed their defiance of the king, they hastened towards assimilation with their English counterparts: the trend towards the Scottish noble being characterised by English education, attitudes and accents accelerated rapidly, developments which would have reduced that sturdy old free-born Scottish gentleman, Patrick Gordon of Ruthven, to despair. High-born Scots now looked to their English rather than their French counterparts for role-models — and in any case, though the English court had relaxed from its peak of "distancing" formality, the French court, for so long regarded as the model for Scots informality, was reaching for a Charles I-like ritualism and keeping of state under the Sun King, Louis XIV.[54]

* * *

Trying to trace so intangible and ephemeral a topic as the history of the etiquette of inter-personal relations is at once frustrating and fascinating, and this paper has left a lot of questions unanswered. The contrast between English codes of formality and Scots informality clearly reached a peak in the time of Charles I. But how far back can traces of such differences be traced? When English descriptions of the Scots in almost ritual fashion commented on the latter's rude and barbarous ways, how far was an element of this the response to a perceived lack of refinement (formality) in Scottish manners? Or, looking forward rather than backwards, how far did Scottish informality survive, increasingly abandoned by the great but preserved lower down in society? The Scots like to pride themselves today on a greater warmth and informality in treating acquaintances and strangers than the colder English. If this is not entirely national myth, perhaps we have here the last bastion of Scots resistance to keeping state. A related myth — or reality — lauds a "democratic" element in Scots society not evident south of the border, referring to greater informality in social relations of men of different classes. Another survival of the distant days of Scottish independence and of a relatively stable and confident hierarchical society in which formality was not seen as necessary to preserve structure?

The sad meanderings of an obscure old laird can lead the historian a long way.

Notes

1. Patrick Gordon of Ruthven, *Ane Short Abridgement of Britane's Distemper, from the yeare of God MDCXXXIX to MDCXLIX*, ed. J. Dunn (Spalding Club, 1844), 77. The spelling of all quotations has been modernised. I have previously touched on the main theme of this essay in *The Scottish Revolution, 1637–44* (Newton Abbot, 1973), 22. It is not clear whether or not these lines of verse were composed by Gordon himself.
2. *Ibid.*, 3–5.

3. *Ibid.*, 4.
4. *Ibid.*, 76.
5. *Ibid.*, 76–7.
6. *Ibid.*, 77.
7. *Ibid.*, 229, 230.
8. J. Cleland, *The Instructions of a Young Noble Man*, ed. M. Molyneux (New York, 1948), 171. Cleland's work is often assumed to be an English manual of behaviour, as it was published in Oxford. But Cleland was a Scot and repeated references make it clear that he is thinking primarily of the Scottish nobility – most obviously when he devotes a whole chapter to supporting James VI's denunciation of the bloodfeud. When the book was reissued in 1607 the point was made by re-titling it *The Scottish Academie*, with the original title relegated to subtitle.
9. Gordon, *Britane's Distemper.* pp. 231-2.
10. G.P.V. Akrigg (ed.), *Letters of King James VI and I* (Berkeley, 1984), 95, 278.
11. R. Kelso, "The Doctrine of the English Gentleman in the Sixteenth Century", *University of Illinois Studies in Language and Literature*, xvi (Urbana, 1929), nos. 1, 2, pp. 79–80.
12. W.L. Ustick, "Changing Ideals of Aristocratic Character and Conduct in Seventeenth Century England", *Modern Philology*, 30 (1932–3), 147–52.
13. L. Stone, *The Crisis of the Aristocracy, 1558–1641* (Oxford, 1965), 750.
14. Kelso, "Doctrine", 81.
15. See Stone, *Crisis*, 583–4.
16. T.K. Rabb, *The Struggle for Stability in Early Modern Europe* (Oxford, 1975), 93.
17. Stone, *Crisis*, 584.
18. D. Starkey, "Court History in Perspective", in D. Starkey (ed.), *The English Court: from the Wars of the Roses to the Civil War* (London, 1987), 3–4.
19. Quoted in *ibid.*, 7.
20. N. Cuddy, "The Revival of the Entourage", in Starkey (ed.), *The English Court*, 178–80.
21. Sir Henry Wotton, *The Life and Letters of Sir Henry Wotton*, ed. L.P. Smith (Oxford, 1966), i, 314–15, quoted (translated from the Italian original) in Cuddy, "Revival of the Entourage", 180.
22. G. Goodman, *The Court of King James I*, ed. J.S. Brewer (London, 1839), i, 30, quoted in Cuddy, "Revival of the Entourage", 178.
23. *Ibid.*, 182.
24. Cited in J. Wormald, "James VI and I: Two Kings or One?" *History*, 68 (1983), 190.
25. *Ibid.*, 190–2,
26. Moryson himself never uses the term "keeping state", but it is interesting that it is at precisely this time that it makes its first recorded appearance in English, in 1599 in a play by Ben Jonson, *Oxford English Dictionary*.
27. Fynes Moryson, *An Itinerary containing his Ten Yeeres Travell* (Glasgow 1907–8), iv, 141, 183, 324–5; Fynes Moryson, *Shakespeare's Europe: A Survey of the Condition of Europe at the end of the 16th century. Being unpublished chapters of Fynes Moryson's Itinerary* (1617), ed. C. Hughes (2nd. edn., New York, 1967), 290; J.P. Cooper, "General Introduction", *New Cambridge Modern History*, iv (Cambridge, 1970), 27.
28. P.H. Brown (ed.), *Early Travellers in Scotland* (Edinburgh, 1891), 102; C. Lowther, *Our Journall into Scotland* (Edinburgh, 1894), 18.
29. Eg, B. Manning, "The Aristocracy and the Downfall of Charles I", in his *Politics, Religion and the English Civil War* (London, 1973), 40–1, cited in K.M. Brown, "Aristocratic Finances and the Origins of the Scottish Revolution", *English Historical Review*, 104 (1989), 48n.

30. See, eg, Brown, "Aristocratic Finances", 46, and Stone, *Crisis*, 750.
31. Brown, "Aristocratic Finances", 46–8, 52–3.
32. K. Sharpe, "The Image of Virtue: the Court and Household of Charles I, 1625–42", in Starkey (ed.), *The English Court*, 228, 233–4, 239.
33. *Ibid.*, 236.
34. E. Hyde, earl of Clarendon, *The History of the Rebellion and Civil Wars in England*, ed. W.D. Macray (Oxford, 1888), i, 108–9.
35. R. Ollard, *The Image of the King. Charles I and Charles II* (London, 1979), 39.
36. *Ibid.*, 28.
37. J. Richards, " 'His Nowe Majestie' and the English Monarchy: the Kingship of Charles I before 1640", *Past and Present*, 113 (1986), 70–96.
38. *Ibid.*, 77–8; C. Carlton, *Charles I. The Personal Monarch* (London, 1984), 62.
39. Richards, " 'His Nowe Majestie' ", 83–6.
40. Carlton, *Charles I*, 62, 64, 107–8, 109, 113, 124.
41. Richards, " 'His Nowe Majestie' ", 78–9; Carlton, *Charles I*, 129–30.
42. Sharpe, "The Image of Virtue", 243.
43. Richards, " 'His Nowe Majestie' ", 93.
44. *Ibid.*, 93–4.
45. Sir James Turner, *Memoirs of his own Life and Times* (Bannatyne Club, 1829), 234. For differing reactions of Scots courtier-nobles after 1603 to Anglicising influences, see K.M. Brown, "Courtiers and Cavaliers: Service, Anglicisation and Loyalty among the Royalist Nobility", in J. Morrill (ed.), *The Scottish National Covenant in its British Context* (Edinburgh, 1990), 155–92.
46. Quoted in B. Galloway, *The Union of England and Scotland. 1603–1608* (Edinburgh, 1986), 140.
47. H. Guthry, *Memoirs* (2nd edn., Glasgow, 1748), 17.
48. Hyde, *Rebellion*, i, 160.
49. Carlton, *Charles I*, 205–6.
50. S.R. Gardiner, *The Hamilton Papers* (Camden Society, 1880), 99–100. See Carlton, *Charles I*, 185.
51. *True Representation of the Proceedings of the Kingdom of Scotland* (1640), pt. 2, p.74.
52. Quoted in Ollard, *Image*, 63–4.
53. T.P. Slaughter (ed.), *Ideology and Politics on the Eve of the Restoration: Newcastle's Advice to Charles II* (Philadelphia, 1984), 45.
54. It is worth noting that as early as 1607 James Cleland had recommended as the model for salutations the "old manner" of the French, "for we have too many new French toys", indicating that he felt that deplorable developments were already taking place in French manners, Cleland, *Instructions*, 177.

7

The Wreck of the Dutch East-Indiaman Adelaar *off Barra in 1728*

COLIN MARTIN

> Hear, oh ye people, and listen, oh ye nations! The great Macneil of Barra having finished his meal, the princes of the earth may dine now!

In this manner, according to tradition, the Macneil's horn-blower each evening proclaimed his master's superiority over the rest of the world from the battlements of Kisimul Castle.[1] But the power of Barra's chieftain depended more upon his isolation than on conventional measures of strength. So long as outsiders neither knew of nor cared about Barra that power was absolute on the island and, if Martin Martin is to be believed, the Macneil (at least in the late seventeenth century) exercised it in a spirit of feudal beneficence.[2]

This happy isolation was shattered in 1728. Among those to scrutinise Barra and its harmlessly megalomaniac chieftain that year was George II, who at the end of August received a report which described the island and its unconventional administration in some detail. Barra, the writer observed with unconcealed disapproval, was "famous even in the Highlands for being barbarous" because its remoteness placed it beyond the normal rule of law. Civil jurisdiction was the prerogative of the sheriff at Inverness, but the great distance "& that too by sea" prevented the exercise of his authority there. The same applied to criminal law, for which the duke of Argyll or his deputy were responsible: courts would not be practicable, declared the report, "without carrying over such force as would be sufficient to maintain the authority of Judicial Proceedings".[3]

The flurry of royal interest was occasioned by a disaster which had taken place off the coast of Barra some months before. On the night of 24/25 March 1728 the Dutch East Indiaman *Adelaar* (*Eagle*), bound from Middelburg to Batavia, had been wrecked on the north-westerly tip of the island with the loss of all 220 on board. A day or so earlier she had been observed off North

Uist, in no apparent distress but sailing dangerously close to the lee shore in a light NNW wind. Sunday 24 March brought a shift of wind to the WSW which heralded a severe overnight storm from the NNW, and the following morning the inhabitants of the nearby village of Greian discovered the ship "intirely beat to pieces, and a great number of the Bodies & some goods floating on the Beech".[4] The ship had evidently attempted to weather Greian Head after becoming trapped in Scurrival Bay by the onshore gale. She just failed to make it, and struck an exposed complex of reefs only 200 yards from the point. Destruction was rapid and total, and for those on board there was little prospect of survival. Among the dead was a woman with two children tied to her, and a "young Gentlewoman, who had in her Breast between her Shift and her Skin, a Letter of Recommendation from her Mother to a Gentlewoman in the East Indies".[5]

The *Adelaar* had been built in the Middelburg yard of the Zeeland Chamber of the United East India Company (VOC) in 1722.[6] Her dimensions, standard for a medium-sized vessel on the Indies route, were (in Amsterdam feet of

Plate 1. Bronze swivel gun recovered from the *Adelaar* wreck site in 1972 (scale 30 cm). The A-VOC cipher on the barrel indicates that the gun originally belonged to the Amsterdam Chamber of the Company

283 mm): length 145 ft; beam 37 ft; and laden draught 15 ½ ft. Cargo capacity was 140 lasts (about 280 tons), which gave the ship a laden displacement of some 700 tons. To protect her from European enemies she carried 36 muzzle-loading guns – ten 12-pounders, twenty 6-pounders, and six 3-pounders. These were of Swedish cast iron except the two 6-pounders adjacent to the compass, which were bronze to reduce magnetic deviation.[7] Eight light breech-loading swivel guns of a type generally regarded as obsolete in Europe were mounted on her upper works, probably to counter the threat of small-boat piracy in Asian waters (Pl. 1).

Between 1722 and 1727 the *Adelaar* made two round trips to Batavia, the VOC's fortified trading post on the north coast of Java.[8] Both voyages were uneventful, with exceptionally low death rates on the outward legs of two and four respectively. In December 1727 the ship was commissioned for a third voyage under Willem de Keyser of Middelburg. It was to be his second command on this prestigious and lucrative run; in 1725/6 he had taken the *Everswaart* to Batavia and back. Early in 1728 Simon Pieter Trouillaert was appointed supercargo, the on-board merchant for the voyage. He would remain at Batavia in the company's service, and was to be accompanied by his wife and child. Other executive members of the crew included the three mates — Bartholomeus Stroobant of Vere (1st), Abraham Meinlever of Middelburg (2nd), and Pieter Bastiaanse of Middelburg (3rd). The surgeon was Jacobus Mierenheuvel of Zierikzee, and Daniel Thijsen of Vere was appointed *ziekentrooster,* or lay chaplain. About 20 passengers – mainly company officials and their families – also sailed with the ship.

60 company soldiers under Captain Pieter Jansen of Franeker were allocated to the *Adelaar* for protection during the voyage and subsequent service in the Indies. Their names and places of origin survive in a muster-roll, which indicates that each was allowed to take with him a chest of personal trade-goods. Only 21 were Dutch, most of the rest coming from Germany or the Southern Netherlands. Three died before the *Adelaar* sailed. Eight crafts-men – four carpenters, three stock-makers, and a sword-cutler – are included in the same list.

Information about the 120 seamen is less complete, being limited to those who wanted to allocate wages to dependants ashore or to people (usually women) from whom they had borrowed money to sponsor their trade chests. Nevertheless, 85 names are listed, with their origins. Dutchmen predominate, though sailors from Bergen, Stockholm, Jutland, Hamburg, Venice, Riga, Danzig, Bremen, Lubeck, Brandenburg, Revel, Copenhagen and the Levant are recorded. The ship's carpenter was Daniel More of Lerwick.[9]

The *Adelaar's* general cargo of cloth, domestic hardware, and tools was intended mainly for European consumption at the Cape and Batavia, while her paying ballast of yellow bricks and lead ingots would have been converted into colonial houses of a kind still to be seen in both places.[10] These items were, however, incidental to the main purpose of the voyage, which was to bring back spices, tea and porcelain for profitable sale in Europe. The most important commodity on the outward leg was cash for the return cargo.

On 6 March (New Style) Captain de Keyser and Supercargo Trouillaert received from the Zeeland Chamber 500 8-mark bars of silver, each stamped with the company monogram, six bars of gold, 32,000 ducatons struck that year at Middelburg, and 450,000 2-stuyver coins. They packed them into 17 numbered chests, after which "two locks were hung on each chest whereof the key of each lock from chest to chest was taken by us and sealed with our usual seal and further nailed round with sail cloth and bound with cords ...". The keys were placed in the last chest, No. 88, which contained the gold.[11] The two men also signed for 200 Spanish 8-real pieces for incidental expenses, and de Keyser took receipt of a portfolio of maps and pilot books for the voyage.[12] On 21 March (N.S.) the *Adelaar* sailed from the roadstead at Rammekens and headed into the North Sea intent on rounding the British Isles north-about, a route frequently chosen in favour of the more direct Channel passage because of the difficulty of beating against the prevailing wind. Two weeks later she struck Greian Head.

At the time the Macneil was in Harris, possibly courting his future bride.[13] A messenger was dispatched with the news and within 48 hours the chief was back on his island, having carefully bypassed the house of Alexander Macdonald of Boisdale at Kilbride on South Uist, close to the Barra ferry. Boisdale, the Macneil knew, had links with the shadowy authorities on the mainland and was clearly to be avoided; in any case the Barra Macneils and the Uist Clanranalds held each other in hereditary mistrust.[14] Once safely in Barra the Macneil placed guards on his own side of the ferry and ordered that no one was to enter or leave the island.

For a week the people of Barra gathered up what had been cast ashore and stripped the dead of valuables and clothing. By the following Sunday, however, timbers from the wrecked ship began to wash up on South Uist. Boisdale, his suspicions already aroused by the unprecedented lack of traffic from Barra, sent a boat to investigate. On its return with news of the wreck he mustered three boatloads of his kinsmen (as tacksman of the ling fishery on South Uist he had at his disposal a fleet of four-oared yoles) and crossed to Greian, determined to exercise his rights and responsibilities of substitute admiralty.[15]

These rights he held on behalf of Alexander Mackenzie, Younger of Delvine, a principal clerk of the court of session who was also admiral depute for the Western Isles. Mackenzie's authority in turn depended upon that of the high admiral of Scotland, the duke of Queensberry. The report set before George II notes that following the Act of Union in 1707 this office operated by virtue of a commission from the admiralty of England, and so was technically a vice-admiralty whose processes were under the ultimate review of the house of lords. The laws of admiralty were (and to some extent still are) complex and virtually uncodified, depending on custom and precedent for their execution.[16] Boisdale thus found himself responsible for administering law of which he had only the haziest knowledge on an island whose proprietor recognised no law but his own.

There was a tense and somewhat bizarre confrontation at the wreck site. The stripped corpses were still unburied after more than a week, and the Macneil informed Boisdale that "if he was to take the goods as Admiral, he behoved to carry the Bodies to Uist also". But after "a great deal of struigle", it was agreed that the Macneil should retain a third of what had been recovered and deliver the remainder to the substitute admiral. In the event the point was academic, for everything had been spirited away and no islander would admit to the slightest knowledge of where it might now be.

All this was duly reported by Boisdale in a letter to his superior in Edinburgh, Admiral Depute Alexander Mackenzie. But although the messenger left Uist on 15 April storms held him up for more than three weeks and he did not arrive at the capital until 25 May. Mackenzie sent him back bearing a letter to the Macneil defining his powers of admiralty, emphasising the penalties that unlawful salvage might incur, and demanding an account of everything that had been recovered. Boisdale was meanwhile ordered to pursue the affair with all vigour.

A few days later Mackenzie dispatched his brother-in-law Eugene Fotheringham, a Leith merchant and shipmaster, to Barra. When he reached the island – presumably with a bodyguard of Boisdale's Clanranalds – he found that the Macneil had gone "off to some Small Isles belonging to him on the south of Barra where he skulked as long as the Gentleman stayed in the Island", and of the island's population (estimated at around 1300 in the 1760s)[17] only three elderly people could be found. From them, however, Fotheringham obtained some documents which had come ashore from the wreck. He also made a careful survey of the site. Although he noted that it was "all surrounded with steep rocks inaccessible to the smallest boat, and the places where most was lying were so surrounded with rocks over which the sea broke even in the best weather as to make it almost impractical to get at these with any boat whatsoever", he also observed that much of the wreckage lay in four to six fathoms of clear water.

When Fotheringham returned to Edinburgh in mid-July Alexander Mackenzie learned the identity of the wreck and recognised its implications. Among the recovered papers was a copy of the receipt signed by de Keyser and Trouillaert for 200 8-real pieces, which named the *Adelaar* and her destination. The ship was clearly an outward-bound Dutch East Indiaman, and therefore almost certainly contained a great deal of treasure.[18]

Alexander Mackenzie now began drawing together a remarkable plan to effect its recovery. First he sought advice from Scotland's most senior lawyers,

Charles Erskine and Duncan Forbes of Culloden, solicitor-general and lord advocate respectively. In particular he asked their opinions on seven key matters:

1. Did the admiral depute have the right to demand an account of the goods already recovered? Could he arrest and imprison the Macneil and his people if they refused? Erskine was cautious about this; Forbes more assertive.

2. Did the admiral depute's jurisdiction override that of the sheriff in enforcing matters of admiralty law? Specifically, could he raise the lieges in order to enforce that law? This worried Erskine, who thought that such action could only be taken with the sheriff's direct authority and participation, but Forbes opined that no deputation from the sheriff was necessary if resistance to admiralty jurisdiction was anticipated.

3. Did the Dutch have any right to claim an interest in the wreck's salvage? If they had, could the admiral depute recover his expenses and a salvage reward? Both advisers believed that the Dutch had no such right but that even if they did expenses and salvage would still be payable.

4. What if the admiral depute engaged in salvage and the Dutch arrived on the scene with the same intention? Should he leave them to carry on alone, or co-operate with them in the enterprise? In either case, was it not his duty to take all recoveries into his custody until their legal status was determined? Erskine and Forbes agreed that the Dutch could not possess overriding powers in this respect, and that while collaboration might be possible (though they questioned its desirability in practice) all recoveries should remain in the admiral depute's custody until adjudication had taken place.

5. What if the Dutch came with authority to salvage signed by the king or council in London? There was firm agreement between the two Scots lawyers on this point: neither the king nor his ministers had the power to grant such authority without reference to the lords commissioners of admiralty and the vice-admiral in Scotland, so the situation could not arise.

6. How should the recovered goods be dealt with? The advisers thought that they should be converted into liquid assets by roup, and then disposed of according to admiralty law.

7. Would the king's duties be payable? No. The goods were wrecked rather than stranded, and therefore not liable to import taxes.[19]

Encouraged by this advice Mackenzie embarked upon his scheme to recover the treasure. He had few financial assets – as heir to the Delvine estate his resources were in anticipated property, not cash. But his rights of admiralty were, he believed, as good as money in the bank, for the issue of shares in the enterprise could buy all the services he required. He found a ready backer in Eugene Fotheringham, who put up most of the money in return for a fifth share of the gross recoveries.

A 25-ton sloop, the *Grizel* of Leith, was purchased and fitted out for sea under the command of John Hay. Fotheringham was made joint master and given a commission of substitute admiralty which empowered him to act independently on Mackenzie's behalf.[20] Since Barra "scarce affords the necessaries of life to the Inhabitants", the sloop was victualled for a long expedition – a supply of candles was the most expensive item – and to disguise its intentions a cargo of meal was loaded into the hold. Financial backing for the voyage and cargo was obtained from Alexander Tait, an Edinburgh merchant to whom Mackenzie was related on his mother's side. At this stage Tait was not apparently made aware of the venture's true purpose.[21]

Recovery of the treasure from the four to six fathoms in which it lay required divers, and through his association with admiralty matters Mackenzie knew that two Englishmen equipped with a patent diving "engine" were currently working on a Spanish Armada wreck off Fair Isle. At the end of July Fotheringham and Hay departed for the Northern Isles to seek out and engage the two wrackmen "on such terms as the Substitute should learn to be the practice in the like cases".[22]

The *Grizel* put into Stromness, and after some difficulty contact was made with the divers. They turned out to be Captain Jacob Rowe of London and his partner William Evans, a shipwright from Deptford. For some time they had been working with little success on the Fair Isle wreck under the mistaken impression that it was the Armada's flagship.[23] The expected treasure had failed to materialise, and they were receptive to the idea that they should join Mackenzie's expedition. But Rowe claimed exclusive rights "in all the British seas" for his diving engine, which he had patented in 1720, and drove a hard bargain.[24] On 19 August a contract was signed at Stromness which reserved Fotheringham's one fifth gross and gave a third of the remainder to Rowe and Evans, payable in kind on recovery. Costs were to be split equally between the parties. Rowe also insisted on using his own sloop, the *Charming Jenny*, for transporting his equipment and crew to Barra.[25]

Back in Edinburgh Mackenzie had been laying plans to neutralise any Macneil resistance to the salvage operation by invoking what he believed to be his right (reinforced by Forbes' opinion, but not by Erskine's) to call out the lieges in support of his admiralty jurisdiction on Barra. The lieges he had in mind were Boisdale's Clanranalds on South Uist and Benbecula, who were under obligation to him and his family. Ranald Macdonald, the late captain of Clanranald, had been out in the '15 and afterwards suffered forfeiture of his estates and exile at St. Germain. During the early 1720s Alexander Mackenzie's father John negotiated the restoration of the Clanranald estates, completing the process in 1725 (most of the intrigue and spade-work was

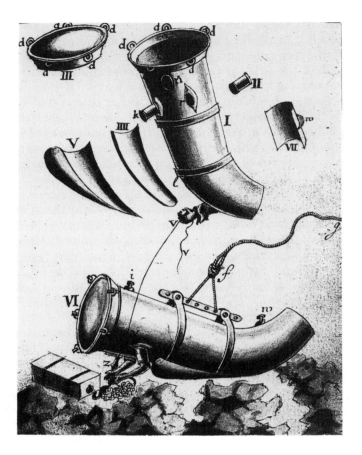

Plate 2. Jacob Rowe's diving engine of c. 1720, from a manuscript probably
attributable to Rowe himself (National Maritime Museum, MS 80/092).

actually conducted by Alexander, John remaining throughout ill and irascible
at Delvine). But before he could return Ranald died at St. Germain without
issue and the chieftainship passed to Donald Macdonald of Benbecula, who
was Alexander Macdonald of Boisdale's father.[26]

This connection enabled Alexander Mackenzie to mobilise 150 "Gentlemen in the Country of South Uist with their travelling weapons" for the Barra
expedition on a promise of £1,500. Because the Disarming Act of 1725
applied to all weapons save those worn by gentlemen for personal defence
on the road it seems clear that the words "gentlemen" and "travelling
weapons" were chosen with care to imply that the raised lieges were no more
than a body of gentry wearing legal sidearms for their journey to Barra in

support of law and order.[27] The reality was undoubtedly quite different – a pack of Clanranald hard-men led by their chieftain's younger son, dirks and pistols in their belts and broadswords on their backs, bent on repaying a family debt of honour with the added inducements of Dutch silver and a chance to mix it with the Macneils.

For Alexander Mackenzie, educated at St. Andrews for a legal career in Edinburgh and life on a Perthshire estate, the West Highlands were wild and unfamiliar territory. "As I want the language and am ignorant of the roads", he wrote to his brother Kenneth on 30 July, "I would wish to have a Discreet Pretty Fellow in my Company".[28] Soon afterwards he left for Barra with 20 companions including his brother John, George Fotheringham (another brother-in-law), and James Stewart, the Gaelic-speaking "Pretty Fellow" whose services he had sought. They probably travelled by Fort William (no doubt encountering General Wade's roadmakers on the way) and through Clanranald country to Loch nan Uamh before embarking for Canna.[29] There they remained windbound until Rowe and Eugene Fotheringham, who had already reached South Uist, heard of their plight and came to pick them up.[30] By late August everything was in place on Barra – the two provisioning sloops, Boisdale's private army, Mackenzie's deputation of admiralty, and Captain Rowe's diving engine. The outsmarted Macneil offered no resistance, though he subsequently exacted a modest revenge by selling boats and local produce to the expedition at inflated prices.[31]

In a manuscript of about 1720 – the date of his patent – Jacob Rowe described and illustrated his diving apparatus and set out workmanlike procedures for its use (Pl. 2).[32] Another description was published by Desaguliers in 1744, and some retrospective information appeared in the *Universal Magazine* a few years later.[33] The machine was a truncated vessel of brass or copper (some versions were built of wooden staves like a barrel) within which the diver lay prone. His arms protruded through sealed sleeves of copper and leather, and he looked down through a small glass port from which he cleared condensation with his nose. A watertight lid secured with butterfly nuts provided entry, and a quick exit if required. The rear part of the vessel was bent upwards to allow the machine to be operated in a slightly head-up attitude, so improving the diver's field of view and providing better arm-room when working on the bottom. It also kept water from gathering around his face in the event of a leak.

Enough lead ballast to create slightly negative buoyancy was fastened beneath the apparatus, which was then suspended by a rope from its mother craft. A life-line provided communication with the surface. The diver could be raised and lowered with relative ease as long as the buoyancy trim was correctly maintained, and this permitted the engine to be brought up from time to time so that air could be replenished through bung holes on its top by means of bellows. Under favourable conditions several hours of underwater work might be conducted in this way, with air changes at half-hourly intervals. For hauling the machine clear of the water, or bringing it up in a flooded condition, a block-and-tackle hoist was employed. Rather surprisingly no arrangement seems to have been made to allow the diver to jettison the ballast for an emergency bale-out.

In effect the engine was an armoured diving dress, although no protection was provided for the arms and the full differential between atmospheric pressure within the vessel and water pressure outside it would be felt on the diver's upper arms where they emerged from the sleeves. This naturally increased with depth. A further effect would be a tendency to push the diver's entire body by way of his arms against the top of the vessel, and a back-saddle was provided to counter this. Even at quite modest depths these effects would have been extremely unpleasant and disorienting, yet it is clear that such devices were frequently employed in up to 10 fathoms of water. But this was close to a diver's physiological limits. Desaguliers reported that Captain Irvin,[34] who dived for Rowe, experienced a strong stricture about his arms at 11 fathoms, and that "venturing two fathom lower to take up a lump of earth with Pieces of Eight sticking together; the circulation of his blood was so far stopped, and he suffered so much, that he was forced to keep his bed six weeks". Another diver died after reaching 14 fathoms.

Depth, however, was not a problem on the *Adelaar's* wreck. Practically everything, including the treasure, lay in less than six fathoms. But it was terribly exposed. The site is open to a 90 degree arc of uninterrupted Atlantic swell which breaks over the reef even when the rest of the sea appears calm. Archaeological investigations have shown that the main area of wreckage lies within a steep-sided gully immediately shoreward of the reef, and it is in here that the bulk of the 1728 operations must have been conducted (Fig. 1). Even with modern diving equipment the site is hazardous and unpredictable, prone to violent surges and explosions of white water as the sea breaks over the reef's central rock (Pl. 3). Rowe's cumbersome engine and its supporting boat would have been unimaginably difficult and dangerous to handle in such a situation, made worse by the tangle of masts and cordage which filled the gully, and "a great number of iron cannon two whereof lay on top of a rock which was dry at Low Water ...".[35]

All these difficulties were heroically overcome. During September, in spite of "a long track of bad weather upon ane high and inaccessible coast [Alexander Mackenzie] did with great hazard to his own & the lives of these Gentlemen Venture out in the Sloop along with the Divers and did cause dive and fish up the goods ..."[36] By the beginning of October the bulk of the *Adelaar's* treasure had been brought safely ashore.

Rowe and Mackenzie's affairs now called them from Barra, though they were "sensible that there were still more money and other valuable Effects which might be recovered". At Eriskay on 5 October instructions were given

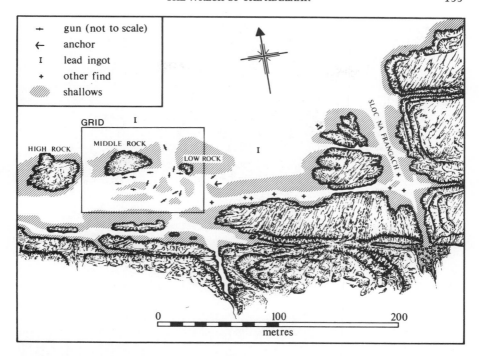

gun (not to scale)
anchor
I   lead ingot
+   other find
shallows

GRID   I

HIGH ROCK   MIDDLE ROCK   LOW ROCK   I

SLOC NA FRANGACH

0   100   200
metres

Figure 1. General survey of the *Adelaar* site compiled in 1972 and 1974. The arbitrary grid encloses the main area of wreckage.

to William Evans and John Hay to continue working on the wreck throughout the winter – a "melancholy prospect" for which they and their men were given extra financial inducements (on account, naturally). Regular reports were to be submitted to Mackenzie via Boisdale, who would keep them supplied with provisions and other necessities.[37] By the end of the month Mackenzie was back in Edinburgh with the recovered treasure, part at least of which was lodged in the Bank of Scotland.[38]

He was not at home on the morning of 28 October when James Lindsay, the admiral macer, thrust a summons into the lockhole of his front door and knocked "six several audible knocks" upon it. A similar document was delivered to the governor and directors of the Bank of Scotland in the "presence of the Tellers and others". The duke of Queensberry, to whom a third summons was to be delivered, was furth of Scotland, and so "three several oysses" for him were cried at the Mercat Cross of Edinburgh and on the pier and shore of Leith.[39] The lords directors of the VOC's Zeeland Chamber and their factor, William Drummond, were suing the lord admiral of Scotland and his deputy in their own court for the restitution of the recovered treasure.[40]

In May reports of the *Adelaar's* loss had reached the VOC's agent in London,

Plate 3. Maolach Sgeir photographed from Greian Head during a north-westerly storm. The remains of the *Adelaar* lie between the reef complex and the shore.

Gerard Bolwerk, and he had passed the information to Middelburg. Mackenzie later claimed to have informed the Dutch at an early stage with a view to co-operating with them, but that his approaches had been ignored.[41] In any event the VOC was slow to respond and it was not until August that a Scottish shipmaster, David Stephenson, was engaged by the directors of the Zeeland Chamber to prosecute their interests in Barra. William Drummond of Grange, whose brother John was a director of the English East India Company, was appointed the VOC's factor in Edinburgh.[42]

Meanwhile the Dutch envoy in London sought and obtained letters of protection from the king through Lord Townshend. These stated what less than a month earlier the solicitor-general and lord advocate of Scotland had so confidently asserted could not be stated – that it was proper "to show the readiness of the Ministry to assist the Dutch India Company, that a Letter be writ to the Duke of Queensberry that he may order his Deputies to give those

who the Dutch shall employ all the Countenance & protection they can... .
Mr. Wade likewise may be ordered, in case it may be necessary to send some
Soldiers aboard the Vessels employed in this business to protect the Dutch
from any insults in case they should land in that or any adjacent Island ..."[43]
By then of course it was too late – perhaps fortunately so. What might have
been the outcome had Wade's troops, charged with upholding foreign
interests on behalf of the crown, come face to face with armed Clanranalds
whose clear duty was to maintain the authority of Scotland's admiralty?

The resolution of the main case before Judge James Graham of Airth took
30 days of court sittings and lasted from 6 November 1728 to 11 July the
following year.[44] Charles Erskine, the solicitor-general, led for the VOC,
assisted by Patrick Grant and others. Alexander Mackenzie's defence was
conducted by Hugh Forbes, Robert Dundas and others, including his brother
Kenneth. At first Mackenzie was eqivocal about what he had recovered, but
in response to a court order of 10 December he admitted to possessing 328
bars of silver, 59 bags of double-styvers, and 300 ducatons. These assets were
lodged in the bank and frozen, mutually exclusive keys being held by
Mackenzie, Drummond, and the clerk of court. The silver was assayed and
the ducatons valued at 5s. 6d. sterling apiece. From the outset the VOC
asserted its right to the treasure in full but accepted that Mackenzie's expenses
and a salvage reward should be paid. The Dutch argument focused on the
extent of those expenses, profound dissatisfaction with Mackenzie's cavalier
approach to accounting, and a well-founded suspicion that not all the
treasure had been declared.

Although the lord admiral and the Bank of Scotland were technically his
co-defendants, Alexander Mackenzie was for all practical purposes on his
own. At first he sought to demolish the Dutch claim in its entirety. What
proof was there that this ship had been the *Adelaar?* Moreover, since no living
creature had survived to maintain continuity of possession, had the vessel
not irrevocably been abandoned by its owners? On both grounds, he argued,
his claim was unassailable.

The VOC countered the first argument by pointing out that documents
recovered from the wreck included receipts signed by the captain and
supercargo of the *Adelaar*. These matched corresponding papers filed ashore,
which were produced together with attested copies in English. Mackenzie's
counsel riposted that this did not amount to proof, pointing out that the wreck
had also yielded a muster-roll of soldiers from a quite different ship. The
remains off Barra could have been, for all he knew, those of a merchantman
from Hamburg, or the East India Company of Ostend.

The question of abandonment gave rise to some nice legal debate. All
agreed that no one had survived the wreck, and much consideration was
given to the status of a hypothetical dog had it come ashore alive. Would it,
until relieved of the burden by the arrival of a VOC representative, have

Plate 4. Wax impressions of the 1728 VOC ducaton from dies at the Zeeland mint, produced in evidence during the *Adelaar* case (Scottish Record Office, ex. AC 9/1203)

retained possession of the company's interests? If so, would the same have applied had the survivor been a cat, or a mouse? Reference was made to a precedent set in 1622 when an ox, as the sole survivor of a shipwreck, was adjudged to have maintained a continuity of ownership "because by the Ox the Owners may be known".[45]

Resolution of both questions came from Middelburg on the backs of two playing cards. They bore obverse and reverse impressions in sealing wax of dies used to strike ducatons that year in Zeeland (Pl. 4). The issues of 1728 were the first coins to bear the Company's bale-mark, which they carried on the reverse. The *Adelaar's* consignment of 32,000 ducatons was made up exclusively of such coins, and no other vessel on which similar coins had been shipped was unaccounted for.[46] "Without any foreign assistance", the concluding argument ran, "the specie bears unbiased witness of the property in question and at the same time affords a proof who are owners of the ship". Continuity of ownership could be maintained by inanimate objects as well as by living creatures, argued the VOC: they had "neither given away nor deserted their right nor had they done any deed or committed any delinquency upon which the same had become forfeited ...".[47] The court accepted both points.

Because so many aspects of the case were unprecedented – not least the use of diving apparatus to effect the recoveries – much legal time was spent in a careful study of maritime codes from Rhodian Law onwards. An act passed by James I in 1429 which laid down that a foreign ship wrecked in Scotland should be treated as a Scottish ship would be treated if lost on the shores of the wrecked ship's nation was regarded as particularly significant by both sides. However, as no precedent involving a Scottish ship wrecked in Zeeland could be found, there was much scope for disagreement. The VOC's counsel naturally emphasised the friendly generosity with which a Zeeland court would view such a situation; equally predictably, Mackenzie's lawyers sought to argue that the Dutch would sieze everything for themselves. Judgement was eventually made in the VOC's favour, with expenses and salvage deductable to the defendants.

The question of determining the extent of these now arose. Captain Rowe had already been paid his full due of £6,266. 13s. 4d. ("there was no cheapening the matter with him"), and the other claims were as follows:

To purchasing a ship and cargo for fishing the wreck £900
To maintaining and paying a guard for six weeks £1,500
To gratifications to several gentlemen in the neighbourhood for their assistance £1,000
To two shipmasters for their pains and service £600
To 25 sailors £660
To charges of advising lawyers £1,000
To incident charges £2,000

which gave a grand total of £13,926. 13s. 4d. The value of the recovered treasure, Mackenzie claimed, was £14,659, of which he by the court's direction already held 20,000 ducatons (this represented, presumably, the bulk of Rowe's and Evans's share, which had already been disbursed).[48]

The VOC strongly disputed these figures, arguing that "the Defender should be more particular ... even though he had thought himself not accountable [to any but himself]". What judge in the world, for example, "can tell whether £1,500 is a Rational expense for maintaining and paying a Guard without he were first informed what sort of a Guard this was, what numbers they consisted of, how many days they Served and where...".[49] After heavy pressure from the court Mackenzie admitted in April 1729 to an additional 10,000 ducatons, 172 silver bars, and the six bars of gold. This accounted for the ingot specie in full, and left a shortfall of only 1,700 of the 32,000 ducatons and £3,845-worth of the £45,000 in double stuyvers. The total estimate of the recovered treasure's value now stood at £23,500.[50]

In response to the VOC's attempts to obtain more specific accounts Mackenzie eventually confessed that none existed: by "laying out of my money in this project I can from Compareing of what remains of my Cash know what I really & Effectually Expended from the beginning to the Conclusion of the Expedition ..."[51] In the face of such ingenuous candour no further argument was possible, and final judgement was passed. Mackenzie received £8,800 for his expenses and a £3,000 salvage award. In strictly legal terms it was not unfair, though hardly generous. There may have been political factors working against him: as a landowner with Highland connections he would have been considered inherently Tory and possibly Jacobite in his leanings. At an early stage in the proceedings Solicitor-General Erskine launched a Whiggish diatribe against him, urging that "the King whose Court this is" should have "full Satisfaction given to his Allies" especially as the defendant was himself "ane officer under the Crown".[52] It cannot have helped Mackenzie's case.

Nevertheless, the VOC was required to pay the costs of the suit, including ten per cent sentence money, though it was entitled to retain the balance. The treasure was not, however, immediately released. While the case had been proceeding, a counter-suit against the VOC was lodged by Captain Alexander Hamilton, who claimed that his ship had been confiscated by the Dutch seventeen years earlier for alleged opium trafficking in the East Indies.[53] His suit was eventually rejected by the lords on 4 April 1732, after which the *Adelaar's* much depleted treasure returned to Holland.[54]

Without doubt Alexander Mackenzie lost heavily on the judgement. His catalogue of expenses, though clearly in part fictitious, concealed monstrous financial naivety and a propensity, in the excitement and urgency of events, to make promises and payments which he could often neither honour nor afford. Rowe's share alone had accounted for more than 75 per cent of his expenses. As for his £3,000 salvage award, more than half evaporated into the pocket of the duke of Queensberry who, though he had resigned from office following the court scandal caused by his eccentric wife Kitty's support for John Gay's banned play *Polly*, nevertheless claimed his admiral's due of £1,500, plus £300 "liquidat expenses". Reluctantly, Mackenzie paid up.[55] A final twist was an attempt by the lord advocate, Duncan Forbes, to exact 10 per cent of the recovered treasure on behalf of the crown. This claim was based on the terms of Rowe's patent, and – happily for Mackenzie – it was not sustained.[56]

Other creditors were less fortunate. Perhaps because of family ties Eugene Fotheringham laid no claim in court to his promised fifth, but Alexander Tait, who had sponsored the voyage to Barra in ignorance of its true purpose, vigorously pursued a claim of £1,000. Although he eventually reduced this to £500, it was still unpaid by 1730 when he was seeking damages as well.[57]

Mackenzie's financial embarrassment and the dashing of his expectations undoubtedly lay behind the harsh (and in the circumstances hypocritical) attitude he adopted towards his former associates, John Hay and William Evans, who had been left on Barra with two dozen men to continue working over the winter. They had endured considerable hardships. From October to May they lived in rented hovels on the exposed coast at Cliad with only deal planks for bedding, burning 725 creel-loads of peat to keep warm. They could only get to the wreck during rare periods of relative calm and, with the

Charming Jenny and the open salvage yoles hauled beyond the beach for security, at the immense labour of dragging the boats and equipment to and from the water's edge. In all, according to Hay's account, they recovered 5,951 ducatons, as well as lead ingots, cordage, brass, ironware, and some broken casks of rotten meat. Boisdale had kept them supplied with meal, ling, cheese, tobacco, salt, and cattle on the hoof, and from the locals they purchased hens, eggs, milk, mutton, potatoes and cabbages. Despite later accusations of "liveing extravagantly", their only luxury appears to have been three dozen bottles of wine which they obtained in January from John MacLeod, who had connections with Belfast.[58]

On 12 November David Stephenson's sloop came to Barra bearing "Mr Peter Richards a diver arrived here from London with permissable letters from his Grace the Duke of Queensberry to take a view or state of the wrack for account of the Dutch East India Company he tarried here till the 14th being very bad weather saw the foulness of the coast took a draught of the west side of the Island Barra and then returned without makeing further enquiry". Richards was the assistant of Jacob Rowe's rival and former associate, John Lethbridge, who had recently carried out successful salvage work for the VOC off Madeira.[59] He correctly surmised that little remained to be done in Barra, and that the VOC's best prospects for recovery lay in the more congenial surroundings of the courts.

Eugene Fotheringham brought the *Grizel* to Eriskay on 28 March 1729 where delivery was taken of 1,530 ducatons, a balance being retained by Hay and Evans according to their interpretation of the previous October's agreement.[60] Another 1,800 ducatons were secreted in the bottom of a barrel of nails aboard the *Grizel*, which set sail for Peterhead on 13 April.[61] Some days later the *Charming Jenny* was hauled down from her winter berthing and on 12 May the salvors departed for Peterhead. From there Evans went on to London, while Hay remained with the ship.[62]

Fotheringham left for Edinburgh on 5 June, and four days later Jacob Rowe touched briefly at Peterhead before taking a herring buss for Stromness, accompanied by Hunter of Lena, one of the divers. On the voyage, Rowe later claimed, Hunter told him that Hay and Evans had conspired to bring home 1,800 ducatons clandestinely in a cask of nails. He also spoke of a number of undeclared Spanish dollars.[63] Further allegations of irregularity followed the discovery of a letter from John Forbes, another of the sailors on Barra, to his brother Thomas in Peterhead. On his return, Forbes wrote, he hoped "to Settle my Self in Some business either Abroad or at home", and in a postscript he claimed to have "brought up at one time in the Enjoine £60 had $\frac{1}{20}$ part to my Self".[64] Finally, it was alleged that when Hay arrived at Leith and was confronted by Mackenzie in John Fentoun's yard, he refused to declare his recoveries and settle matters "in an Aimiable Manner".[65]

On the basis of these claims Mackenzie and Rowe brought actions against

Hay and Evans. John Forbes of Peterhead, who was 22, was persuaded to give evidence against his former shipmates – as a common sailor he had not been authorised to dive in the engine, and was threatened with action if he did not co-operate. He attested that "ane day when they Drag'd up some money Hunter of Lena stood by haveing on him a pair of wide sailors bretchers with pockets in them into which Evans from time to time clandestinely put his hands-full of money".[66] Another sailor, James Sinclair, who at 67 seems rather old to have been engaging in this sort of thing, supported Forbes' testimony.[67] But the questioning was leading and full of innuendo. Ingenious but dubious attempts were made to calculate a higher figure than that admitted by Hay and Evans. The dimensions of the boxes and other containers (including a tea caddy) into which the ducatons had been gathered, how often they had been filled and to what extent, were minutely considered by the court. Four or five loads of "louse money ... carried home on Highland mens backs to their quarters" were miraculously quantified to the last coin. But even on this questionable evidence it could only be concluded that 128 ducatons remained unaccounted for.[68]

Hay had in any case already specified his recoveries in full to Alexander Mackenzie's uncle: he had not declared them at the meeting in John Fentoun's yard, he explained, because he "did not think that Mr McKenzie in that Temper would bear me wth patience". As to the "Little Matter" of the ducatons in the barrel of nails, Hay continued, the subterfuge had been instigated by Mackenzie himself, "Desireing that all things should be kep't quiet ... till I am settled with the Dutch".[69] Mackenzie won his suit, though Hay successfully counter-claimed for his not inconsiderable expenses and 14 months back pay.[70] But Mackenzie, convinced that far larger sums were being hidden from him, continued to hound Hay and Evans. No doubt there had been some embezzlement – it would be out of keeping with human nature to suppose otherwise – but it cannot have been great. Mackenzie's own testimony shows that the bulk of the treasure had been recovered when he left Barra in October 1728, and that he knew there was little more still to find nine months later is evident from his favourable response to a request by the Macneil of Barra, written on 30 June 1729, for permission to fish "on all wrecks in his bounds", including the *Adelaar*.[71]

On 28 January 1730 William Evans wrote to Mackenzie from Deptford with undisguised contempt and anger on hearing of "Mr. Hay's malicious and undeserved imprisonment, he being a man that has stood up soe much for your honour and reputation far beyound what you deserved ... in my opinion you are not capable of making him satisfaction for the service he has done you and the heard ship he has suffered in your Dishonorable service ...".[72] By then Mackenzie, even had he wished it, was in no position to give satisfaction to anyone. The previous year, in a desperate attempt to recover his fortune, he had used his rights of admiralty together with those granted by Charles I to the duke of Argyll in respect of the Tobermory wreck, to engage with Captain Rowe in a venture to recover its elusive (because illusory) treasure. It had ended in total failure and a new crop of debts.[73] "...if I once had wrought my way out of this perhaps I will take a little more care of myself in time comeing", he wrote despairingly to his brother John on 23 April 1731, "& I hope you may also learn a lesson from it also with this advantage that it is not att your own but my Expense that you'll grow wise ...".[74]

Alexander Mackenzie inherited Delvine in 1731, but with annuities payable to twelve surviving siblings (eight of them sisters, including five who never married) and a mother who was to outlive him, his finances were beyond recovery. The estate was transferred to John before he died at the age of 42, bankrupt and blind, in 1737.[75]

Jacob Rowe and William Evans, who had had the good sense to take their share in cash before they left Barra, fared rather better. But they fell out with one another over the division of expenses within their partnership, while Evans was sued by Captain Simon Fraser of Broadland, who had been an investor in the abandoned Fair Isle venture and now not unreasonably sought a cut of the Barra profits.[76] A more unusual claim was put in by Robert Sinclair of Quendale, another of the Fair Isle investors, who had agreed to join the Barra expedition as a third sharer with Rowe and Evans. But his business in Shetland as a commissioner of supply delayed him and he missed the rendezvous at Orkney because the English ship he had engaged to take him there did not sight land until they reached Flamborough Head. From there a collier brought him to Newcastle, where he boarded a ship bound for Fraserburgh. Three months after signing the agreement he caught up with events in Edinburgh just as the *Adelaar* action was getting under way, and determined to seek a slice for himself. Rowe settled out of court and Sinclair got £120 "in consideration of the damage I entertained and danger I underwent in endeavouring to play my part in the said agreement".[77]

Alexander Macdonald of Boisdale stood briefly in the spotlight of history in 1745 as the man "who spoke very discouragingly" to the Young Pretender when he landed on Eriskay, and refused to bring the Clanranalds out in the Jacobite cause.[78] When the prince was on the run in South Uist the following year, however, Boisdale helped him, and spent a night drinking with him in the cave at Coradale.[79] For his alleged Jacobite sympathies Boisdale was held prisoner in London, together with the Macneil of Barra. In common adversity they may (one hopes) have forgotten former differences and reflected upon a changing world. Both were to lose sons fifteen years later in Canada, fighting in Fraser's Regiment for an empire and a cause which their fathers, in their own youth, could scarcely have comprehended.

The *Adelaar* site was rediscovered and investigated by the fledgling Scottish Institute of Maritime Studies in 1972 and 1974 (Pl. 5). This essay is offered in recognition of Christopher Smout's many contributions towards making

Plate 5. Lead ingots from the *Adelaar* in a gully bottom off Maolach Sgeir.

the Institute a focus of interdisciplinary studies into humankind's relationship with the sea. It also seeks to illustrate his belief, so amply demonstrated by his work, that within the chaos of history (as of shipwrecks) there are threads which can be drawn together. On occasion such connections can be very close to home. Alexander Mackenzie and his younger brothers, Kenneth and Thomas, matriculated at St. Andrews University in 1711 and have left a remarkable record of their years there.[80] Kenneth, moreover, went on to become professor of law at the University of Edinburgh, and to found a cadet branch of his family at Dolphington in Lanarkshire.[81] In October 1991 the daughter of a Dolphington Mackenzie matriculated at St. Andrews, so completing a 280-year circle of historical coincidence.

Notes

Dates are Old Style unless otherwise indicated, while monetary values other than Dutch ones are expressed in Sterling.

1. Moncreiffe of that Ilk, in his foreword to R.L. Macneil, *Castle in the Sea* (London and Glasgow, 1964), 6.
2. Martin Martin, *A Description of the Western Highlands of Scotland* (Glasgow, 1884), 91–100.

3. Public Record Office [PRO], SP 100/24/685.

4. National Library of Scotland [NLS], MS 1490/6–7.

5. *Caledonian Mercury*, 1 July 1728.

6. The *Adelaar's* history and statistics were kindly extracted from the Algemeen Rijksarchief [ARA] in The Hague and summarised for me by Dr. E.S. van Eijck van Heslinga, through the good offices of Professor J.R.Bruijn. The main sources are ARA, KA (Kamer Zeeland) 4006/8316 (papers concerning the *Adelaar* process, 1728– 1735); ARA, KA 18 and 19 (minutes of the Zeeland Chamber); ARA, KA 4390 and 4390a ("Uitloopregister" of the VOC); and ARA, KA (Collectie Radermacher) 84. There is a contemporary model of the ships *Padmos* and *Blydorp*, built in 1722 to the same specifications and dimensions as the *Adelaar*, in the Prins Hendrik Maritime Museum, Rotterdam.

7. The trunnion faces of cast-iron guns examined on the *Adelaar* wreck site in 1972 bear the distinctive "F" mark of the Finspong foundry. One of the bronze 6-pounders was recovered in 1728, the other in 1972, together with one of the swivel guns.

8. For the workings and historical background of the Dutch East India Company see Kristof Glamann, *Dutch-Asiatic Trade, 1620–1740* (Copenhagen and The Hague, 1958), and C.R. Boxer, *The Dutch Seaborne Empire* (London, 1965).

9. The *Adelaar's* muster-lists were kindly obtained for me by Ms. Lous Zuiderbaan. They are from ARA, KA (Kamer Zeeland) 9370 (soldier-roll); *ibid.*, 9439 (soldiers' payment roll); and *ibid.*, 9814 (sailors' request-book).

10. Full cargo lists, with attested English translations, are preserved among the warrants of the *Adelaar* litigation: Scottish Record Office [SRO], AC 9/1203/72 (original) and /73 (translation) includes cloth, clothing, and soldiers' accoutrements; while *ibid.*, /76 (original) and /75 (translation) lists hardware, tools, and building materials.

11. SRO, AC 9/1203/74 (original) and /71 (translation) is the ship's inventory of specie. This document is of numismatic significance as the only surviving example of its kind. Treasure was supplied to VOC ships by outside contractors, so detailed bills of lading were not held by the company, which noted only the total sum consigned to each vessel. Its production in court and subsequent deposition renders this one unique. See A. Pol, "Tot gerieff van India: Geldexport door de VOC en de muntproduktie in Nederland, 1720–1740", *Jaarboek voor Munt-en Penningkunde*, 72 (1985), 65–195, and A. Pol, "For the Convenience of the Indies: Coin Production in 18th-Century Holland for Internal Circulation and for Exportation", in I.A. Carradice (ed.), *Proceedings of the 10th International Congress of Numismatics* (London, 1986), 583–89. I am grateful to Dr. Pol for pointing out to me the significance of this document.

12. SRO, AC 9/1203/79 and /81.

13. NLS, MS 1490/6–7. Roderick Macneil (1693–1763), 39th by the family's reckoning (though this has been disputed), was nicknamed "Dove of the West" because of his kindness and charm of manner. He married Alice MacLeod of Luskintyre (A. Mackenzie, *History of the MacLeods* [Inverness, 1889], 245–6), probably about 1728, since their only son Roderick was born in 1730, as his matriculation record at Aberdeen University shows (pers. comm., Professor Ian Macneil of Barra). It is not known when Roderick 39th succeeded, although his father, Roderick Dubh, was alive in 1717 and had died by 1745 (Macneil, *Castle in the Sea*, 113–14). Professor Macneil, the present chief, believes that the Harris connection makes it virtually certain that the Macneil of our story was indeed Roderick 39th.

14. The Clanranald Macdonalds drove the Macneils from their South Uist lands in 1601, though in 1653 Gilleonan, Roderick 39th's grandfather, married Clanranald's daughter Catherine (*ibid.*, 118).

15. NLS, MS 1490/6–7. Details of the ling fishery in 1764 (four years before Boisdale's

death) are provided in Margaret M. McKay (ed.), *The Rev. John Walker's Report on the Hebrides of 1764 and 1761* (Edinburgh, 1980), 81–82.

16.   PRO, SP 100/24/685. This contemporary perception of the Scottish admiralty from a Westminster viewpoint is at odds with a description of the office given in the introduction to the SRO's admiralty court catalogue, which notes that "Clause 19 of the Treaty of Union provided for the continuance of the Court of Admiralty in Scotland, with the same powers and subject to the like review of its judgements, until the Parliament of the United Kingdom should make such regulations and alterations as should be judged expedient for the whole kingdom". In 1830 the admiralty court of Scotland was subsumed by the court of session where, in 1972, my colleagues and I brought an action against interlopers who sought to contest our possession of the *Adelaar* wreck site. They withdrew before a judgement was given.

17.   McKay, introduction to *Walker's Report*, 26.

18.   See n. 11 above. The other recovered document (SRO, AC 9/1203/82–3) was a soldier-roll for the VOC ship *Noordvreek*. Fotheringham is named as the agent sent to Barra in SRO, AC 9/1203/33/7.

19.   NLS, MS 1490/3 (Alexander Mackenzie's "Quaries anent the Eagle of Zeland"); *ibid.*, /4 and /33 for Erskine's and Forbes' answers on 5 August and 27 July respectively.

20.   SRO, AC 8/393.

21.   NLS, MS 1490/18 ("outrige in the Grizle sloup"); *ibid.*, /85 and /86 for Tait's involvement and the cargo of meal.

22.   SRO, AC 7/37/482.

23.   SRO, AC 8/392 (Jacob Rowe vs. William Evans). The Fair Isle wreck was that of *El Gran Grifón*, flagship of the Armada's squadron of supply ships; see Colin Martin, *Full Fathom Five: The Wrecks of the Spanish Armada* (London, 1975), 160–64.

24.   Patent No. 431, 1720. The rights on his invention were exclusive until 1734.

25.   SRO, AC 8/393; AC 7/37/482–3.

26.   A. Mackenzie, *History of the Macdonalds and Lords of the Isles* (Inverness, 1881), 427–28. The negotiations were conducted on behalf of the exiled Ranald Macdonald of Clanranald by Mrs. Penelope Macdonald (née Mackenzie), widow of his elder brother Allan who was killed at Sheriffmuir. Various letters from Alexander Mackenzie to his father John concerning these matters are preserved among the Delvine Papers (see esp. NLS, MS 1128/207).

27.   SRO, AC 7/37/483. For the Disarming Act, see William Taylor, *The Military Roads in Scotland* (Newton Abbot, 1976), 18–20. As one of the conditions of Clanranald's restoration Alexander Macdonald of Boisdale was present at the surrender of arms to General Wade's troops at Castle Brahan on 28 August 1725 (NLS, MS 1128/236). It is probable that, in line with others who were not active Hanoverian supporters, he handed over no more than a token number of weapons, perhaps unserviceable ones imported as scrap for the purpose (Bruce Lenman, *The Jacobite Risings in Britain 1689–1746* [London, 1980], 210).

28.   NLS, MS 1128/390.

29.   On 20 July 1728 Wade was at Blair Atholl, from where he wrote to Henry Pelham that "I am now with all possible dilligence carrying on the new road for wheel-carriages between Dunkeld and Inverness ..." (NLS, MS 7187/102). Richard Graham, writing to Alexander Mackenzie from Glasgow on 15 October 1729 about the best route to Mull, notes that "you have Genll Wades new roads all the way to Fort Wm " (NLS, MS 1491/75). Loch nan Uamh was the usual point of departure for the Outer Isles – cf. the itinerary of Prince Charles Edward in 1745–6 – while Canna with its "fine Harbour: much frequented by the Ships which pass through the Hebrides"

(McKay, *Walker's Report*, 229) was an important staging-point on the route.

30. SRO, AC 7 37/483.
31. SRO, AC 9/1142/9; AC 7/37/484.
32. National Maritime Museum, MS 80/092.
33. J.T. Desaguliers, *A Course in Experimental Philosopy* (London, 1744), ii, 215 and Plate XX; *Universal Magazine*, 13 (September 1753), 128–29.
34. Probably William Irvine, customs inspector at Lerwick.
35. NLS, MS 1490/6–7. A folk-memory of the wreck and its location is recorded by John MacPherson, *Tales of Barra told by the Coddy* (Edinburgh, 1960), 123. The Coddy named the spot "Mollachdag", which he translates as "the cursed rock", although Mr. Malcolm McAulay of Castlebay has informed me that it is more properly known as "Maolach Sgeir", or "the cursed reef". The location of the reef was pointed out to my colleagues Chris Oldfield, Simon Martin and Tony Long by Mr. John MacLean of Cliad and there, on 23 March 1972, they found the *Adelaar's* remains. It is appropriate here to acknowledge with gratitude the work they subsequently put into the project, and additionally to thank my brother Simon for his help with research.
36. SRO, AC 7/37/484–5.
37. NLS, MS 1490/9–10.
38. SRO, AC 7/37/485.
39. SRO, AC 9/1203/4–6.
40. SRO, AC 1203/33.
41. *Ibid.*, /33.
42. SRO, GD 24/1/464 D (Abercairny Muniments) fo. 69 forward contains extensive correspondence from William to John Drummond about the case.
43. PRO, SP 100/24/685.
44. The action is documented in SRO, AC 7/37/450–710 (Decreets) and AC 9/1203/1–86 (Warrants). AC 9/1203/85 lists the diets of court, while *ibid.*, /32 and /33, which are printed pamphlets, summarise the arguments of the VOC and Alexander Mackenzie respectively. There is another account of the case in NLS, MS 1192/1–287.
45. SRO, AC 1203/32/17. That a dog could be vested with legal rights and responsibilities is clear from an action brought by Lord Tankerville in the 1740s against "a dog – the property of the Earl of Home", which he accused of salmon poaching. The dog won (Lord Home, *Border Reflections* [London, 1979], 16–17).
46. SRO, AC 7/37/466 makes it clear that all the officially consigned ducatons had been struck in 1728. Not one of the 28 ducatons recovered by ourselves in 1972 and 1974, or the 10 delivered to the receiver of wreck by our rivals in 1972 (report by Dr R.B.K. Stevenson), carries this date. It seems likely that the full consignment, still probably packed in its boxes, was recovered in 1728. All other ducatons on the ship will therefore have been "unofficial", and hence illegal, because – as Dr. Arent Pol informs me – the ducaton was at this period exclusively reserved for the East Indies trade.
47. SRO, AC 7/37/503 and /513.
48. SRO, AC 9/1203/44.
49. *Ibid.*, /50.
50. *Ibid.*, /39.
51. SRO, AC 1203/53.
52. *Ibid.*, /34.
53. SRO, AC 7/36/24.
54. SRO, AC 9/1203/63.
55. NLS, MS 1490/83. The *Polly* episode, which caused Queensberry to resign the

admiralty of Scotland, is described in Romney Sedgwick (ed.), *Lord Hervey's Memoirs* (London, 1952), 52–54.

56. SRO, AC 9/1203/35–6.

57. NLS, MS 1490/86.

58. NLS, MS 1490/21–23 (John Hay's Barra Journal from 7 October 1728 to 29 April 1729); SRO, AC 9/1142/9 (Hay's claim of expenditure and dues for the same period). There was much argument as to the authenticity of these documents. The Journal is sufficiently dog-eared to carry conviction, while the tendency of Hay's writing to deteriorate as the weather he recorded became increasingly awful can scarcely have been contrived. Moreover, he accurately describes, without understanding what was happening, the lunar eclipse of 3 February 1728/9. His list of payments, on the other hand, is undoubtedly a subsequent compilation, though the outlays seem reasonable enough. The mention of potatoes on Barra in 1728 is interesting – this is 15 years before the earliest reference to the vegetable previously known for the Outer Isles (T.C. Smout, *A History of the Scottish People 1560–1630* [London, 1969], 251–52). Quite substantial quantities ($4\frac{1}{2}$ bolls in total) were involved. That the divers were accommodated in traditional black houses is evident from frequent mention of clay to repair the hearths (cf. T.C. Smout, *A Century of the Scottish People 1830–1950* [London, 1986,], 79).

59. Hay's Journal (see n. 58), 27 November 1728. Lethbridge possessed diving apparatus similar to Rowe's, and claimed to have invented it first (*Gentleman's Magazine*, 19 [1749], 411). Rowe hotly disputed this, and on 20 November 1728 (NLS, MS 1491/92–93) wrote that his patent "hath lately been invaded by one John Lethbridge, who formerly was my servant; but now is in the service of the Dutch". For Lethbridge's career see John S. Amery, "John Lethbridge and his Diving – machine", *Transactions of the Devonshire Association*, 12 (1880), 489–96, and Zelide Cowan, "John Lethbridge, Diver", *History Today*, 28 (December 1978), 825–29. The Madeira wreck was that of the *Slot ter Hooge*, also of the Zeeland Chamber, which was lost off Porto Santo in 1724. The site was rediscovered in the early 1970s (Robert Sténuit, "The Treasure of Porto Santo", *National Geographic*, 148, 2 [August 1975], 260–75). Among Sténuit's recoveries were silver bars stamped with the Zeeland Chamber's monogram, presumably similar to those shipped aboard the *Adelaar* four years later. Dr. Sténuit had himself intended to search for the *Adelaar's* remains, but when he heard that I and my colleagues had found them he not only withdrew his interest but also most generously provided us with the fruits of his own researches.

60. NLS, MS 1490/21–32 (Hay's Journal).

61. *Ibid.*, /87.

62. SRO, AC 9/1105/3 and /6; NLS, MS 1490/21–32.

63. SRO, AC 9/1105/7.

64. SRO, AC 9/1105/4, 2 February 1729.

65. SRO, AC 9/1105/3.

66. NLS, MS 1490/90.

67. NLS, MS 1490/92.

68. NLS, MS 1490/88.

69. SRO, AC 9/1105/6.

70. SRO, AC 9/1142.

71. NLS, MS 1128/405.

72. NLS, MS 1490/227.

73. NLS, MS 1491/96–113. For an account of the Tobermory venture see Alison McLeay, *The Tobermory Treasure* (London, 1986), 49–65.

74. NLS, MS 1128/347.

75. The final years are chronicled by his wife in her letters to his brother John (NLS, MS 1129/1–65). On his death Alexander Mackenzie's debts exceeded his funds by £469. 6s. 9d. (NLS, MS 1129/300–03). Delvine was transferred to John in February 1736 (NLS, MS 1128/285–98), who became a noted improving landlord (*Old Statistical Account*, 9, XXXIII (Caputh), 496), founding the planned village of Spittalfield (R.N. Millman, *The Making of the Scottish Landscape* [London, 1975], 107 and 159). In happier circumstances Alexander might have done the same. He clearly loved Delvine, and in the early 1720s was occasionally concerned with its day-to-day management. In a letter to his father on 13 March 1720 he speaks of "...the new inclosure of Ash on the South Side ... along by the side of the middle ditch" (NLS, MS 1128/55). This enclosure had reached maturity by 1755 when William Roy recorded it (*The Military Antiquities of the Romans in North Britain* [London, 1793], pl. XVIII), and it still appears as a crop-mark to aerial archaeologists – myself among them – who survey the Roman legionary fortress at Inchtuthil, of which Alexander Mackenzie's "middle ditch", later recorded by Roy, was an adjacent element (Lynn F. Pitts and J.K. St. Joseph, *Inchtuthil: The Roman Legionary Fortress* [London, 1985], 244–6). In 1762 Alexander's daughter Margaret married George Muir of Cassencary and in due course (John dying childless) Delvine became the seat of the Muir-Mackenzie family.
76. SRO, AC 8/398; *ibid.*, 9/1182.
77. NLS, 1490/19–20.
78. Bishop Forbes, *The Lyon in Mourning* (Edinburgh, 1895), i, 205.
79. *Ibid.*, i, 269: "Boisdale was once a whole night with the Prince upon Coradale, and was very merry with him ...". A later reference to this occasion (ii, 97) notes that "he [the prince] still had the better of us, and even of Boystill himself, notwithstanding his being as able a boulman as any in Scotland".
80. NLS, MS 1128/1–13. See William Croft Dickinson, *Two Students at St. Andrews, 1711–1716* (Edinburgh and London, 1952).
81. A. Mackenzie, *History of the Mackenzies* (Inverness, 1894), 613–14.

8

Royal Day, People's Day: The Monarch's Birthday in Scotland, c. 1660–1860

CHRISTOPHER A WHATLEY

> Sing, then, how on the fourth o' June
> Our bells screed aff a loyal tune;
> Our ancient castle shoots at noon,
> Wi' flag-staff buskit,
> Frae which the sodger blades come down
> To cock their musket.
>
> On this great day the city-guard,
> In military art weel lear'd,
> Wi' powdered pow, and shaven beard,
> Gang through their functions;
> By hostile rabble seldom spar'd
> O' clarty unctions.

Robert Fergusson's poem, "The King's Birthday in Edinburgh" (1772), from which these stanzas are taken, is well-known to students of Scottish literature. "The Riot", Chapter X of John Galt's novel, *The Provost* (1822), also describes the events of King George III's birthday, which was "ushered in with the ringing of bells, and the windows of the houses adorned with green boughs", and culminated in a riot during which the provost was felled by a dead cat which was hurled at him. Autobiographical sources too indicate that this was a day of considerable violence: after having been knocked down during a riot on the monarch's birthday in Aberdeen, the weaver and botanist John Duncan declared that he had "aye It keepit oot o' mobs since".[1]

The event which is portrayed here by contemporary writers is, however, less familiar territory for historians in Scotland. Indeed, it is really only the riots which occurred in Edinburgh at the time of King George III's birthdays in 1792 and 1796 which have received any serious attention.[2] The purpose, then, of what is very much an exploratory paper is to begin to recover what

Plate 1. The King's Birthday Riot in Perth in 1819. (Drawn by D. O. Hill and
published in *The Ancient Capital of Scotland* (1904), by S. Cowan).

in fact appears to have been a remarkable day in Scotland from the
Restoration until the mid-Victorian era. This will be done by widening and
extending the investigation and demonstrating that the monarch's birthday
was celebrated not only in Edinburgh, but as its inclusion in Galt's novel and
the reference to Aberdeen suggest, throughout much of Lowland Scotland.
An equally important consideration is what "meaning" and significance to
attach to these celebrations, for those who sponsored them, and in particular
for the "hostile rabble" referred to by Fergusson. It will be suggested that the
portrayal of the disorders which followed the official proceedings as simply
drunken and boisterous behaviour on the part of the "lower orders" does not
convey the full significance of the monarch's birthday in Scotland.

Judged by the sums of public money spent on it, and the colour and noise
which were part and parcel of the festivities, it is unlikely that any other
single public occasion was better known to the inhabitants of the larger
Scottish towns such as Edinburgh, Glasgow, Dundee and Aberdeen. Even in
smaller towns such as Greenock, Renfrew, Lanark, Cupar and Crieff, the day
was also publicly celebrated. In Perth, from early in the morning, "the fronts
of the houses were profusely decorated with boughs and flowers, the principal
streets presenting the appearance of an avenue in a wood".[3] Town and gown
united in St. Andrews, where throughout the eighteenth century the university played its part by contributing to the cost of the festivities, as in June
1719 when it resolved to pay "eight shillings Str: to the Town Treasurer as
their proportion of 24 pd weight of powder spent at ye solemnity on his
Majesties birthday".[4] Individual employers too sometimes marked the occasion, as at Cockenzie saltworks, again in 1719, when the manager provided
a total of £10. 8s. (Scots) for two barrels of ale, four bottles of claret and two

corfs of coal for a bonfire.[5] In June 1797, the workers at Clyde Iron Works heard "repeated discharges of artillery", and drank "appropriate toasts in porter, which were liberally dealt out to them by Mr Edington, the proprietor".[6] Later, and further north, in 1814, the "public-spirited" proprietors of Ruthven Printfield, near Perth, were reported to have entertained some 800 of their workers to a dinner, whisky punch, music and dancing. During the afternoon, "the entertainments were diversified by loyal songs and corresponding sentiments".[7]

Unfortunately, the inconsistent nature of most burghs' accounting systems can make it difficult to distinguish monies laid out on the monarch's birthday from other "solemnities and entertainments", and in some cases it is largely a matter of luck as to whether information about this sort of expenditure can be obtained. Even so, some hard data can be found, and while the sums which were spent are not in themselves large, in the burghs it seems that few other items of publicly funded festivity received as much financial support. Certainly, very few had the distinction of being listed separately, sometimes at least, in town treasurers' account books. Dundee provides a good example. In 1717–18, for instance, while only £11. 11s. 2d. (Scots) was laid out on the customary occasion of the magistrates' riding of the town's marches, £84. 14s. (Scots) was spent on the king's birthday. By the 1760s, in the region of £30–£40 sterling was being devoted to the day's festivities.[8]

As this suggests, and as will be confirmed as the essay develops, the occasion of the monarch's birthday often provided a bigger annual public spectacle than any other in the Scottish urban calendar. Fairs, New Year and Handsel Monday were also regular holidays, but they had little of the formal civic ceremonial of the royal birthday. This conclusion is in accordance with contemporary claims, not only in Edinburgh, where there is no doubt that it was "one of the great holidays", but also in more modest urban centres such as Perth, where it was "held by every body as a holiday".[9] This continued long into the Victorian era, in towns both big and small, from Edinburgh to Auchterarder.[10] Even in grinding industrial towns such as Dundee, where commerce slept on 28 May 1841, the anniversary of Queen Victoria's birth, the mills were reported to have "dropped work in the afternoon".[11] In Edinburgh in May 1865, on the anniversary of Queen Victoria's birth, it was reported that the people were "gaily dressed", while rail and steamship excursions were "largely patronised by all classes of the community".[12]

Although the details varied from place to place, in the later seventeenth and eighteenth centuries, certain features appear to have been common to both large and small towns: flags were hoisted, bells rung, bonfires and candles were lit, cannon and small-arms fire were discharged, and loyal toasts were drunk. These, however, were not formless demonstrations. Prior to 1707, the Scottish parliament and privy council issued edicts which insisted that the day be recognised, and precise instructions on how it should be celebrated. In 1690, for instance, the privy council ordered that 4 November, "being the birthday of our dread sovraigne" (King William II), be celebrated with "all solemnity and tokens of joy and particularly with putting on of bonfires and ringing of bells and fyring of guns from their Majesties castles and forts".[13] A similar instruction was issued on 1 November 1700, when Edinburgh town council was informed that the high commissioner would be arriving at the council chamber in mid-morning and "be present at the Solemnity upon the Theater to be Erected at the Cross".[14] At this time the guns of Edinburgh Castle were to be fired and "the music bells rung". Similar patterns were established elsewhere. Even much later in the century, in Perth, at twelve o' clock, "The bells were set a ringing; the great guns fired a royal salute; the military fired a *feu de joie*; and the whole town turned out to see the sights, and give vent to their ardent feelings of loyalty". In the afternoon the magistrates, attended by a band of music, assembled in the council chambers, while a body of troops stationed in the street fired a volley every time a toast was drunk. "No cost was spared on wines and sweetmeats; and every officer was presented with a burgess ticket".[15]

Strenuous efforts too were made by the Scottish parliament and privy council to ensure that the anniversary was honoured.[16] In the seventeenth century at least, ministers proclaimed the day from their pulpits, as at Elgin in 1685, when a "proclamatione for an anniversary thanksgiving in commemoration of his Majesty's happy birthday" was read. The burghs followed suit. In Dundee in May 1716, for example, the inhabitants were ordered to have their windows or closes illuminated between 9.30 and 11 pm. Each family "faylzeing so to doe" was to be fined £5 Scots.[17] Few apparently were. And less than a hundred years later the problem the authorities had was to put a stop to some of the ways in which their inhabitants were celebrating the day.

The roots of the monarch's birthday celebrations are almost certainly to be found in England in the last quarter of the sixteenth century, where there developed "a new national, secular and dynastic calendar centring on the anniversaries of the Protestant monarch".[18] Although Scotland was bound to England by regal union in 1603, the English royal calendar does not appear to have been adopted in Scotland until the Restoration of Charles II. It was at this time, when there was in Scotland a considerable "sentiment for royalty",[19] that the king's birthday was first celebrated publicly north of the border. The celebrations, which were marked in Edinburgh by a "voylie of cannoun" from the castle, assumed immense significance from the very outset, as immediately after the cannon had been discharged, a storm of thunder and lightning broke, "the lyke quhairof wes not sene by the space of many yeiris befoir". Thereafter, "the Lord sent doun the first and latter rayne for refresching the crop and cornes of the ground", which had been "parched with drouth".[20]

The monarch's birthday was one of a whole series of English celebratory events which were imported by the authorities into Scotland. Apart from the monarch's birthday, other regal occasions which were publicly saluted were the monarch's accession, coronations, the queen's birthday, the prince of Wales' birthday and sometimes too that of a royal princess. Rightly, this has been described as "orchestrated festivity".[21] In Scotland as in England it tapped a "vocabulary of celebration" which was widely understood. The beating of drums called the community to attention and announced in dramatic fashion an event of some importance; the pealing of bells reinforced this but in addition lifted hearts and conveyed a sense of joy; music, provided either by pipes or fiddles, also raised spirits and contributed to the sense of festival; the hoisting of flags created spectacle, their colours, designs and emblems providing an unambiguous reminder of what all the noise was about. And although bonfires could perform a variety of functions, it seems most likely that they were an expression of honour, approbation and good will. Not that the full range of "celebratory equipment" was used on every occasion. Events of lesser importance could be marked simply by hoisting a flag or set of flags: Dundee town council, for example, thought it quite sufficient in 1730–31 to spend a modest 14s. (Scots) "putting out a Flag on the Queens Birthday".[22]

As far as formal demonstrations of loyalty to the monarch and attachment to the British state are concerned, there is little apparent difference between Scotland and England after the accession of George III. Public opinion north of the border also inclined "towards [British] national self-congratulation and show", as is to be seen in the orchestration by the civic authorities in towns such as Dundee of rejoicing following reports of the naval and military victories of Britain and her allies.[23] Scotland too shared in the growing adulation of King George III, who from the 1780s became a symbol of British patriotism, and was later in his reign portrayed as "a wise, Lear-like patriarch" and "celestial guardian" of the nation, increasingly distanced after his illness in 1788–9 from the corrupt world of day-to-day politics.[24] Although civic support for the occasion waned in the early nineteenth century, it was not withdrawn altogether, and some burghs, such as Linlithgow, continued to pay for the bells to be rung and wine and glasses with which to toast the king's health.[25] In Dundee in 1840, although the bells were not rung, the union flag was hoisted on the old steeple, and the troops then stationed in the town's barracks fired a *foi-de-joie*.[26]

Where Scottish experience does seem to have diverged somewhat is in the period shortly after the Restoration until the latter part of George III's reign, when the monarchy in England attracted less sympathetic public support.[27] As has been indicated, in Scotland the monarch's birthdays were regularly celebrated in public by the country's civic leaders, and, it appears, with a considerable degree of popular enthusiasm, while south of the border such anniversaries often ended in disturbances occasioned by political and religious rivalry.

Hard evidence which would explain this apparent difference is not easy to find. As far as the first half of the eighteenth century is concerned, it seems highly likely that civic enthusiasm for royal birthdays was linked with a concern to counter the image, long held by Englishmen, that underneath every Scotsman's kilt there lurked a Jacobite.[28] The Scots may have been cool – and occasionally hostile – towards the English, but they were loyal Britons. The sanctity of the union of parliaments had faced Scottish-led challenges, while respect for the agents of Westminster government – principally customs and excise officers – had been slow to materialise,[29] and Scottish fidelity had therefore to be underlined. With perhaps one in four Scots of military age serving with the British army and navy,[30] they had just cause to trumpet their commitment.

With the growth of British national consciousness,[31] it can reasonably be assumed that the reasons adduced for the growing popularity of public shows of support for the monarch in England in the last two decades of the century apply in the Scottish case too (although, as has been indicated, as far as celebrating the monarch's birthday was concerned, the Scots had a head start). These include an increased familiarity with royal cum national celebration; the reportage and incitement of the London and provincial press; increased urban affluence and civic pride and emulation; and above all the wartime context, with the king becoming the prime symbol both of Britain's national identity and "her singular success in resisting French domination".[32] It is notable that some of the largest public turnouts on the king's birthday occurred during the wars with France: in Glasgow in 1795, for instance, more than 20,000 people were reported to have turned out to watch the Glasgow Royal Volunteers being reviewed on the Green.[33]

Threats to the existing social order from within may have further encouraged demonstrations of "loyalty and affection". In 1820, the year of the so-called "Radical War" in Scotland, the number of spectators at a grand military display on Glasgow Green was reported to have been 50,000: "the number of carriages, filled with all the beauty and fashion of this city and neighbourhood, were greater", thought the *Glasgow Courier*, "than on any former occasion".[34] If it is true, as has recently been claimed, that the radical-tinged events of 1819 and 1820 in Scotland "were more extensive and more serious than anything in England, not excluding Peterloo",[35] then loyalist demonstrations of this sort take on an even greater significance and show how strong was the counterbalancing force in favour of the status quo. By both tapping and nurturing patriotic feelings amongst the working classes, those paternalistic employers who provided royal birthday entertainments for their employees were able to serve their workplace interests as well as contribute to the maintenance of social order.

The feature of the monarch's birthday in Scotland with which this essay is mainly concerned, however, is the rioting which accompanied it. Drunkenness and boisterous behaviour-saturnalia – had been an integral part of the day's celebrations from the start. Indeed, according to one disapproving contemporary, the restoration of King Charles II had brought about a general "spirit of extravagant joy", and that under "the colour of drinking the king's health, there were great disorders and much riot everywhere".[36] The diary entry of John Nicoll, WS, for 29 May 1661, the date both of King Charles II's restoration to the throne and his birthday, records that while this was "solemplie keipit a solempne day in all the churches of Scotland", in Edinburgh a great feast was prepared by the town authorities, during which there was "great mirth and melodie", with "trumpettis sounding, cannones roring, bailfyres birning, drumes touking, men, wemen, and chyldrene, dancing and drinking the Kinges helth, and quhat ellis could be invented wes performit for the Kinges majesties honor".[37]

Indeed, it could hardly have been otherwise, given the large quantities of claret and other alcoholic beverages which were consumed. In Dundee in the mid-1720s, for example, the town council bought some 57 bottles of claret and eight of white wine, mainly for the enjoyment of the official party.[38] It is not surprising then to discover that, in June 1802, Lt. Col. George MacKenzie of the Ross and Cromarty Rangers admitted that after attending the "entertainment" given by the provost and magistrates of Aberdeen, he "found himself a good deal affected by the quantity of wine he had been induced to drink", and claimed that on his return to barracks he had fallen into a deep sleep.[39]

Those uninvited by the provosts and magistrates to the town house gatherings had to devise their own entertainments, as in 1814 when a party of "gentlemen of all professions" had left Dundee and sailed over the Tay to attend a celebration dinner in an inn at Newport. On his arrival back in Dundee, their "croupier", it was reported, "found much difficulty in accounting for the last two hours", and was of the "decided conviction that he had driven across the river in a coach".[40]

As far as the lower orders were concerned, for much of the eighteenth century at least, their appetites for liquor were whetted, occasionally by public fountains which were ingeniously adapted to flow with wine, or with the dregs of wine (sometimes accompanied by empty glasses) specially purchased for the occasion and distributed freely, if almost certainly thinly, amongst the crowds which gathered around the towns' crosses to watch their social superiors perform their patriotic duties. The quantity of alcohol consumed per head must have been fairly substantial at Ruthven bleachfield in 1814 though, as it was reported that the bowl of punch, into which ten ankers of whisky had been poured, "could not be got emptied, even on the near approach of Sunday".[41] A reasonable claim to be top of this particular league, however, came from Glasgow, where the king's birthday was so widely celebrated by the "multitudes" that "probably a greater quantity of wines, rum-punch, and other liquor was consumed in it than in any other city of equal extent in the British Empire".[42]

In the immediate post-Restoration period there is no evidence to suggest that the king's birthday celebrations were anything other than drunken, disorderly affairs. Although, as Christopher Smout has shown, riot was an integral part of urban life in late seventeenth-and early eighteenth-century Scotland,[43] the king's birthday does not appear to have been distinguished by much violent social confrontation. As far as the authorities were concerned, of course, it was designed to be a day of formal if exuberant ceremonial in which all ranks gazed in rapture, metaphorically at least, at their Caesar.[44]

Long before the end of the eighteenth century, however, intimidating and aggressive behaviour on the king's birthday had become commonplace. Indeed, anything else was unusual. Distinctive for this reason were the manners of the tradesmen of the small village of Kilconquhar, in north-east Fife, whose minister reported in his return for the *Statistical Account* on their "perfect order, decorum, and loyalty" both on the procession and during the later festivities on the king's birthday there, at a time when "confusion and disorders" were the norm in other parts of the country.[45]

Two decades or so later, in the eyes of one contemporary, James Peddie, the monarch's birthday riot had become a benchmark by which the severity of other riots could be judged. Thus, following a violent clash in Glasgow's Saltmarket in June 1820 between the local inhabitants, police and the military, described in one newspaper as having had a more dreadful appearance "than was ever witnessed on the streets of this city", Peddie reported to the lord advocate that it was his impression that he had not seen in the crowd "so much outrageous disposition" as was "repeatedly ... displayed on an ordinary King's Birthday Night".[46]

Reports abound of both low level violence and much angrier clashes between sections of the crowd and the authorities. A "normal" monarch's birthday ended in the manner described by Fergusson. More often than might be expected, however, king's birthday rioting took a more serious turn and troops had to be called on to restore order. This is reflected in Galt's account, where the provost thought it prudent to send to Ayr for a regiment of soldiers, "the roar of the rioters without, being all the time like a raging flood".[47] Reference has already been made to the events in Edinburgh of November 1792, when disturbances went on over a two day period, and 1796. Disorders on this sort of scale, however, occurred elsewhere too. In Aberdeen in 1802, "a number of innocent persons were killed or injured" in a skirmish with the military.[48] Glasgow in 1819 saw what was probably the worst outbreak of king's birthday rioting in the city's history. The "most harmless" amusement of the "degraded mob" was the firing of guns and pistols. In the heart of the town large bonfires were lit, fuelled with the roofs, doors and contents of several old houses, as well as a vast range of other combustible material which included lamp-posts, police-boxes, horse-carts, hurleys, sign-boards, and full tar barrels. Numerous windows were broken as the crowd took over the streets and embarked on what appeared to be an orgy of destruction which included breaking into at least one shop and stealing cash and rum, which was then consumed on the Green.[49]

The following year, in Aberdeen, two companies of the 80th Regiment of Foot were required to break up a crowd which had set a huge bonfire going in front of the town house, and begun to stone the provost and magistrates inside, despite attempts on the part of the latter to read the Riot Act.[50] In 1821 Glasgow was once again to the fore when a battle broke out between a section of the crowd which had set a fire going against the wall of the town jail, and the magistrates and a party of soldiers. Ultimately, having been subjected to treatment which would "have disgraced barbarians", the cavalry mounted a charge during which numerous injuries and some fatalities occurred, as Hutchesontown bridge, across which they were escaping, collapsed.[51]

It is at present impossible to say precisely when the apparent antagonism between ruled and rulers reported here first manifested itself. It is conceivable – but unlikely – that it had always been there, but had gone unreported. Certainly, the day had always been one of riot and disorder – yet there is little to suggest that this was particularly troublesome. By the early 1730s, however, concern was evidently being felt by the authorities. In 1734, for instance, Lanark burgh council stationed lookouts in several parts of the town "for preventing former abuses", which in the previous year had included the throwing of a stone through Lady Auchtyfradle's illuminated window.[52]

Some apprehension was evidently felt in Stirling too, again in 1734, with the appearance in the town council's minute book of a frustratingly terse reference to an action which had been raised by the procurator fiscal "agt Severalls for the late Disturbances and abuse on the Kings birth night".[53] Fergusson's poem suggests that an element of violence which was targetted against those in authority had become the norm in Edinburgh by the early 1770s, if not earlier.

An indication that violence and disorder were new, or at least becoming more noticeable in Glasgow – but later on – is to be found in the comments of newspapers such as the *Glasgow Mercury*, which on 5 June 1792 followed its disapproving comments on the rioting which had concluded the king's birthday celebrations of the previous day with the remark that this "outrage" had "been too conspicuous for *some time past*".[54] And although the reflections of an unknown Dundee-based journalist in 1845 about some vaguely-defined time in the past should certainly be treated with caution, it is at least worth noting that after an unusually peaceful queen's birthday celebration in

Dundee, it was remarked that the evening "bore some resemblance to the old Fourth of June – it had all the loyal display of merriment without apparently any disposition to proceed to riot and outrage, as was formerly the case".[55]

If there are some questions about what had happened before c. 1730, there are none later. The monarch's birthday continued to bring considerable disorder in its wake until at least the third decade of Queen Victoria's reign. Examples abound: in 1838 David Christie of Balhousie in Perth complained that a Perth mob had on the night of the queen's birthday not only indulged themselves "in the destruction of the property belonging to the lieges in the Landward part of the East Church Parish of Perth", but also tore down the fencing on his farm which adjoined the North Inch.[56] In 1839 in Dundee, an attempt was made by a crowd to find a boat to burn, and while they did not succeed in so doing, or indeed in setting fire to a tar barrel, it was noted by one Dundonian that there "was a gae row for a' that and the Provost got his head cut by some rascal or other who was afterwards sent to the Bridewell for 90 days for his trouble".[57] In Kelso in 1854 a crowd rolled a burning tar barrel onto Kelso bridge and tore down the toll-gate.[58]

However, prompt intervention by the police appeared to be preventing most disorders from getting out of control, and by the 1860s there were also distinct signs that former habits were changing. In May 1860, in Edinburgh, a "large proportion of the juvenile and adolescent population" had employed themselves "very assiduously in the combustion of gunpowder in all available forms", but *The Scotsman* announced, there had been no disturbances, "a result scarcely less gratifying than unprecedented".[59] In Perth in 1861 the same newspaper reported that, although some squibs had been set off in the High Street, and some "halting" had occurred, there was "no breach of the public peace".[60] It was the same in the smaller towns. In Anstruther in 1864, there was "little outward noise of firing of guns as in former years", while, unusually, "the streets presented a quiet and peaceable aspect".[61] The queen's birthday was observed in 1865 too, but there were no casualties and an obviously relieved *East of Fife Record* correspondent felt able to pronounce that "the foolish and dangerous amusements of bonfires and firing of guns seems now to be given up on such occasions, and is certainly an improvement".[62] In this respect at least, the concept of a (slow) "transition to order" in mid-Victorian England[63] seems applicable to Scotland too.

It is not intended here to discuss further the disappearance of riot on the monarch's birthday in Scotland. Instead, the rest of this essay attempts to discover the "meaning" of the disturbances which took place.

Rioting on the monarch's birthday was not uncommon in England – indeed, a Wilkite crowd in London on the king's birthday in 1771 had caused so much damage that the Royal Academy had to abandon its plans for further exhibitions of royal splendour.[64] Yet there are relatively few accounts of monarch's birthday riots in the second half of the eighteenth century and by the early nineteenth they appear to have been rather tame affairs.[65] The tenor of royal celebrations was changing, and around the turn of century they became noticeably more orderly, with the replacement of "licensed exuberance" by acts of civic charity. Officially, there was a move in this direction in Scotland too, and by and large, as has been seen, there was a diminution of local authority support for royal birthday celebrations. Yet there is no sign of parallel decline in the incidence of riot and disorder north of the border.

Unlike London, where in the early Hanoverian period the riots which marked royal anniversaries were inspired by Tory sympathies and tinged with popular Jacobitism,[66] Scottish king's birthday riots appear to have had little to do with support for the Stuart cause. It is true that the birthday of the "Old Pretender" in 1708 was "signalised by defiant demonstrations in favour of the exiled family", in Edinburgh and Leith in particular,[67] but mass demonstrations in favour of the Stuarts such as this, which happened in the wake of an immensely unpopular union settlement,[68] do not seem to have been common. Indeed, in Dundee in 1745 the birthday of the Hanoverian George II was marked by the crowd chasing the temporary Jacobite governor out of the town.[69] Throughout, what is striking about the Scottish "mob" is its apparent loyalty to the Hanoverian succession.

Close scrutiny indicates that several interconnected factors may account for the rioting which marked the late afternoon and evening of the regal birthday. The timing is important. The latter part of the day was when those who had been at work could get onto the streets and swell the crowd which was steadily becoming more inebriated. Indeed, in the nineteenth century the degree of disorder tended to be greater when the king's birthday fell on a Saturday, which for the bulk of the working classes was when their wages were paid, and the start of the weekend break. On whatever day it fell, however, as was indicated earlier, the monarch's birthday was, for many thousands of town-based Scots, a holiday, a period of release from their normal routines, which became increasingly regimented with the march of industrialisation. The noise of the bells, small arms and cannon fire which had been heard for much of the day fulfilled their purpose in arousing public emotions, but in combination with liberal quantities of drink, are likely to have weakened the usual restraints on behaviour. Furthermore, for the mass of the onlookers, the formal climax of the day also occurred late in the afternoon, when the magistrates and their guests assembled at town crosses throughout Scotland to drink a variety of loyal toasts.

What the watching crowds were also being treated to was an unashamed display of local ruling class privilege and military-backed power. One of several surviving guest lists from Perth reveals that prominent amongst the party which at six o'clock in the evening of 4 June 1761 joined with the "Magistrates & Town Council attended by the Military Officers" were the sheriff of Perth, the collector of customs, the supervisor and officers of the excise, the deacons and conveners of the trades, schoolmasters, lawyers, merchants and principal tradesmen.[70] After drinking the health of the king and other members of the royal family, "at the Discharge of the Small Arms by the Dragoons", a procession filed along to the council chamber where further toasts were drunk and the freedom of the town was conferred upon "Colonel Hale and other Strangers then present".[71] Pipe or fiddle music accompanied the evening's feasting and drinking in the town house which in Dundee at least was properly cleaned each year only for this occasion.[72] During the hey-day of the burgh-sponsored celebrations, guests could select from a range of foodstuffs, which, depending on date and place, could include bacon hams, tongues, oysters, bread and various sweetmeats.

The fact that, as in Lanark, "soldiers of some kind were always present" and the musketry "never omitted"[73] may have engendered antagonism, as their presence reinforced the growing distance between master and man, rulers and ruled, and at the same time undermined respect for the civic powers, whose overbearing vanity on such occasions (reflected in *The Provost* in the person of Provost Pawkie) the crowd may have been anxious to prick. And as the gulf between the classes in urban Scotland grew, with the middling classes engaging with their counterparts elsewhere in early modern Europe in a process of spatial and cultural differentiation,[74] so in dramatic fashion the "mob" on the monarch's birthday may have been reminding their social superiors of the continued existence of a valid and energetic plebeian culture. Certainly, at no other time in the year in Scotland were the urban authorities so regularly and forcefully made to recognise the existence and sometimes the grievances of the underprivileged in their rapidly industrialising society. There are strong similarities between this function of the monarch's birthday riots in Scotland and instances of disruptive or anti-social rituals found elsewhere in Britain, which were designed to demonstrate the strength and importance of the "powerless" within the social hierarchy, particularly at times of real or threatened deprivation.[75]

This was done in a variety of ways. Physical intimidation played a large part. Threatening demands were made for money,[76] an action which momentarily overturned rank and authority and reminded the better off of their obligations towards the relatively poor.[77] It is notable that in Glasgow the worst king's birthday rioting in the early 1800s took place in Barony parish, the city's desperately overcrowded working class heartland. It may be speculated that such reminders may in some way have been legitimised in the popular mind (in Edinburgh at least) by the fact that in 1660 the "pure pepill of Scotland", clothed in traditional blue gowns, had received their pensions at Holyrood Church on the king's birthday.[78]

Temporary reversals in social status were sought too. In Edinburgh in 1823, "a number of loose fellows assembled as usual on the bridges, and annoyed passengers, by calling for hats off"[79] in Glasgow, in 1839, it was reported that "Many of the citizens were struck and grossly abused, in the vicinity of the Cross, the common method of annoyance being to tear their coats to pieces, and their hats".[80] Attacks on private property, either by throwing stones through windows, or removing palings or other fixed and moveable items to add to the fire, were further assaults on privilege.

The well-known practice of throwing squibs, garbage, cod-heads and dead cats which were grotesquely distended as they were hurled around by the crowd was a widely used form of humiliation. In Glasgow on 4 June 1792, for instance, the *Mercury* reported that the night had ended in a "most riotous manner" with a "loose disorderly rabble" throwing "brick bats, dead dogs and cats, by which several of the military were severely cut".[81] If, as seems to have been the case, soldiers on ceremonial occasions such as this customarily surrendered their stock of 18 ball cartridges for three blanks, they would have been tempting targets for taunting crowds.[82] Individuals too were singled out, as in Edinburgh, where a charivari-like ritual was observed, in which:

> unpopular persons were absolutely seized and carried to the ... Square, and there burghered, as it was called – that is, had their bottoms brought hard down upon the ridge of the box three times, with severity proportioned to the caprice of the inflictors, or determined by the degree of resistance made by the sufferer.[83]

Thereafter, the town guard was pelted with missiles, and dispersed, before the "mob" rampaged, unchecked, through the city's streets. It was much later in the evening, either after the crowd had exhausted itself, or when the military or fire-hoses were brought in to cool things down, that order was restored, and the streets in the hearts of towns such as Glasgow, Edinburgh and Aberdeen became, once again, battle-free zones. Rituals such as this, however, which included burning effigies of unpopular members of the community, or attacks on their persons or property, continued well into the nineteenth century. In Arbroath as late as 1865, for example, a "house of evil repute" in Marketgate was attacked and set on fire, while the police and firemen who had arrived to restore order were confronted by a stone-throwing crowd in which youths were prominent, and who, on the advice of some women, cut the fire hoses.[84]

What this also suggests is that the monarch's birthday riots functioned as a form of social politics,[85] occasions when the use of violence in the pursuit or the rectification of a specific local grievance was deemed by the crowd to be appropriate, their resort to force sanctioned in some way by the monarch to whom they were paying homage. Perhaps there were echoes in Scotland of what had been believed by peasants in seventeenth-century France, that the good monarch knew nothing of the iniquities his people endured at the hands of local intermediaries. By the early nineteenth century, George III was being portrayed as the "Father of his People", while the prince regent was seen in a similar light, with petitions being sent from handloom weavers and others at times of distress.[86]

What is more difficult to determine is the extent to which king's birthday rioting was inspired by the emergent political radicalism of the 1790s. A chronicler of Perth, George Penny, did associate what he saw as the degeneration of the day in the late eighteenth century with the appearance of "Democrats",[87] but his obsessive hostility to political reform of virtually any sort evidently caused him to forget that dead cats and other missiles had been hurled around for years. The well-known king's birthday riot in Edinburgh in 1792 also seems to have drawn in part for its inspiration on democratic notions,[88] with the crowd's targets being specific, unpopular politicians, who were representives of Scotland's notoriously undemocratic system of political representation – notably Henry Dundas, Scotland's political overlord, and his nephew Robert Dundas, Scotland's chief law officer, as well as James Stirling, lord provost of Edinburgh.

On the other hand, in Glasgow around the same time, the "rabble" was said to have burned effigies of John Wilkes and Thomas Paine.[89] During the post-Napoleonic War years too, it was the patriotism of the "mob" which was remarked upon by middle class contemporaries. After an ugly incident on the king's birthday in Dundee in 1817, reference was made to the "noisy loyalty of the young",[90] and in Aberdeen in 1820 to the spirit of "good humoured loyalty" which had preceded the attack on the town house.[91] The editor of the *Dundee, Perth and Cupar Advertiser* in 1851 may have been anxious to sweep away the bonfires, squibs and "miniature cannon" which contributed to the "fiery ordeal" which the queen's birthday had become in Dundee, but he did not doubt that they were used as a means of expressing "Scotland's loyalty".[92]

Nevertheless, patriotism and support for the monarchy and radicalism were not necessarily incompatible,[93] and indeed artisan along with middle class parliamentary reformers in Glasgow in 1830 claimed that the king was on their side.[94] At this stage, however, there is insufficient evidence to link the king's birthday riots of the 1790s and 1810s with widespread popular support for a programme of political reform, let alone with republicanism. The occasion of the monarch's birthday almost certainly heightened awareness amongst the lower orders of the gulf between them and their social superiors during a period of profound economic and social change. It also provided an opportunity in times of acute suffering, or in the face of a specific injustice, for them to express their disapproval loudly and, not infrequently, forcefully. Occasionally, as in Edinburgh in 1792, this could incorporate radical aspirations, but in general the day seems to have functioned as a confirmation of the status quo and not as a challenge to it.

For notably, in spite of the growing distaste with which the "respectable" classes viewed the king's birthday "mobs", and indeed the physical discomfort which some of their number felt when they were abused by them, there is little sign that middle class opposition to the proceedings was based on any sense of threat from below. Indeed, there were those who recognised that no matter how unpleasant and intimidating they were, the crowd's activities fulfilled a necessary social function. Amongst the most perceptive observers of this was Robert S. Rintoul, the radical editor of the *Dundee, Perth and Cupar Advertiser*. In response to a complaint about the riotousness of the day, Rintoul pointed out that the "privilege which the rabble have to be riotous on the King's Birth-day" had been enjoyed "past all memory of man". The burgh's "constitution", he argued, had been sanctioned by "long-tried expediency" and the right of "blackguard boys" to insult the "respectable inhabitants with impunity" was firmly established. Should a single "pin" of the "venerable fabric which we inherit from our ancestors" be removed, the whole would "tumble down" and "throw everything into anarchy and confusion".[95] In other words, in Scotland, no less than in other societies in which there were visible inequalities in wealth, status and power, the prevailing social order could not survive without a safety-valve, "a means for the subordinates to purge their resentments and compensate for their frustrations".[96] Although detailed investigation into the social composition of those "subordinates" has not yet been carried out, the indications are that over time they were increasingly less likely to have been respectable artisans who could channel their grievances through their unions, clubs and reform societies, but rather "trade lads", the unskilled, inarticulate and dispossessed, the stragglers on Scotland's march to industrialisation.

In general terms though, what had happened on the monarch's birthday was that the formal ritual was taken over and turned into popular ritual, and the "world turned upside down", the crowd's actions legitimised by their adoption of traditional forms of behaviour.[97] The bonfires, which had once been under the control of the authorities, who had provided money for the fuel, were appropriated by the crowd and increasingly became points of conflict. Indeed, the tar barrels which were rolled along the streets before being set on fire on or near sites which were usually the preserve of the authorities, such as the town houses, were turned into weapons and directed against those who formerly sponsored the use of fire.[98] The way in which the day unfolded was by no means spontaneous, but developed along the lines of an alternative pre-arranged programme which in some respects was devised as carefully as that of the authorities in the seventeenth and eighteenth centuries. Supporting this, and underlining the importance of the day in the urban calendar, is Chambers' account of boys in Edinburgh beginning to save for it six months in advance, while "for a good many weeks, nothing was thought of but the day, and nothing was done but making preparations for it".[99]

Just as one swallow does not make a summer, so the value of this highly speculative preliminary study of one form of riot is limited. Its longevity does, however, seem to highlight the absence of a serious class-based challenge to paternalist rule in Scotland: monarch's birthday riots point to the existence of an active plebeian culture, but the form they took was always conservative, drawing on the traditional sanctions of force, ridicule, shame and intimidation. They could be angry and rage against ruling class hegemony, but they provided no alternative.[100] The essay also seems to have something of significance to say about the little-explored world of popular culture in Scotland. This, it has been asserted recently, was "ritually impoverished" in the central Lowlands and south east.[101] The evidence examined here suggests that this judgement may be premature.

It is true that Calvinism in Scotland curbed many communal recreations. Yet official proscription did not necessarily sound the death-knell of the more exuberant elements of popular culture, or confine them to the Highlands and the northern margins of Lowland Scotland, but may instead have caused them to seek other outlets. The monarch's birthday in Scotland acquired many of the features of the "carnivalesque", the rather more modest northern European equivalent of the great carnivals of the south, Italy, Spain and France.[102]

It involved large numbers of people and attracted visitors from the surrounding countryside; not only was it looked forward to for many months, but Fergusson's reference to tales told the next day "O' crackit crowns and broken brows" suggests that it was remembered afterwards too amongst part of the populace. It was a time of release, a drunken, disorderly, abandoned affair, cruel, violent, fiery, irreverent, which incorporated "rites of protest". Denied the rich repertoire of festival which punctuated the English urban calendar, the "lower orders" in Scotland's towns found their own festive opportunity and by their own efforts shaped it to suit their own ends.

Notes

I would like to express my sincere thanks to Kenneth Simpson of Strathclyde University for discussing this topic with me at length, and to my colleague William Knox for commenting on an earlier draft of the essay.

1. W. Jolly, *The Life of John Duncan, Weaver and Botanist* (n. p., 1883), 73.
2. K.J. Logue, *Popular Disturbances in Scotland, 1780–1815* (Edinburgh, 1979), 133–47.
3. G. Penny, *Traditions of Perth* (Perth, 1836; Coupar Angus, 1986 ed.), 38.
4. University of St Andrews Archives, UY 452.3, University Minutes, vol. 3, 1718–1726, 28 May 1719. I am indebted to the University Archivist, Mr. Robert Smart,

for drawing this and other similar eighteenth-century references to my attention.

5.   C.A. Whatley, "A Saltwork and the Community: the Case of Winton, 1716–1719", *Transactions of the East Lothian Antiquarian and Field Naturalists' Society*, 18 (1984), 53.

6.   *Glasgow Courier*, 8 June 1797.

7.   *Dundee, Perth and Cupar Advertiser*, 10 June 1814.

8.   Dundee Archive and Record Centre [DARC], Burgh Treasurer's Account Books, 1693–1733; 1733–55; 1755–78; 1778–1815.

9.   R. Chambers, *Traditions of Edinburgh. Vol. 2* (Edinburgh, 1825), 221; Penny, *Traditions of Perth*, 38.

10. *The Scotsman*, 25 May 1860; 24 May 1862; 25 May 1865.

11. *Dundee, Perth and Cupar Advertiser*, 29 May 1841.

12. *The Scotsman*, 19 May 1865.

13. *Register of the Privy Council of Scotland, Third Series, XV, 1690* (Edinburgh, 1967), 511.

14. Scottish Record Office [SRO], Acts of the Privy Council, PC1/52, 1699–1703, 159.

15. Penny, *Traditions of Perth*, 38.

16. T. Thomson and C. Innes (ed.), *The Acts of the Parliaments of Scotland* (Edinburgh, 1814–75), vii, p. 376: "Act for keiping the anniversarie thanksgiveing for the K. Majesties birth and restauration". *Register of the Privy Council of Scotland, Third Series, X, 1684–85* (Edinburgh, 1927), 36–8.

17. W. Cramond (ed.), *Extracts from the Records of the Kirk Session of Elgin, 1584–1779* (Elgin, 1897), 311; DARC, Council Minute Book, vol. VIIIa, 1716–42, 24 May 1716.

18. D. Cressy, *Bonfires and Bells: National Memory and the Protestant Calendar in Elizabethan and Stuart England* (London, 1989), p. xii.

19. R. Mitchison, *Lordship to Patronage: Scotland, 1603–1745* (London, 1983), 70.

20. J. Nicoll, *A Diary of Public Transactions and Other Occurrences, Chiefly in Scotland, From January 1650 to June 1667* (Edinburgh, 1836), 290.

21. Cressy, *Bonfires and Bells*, 67–92.

22. DARC, Burgh Treasurer's Account Book, 1693–1733.

23. L. Colley, "The Apotheosis of George III: Loyalty, Royalty and the British Nation 1760–1820", *Past & Present*, 102 (1984), 99; and see, for example, DARC, Burgh Treasurer's Account Books, 1755–78.

24. Colley, "Apotheosis", 102.

25. "Accompt of Expenses of the Kings Birth Day, April 1826" (Linlithgow), document in possession of the author.

26. *Dundee, Perth and Cupar Advertiser*, 29 May 1840.

27. Colley, "Apotheosis", 95.

28. T.C. Smout, "Problems of Nationalism, Identity and Improvement in later Eighteenth-Century Scotland", in T.M. Devine (ed.), *Improvement and Enlightenment* (Edinburgh, 1989), 8–9; L. Leneman, "A New Role for a Lost Cause: Lowland Romanticisation of the Jacobite Highlander", in L. Leneman (ed.), *Perspectives in Scottish Social History: Essays in Honour of Rosalind Mitchison* (Edinburgh, 1988), 109.

29. See P.W.J. Riley, *The English Ministers and Scotland, 1707–1727* (London, 1964); C.A. Whatley, "How Tame Were the Lowlanders during the Eighteenth Century?", in T.M. Devine (ed.), *Conflict and Stability in Scottish Society, 1700–1850* (Edinburgh, 1990), 6–14.

30. A. Murdoch, "More 'Reluctant Heroes': New Light on Military Recruitment in North East Scotland", *Northern Scotland*, 6 (1985), 164, 168.

31. L. Colley, "Whose Nation?: Class and National Consciousness in Britain, 1750–1830", *Past & Present*, 113 (1986), 100–101.

32. Colley, "Apotheosis", 113.
33. *Glasgow Mercury*, 5 June 1795.
34. *Glasgow Courier*, 25 April 1820.
35. W.H. Fraser, "Patterns of Protest", in T.M. Devine and R.M. Mitchison (ed.), *People and Society in Scotland, Vol. 1, 1760–1830* (Edinburgh, 1988), 286.
36. O. Airy (ed.), *Burnet's History of My Own Time. Part 1* (Oxford, 1897), 165–6.
37. Nicoll, *Diary*, 335.
38. DARC, Burgh Treasurer's Accounts, 1693–1733.
39. SRO, Justiciary Court Records, JC 26/319, Daniel Ross v Col. Mackenzie & others, 16 December 1802. Ann Miller kindly brought this case to my attention.
40. *Dundee, Perth and Cupar Advertiser*, 10 June 1814.
41. *Ibid.*
42. "Senex", *Glasgow, Past and Present, Vol 1* (Glasgow, 1849), 259.
43. T.C. Smout, *A History of the Scottish People, 1560–1830* (London, 1969; 1981 ed.), 205–12.
44. See "Ode on his Majesty's Birth-day", *Scots Magazine* (October 1739), 475–6.
45. Sir J. Sinclair (ed.), *The Third Statistical Account of Scotland, 1791–1799*, X (Wakefield, 1978), 459. Paula Martin kindly drew my attention to this source.
46. *Glasgow Courier*, 29 June 1820; SRO, Lord Advocate's Department, AD 14/20/225, James Peddie to Lord Advocate, 3 July 1820.
47. Notably, *The Provost* has been described as "one of the first political novels and ... one of the most sharply observed". See P.H. Scott, *John Galt* (Edinburgh, 1985), 59.
48. SRO, JC 26/319, Ross v Mackenzie & others, 1802.
49. *Dundee, Perth and Cupar Advertiser*, 11 June 1819; Senex, *Glasgow*, 258–60.
50. SRO, Lord Advocate's Department, AD 14/20/147, Papers concerning King's Birth-day riot in Aberdeen, 24 April 1820.
51. *Glasgow Courier*, 24 and 26 April 1821; 23 April 1822.
52. A.D. Robertson, *Lanark: The Burgh and its Councils. 1469–1880* (Lanark, 1974), 189. I am grateful to Dr. Ian L. Donnachie for this reference.
53. Central Region Archives, B 66/22, Stirling Council Minutes, 1732–39, 26 November 1734.
54. *Glasgow Mercury*, 5 June 1792. Author's emphasis.
55. *Dundee, Perth and Cupar Advertiser*, 27 May 1845.
56. Perth Archive Centre [PAC], PE 16/68, John McWhannell to Provost of Perth, 12 June 1838.
57. University of Dundee Archives, MS 58, Papers of Robert Leighton, 1822–69, Jeffrey Inglis to Robert Leighton, 25 May 1839.
58. C. Martin, "Kelso Bridge is Falling Down", *Scots Magazine*, 84 (1965–66), 70–2.
59. *The Scotsman*, 25 May 1860.
60. *Ibid.*, 25 May 1861.
61. *East of Fife Record*, 27 May 1864.
62. *Ibid.*, 26 May 1965.
63. J. Stevenson, *Popular Disturbances in England, 1700–1870* (London, 1979), 275–300.
64. Colley, "Apotheosis", 96.
65. *Ibid.*, 119.
66. N. Rogers, "Popular Protest in Early Hanoverian London", *Past & Present*, 79 (1978), 70–4; R.B. Shoemaker, "The London 'mob' in the Early Eighteenth Century", in P. Borsay (ed.), *The Eighteenth-Century Town: A Reader in English Urban History, 1688–1820* (London, 1990), 210.
67. P. Hume Brown, *History of Scotland* (Cambridge, 1911), iii, 130.

68. For a recent study, see J.S. Gibson, *Playing the Scottish Card: The Franco-Jacobite Invasion of 1708* (Edinburgh, 1988).

69. A.M. Smith, "Dundee in the '45", in L. Scott-Moncrieff (ed.), *The '45: To Gather an Image Whole* (Edinburgh, 1988), 102.

70. PAC, B59/33/16, "List of Persons to be invited to the Council house on the King's Birthday 4 June 1761".

71. PAC, B59/33/17, Report on King's Birthday, Perth, 4 June 1761.

72. This information is derived from the Treasurer's Account Books listed in note 8, above.

73. Robertson, *History of Lanark*, 167.

74. P. Burke, *Popular Culture in Early Modern Europe* (London, 1978; 1983 ed.), 270–81; for Scotland, see S. Nenadic, "The Rise of the Urban Middle Classes", in Devine and Mitchison (ed.), *People and Society*, 109–26.

75. B. Bushaway, *By Rite: Custom, Ceremony and Community in England, 1700–1880* (London, 1982), 168.

76. Chambers, *Traditions of Edinburgh*, 226.

77. J. Bohstedt, *Riots and Community Politics in England and Wales, 1790–1810* (Harvard and London, 1983), 6.

78. Nicoll, *Diary*, 291.

79. *Glasgow Courier*, 26 April 1823.

80. *Scottish Guardian*, 28 May 1839.

81. *Glasgow Mercury*, 5 June 1792.

82. SRO, JC 26/319, Evidence of Lt. Col. George McKenzie, 5 June 1802.

83. Chambers, *Traditions of Edinburgh*, 227.

84. *Arbroath Guide*, 27 May 1865. I am grateful to Iain Flett (DARC) and Alastair M. Sutherland (Angus District Libraries) for drawing my attention to this source.

85. Bohstedt, *Riots*, 4–5.

86. Y.M. Bercé, *History of Peasant Revolts: The Social Origins of Rebellion in Early Modern France* (London, 1986; 1990 ed.), 249; Colley, "Apotheosis", 120; J.D. Young, *The Rousing of the Scottish Working Class* (Edinburgh, 1979), 59–60.

87. Penny, *Traditions of Perth*, 39.

88. Logue, *Popular Disturbances*, 144–5.

89. Senex, *Glasgow*, 258.

90. *Dundee, Perth and Cupar Advertiser*, 6 June 1817.

91. SRO, Lord Advocates Department, AD 14/20/147, Papers concerning King's Birthday riot in Aberdeen, 1820.

92. *Dundee, Perth and Cupar Advertiser*, 23 May 1851.

93. See H. Cunningham, "The Language of Patriotism, 1750–1914", *History Workshop Journal*, 12 (1981), 8–33.

94. F.A. Montgomery, "Glasgow and the Struggle for Parliamentary Reform, 1830–1832", *Scottish Historical Review*, 61 (1982), 137–8.

95. *Dundee, Perth and Cupar Advertiser*, 6 June 1817.

96. Burke, *Popular Culture*, 201.

97. Shoemaker, "London", 211.

98. SRO, AD 14/20/147, Papers concerning King's Birthday riot in Aberdeen, 1820.

99. Chambers, *Traditions of Edinburgh*, 221.

100. See E.P. Thompson, "Eighteenth-century English Society: Class Struggle without Class?", *Social History*, 3 (1978), 133–165.

101. R.A. Houston and I.D. Whyte, "Introduction: Scottish Society in Perspective", in Houston and Whyte (ed.), *Scottish Society, 1500–1800* (Cambridge, 1989), 34.

102. Burke, *Popular Culture*, 178–204.

9

Railway Mania in the Highlands:
The Marquis of Breadalbane and the Scottish Grand Junction Railway

C.J.A. ROBERTSON

In the mid-1840s two seemingly unrelated trends made their impact on the economy of Scotland. One, long apparent and increasingly becoming more serious, was the over-population and lack of resources in the Highland economy, which led to a Malthusian crisis in the famine of 1846. The other, of more sudden growth, was the outbreak of enthusiasm for investment in railways which became known as the Railway Mania. This first gave Lowland Scotland the essential structure of its rail network, and then developed into a speculative craze which led in turn to financial chaos and economic crisis. The two trends came together in the activities and on the estates of John Campbell, 2nd marquis of Breadalbane.

* * *

Breadalbane's impact on British life was what might have been expected of a high ranking peer with reasonable abilities and a sense of public duty. He entered the house of commons at the age of 24, representing Okehampton (as Lord Glenorchy) from 1820 to 1826, and Perthshire (as earl of Ormelie) from 1832 until he succeeded to the marquisate in 1834. From 1848 to 1852, and again from 1853 to 1858, he served as lord chamberlain of the household. At intervals, various forms of public recognition came his way — KT in 1838, lord lieutenant of Argyll in 1839, member of the privy council in 1848.[1]

But in Scotland Breadalbane was more significant. Apart from his rank and ancestry, of which he was notoriously proud,[2] the extent of his property assured him of importance. Bateman's survey of 1883 found that his 438,358 acres made him the second most extensive landowner in Scotland (with only one third of the acreage of the duke of Sutherland, but a little more than the duke of Buccleuch); he owned a seventh of Perthshire and a twelfth of Argyll. However, a gross annual value of £58,292 placed him only ninth in Scotland in terms of landed wealth.[3] From his palatial and vastly expensive new mansion at Taymouth Castle, Kenmore, he influenced the social and economic life of central Scotland. In his position as "by far the most outstanding man among the laity"[4] of the Free Church after the Disruption, he affected the religious life of the whole country. He was not an outgoing man – "beyond the celebrity attaching to the name of one in his position, he was little known"[5] – and as "a man of austere cast of countenance and commanding presence"[6] he was perhaps more likely to be respected than held in great affection. But of his importance in the southern Highlands there could be no doubt.

Economic change was being forced upon the Highlands, both from within and from without. Within was the inexorable pressure of rising population upon resources stretched to breaking point; of crofts subdivided to the point where family self-sufficiency, even on potatoes rather than oats or barley, was impossible; of a growing army of landless cottars whose place in Highland society was at best unclear; of the failure of the kelp industry on the western coast; of the falling prices obtainable for the crofters' cattle; of their consequent failure to keep up with rent payments, and the steady growth of arrears in the rent books. Without were the changes brought about by industrialisation and growing wealth on the Lowland and English economy and society in which Highland landowners were increasingly inclined to move; and the growing range of consumer items and other tempting ways to spend money, to gratify which they would have to increase the income they derived from their estates. Highland landowners were having to regard their estates as commercial enterprises rather than feudal possessions, and to consider how to maximise the revenue that could be obtained from them. The Breadalbane estates, located close to the more prosperous Lowlands, were in the front line of change, and the marquises turned their attention both to increasing their agricultural revenue and to considering other possible sources of income.[7]

The Breadalbanes had tackled estate improvement from the late eighteenth century. The 4th earl, who was created marquis in 1831, had ended runrig, limited cattle to the number which could be over-wintered, and encouraged drainage, crop rotation and the cultivation of potatoes.[8] At one time he had considered banning sheep in the hope of improving the soil and thus achieving both higher rents and greater employment,[9] but eventually he introduced the Cheviot (for "the good of the people", according to the minister of Glenorchy).[10] Co-operative tenants were encouraged with fifteen year leases; unco-operative ones were expelled. This policy was extended to encompass substantial clearances in the early nineteenth century, particularly in Glenorchy, with consequent depopulation and large-scale emigration.[11]

The 2nd marquis continued the policy of clearances, evicting some 2,500 people from areas including Glenorchy, where the population fell from 1,806 in 1831 to 831 in 1841, Glen Quaich and the Braes of Taymouth. A hostile pamphleteer accused him of totally clearing Glen Etive and Luing, and of reducing the military potential of the estates from the 1600 men raised by the 4th earl during the Napoleonic Wars to a maximum of 150 men in the 1850s. He concluded:

> I believe that your Lordship has done more to exterminate the Scottish peasantry than any man now living; and perhaps you ought to be ranked next to the Marquis of Stafford [later duke of Sutherland] in the unenviable clearing celebrities.[12]

Not surprisingly, the contributors to the *New Statistical Account* from parishes in which Breadalbane was a significant landowner tended to say little that was hostile to clearances. Several merely noted a fall in population, an increase in emigration, or the enlargement of farms; the minister of Ardchattan did refer specifically to both the "uniting of farms" for sheep and the enlargement of the marquis's deer forest.[13] The minister of Kenmore, in suggesting that there were no clearances in his parish at least, clearly thought that the marquis was too soft:

> The policy of the Noble family of Breadalbane, for many years has been to retain, for the most part, their poorer tenants and dependants on the property, and to make provision for them by means of pensions, cheap crofts and otherwise. Here, therefore, at the very door, is exhibited a significant exemplification of one of the most important truths of political economy; – that the more prominently you hold out the prospect of making provision for people, and do actually provide for them, you tamper with the salutary spirit of independence, and in so far help to widen the domain of pauperism.

He believed that it was "the duty of at least many of the young to betake themselves to other scenes".[14]

The Breadalbane policy was to transform their lands from a feudal patrimony into a commercial enterprise aiming at profitability in a market economy. Having cleared the superfluous poor in favour of the more profitable sheep, reasonable consideration was given to those tenants who remained. Grants of up to two-thirds of the costs were given for draining and ditching; holdings were consolidated; enclosure encouraged; leases of up to nineteen years granted; agricultural societies and prize competitions founded.[15] Overall, between 1834 and 1848 the marquis spent £42,762 on estate improvements.[16]

* * *

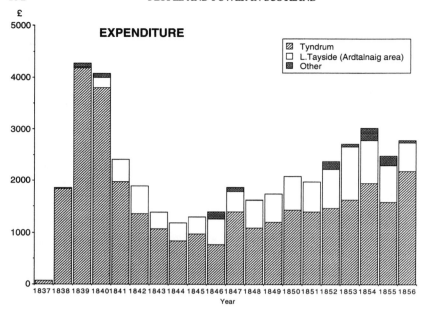

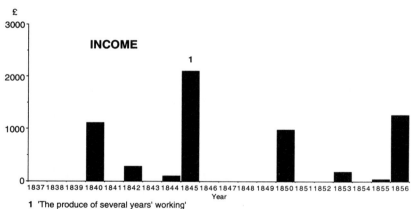

Sources: SRO, Breadalbane Muniments, GD112/18/13/4/21, 'Statement of outlay on Mineral trials in Breadalbane';
GD112/18/1/3/29, 'Continuation of statement on Outlay on Mineral Trials in Breadlabane from 1845 to 1856';
GD112/18/1/8/4, Lawrence Davidson W.S., 'Memorandum and Report to the Marquess of Breadalbane on Mr.
Wyllie's Acc^{ts} from Mart' 1844 to Mart' 1856'.

Figure 1. Breadalbane mineral trials, 1837-56: income and expenditure.

Breadalbane's hopes of profit were not restricted to the agricultural potential of his lands. Himself a keen amateur geologist, to the extent that his personal collection of fossils and minerals was displayed at the Great Exhibition,[17] he had great hopes of developing the estate's mineral resources. He started in

1838 by reopening the lead mines at Tyndrum, which had originally been worked in the mid eighteenth century by Sir Robert Clifton, but had been closed for forty years.[18] This began a pattern of expenditure on mineral trials which lasted for the rest of his life, and which did little but lose him money. The main search was at Tyndrum, where Breadalbane hoped to find commercial quantities of gold and silver as well as lead, but where in 1841 Lord Cockburn saw only "wretched mining, in reference to science, and, I suspect, in reference to profit".[19] Further investigations took place near Killin and Lochearnhead, in Glenorchy, and around Ardtalnaig on the south side of Loch Tay, where lead had been mined in the previous century. Here the marquis opened the Tomnadashin copper mine, which was so unprofitable that it was closed immediately when he died; apart from a little copper, it produced just enough gold to make a few trinkets for Breadalbane's personal use. Ardtalnaig was an unsuccessful area for economic enterprise; among the other failures there were a meal mill, a lint mill, bobbin-making, distilling and farina-making.[20]

Figure 1 indicates the steady drain on Breadalbane's finances through mineral searches, and the small amounts of compensating income which came from exploiting discoveries. To bolster his own conviction that his lands contained minerals suitable for profitable exploitation, Breadalbane brought in a procession of experts from England and Germany to analyse the deposits. Their generally gloomy reports were never enough to deter the marquis from continuing his quest.[21]

The report made in 1854 by Thomas Rowlandson was perhaps the most comprehensive. He confirmed the presence of ores of lead, iron, copper, chrome, sulphur, zinc and even gold and silver, but most of them, he considered, were not commercially viable. Lead was the commonest ore, but:

A very large number of the lead veins in different parts of your Lordship's property, whilst being extensive in both length & breadth and sufficiently impregnated with ore to tempt speculation, are not sufficiently so to lead to any sanguine expectation of eventual profitable results.[22]

The best prospects for lead were at Tyndrum, and even there an initial expenditure of £2,000 over four years would be called for. Other minerals which might pay their way included lead at Glenorchy and Lochearnhead, and copper, with associated sulphur and possibly potash, near Ardtalnaig. Among those rejected for development were the low grade gold and silver ores of Tyndrum, the zinc of Seil and Tyndrum, and the iron pyrites of Seil and Tomnadashin. Chrome ore in Glen Lochay would be expensive to work, and imports from the USA were cheap. Glen Lochay iron ore might conceivably be charcoal-smelted on site; the vein in Glen Quaich could not, since

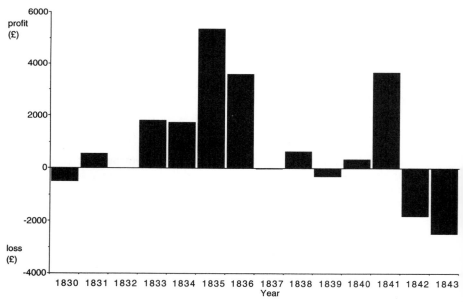

Source: SRO, Breadalbane Muniments, GD112/18/27/14/5, 'Table of Sales Expenses & Profits of
Easdale Quarries from 1818 to 1843'.

Figure 2. Easdale Quarries, 1830-43: production and profits.

neither fuel nor limestone was readily available.[23] Breadalbane was still undiscouraged; in the following year he was reportedly attempting to mine gold and silver on a new site, in Strathyre, where once again the workings were abandoned on his death.[24]

At the western end of Breadalbane's possessions lay a different type of mineral deposit which had long been profitably worked – the slate quarries on the islands of Easdale, Seil and Luing. The substantial demand for roofing slates from the expanding urban centres of industrialising Britain ensured a market, even although there was local competition from Ballachulish, English consumers tended to prefer the larger Welsh slates, and much of eastern Scotland used pantiles. Easdale's profitability fluctuated markedly, with the intense depression years of 1842–43 leading to substantial losses (see Figure 2). By 1845 Easdale had 109 customers scattered in 44 locations, almost all coastal, all around Scotland.[25] In the spring of 1845 Breadalbane's chamberlain, Sir Alexander Campbell of Barcaldine, undertook a tour of the east and south-west coastal towns of Scotland on behalf of Easdale. He found that most towns were supplied completely from either Easdale or Ballachulish, though Berwick, Ayr and Greenock preferred Welsh slates, and that diverting orders from Ballachulish was difficult, since their discount on one year's trade was only given if a further order was placed for the following year. Even so, he returned with a satisfactory amount of new orders and hopeful promises.[26]

More quarrying, this time for granite, took place at Barrs on the remote north side of Loch Etive, and at a smaller site across the loch at Inverliever. In 1844 Breadalbane ended the contract of the unsatisfactory tenant at Barrs, Walter Gardiner, and put the quarry under the direction of Sir Alexander Campbell. A manager, Archibald Stewart, was appointed and immediately sent on a clandestine tour of Aberdeenshire to learn how to run a granite quarry.[27] One problem was the lack of local men with any knowledge of either blasting or stone dressing. Stewart managed to entice one skilled dresser from Aberdeen,[28] but he appears to have led a lonely existence. Within a fortnight of his arrival, Stewart noted that "one man can do very little work in a quarry alone", and three months later he had to report that "I am sorry to say that the Aberdeen man ran off yesterday ... and would not be prevailed upon to stop any longer".[29] In the nine months from October 1844 to June 1845 Barrs and Inverliever produced an income of a mere £148 against an expenditure of £141.[30] The main market was in Glasgow, both for major works such as harbour improvements and for causeway setts for road paving, but in 1844 this market was quiescent,[31] and two years later the rejected William Gardiner, now quarrying at Bonawe, beat Barrs to a major contract for stone for extensions to the Broomielaw.[32] As it stood, Barrs was not a source of great profit to the marquis.

* * *

More profit might be anticipated from the town of Oban, of which Breadalbane had in 1837 purchased the northern part. The town had become a burgh
of barony in 1820 and a parliamentary burgh (with 33 electors) in 1833;[33]
its prosperity was to be linked to the growth of a west Highland tourist boom,
helped a little by writers such as Johnson, Boswell and Thomas Pennant, and
a great deal by Sir Walter Scott. Mull in 1840 was reported to be full of
tourists:

> They fill every conveyance, and every inn, attracted by scenery, curiosity,
> superfluous time and wealth, and the fascination of Scott ...[34]

The ruins of Iona, though sadly decayed and neglected, appealed to the
Victorian taste for the picturesque; Staffa, boosted by Mendelssohn's visit in
1830, catered for those seeking the sublime. Oban was the port of departure
for these islands and the spreading Hebrides beyond.

The first steamship, Henry Bell's pioneering *Comet*, had reached Oban in
1812. Twenty years later, regular services ran from Glasgow to Oban and
on to Tobermory, Fort William and Inverness.[35] Even so, in 1840 Cockburn
noted that Oban was "the gem of sea villages ... no manufactures, no trade,
and scarcely any bustle".[36] The advent of faster steamships in 1841[37] may
have caused the change he noted five years later:

> It is becoming a great steamboat station, – too great. Each landing creates a
> flutter which disturbs its solitude. It seems fuller of strangers than of natives.[38]

However, the journey from Glasgow involved either a tedious eleven-hour
journey by the Crinan Canal or an even longer and often dangerous trip
round Kintyre. One commentator observed that the canal could only take
steamers which were too small to venture into the Atlantic in bad weather,
and that most passengers were hauled through the canal by horse barge:

> From the many delays caused by the passing through of the locks, many of the
> passengers usually walk from Ardrishaig to Crinan.[39]

Breadalbane added to the town's growth with a feuing plan for his land which
marked "the beginning of villadom".[40] In 1845 he commissioned six assorted
designs for villas from a local builder; construction started two years later.[41]

It also appeared that a tourist attraction might be developed at the eastern
end of Breadalbane's estates. The discovery of a mineral spring at Moness,
near Aberfeldy, led to visions of a new spa. Mineral analysis of the water
showed that it had an iron content similar to that of Tunbridge or Harrogate,
but that "organic matter" gave it an unpleasant colour.[42] One of
Breadalbane's German mineralogists advised that the organic matter was
probably only on the surface, and a pipe might be sunk to the spring below.

All that would then be required would be

> to embellish the place by the construction of secret walks to Aberfeldy and the
> falls of Moness, as motion is requisite for the wholesome influence of the waters
> which are rather difficult to digest... . The fine situation of the village of
> Aberfeldy recommends itself strongly as a place of public resort and a Highland
> spa.[43]

* * *

The development of all this economic potential would require improved
transport, and in the 1840s this suggested the promotion of a railway.
Traditionally the trade in sheep and cattle had transported itself; the Breadalbane lands lay across the line of all the main drove roads from the north and
west to the fair at Crieff and the great Tryst at Falkirk. Every year 8,000 cattle
and 40,000 sheep passed along the road from Oban, and at Tyndrum they
met a further 9,000 cattle and 70,000 sheep coming by Dalwhinnie from
the north; yet more went by Glen Lyon or Tummel and past the eastern end
of Loch Tay.[44] But although droving reached its peak in the 1830s, it was
becoming more difficult to fit into a changing pattern of agriculture. With
the growth of turnpike trusts, roads were made up and thus rendered
unsuitable for hooves. Enclosure meant that roads were fenced in and beasts
could not straggle in search of grazing; and pressures on land meant that
even traditional grazing sites which had long been free now had to be paid
for. Railway transport would also reduce the loss of weight on the journey.
The later nineteenth century was to see a pattern of drove road closures, the
decline of Falkirk Tryst, and a general transfer of the trade in animals to the
railways.[45]

For other traffic Perthshire's roads were much improved from the 1820s,
when they had been in a notorious state of disrepair.[46] By the 1840s
Breadalbane's Perthshire estates had "ample and various means of communication", with roads and bridges "in excellent repair", and turnpikes from
Aberfeldy to Killin, Logierait and Dunkeld, the latter two joining the great
road from Perth to Inverness.[47] Roads in Argyll, a county without turnpikes,[48] were more varied: a typical report from Muckairn noted that the
parish was traversed by a "good county road" from Oban to Inveraray, but
had "no other roads which deserve the name".[49]

Rail transport, however, could offer facilities which even improved roads
could not – in particular the rapid and economical transport of heavy or
bulky goods. Agriculture would be helped by the importation of fertilisers and
by access to markets for any surplus production. The whole area would
benefit by the availability of cheap coal: in Kenmore, for instance, coal cost
twice as much as in Perth, and most of the fuel used was peat "procured at
a vast cost in time and labour" equivalent to bringing coal for twenty or thirty

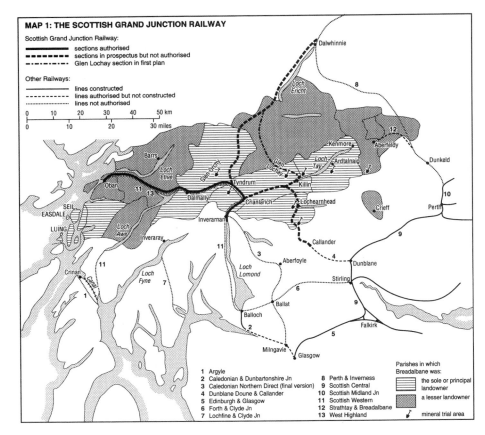

MAP 1: THE SCOTTISH GRAND JUNCTION RAILWAY

miles.[50] If the marquis's hopes for his minerals were to be realised, he would need cheap coal supplies for smelting and cheap transport to take away the production. As the minister of Killin had noted of the Tyndrum minerals, "the great distance from coals and from the market may render them less valuable".[51] Easdale and Barrs perhaps had less need of a railway, since their produce could be sent out by water. But sea journeys round the Mull of Kintyre to Glasgow, or round Cape Wrath to east coast markets, were long and often dangerous. Conveyance by rail, even with an initial short journey by water, would save time and perhaps expense to established markets, and allow direct access to new inland customers. Oban could become both a major tourist centre and the principal port for the whole of the western Highlands and the Hebrides, and Aberfeldy's tourist potential might also be developed. Cheap transport might even encourage some of the surplus crofting population who had survived the clearances to move away in search of more profitable employment.

For all these reasons, in 1845–46 Breadalbane initiated the promotion of two railways affecting his estates. One, the Strathtay & Breadalbane, was a short branch with a modest share capital of £120,000, running from the proposed Perth & Inverness at Dalguise along Strathtay to Aberfeldy.[52] The other, the Scottish Grand Junction, with a proposed share capital of £1,000,000, was one of the largest mania projects in Scotland. Its prospectus envisaged a main line from Oban to Callander, where it would connect with the projected Dunblane Doune & Callander and thus with the rest of the Scottish railway system; branches would run from Crianlarich to the head of Loch Lomond (connecting with the loch steamers) and from Tyndrum by Loch Ericht to Dalwhinnie (connecting with the Perth & Inverness).[53] The project thus formed a cross covering most of the Breadalbane estates (see Map 1); surprisingly, the Loch Lomond branch was not continued to Balloch, which would have created a complete and direct through route from Oban to Glasgow.

* * *

Breadalbane was unique among Scottish aristocrats in the extent of his support for railways. During the mania he appeared on the committees of four eventually successful companies, one which was partially built, three which were authorised but not constructed, and several total failures (see Map 2).[54] Had all the mania railways with which he was connected been built, he would have been a director of a system stretching from Glasgow to Inverness and from Oban to Forfar and Falkirk. Most peers, however, held back from open involvement, and the exceptions almost invariably committed themselves only to lines which passed through or near their own estates. Among these were the earl of Eglinton, chairman of the Ardrossan and director of the Ayrshire;[55] Lord Belhaven & Stenton, coalowner at Wishaw, director of two small railways over which his coal would reach the Clyde, and chairman of the provisional committee of the Caledonian before authorisation;[56] Viscount Kinnaird, chairman of the Dundee & Perth;[57] Lord Wharncliffe, chairman of the Scottish Midland Junction; and the earl of Leven, director of the Edinburgh & Northern. No other peer became a director; few others allowed their names to go on to the committees of more than a single project.[58]

Breadalbane's most successful company was the Scottish Central, running from Perth through Stirling to meet both the Caledonian and the Edinburgh & Glasgow near Castlecary, and offering the only through link between northern and central Scotland. Of this he was chairman until 1849 and a director until his death, apart from brief periods of resignation when he fell out with his fellow-directors. The Central was for long the target of takeover bids by both the Caledonian and the Edinburgh & Glasgow, and Breadalbane, who on the whole favoured the company retaining its independence, found

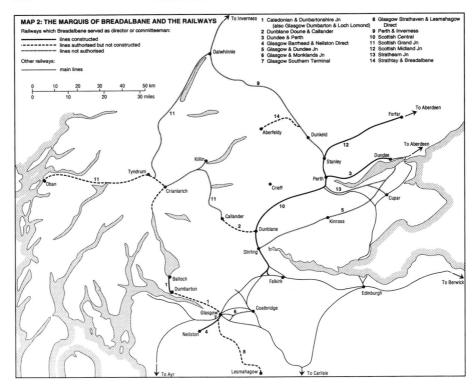

MAP 2: THE MARQUIS OF BREADALBANE AND THE RAILWAYS

Railways which Breadalbane served as director or committeeman:

— lines constructed
- - - - lines authorised but not constructed
········· lines not authorised

Other railways:
— main lines

1 Caledonian & Dunbartonshire Jn
  (also Glasgow Dumbarton & Loch Lomond)
2 Dunblane Doune & Callander
3 Dundee & Perth
4 Glasgow Barrhead & Neilston Direct
5 Glasgow & Dundee
6 Glasgow & Monklands Jn
7 Glasgow Southern Terminal

8 Glasgow Strathaven & Lesmahagow
  Direct
9 Perth & Inverness
10 Scottish Central
11 Scottish Grand Jn
12 Scottish Midland Jn
13 Strathearn Jn
14 Strathtay & Breadalbane

that it took up most of the time that he could devote to railways.[59] His support for two connecting railways, the Scottish Midland Junction and the Dundee & Perth, involved little more than allowing his name to appear on the provisional committee. But the Perth & Inverness was of more direct interest to him, and its rejection was a substantial disappointment. Parliament, doubtful whether locomotives could cope with the gradients over the Drumochter pass and unpersuaded that a railway could pay in such an unpopulated countryside, threw out a serious and well-designed plan remarkably similar to the successful Highland Railway of two decades later.[60] This left the Strathtay & Breadalbane successfully authorised but unconnected to any other railway. Attempts to extend it to link to the Scottish Midland Junction failed in both 1847 and 1848, and it remained unbuilt.[61]

To the west were schemes to link Argyll to the markets of Glasgow and beyond. Breadalbane was on the committees of both the Glasgow Dumbarton & Loch Lomond of 1844 and its successor in the following year, the Caledonian & Dunbartonshire Junction. Both planned to connect Glasgow to Balloch and the steamer service on Loch Lomond, thus bringing steam transport within ten miles of the mines at Tyndrum.[62] But above all there was the project which promised to link almost all his economic interests to each other and to outside markets in all directions – the Scottish Grand Junction.

*   *   *

The Scottish Grand Junction was only one of many railways promoted beyond the Highland line, but it was alone (apart from the little Strathtay & Breadalbane) in achieving authorisation. It was not even the first scheme projected to reach Oban. The prospectus of the Scottish Western, issued early in August 1845, proposed to spend £600,000 on a line from Oban by Crianlarich to Balloch, thus establishing a complete rail route to Glasgow: a month later its shares had been applied for five times over.[63] But within a week it was reported that Breadalbane and other landowners were "of opinion that the Scottish Western Railway scheme is not a suitable one for the country", and that they were preparing their own project, which would connect to the Scottish Central and the Caledonian.[64] At the same time, some supporters of the Caledonian & Dunbartonshire Junction proposed the West Highland, at a cost of £300,000, from Oban to the head of Loch Lomond, where it would connect with the boats to Balloch – a project which rapidly disappeared into the Highland mists.[65] Another scheme, the Caledonian & Great Northern, came before the public on 3 September. This was a typically vague and inadequately surveyed mania project, running from the Caledonian & Dunbartonshire Junction at Milngavie through the Trossachs and then "by the most direct route to Inverness", with branches to Oban and Crieff. The prospectus named as engineers the prestigious English firm of Locke and Errington who had designed the Caledonian, but they denied any knowledge whatsoever of the project.[66]

The original Grand Junction prospectus, issued on 13 September,[67] combined elements of all these schemes. The company was initially projected as the Scottish Direct Northern & Western, but the name was changed at the suggestion of company solicitor Archibald Reid, whose explanation indicated one of the confusions of the mania:

> There is a great deal in a *name*, and there are so many Westerns, Northerns, and Direct Northerns, that without some name strongly distinctive this new scheme would be constantly confounded with one or other of the more ephemeral ones of the day.[68]

Highland promotions were of two kinds – those projected by local landowners and their professional advisers, and those planned by railway interests from elsewhere, often from Glasgow. The original Scottish Western committee was largely composed of landowners on or near the route, with a few Glasgow names – Lord Provost James Lumsden, Alexander Baird of Gartsherrie, John

Bain of Morriston – which would encourage the city's investors. They later strengthened their appeal to established railway interests by acquiring five Edinburgh & Glasgow directors, including the most prominent figure in Scottish mania promotions, John Learmonth.[69] The Grand Junction's committee contained fewer local names; of the ten men originally approached by Reid, only Alexander Campbell of Monzie joined.[70] Apart from Breadalbane, the active promoters were mostly Glasgow merchants and industrialists who were already well-known in the railway world. They included Mark Sprot, William Houldsworth, John Tennant and two more of the Baird brothers of Gartsherrie, William and Robert; three appeared on the committee of the Caledonian, and there were further strong associations with Caledonian-backed companies.[71] A familiar rivalry appeared in the choice of engineers; the Western had the leading Scottish engineer, John Miller, who had designed the Edinburgh & Glasgow, the Ayrshire and the North British, while the Grand Junction announced the appointment of Locke and Errington.[72]

In spite of all these names, the Grand Junction was, as a committeeman reminded him, very much Breadalbane's creation:

> The Provisional Committee were induced to join it very much by the request of your agents... . In all the arrangements your Lordship's wishes have been carefully consulted, while at the same time no landed proprietor could possibly benefit more by any undertaking than your Lordship would by this if it were carried... . In public estimation, & not without good grounds, your Lordship is identified with the Railway, & indeed it has been a matter of complaint by many that it was entirely your Railway and managed not as an ordinary mercantile concern, but in deference & indeed complete subservience to your wishes.[73]

From the tone of this letter, it is clear that by the end of 1845 the scheme was running into trouble, but in the late summer the prospectuses of both it and the Western had been optimistic about the future. The concentration in both companies was on goods traffic, emphasising the livestock droves to Falkirk, from which the Grand Junction in particular, serving both Oban and Dalwhinnie and linked to Falkirk via Callander, would be well placed to profit. Both companies expected a large mineral traffic, of coal into the area and of lead and slate out, although only the Western pointed out that most of the mines belonged to Breadalbane. Both made much of Oban, "well-known as the principal port and central market of the Western Highlands and Islands":[74]

> It cannot fail also to become the favourite resort of those numerous parties of pleasure and for recreation from the large Manufacturing Towns now so much adopted on existing Railways.

The "well-known inconvenience and delay to which passengers are now subjected by the [Crinan] canal" led the Scottish Western to include in its final version a detached branch from Ford, at the south end of Loch Awe, to Ardrishaig or Lochgilphead; the two sections of the railway would be connected by steamers on Loch Awe.[75] It also spawned an abortive scheme for the £90,000 Argyle Railway across the Crinan isthmus, which, it was claimed, would save two hours on the journey for an annual total of 20,000 passengers, 24,000 sheep and 30,000 tons of goods.[76] In north Cowal some of the landowners proposed a line from Oban to Helensburgh via Inveraray and Kilmun, with ferries across both Loch Fyne and Loch Long. This developed into another ephemeral project, the Lochfine & Clyde Junction from Strachur to Dunoon.[77] The clear advantage, however, would lie with a through railway to Oban, which would save four hours on the journey from Glasgow using the Loch Lomond boats, and five hours if there was a continuous rail link.[78]

Those acquainted with the terrain may have been surprised to learn that the Grand Junction route

> for the most part ... is a dead level, and the surface is so regular that the cost of construction will be much below the average of railway undertakings,[79]

but there were in fact few severe engineering problems. The one exception was the heavy gradients on the Loch Lomond branch, which it was decided to overcome

> by means of an application of the atmospheric principle, to be worked by water power, of which, as it happens, the proprietors have on the spot an unlimited command.[80]

Not everyone was impressed. One correspondent to the *Scottish Railway Gazette* resorted to heavy-handed sarcasm:

> One would think in reading the prospectus of this "grand" affair that Argyle, Perth and Inverness-shires were a sort of Scottish Midland Counties – that Tyndrum was the Derby of Scotland, and destined to be a great focus for her railways – while Dalmally was a Leeds at least, and Oban nothing short of a northern Liverpool. Another railway, the "Scottish Western", had already offered to supply the wants of these great commercial seats, but they are prizes, it seems, much too rich to be snapped up without a struggle; and now these rival lines are competing, who shall be at the cost of enlivening the wastes of Glenorchy with the stoker's lonely whistle, and scaring the wild deer of Glenfillan with the rattle of empty trains. And men look on, too, and talk gravely of these schemes as benefits to the public, and little Potosi-mines *in petto* to the shareholders. Can human folly or gullibility go further?[81]

And even some local opinion saw the scheme as a folly of the mania:

> For what purpose such lines as that from Dalwhinnie to Callendar, and through
> Argyleshire to Oban, are projected but to fill lawyers' and surveyors' pockets,
> we know not. Like land-marks indicating the height of some extraordinary tide
> or swell of the sea, they may however be useful to record the height to which
> the railway mania had attained in the year of grace 1845.[82]

* * *

The first signs of the collapse of mania enthusiasm for railways came with a
fall in share prices in the autumn of 1845, which weeded out many of the
weaker projected schemes before they could be submitted to parliament.
Although railway shares stabilised for the first two-thirds of 1846, they
declined steadily thereafter, until at the end of the decade they stood at less
than 40 per cent of the peak of July 1845.[83] In these conditions, many
projects found that subscribers who had cheerfully promised to take their
shares were now unwilling or unable to pay their calls, and that even raising
the deposit required before a scheme could be considered by parliament might
be difficult or impossible. Promoters had to adjust from a financial climate in
which anything seemed possible to one in which the main aim was survival.

The Grand Junction projecters, however, remained optimistic, seeing no
immediate need for retrenchment, and instead turned to eliminating the
competition. The relatively inexperienced promoters of the Scottish Western
were not a serious problem: rumours of amalgamation were afoot by October
1845, and in the following month the Western agreed to withdraw; in return
the Grand Junction paid all its expenses and offered its shareholders either
repayment of their deposits plus 5 shillings for each share, or this offer on
half their shares with the other half being converted into shares in the Grand
Junction (at the rate of two Western for one Junction). This, it was hoped,
might attract "some of the very respectable men on their committee and help
get off some shares".[84] Almost all the Western shareholders took the offer of
shares, though incompetence in the Junction office meant that the deposits
were not repaid until January 1846.[85] The *Scottish Railway Gazette* was now
convinced that the Grand Junction would be built:

> There is no doubt that it will be carried out; and it is precisely one of those
> schemes which Parliament will be most inclined to support, as it is not a mere
> scheme for speculative purposes, but one intimately identified with the improve-
> ment of the country and the good of the people.[86]

The promoters of the Caledonian & Great Northern were originally hostile,
but soon decided that co-operation was better than competition. They cut
their plan to a line from Milngavie through the Trossachs to Crianlarich, and

renamed their company the Caledonian Northern Direct. They also strengthened their appeal to investors by acquiring the duke of Montrose as chairman and concluding an arrangement by which the mighty Caledonian company would work the line, although as engineers they had to settle for the minor Glasgow firm of Gordon and Hill.[87] From the point of view of the Grand Junction, this line now only competed with its Loch Lomond branch, while it offered an all-rail route to Glasgow. Even so, Breadalbane was reported to be so opposed to the scheme that his men were instructed to block the activities of the other company's surveyors.[88]

To many supporters, amalgamation of the two companies now seemed necessary, in the hope of helping their standing in a discouraging money market.[89] Some potential customers disliked the Loch Lomond break in the Grand Junction route to Glasgow, and threatened to keep using the Crinan Canal unless a complete rail link was assured.[90] Admittedly one committee member believed that an extra hour on the Loch Lomond route would be well worth while for a saving of £300,000 on total construction costs and a reduction of one third in fares; he also thought that carriages might be conveyed down the loch on boats as in America.[91] Engineer George Martin favoured amalgamation only if the Caledonian Northern Direct could be built within £8,000 of its estimate.[92]

Another attraction of amalgamation, given the Northern Direct's agreement with the Caledonian, was the chance of persuading that company to take over the amalgamated concern. The collapse of the mania, and the consequent tightness of money, meant that for many projects the only chance of survival was to be taken over by a well-established large company, preferably with a guaranteed rate of interest on the shares. Joseph Locke put the argument succinctly:

> Railway affairs just now are not only so critical but so desperate that it seems but a hopeless task to endeavour to resuscitate even the most promising of them... . It appears to me advisable to make any arrangement you can, *with any parties*, so as to lessen (by dividing) your responsibilities for the expenses already incurred.[93]

Locke himself was closely identified with the Caledonian. Its chairman John James Hope Johnstone noted that

> their Board had never yet taken shares in any other line, although they had promised to do so in one or two instances, if necessary,

but also said that he would consider recommending the Caledonian to take 500 shares in the new joint company if the amalgamation with the Caledonian Northern Direct went through.[94]

In November 1845 a draft of amalgamation proposals envisaged the Grand Junction paying one-third of the parliamentary deposits for a united company, which in turn would complete the buy-out of the Scottish Western.[95] There were some cautionary notes; both Breadalbane and the Caledonian were unhappy about the proposed gradients on the Caledonian Northern Direct, and wanted Locke brought in to revise them.[96] Even so, the companies seemed likely to get together, even if it was not clear that two weak companies could add up to one strong one. But it never happened. The problem was partly an inability to agree terms, caused largely by the stubbornness of the two noble chairmen, each of whom was convinced of the superiority of his own line.[97] Partly it was the alternative possibility of salvation for the Grand Junction by sticking to the Loch Lomond route and offering parliamentary support to any Glasgow-Balloch line which would take 5,000 Grand Junction shares.[98] And partly it was the unwillingness of the Caledonian Northern Direct to see the projects sink or swim together; since both companies would have to go to parliament separately in any case, they wanted any arrangement to be conditional on both passing in 1846, and were unwilling to chance having to contribute to the expenses of the Grand Junction if it failed.[99] According to Grand Junction committeeman Strachan Popham:

> Had both Coys. sufft. funds the terms wd. be fair enough.... What divides us is the risk of being thrown out of Parlt. & being saddled with increased expences in case of failure.[100]

Two days later, however, he was firmly blaming the rival company: "I can only account for their conduct from the different interests in their *numerous* Committee".[101] And at least one committeeman hoped for a Caledonian takeover of the Grand Junction without any involvement of the Northern Direct, which he thought might happen if Breadalbane proposed it.[102]

In January 1846, however, agreement was reached on co-operation, though not on amalgamation. The Caledonian Northern Direct agreed to provide a line from Ballat to meet the Grand Junction at Inverarnan, and to abandon its plans further north. It also agreed to take 1,500 Grand Junction shares. Meanwhile, it had reneged on the working arrangement with the Caledonian and was falling prey to the blandishments of the Edinburgh & Glasgow, whose empire-building chairman (and Grand Junction director), Peter Blackburn, took over its chair early in 1846. The Edinburgh & Glasgow also took over the 1500 Grand Junction shares, which it later surprisingly claimed to have sold without making a loss.[103]

It was all too late. The Caledonian Northern Direct was in severe financial trouble. A shareholders' meeting on 14 April 1846 learned that, of the company's original 24,000 shares, the deposits had been paid on only 11,566. Of the 53 members of the provisional committee, 22 had failed to pay the deposit on their allocation, while the rest only held 2154 shares between them. Although the *Scottish Railway Gazette* considered that "the scheme was in every respect a *bona fide* one and at least merited success", it was clear that a company which could not pay its parliamentary deposit could not go on. The committee, however, wished to raise another £500 and continue; the disillusioned shareholders divided between those who wished to wind up the company immediately, and those who preferred to wait for the Dissolution Bill going through parliament. The latter carried the vote by 1875 to 1080.[104] The company's bill, which had passed its second reading in March, was withdrawn, and the concern slumped into apathy. Eventually, in August, it was wound up by 4390 votes to 550, leaving the Scottish Grand Junction without any hope of a rail link to Glasgow.[105]

Meanwhile, the Grand Junction was also facing financial difficulties. With the bursting of the mania bubble in October 1845, the market in railway shares and scrip collapsed. Although the Grand Junction's £1,000,000 share capital had initially been handsomely over-subscribed, "about the time when the shares were allocated ... the recent great change in the money market took place", and the committee became aware that many of their shareholders either could not or would not pay their calls.[106] An undated memorandum in Breadalbane's papers notes that at one point a group of applicants who should have paid £65,300 had actually produced only £3,500.[107] By January 1846 only £75,000 had been subscribed; another £125,000 was required to satisfy parliamentary standing orders, and £70,000 beyond that even to construct a line from Oban to Loch Lomond.[108] Prices for Grand Junction shares, with a deposit of 50 shillings paid up, started to be quoted in the press in February 1846. Although there were short bursts of relative enthusiasm at the beginning of the parliamentary sessions in both 1846 and 1847, the quoted price never exceeded 60 per cent of the paid-up value, and was usually much lower. After the price crashed in the autumn of 1847 it seems that the shares were hardly traded at all (see Figure 3).

The committee had to reconsider their plans:

> Owing to the late panic the applicants for stock failed to take up their shares, it is consequently out of the power of the Committee to proceed with the undertaking as originally intended.[109]

One possibility, of simply cutting losses and winding up the company, might lead to both practical and ethical problems:

> Breaking up will involve us in a host of difficulties. How can we *practically* enforce payment of a proportion of the expences from all the shareholders & Provisional Committee – & we cannot take more than a just proportion of the deposits we have in hand, & what a fraction this will prove of the sum required!

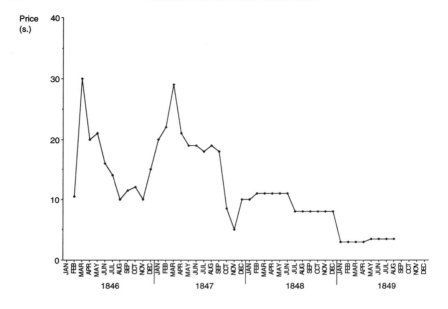

Source: *Glasgow Herald* 1846-49, price given on first Friday of each month.

Figure 3. Scottish Grand Junction share prices, 1846-49 (Shares with 50s. deposit paid).

> How can we either face the public – we found a flourishing Cy. in the field [the Western], prepared to go to Parlt; we forced them to retire & then became disillusioned ourselves in the face of obstacles that have often been surmounted in similar cases – we should not act *right*, if we give in.[110]

Another temptation was to look to Breadalbane to rescue the concern single-handed. In December committeeman James Forsyth of Dunach observed that only £8,000 had been raised while £15,000 had already been spent on "our unfortunate railway". In a mixture of pleading and implied threats, he tried to persuade Breadalbane to provide a personal guarantee for up to half the total expenses, on the grounds that if the company failed before even going to parliament:

> [it] would raise a perfect storm of outcry, & ... your Lordship would suffer more in public opinion than the whole money is worth ... . I think it is quite clear that to satisfy your Lordship's own sense of what is right, you would in such circumstances contribute by far the greatest proportion, perhaps two thirds or three fourths of the whole claim.[111]

A memorandum prepared for Breadalbane advised caution:

> The suggestion that Lord Breadalbane should take 5000 shares [i.e £125,000 face value] is thus tantamount to his taking on himself very nearly *all* that will be required for satisfying standing orders.... . Most certainly, his Lordship should not accede to that suggestion.

Even paying half of the sum required to go to parliament (£67,500) was "an extent of liability, which Lord Breadalbane in prudence, ought not to undertake". At most he might consider taking a further 1350 shares (£33,750), if the rest of the provisional committee took 150 shares each; but he might have to help some committeemen to meet this commitment. If the project failed, he would probably have to meet up to a quarter of the total losses.[112]

A more optimistic, if less likely, proposal suggested that, since a railway alone was unlikely to pay, the company should expand by building quays and running shipping services from Oban.[113] And any hope of a Caledonian takeover had been killed, first by the Caledonian Northern Direct's defection to the Edinburgh & Glasgow, and then by its subsequent collapse. In public the committee maintained an attitude of optimism. An anonymous pamphlet issued in January 1846 in support of the scheme, quite possibly by the committee itself, claimed that the cost of the line would be "exceedingly moderate", since the engineering was easy, the landowners favourable, the land inexpensive, the labour cheap and readily available, and the competition from roads non-existent.[114]

In practice, the Grand Junction curbed its ambitions. In January 1846 the proposed sections from Crianlarich to Dalwhinnie and Callander were abandoned, probably to the satisfaction of Breadalbane's Scottish Central, which could now anticipate carrying all the traffic between Inverness and central Scotland. This left a 46 mile line from Oban by Tyndrum to the head of Loch Lomond, with no connection to any other railway, though Campbell of Monzie consoled himself that the Loch Lomond boats had carried 30,000 passengers in the previous year. The cost of the reduced plan was estimated at £322,000, or about 7000 per mile, and the share capital was accordingly reduced to £350,000. And another five men joined the committee, all of whom later became part of the twelve-man directorate after the authorisation act.[115]

Even so, money remained short. Once a mania promotion was seen to be in financial difficulties, its subscribers became chary of throwing good money after bad. Many would refuse to pay calls, forfeiting their share allocation and writing off any money already paid. In the event, Breadalbane had to agree to take a further £75,000 of stock to enable the Grand Junction to raise its parliamentary deposit.[116] Surprisingly, the bill then went through parliament with little difficulty, largely because all the landowners concerned were in favour and the bill was unopposed. The directors named in the act were six Argyll landowners, a banker from Oban, and five Glaswegians, all with considerable railway experience. Among them were Edinburgh & Glasgow chairman Peter Blackburn and his deputy Henry Dunlop (though neither appears to have been active in promoting the Grand Junction): of the Caledonian interest, only one representative remained.[117] By this time even Breadalbane may have been losing faith; although he had chaired the committee of management before the act, he was unwilling to head the new board of directors. Indeed, no one wanted the position, which was reluctantly accepted by Glasgow merchant William Graham of Lancefield with the comment that "the duties were not at present likely to be arduous".[118]

At this stage the shareholders were still cautiously supportive. A meeting held under Lord Wharncliffe's Act (which ruled that shareholders had to reaffirm their desire to go on with a project before its bill was given its final reading) voted in favour by 6752 to 349, perhaps encouraged by Campbell of Monzie's promise that the directors would only build the line if they were sure that it would pay.[119] But affairs went no further. The first shareholders' meeting after the act, although making conventionally optimistic noises about the long term prospects, agreed not to start on construction and to make no calls for the moment.[120] In practice, this was close to a decision to abandon the scheme. In the aftermath of the mania, as the economy sank into recession and railway shares slumped in public estimation, a company which failed to start work as soon as it legally could very rarely was able to come back to construction at a later date.

By April 1847 the directors were making no attempt to hide their financial desperation; as a last hope they turned to the government. They suggested that either the government should take over all the shares at par (which would have meant a price of under £1 for shares with £2.10s. paid on them), or it should take three-quarters of the shares and divide the profits with the existing shareholders, or it should lend the company £300,000 at $3\frac{1}{2}$ per cent interest on the security of the railway itself.[121] The railway press remained optimistic:

> We understand the Government are willing to entertain the proposals, as they are beginning to see that the destitution in the Western Highlands is likely to extend into another year, and they consider the formation of this line will, in a great measure, assist in averting the distress. The shareholders may therefore congratulate themselves with the prospect of getting this railway made at an outlay of £5 per share.[122]

But, although the government had occasionally been willing to help out transport enterprises which it saw as essential for national security, no such considerations applied to the isolated Grand Junction, and it is not surprising that no help was forthcoming. In 1851 a further appeal for government construction was made by a group of Highland landowners with the support of Glasgow town council, partly in order to provide employment in a severely depressed area. The government's decision not to act was in effect the death knell of the Grand Junction, since the five year period in which it could exercise compulsory powers to purchase land ran out in July.[123]

The final hope came in March 1852, when MP John Stuart moved for government money to build a railway from Oban to Glasgow. The Scottish Grand Junction, which had been "an incomplete communication" since it used the Loch Lomond boats, he clearly regarded as dead: "he needed not say that this was a defective proposal, and failed". A through railway would help to relieve distress throughout the western Highlands, which government-aided emigration schemes had failed to do. The estimated cost was £500,000, of which local proprietors would supply 40 per cent if government produced the rest. Since Irish railways had received £973,000 from public funds, Scotland deserved some assistance as well. The proposal met a generally hostile reception, largely on the grounds that Stuart was suggesting a line which "would cost so much money that it would not pay any private undertakers to do it, and therefore it ought to be paid for out of the public purse". Disraeli, as chancellor of the exchequer, insisted that the proprietors should actually expend their 40 per cent of the costs before coming to parliament to ask for help (which they might or might not get), and the proposal was finally killed by a motion for adjournment.[124]

All that remained were the last rites of the Scottish Grand Junction. Although any realistic hope of construction had long vanished, the company dragged out a moribund existence until 1852. Then, at a special meeting representing 34.9 per cent of the shares, there was a majority of 2,931 to 550 for formal abandonment. In its $5\frac{1}{2}$ year career the company had received an income of £26,388, almost all for the parliamentary deposit: it had spent £22,136 and had nothing at all to show for its efforts. The local proprietors who had supported construction did not now oppose abandonment: "there is reason to infer", reported the Board of Trade, "that its construction is not considered a matter of much importance as far as local interests are concerned".[125] Breadalbane's railway eventually foundered in face not of hostility but of almost universal apathy.

The speculative atmosphere of the railway mania allowed the projection of schemes which would previously have been considered improbable or even farcical. Its collapse enforced reconsideration of both the likelihood of profitable traffic and the financial resources of investors; in the event the Grand Junction was only one of many projects which passed parliament in 1846 but remained unbuilt. Indeed, had Breadalbane introduced his project a year earlier, it is probable that it would have been authorised in the summer of

1845 and would have started construction before the financial crisis – and every Scottish company which in fact kept to that timetable eventually came through to commercial operation. It may be doubted whether the Scottish Grand Junction could, in the short run at least, have generated enough traffic to be profitable. But many a railway, while not providing its shareholders with much in the way of dividends, was invaluable to the area through which it passed; counter-factual historians may wish to calculate the impact of the construction and operation of a major railway project on the agriculture, tourism and general prosperity of the post-famine central Highlands.

The Breadalbane estates did eventually get their railway, when in 1880 the Caledonian-sponsored Callander & Oban was opened along much of the route originally proposed by the Grand Junction. But by that time Breadalbane was dead, the estates had passed after a long legal battle to a distant cousin, Barrs quarry had closed in 1849[126] and the Tyndrum mines in 1862, and the opening in 1870 of the railway from Dingwall to Strome Ferry had ensured that Skye rather than Mull became the Hebridean focus of Victorian tourism. The marquis had made his mark on railway development, notably through the success of the Scottish Central, but his Scottish Grand Junction became merely the most grandiose failure of the Scottish railway mania.

Notes

Note: the Breadalbane Muniments in the Scottish Record Office [SRO] are at the time of writing in process of being catalogued. Hence full catalogue references can be given in some areas (eg., GD112/18, which deals with minerals); but for GD112/53 (railway material) no more detailed references are yet available.

1. *Dictionary of National Biography* [*DNB*], viii, 386; W.A. Gillies, *In Famed Breadalbane* (Perth, 1938 ed.), 211; J. Christie, *The Lairds and Land of Loch Tayside* (Aberfeldy, 1892), 14.
2. Gillies, *Breadalbane*, 211.
3. J. Bateman, *The Great Landowners of Great Britain and Ireland* (4th ed. 1883; repr. Leicester, 1971), 55. If Buccleuch's English holdings are included, he rises to second place in terms of acreage in the British list with Breadalbane third. In terms of value, those ahead of Breadalbane were the noble houses of Buccleuch, Seafield, Fife, Sutherland, Stair, Hamilton, Richmond & Gordon, and Dalhousie.
4. *DNB*, viii, 386.
5. W. Norrie, *Dundee Celebrities of the Nineteenth Century* (Dundee, 1873), 221.
6. Gillies, *Breadalbane*, 211.
7. For the early nineteenth-century highland economy, see, for instance, T.M. Devine, *The Great Highland Famine* (Edinburgh, 1988), ch. 1; M. Gray, *The Highland Economy 1750–1850* (Edinburgh, 1957), chs. 2–4.
8. Gillies, *Breadalbane*, 199–200.

9. M.M. Macarthur (ed.), *Survey of Lochtayside* (Edinburgh, 1936), introduction, p. xxiii.
10. *Old Statistical Account*, Glenorchy & Inishail, 339.
11. E. Richards, *A History of the Highland Clearances* (London, 1982), i, 212. In 1819 Robert Southey found that some at least of the cleared crofters had been resettled in improved circumstances elsewhere on the estate. A. Mackenzie, *History of the Highland Clearances* (1883; repr. Perth, 1986), 216–17.
12. R. Alister, quoted in Mackenzie, *Highland Clearances*, 347–N8.
13. *New Statistical Account* [*NSA*], vii (Argyll), 502 (Ardchattan); see also *NSA*, x (Perthshire), 770 (Dull), 1090 (Killin); *NSA*, vii, 69 (Kilninver & Kilmelfort).
14. *NSA*, x, 484 (Kenmore). The ministers of Killin and Dull also suggested that noble hand-outs were encouraging pauperism (*ibid.*, 1094 [Killin], 782 [Dull]).
15. *NSA*, vii, 69 (Kilninver & Kilmelfort), 76 (Kilbrandon & Kilchattan), 100 (Glenorchy & Inishail); *NSA*, x, 473–5 (Kenmore), 1091 (Killin). Even for the poor there are numerous comments on the provision of pensions, and of "liberal donations", on top of which Breadalbane might, in a parish such as Glenorchy, find himself paying over 80 per cent of the costs of formal poor relief (he contributed £61 to a total poor fund of £75.8s.); *ibid.*, and *NSA*, vii, 102 (Glenorchy & Inishail).
16. SRO, Breadalbane Muniments, GD112/12/5/3/25, Davidson & Syme WS, "State of Sums Expended on Improvements upon the Entailed Estate of Breadalbane from Martinmas 1834 to Martinmas 1852".
17. SRO, GD112/18/9/8/1, C.H.G. Thost to Sir Alexander Campbell, 8 Feb. 1851.
18. Gillies, *Breadalbane*, 212; Christie, *Lairds and Land*, 11.
19. Henry, Lord Cockburn, *Circuit Journeys* (Edinburgh, 1888), 105.
20. Christie, *Lairds and Land*, 82; Gillies, *Breadalbane*, 212.
21. Eg., SRO, GD112/18/1/3/12, Prof. Thomas Thomson to Breadalbane, 25 Jan. 1838; GD112/18/4/1/8–9, Dr. A. Fyfe, "Analysis of supposed copper ore found near Taymouth", Apr. 1840; GD112/18/4/l/24, F. Odernheimer, "Report of assay of lead ore from West Corabuie vein and of grey copper ore from Tomnadashin", 10 Oct. 1840; GD112/18/4/1/22–23, J. Barratt to Breadalbane, 28 Oct. 1843; GD112/18/1/35/5, F. Odernheimer to Breadalbane, 30 Nov. 1845; GS112/18/8/9/36–7, S. Reichendorf, "Report on lead mines at Tyndrum", 1 May 1847; GD112/18/8/9/40, G. Roberts & J. Crerar, "Memorandum on Tomnadashin mineral trials", 11 Jan. 1848; GD112/18/1/3/34, C.H.G. Thost, "Description of the Mineral Fields in the Marquisate of Breadalbane", 2 Apr. 1855; and many others.
22. SRO, GD112/18/8/12, Thomas Rowlandson, "Survey of Lord Breadalbane's Scottish property" (1854), 37.
23. *Ibid.*, 37–58.
24. A. McKerracher, *Perthshire in History and Legend* (Edinburgh, 1988), 90.
25. SRO, GD112/18/13/4/5, List of Easdale Customers, Jan. 1845.
26. SRO, GD112/18/24/2/3, "Abstract from the Journal of Sir Alexander Campbell in as far as regards the Customers of the Easdale Slate Quarries", 1845.
27. SRO, GD112/18/3/2/3–4–5–6–15–24–41, Archibald Stewart to Sir Alexander Campbell, 18 Apr. 1844, 20 Apr. 1844, 4 May 1844, 10 May 1844, 4 July 1844, 10 Aug. 1844, 14 Feb. 1845.
28. SRO, GD112/18/3/2/20, Stewart to Campbell, 19 July 1844.
29. SRO, GD112/18/3/2/23, Stewart to Campbell, 2 Aug. 1844; GD112/18/3/2/29, *ibid.*, 18 Nov. 1844.
30. SRO, GD112/18/3/7/1, Account: "Inverliever and Barrs Quarries".
31. SRO, GD112/18/3/2/29, William Bald (engineer to the Clyde Trustees) to Sir Alexander Campbell, 17 Sept. 1844.
32. SRO, GD112/18/3/7/6–7–9–12–13, Archibald Stewart to Sir Alexander Campbell,

22 May 1846, 23 May 1846, 12 June 1846, 1 May 1846, 1 Apr. 1846. Stewart considered that Gardiner could only have won the contract by lying to the customer.

33. Hugh Shedden, *The Story of Lorn, Its Isles, and Oban* (Oban, 1938), 216; Alexander M. Faichney, *Oban and the District Round* (n.p., 1902), 84–5.

34. Cockburn, *Circuit Journeys*, 83.

35. Faichney, *Oban*, 67–8.

36. Cockburn, *Circuit Journeys*, 78.

37. Shedden, *Story of Lorn*, 229.

38. Cockburn, *Circuit Journeys*, 288.

39. Aberdeen University, O'Dell Collection, OD.C2.Sco, Anon, *Statement in Relation to proposed Highland Lines of Railway and to the proposed Scottish Grand Junction Railway* [1846], 6.

40. Shedden, *Story of Lorn*, 234.

41. SRO, GD112/18/13/6/7, Account of Peter McNab, Oban, to Lord Breadalbane per James Mudie, factor, Easdale.

42. SRO, GD112/18/1/5/28, A.W. Fyfe MD, "Analysis of Aberfeldy water", 17 June 1844.

43. SRO, GD112/18/1/5/26, F. Odernheimer, "Report of the Mineral Spring at Moness near Aberfeldy", 25 Sept. 1845.

44. A.R.B. Haldane, *The Drove Roads of Scotland* (Edinburgh, 1968), 207 and endpapers map; *Herapath's Railway Journal* [*HRJ*], 8 Oct. 1845, Scottish Grand Junction Railway prospectus.

45. Haldane, *Drove Roads*, 208–219. In 1844 Breadalbane himself helped to make the drovers' life more difficult by closing the traditional overnight stance at Inveroran, making the journey between the stances at Kingshouse and Clifton too long for a day's droving. The drovers took him to court, but finally lost in the house of lords. (*Ibid.*, 212–213).

46. A.R.B. Haldane, *New Ways through the Glens* (Newton Abbot, 1973 ed.), 170–1.

47. *NSA*, x (Perthshire), 477 (Kenmore), 697 (Logierait), 776 (Dull), 1091 (Killin). One link which had not been built was the 1807 proposal by the 4th earl for a road from Ardeonaig by Glen Lednock to Comrie and Dunblane, which was to bring in coal and lime to Loch Tayside; no contractor had been prepared to do the job for less than twice the estimate. Haldane, *New Ways*, 94–5.

48. *NSA*, vii (Argyll), 36 (Inveraray).

49. *NSA*, vii (Argyll), 52 (Muckairn). Pressure from both marquises had also led to improved postal services throughout the estates: the 2nd marquis himself paid for the mail cart service between Kenmore and Tyndrum. A.R.B. Haldane, *Three Centuries of Scottish Posts* (Edinburgh, 1971), 64, 132, 135.

50. *NSA*, x (Perthshire), 485–6 (Kenmore).

51. *NSA*, x (Perthshire), 1081 (Killin).

52. *Scottish Railway Gazette* [*SRG*], 18 Oct. 1845, Strathtay & Breadalbane prospectus.

53. *SRG*, 11 Oct. 1845, Scottish Grand Junction prospectus. The original plan had taken its Dalwhinnie branch by Glen Lochay and Killin to join the main line at the head of Glen Ogle. Earlier correspondence in the *Scottish Railway Gazette* had suggested lines from Killin to Dalwhinnie, and from Stirling by Tyndrum to Fort William. The journal itself favoured Callander – Killin – Dalwhinnie (linking to the Perth & Inverness), and Laggan – Fort Augustus – Inverness (*SRG*, 12 July 1845, 19 July 1845).

54. The successful companies were the Dundee & Perth, Glasgow Southern Terminal, Scottish Central and Scottish Midland Junction; partially built, the Caledonian & Dunbartonshire Junction; authorised but unbuilt, the Dunblane Doune & Callander,

Glasgow Strathaven & Lesmahagow Direct, Scottish Grand Junction and Strathtay & Breadalbane; unauthorised, the Glasgow & Dundee Junction, Glasgow & Monklands Junction, Perth & Inverness and Strathearn Junction. In 1848 he also joined the board of the Glasgow Barrhead & Neilston Direct (*Bradshaw's Railway Guide* and company prospectuses in *SRG* and *HRJ*, 1845–48).

55. Eglinton was the proprietor of Ardrossan harbour, and in 1847 resigned from the Ayrshire to promote the rival Glasgow Kilmarnock & Ardrossan which would give his harbour a more direct connection to Glasgow (*SRG*, 12 Apr. 1845; *Bradshaw's Railway Guide*, 1945).

56. The two companies were the Wishaw & Coltness and the General Terminus & Glasgow Harbour. He was also on the provisional committees of eight failed mania projects associated with the Caledonian interest, but he left the Caledonian itself when its act was passed (*Bradshaw's Railway Guide* and company prospectuses in *SRG* and *HRJ*, 1845–46).

57. He was also chairman of the failed Scottish North-Western (*SRG*, 30 Aug. 1845).

58. *Bradshaw's Railway Guide* and company prospectuses in *SRG* and *HRJ*, 1845–46.

59. *SRG* and *HRJ*, 1846–49. I hope to deal fully with the history of the Scottish Central in this period in a forthcoming book on the Scottish railway mania.

60. J. Mitchell, *Reminiscences of my Life in the Highlands* (London, 1883), ii, 158–165; *HRJ*, 5 Apr. 1845.

61. SRO, GD112/53, Archibald Reid to Breadalbane, 10 Mar. 1847; *SRG*, 24 July 1847, 2 Sept. 1848; *Edinburgh Gazette*, 13 Nov. 1846, 16 Nov. 1847.

62. *HRJ*, 4 May 1844; *SRG*, 19 Apr. 1845.

63. *SRG*, 9 Aug. 1845, 13 Sept. 1845.

64. *Caledonian Mercury*, 21 Aug. 1845.

65. *Glasgow Constitutional*, 13 Aug. 1845, 16 Aug. 1845, 20 Aug. 1845.

66. *SRG*, 6 Sept. 1845, 27 Sept. 1845. The line was also referred to as the Caledonian & Grand Northern, and was stated (inaccurately) by one hostile writer to be a former title of the Scottish Grand Junction (*SRG*, 27 Sept. 1845).

67. *HRJ*, 14 Sept. 1845.

68. SRO, GD112/53. Archibald Reid to Breadalbane, 30 Aug. 1845; GD112/53, Draft Prospectus of the Scottish Direct Northern and Western Railway, Sept. 1845. The scheme had also earlier been referred to as the Western & Northern (*ibid.*, James Graham to Breadalbane, 25 Aug. 1845; *SRG*, 27 Sept. 1845).

69. *SRG*, 16 Aug. 1845, 30 Aug. 1845. It is unlikely that any of these extremely busy men took an active part in promoting a scheme which they only joined at a late date, and their participation may simply have reflected their almost automatic opposition to any scheme associated, however remotely, with the Caledonian.

70. SRO, GD112/53, Reid to Breadalbane, 31 Aug. 1845.

71. Others included Alexander Downie, William Leckie Ewing, Robert Stewart of Carfin, John Stirling of Kippendavie and Patrick Maxwell Stewart MP. Of the committee, five were directors of the Caledonian & Dunbartonshire Junction, and five of the Glasgow Garnkirk & Coatbridge, both Caledonian-backed companies (*SRG*, 11 Oct. 1845).

72. *Ibid.*; *SRG*, 16 Aug. 1845.

73. SRO, GD112/53, James Forsyth of Dunach to Breadalbane, 29 Dec. 1845.

74. *SRG*, 11 Oct. 1845 (Scottish Grand Junction prospectus).

75. *SRG*, 16 Aug. 1845 (Scottish Western prospectus).

76. *HRJ*, 4 Oct. 1845 (Argyle prospectus).

77. SRO, GD112/53, Dugald McDougall of Gallanach to Breadalbane, 10 July 1845; Lochfine & Clyde Junction prospectus (in author's possession). Neither the Argyle nor the Lochfine & Clyde Junction got so far as to deposit their plans for parliamentary consideration.

78. Anon., *Statement*, 6.
79. *SRG*, 11 Oct. 1845.
80. Anon., *Statement*, 11.
81. *SRG*, 27 Sept. 1845.
82. *Perthshire Courier*, quoted in *Inverness Journal*, 14 Nov. 1845.
83. A.D. Gayer, W.W. Rostow & A.J. Schwartz, *The Growth and Fluctuation of the British Economy 1790–1850* (Oxford, 1953), ii, 375. Gayer *et al.*'s index of the prices of leading railway shares gives the following figures for June and December of the mania years (June 1840 = 100): 1844, 119.6 & 128.1; 1845, 165.3 & 133.9; 1846, 142.6 & 128.5; 1847, 122.0 & 105.3; 1848, 100.2 & 85.0; 1849, 79.1 & 63.8.
84. *HRJ*, 4 Oct. 1845, 5 Nov. 1845; *SRG*, 1 Nov. 1845; *Edinburgh Evening Courant*, 1 Nov. 1845; GD112/53, Notes; GD112/53, James Forsyth to Sir Alexander Campbell, 20 Dec. 1845.
85. *SRG*, 8 Nov. 1845, 13 Dec. 1845, 27 Dec. 1845.
86. *SRG*, 8 Nov. 1845.
87. *Edinburgh Gazette*, 31 Oct. 1845; *SRG*, 30 Aug. 1945. The Caledonian Northern Direct's line from Inverarnan to Ballat, near Balfron, was undisputed; from Ballat to Milngavie it was challenged by a proposed branch of the Forth & Clyde Junction.
88. *Edinburgh Evening Courant*, 29 Nov. 1845.
89. SRO, GD112/53, S.I. Popham to Sir Alexander Campbell, 15 Dec. 1845.
90. SRO, GD112/53, Donald Campbell, Tobermory, to Breadalbane, 27 Mar. 1846.
91. SRO, GD112/53, S.I. Popham to Sir Alexander Campbell, 17 Dec. 1845.
92. SRO, GD112/53, George Martin to Sir Alexander Campbell, 8 Dec. 1845. Martin had been assistant engineer to Miller on the Scottish Western, but transferred to the Grand Junction when that company was wound up.
93. SRO, GD112/53, Joseph Locke to Breadalbane, 15 Dec. 1845.
94. SRO, GD112/53, James Forsyth to Sir Alexander Campbell, 29 Nov. 1845.
95. SRO, GD112/53, draft amalgamation proposals, 27 Nov. 1845.
96. SRO, GD112/53, Forsyth to Sir Alexander Campbell, n.d.
97. SRO, GD112/53, Montrose to Breadalbane, 29 Oct. 1845.
98. SRO, GD112/53, Notes, n.d.
99. SRO, GD112/53, George Crawford to Sir Alexander Campbell, 10 Dec. 1845.
100. SRO, GD112/53, Popham to Sir Alexander Campbell, 15 Dec. 1845.
101. SRO, GD112/53, *ibid.*, 17 Dec. 1845.
102. SRO, GD112/53, James Forsyth to Breadalbane, 29 Dec. 1845.
103. *SRG*, 31 Jan. 1846, 18 Apr. 1846, 18 Sept. 1847.
104. *Edinburgh Evening Courant*, 18 Apr. 1846; *SRG*, 18 Apr. 1846.
105. *SRG*, 23 May 1846, 8 Aug. 1846.
106. Anon., *Statement*, 5.
107. SRO, GD112/53, Note of Scottish Grand Junction share allocation.
108. SRO, GD112/53, "Memorandum as to the Scottish Grand Junction Railway", Jan. 1846.
109. SRO, GD112/53, Note of Scottish Grand Junction share allocation.
110. SRO, GD112/53, Popham to Sir Alexander Campbell, 15 Dec. 1845.
111. SRO, GD112/53, James Forsyth to Breadalbane, 29 Dec. 1845.
112. SRO, GD112/53, "Memorandum as to the Scottish Grand Junction Railway", Jan. 1846.
113. SRO, GD112/53, William Robertson, Kinlochmoidart, to Breadalbane, 27 Feb. 1846.
114. Anon., *Statement*, 2–3, 10–12.

115. *Ibid.*, 12; *SRG*, 9 Jan. 1846, 17 Jan. 1846.
116. *SRG*, 17 Jan. 1846.
117. Act 9 & 10 Vic. c.137, 3 July 1846. Four of the twelve had been members of the Scottish Western provisional committee. Neither Blackburn nor Dunlop had been on the original Scottish Grand Junction provisional committee.
118. *SRG*, 1 Aug. 1846.
119. *SRG*, 4 July 1846.
120. *HRJ*, 15 Aug. 1846; *SRG*, 1 Aug. 1846.
121. SRO, GD112/53, Scottish Grand Junction directors' minutes, 7 Apr. 1847.
122. *SRG*, 12 Apr. 1851.
123. *SRG*, 20 Mar 1852, quote from Sir George Strickland Bt., MP for Preston. Stuart, MP for Newark, owned land at Kinlochleven and had been born on his father's estate at Ballachulish (M. Stenton, *Who's Who of British Members of Parliament* [Brighton, 1976], i, 366).
124. *SRG*, 10 Apr. 1847.
125. Parliamentary Papers, 1852(26–2)XLVIII, *Report of the Board of Trade on the Abandonment of the Scottish Grand Junction.* The expenses broke down as £9681 for parliamentary costs, £4249 for legal costs, £5146 to the engineers and £3062 miscellaneous.
126. SRO, GD112/18/3/3/38, Testimonial to James Ross, 5 Nov. 1849.

10

Whatever Happened to Radical Scotland? The Economic and Social Origins of the Mid-Victorian Political Consensus in Scotland

WILLIAM W. KNOX

Coming as it does between the turbulent years of Chartism and the rise of socialism in Scotland, the third quarter of the nineteenth century has been seen by some historians as a period of class collaboration and political consensus.[1] The class antagonisms of the Chartist era, which threatened to undermine the political system, gave way to a more harmonious and stable relationship between capital and labour based on a shared commitment to the values and ethos of liberal capitalism. In this scenario of historical development stabilisation was closely identified with the emergence of an élite upper stratum of the working class — the labour aristocracy — whose earnings, lifestyle, status and values isolated it from the rest of the working class and pushed it into the arms of the middle class. Under bourgeois influence and patronage the labour aristocracy actively sought to be incorporated into the major institutions of the British state and accepted a framework of industrial relations based on conciliation rather than conflict. Consequently accommodation to liberal capitalism rather than confrontation characterised the Scottish labour movement in this period.

Although the thesis of the labour aristocracy no longer carries the academic weight it once had in explaining mid-Victorian social and political relationships, and has been rejected by, at least, one of the original proponents,[2] its demise does not absolve historians from seeking the origins of stabilisation or consensus. In this period formerly powerful alternatives to industrial capitalism, such as the co-operative societies of the Owenites, the trade guilds of the builders, and the Chartist land banks, lost their appeal for workers. The legitimacy of private property and the permanency of the industrial system was accepted by Scottish workers. The third quarter of the nineteenth century also witnessed important changes in the conduct and language of political struggle within the working class. The Chartist period saw the language of politics as primarily one of conflict as captured in the shibboleth "peacefully if we may, forcibly if we must", and there were reports of workers arming themselves for the overthrow of the state.[3] Although the violence of Scottish Chartism can be exaggerated,[4] there is no doubt that after 1850 working class politics were more strongly based on prevailing ideology and working through mainstream institutional channels as a means resolving socio-economic grievances. The concern was less with *The Rights of Man* and more on the right of the respectable working class householder to a share in political power through the vote.

The explanation of this transformation has to be placed in the context of a more comprehensive and dynamic thesis than that offered by proponents of the labour aristocracy thesis. As the stabilisation of political and social relationships is systemic, rather than specific to the particular stratum, it has to be located within a wider economic and social perspective. Central to this approach is the idea of recomposition. This paper will argue that changing economic and social forms led to a remaking of the Scottish working class in terms of occupational structure, trade union strategies and political practice after 1850. Although the paper places the emphasis on change within the working class, at the same time, it recognises that the process of recomposition was incomplete due to the existence of pre-industrial craft forms and the continuing impact of what Christopher Smout has called the "radical political tradition" on the consciousness of Scottish workers.[5] The duality of old and new forms of production existing side-by-side in industrial society led at times to contradictory patterns of political and workplace behaviour. In spite of this, the changing nature of the Scottish working class is unmistakeable and it is this which provides the key to understanding the process of stabilisation in mid-Victorian Scotland.

The Changing Economic and Occupational Structure

The obvious starting point for such a study lies in the changing nature of the Scottish economy and its impact on the occupational profile of the country. Prior to 1850 the industrial structure of the economy was rather narrowly based, with around nine out of ten workers in manufacturing employed in textiles. The main engine of economic growth and technological change was the cotton industry. The mechanisation of spinning obliged a transition to the factory system, although the abundance of cheap labour in the weaving sector delayed transition to power-loom weaving until the 1850s. In spite of its narrow base, manufacturing was heavily orientated towards export markets and thus subject to extreme fluctuations in trade.[6] The relative backwardness of manufacturing industry had a retarding effect on the primary sector of the economy. Coalmining was based on local markets, and miners often retained a connection with the land. Dual occupations were also not uncommon among manufacturing workers.[7] Transportation was similarly underdeveloped.[8] The uneven development of the industrial economy, as we will show, had a corresponding effect on workers' activity and organisation.

Between 1850 and 1880 the Scottish economy experienced a transition to a broader industrial base. These decades witnessed the mushroom growth of shipbuilding on the Clyde and the equally impressive development of the coal and iron industries. From only 3 per cent of the total British labour force in shipbuilding in 1831, the Clyde's share grew to 21 per cent (and that of Scotland to 26 per cent) by 1871. In that year the Clyde accounted for 48 per cent of the shipbuilding output of British yards.[9] The coal industry saw massive rises in output from 7.4m tons in 1854 to 38.8m in 1914, with an equally spectacular rise in employment. The west of Scotland became the main producing area of coal in Scotland with Lanarkshire and Ayrshire accounting for 70 per cent of Scottish output by 1870.[10] Capitalising on Neilson's invention of the hot blast furnace, Scottish ironmasters were producing the cheapest pig iron in the world. Output of pig iron manufacture increased from 797,000 tons in 1854 to a peak of 1,206,000 in 1869/70.[11] The growth of engineering complemented developments in shipbuilding and other transport industries, particularly the railways. The Springburn district of Glasgow became the world's leading manufacturer of locomotives. Textiles, as an employer of labour, were still important to the economy. By the 1850s the power-loom had been introduced to weaving bringing about the demise of the hand-loom weaver in all but the fanciest aspects of the trade.

The massive surge in economic growth in the third quarter of the nineteenth century was export led. As early as 1847 two-thirds of Scottish pig iron was exported; indeed, between 1830 and 1870 Scotland was supplying 50 to 90 per cent of British pig iron exports.[12] In the engineering industry recurring economic crisis was overcome by diversification in product line and by selling its products in export markets.[13] Glasgow's economy was more dependent on overseas trade than any other British region.

The concentration of economic historians on industrial successes has perhaps overshadowed the small scale nature of much of Scottish business. As Rodger shows in his study of mid-Victorian Scottish industry, half the firms in urban areas in this period employed fewer than five workers and three out of every four firms less than nine. Only 10 per cent of Scottish firms employed more than twenty workers. He also found that in terms of the numbers employed the largest firms were to be found in textiles with a mean workforce of 662. However, he also notes that 60 per cent of the industrial labour force was concentrated in plants of a hundred or more workers.[14] The duality of the industrial structure in Scotland in mid-century was, therefore, evident, and this perhaps helps to explain the fragmentation of the working class; a phenomenon which we will examine later in the paper.

However, the rapid expansion of the Scottish economy increased the demand for labour, which became insatiable in times of economic boom. The number of metal workers increased from 60,800 in 1851 to 210,000 in 1901, as did those in mining from 48,100 to 127,000 over the same period, and there were similar gains in the other main branches of industry, with the exception of textiles which lost 67,000 jobs. At a macro level there was a sharp fall in the numbers working in agriculture from around 30 per cent of the total working population to just over 19 per cent in the thirty years after the 1851 Census, with corresponding rises in employment in the other main sectors of the Scottish economy. The Strathclyde region showed the largest fall of those working in agriculture from 16.27 per cent of total working population in 1851 to just 7.43 per cent in 1881. By the latter date half the working population of Strathclyde was employed in manufacturing.[15]

The expansion of the economy and the labour market, as well as the changing occupational profile of the country, had important political and social implications. Much of the industrial and political protest prior to 1850 had centred on groups of workers deskilled and impoverished by industrial change such as the hand-loom weavers. The introduction of power-loom weaving in the 1850s saw the demise of this group of workers and their absorption in other forms of industrial employment. Those workers at the frontier of technological change such as cotton spinners also suffered a decline in numbers and a change in the sexual composition of the labour force. After the strike of 1837 spinning in Scotland was increasingly feminised. By the 1880s two-thirds of the workforce were women[16] who, although not entirely passive, were unorganised. The militancy of the cotton spinners was broken in the new sexual division of labour. Of those workers associated with the pre-industrial modes of organisation only the colliers remained. They continued to prove militant in times of rising prosperity, but the militancy tended to be confined to the large and integrated coal and iron combines, such as the Dixon enterprises of Lanarkshire. The average figure for west Lanark was in 1873 around 136.9 men per pit, although in districts like Old Monkland in 1864 it was only 45.6 men per pit. It was not until after 1880 that a workforce of around 300 was common for a colliery.[17] Thus as the labour force changed in composition the threats to the industrial order diminished and it assumed a permanency among the workers as they became attuned to bargaining by "playing the market".[18]

The Material Condition of the Working Class

The stability of a social system lies in its ability to deliver an increasing amount of goods and services to a growing population, rather than solely in the ability of corporate powers to manufacture consensus by broad and binding agreements between them on policy. The first phase of industrialisation saw many workers experience a decline, or at least stagnation, in living standards and that fuelled much of the industrial and political protest of the 1830s and 1840s. Levitt and Smout, in their study of poor law returns in 1843, point to a low wage economy, in spite of regional and occupational variations. The average weekly wage for Scottish stonemasons in 1843 was 15.63 shillings, with colliers receiving 15.51 and millwrights 14.00 shillings respectively. Those male workers in the lowest categories of employment were estimated to earn an average of 5.79 shillings a week, or around a third of the skilled rate.[19]

Although the evidence is patchy, the third quarter of the nineteenth century saw a substantial improvement in money wages and living standards for the majority of Scottish workers and their families. During the 1848 depression colliers' wages had reached a nadir of 10s. weekly,[20] but by 1863 wages averaged between 4s. and 4s. 9d. per day in the Glasgow area, and by 1880 hewers were receiving around 25s. 3d. per week at a time of falling prices.[21] In the more skilled trades wages were much higher than in mining. Burgess notes building wages in Scotland reached parity with England in the 1850s, which eroded the differential advantage Scottish employers had over the English by as much as 15–25 per cent.[22] Indeed, between 1843 and 1880 stonemasons in the Glasgow area saw their money wages increase by around 35s., or 230 per cent, for a reduced working week of 43 hours.[23]

Engineering and shipbuilding workers also experienced rises in wages. According to the evidence of the Amalgamated Society of Engineers [ASE] given in the Report on Trade Unions (1867), average minimum wages increased on a much reduced working week from 18s.–34s. in 1851 for 63–57 hours of work, to 22s.–36s. in 1866 for 60–56 hours, and in 1880 24s.–36s. for 54 hours.[24] Figures for the Glasgow area over the same period would appear to confirm the ASE's estimates. Weekly rates for fitters were said to be 28s. 9d. in 1866 for 60 hours of work. Fourteen years later the respective figures were 31s. 9d. for 54 hours, although workers on piece could earn more. Shipyard riveters on the Clyde were said to earn 25s. 10d. in 1866 for a 60 hour week, but this rose sharply in 1880 to 40s. for those on piece, although the hours of work are unspecified.[25] Even among certain sections of the unskilled wages were rising. Pan men in the sugar refining industry were earning as much as skilled men, with earnings estimated to be between 30s.–40s. per week in 1866, and machine men in paper manufacture in 1863 were getting between 19s.–21s., although in both cases the hours of work are not specified.[26]

Although earnings of a broad range of trades were increasing over the third quarter of the nineteenth century and the economy was expanding rapidly, it was susceptible to violent fluctuations associated with the trade cycle. The shipbuilding industry, for example, suffered seven major cycles averaging seven to nine years between 1822 and 1879.[27] These recurring crises after 1850, however, did not have the same impact as those which occurred during the first phase of industrialisation. Part of the reason lies in the diversification and expansion of the economy, which meant that the impact of unemployment was more uneven than in the period of cotton's dominance, and the more liberal interpretation of the poor laws after 1845 which provided assistance for the able bodied poor. These developments ensured that, in spite of short-term fluctuations, workers were able to perceive themselves as beneficiaries of the workshop of the world. This appears to be borne out by the declining rate of out migration in these decades. Although the gold discoveries in Australia and New Zealand in the 1850s led to a substantial rate of out migration of young men in the early 1850s, the 1860s and 1870s saw this slow to a trickle.[28]

Changes in the Workplace

The growth of the Scottish economy also witnessed a seachange in employer attitudes towards labour. The Gradgrind image of employers born of the cut-throat competition of the cotton trade in which labour was seen as a mere commodity, gave way to a self-confident bourgeoisie mindful of civic responsibilities and with paternalistic concern for their workers. Although few studies exist in Scotland of paternalism, Patrick Joyce, in his study of the Lancashire cotton industry, has convincingly demonstrated how a paternalistic strategy was used by employers to obtain the social adhesion of the workforce.[29] Paternalism was expressed in the notion of the indivisibility of the relations between master and man, as well as in the idea of the workplace and the locality as a community. This was given practical expression in times of crisis such as the cotton famine of the early 1860s, or in times of personal distress. Lothian coalowners provided small pensions for widows of colliers killed in mining accidents and made provision for men incapacitated through industrial injuries.[30] The assistance in times of distress was complemented by civic benevolence. The cotton thread manufacturers of Paisley donated hospitals, churches, schools and other civic institutions to the town. Lothian coalowners donated libraries, schools, bowling greens and parks to the mining communities. These acts of benevolence, along with company housing, extended the power of the employer beyond the factory gates and helped build up identification with the community, and naturally with the leading employers, since they personified the community, among the workers. An example was the monument of the shipyard workers of Dumbarton to the memory of their employer William Denny, shipbuilder. Another might be found in the workers of Coats, cotton thread manufacturers of Paisley, parading the streets of Edinburgh on an away day excursion with their company banners, or turning up in their "hundreds ... late at night" in 1857 to welcome James Coats and his American bride back from their honeymoon. The *Paisley Herald* described the scene:

> The deafening shout of the multitude when the first carriage came in sight, the music of instrumental bands ... there was also artillery to fire midnight salvoes, after which the carriage horses were unyoked, [and] a great army of Ferguslie workers pulled the first carriage up to Woodside House where his father lived.[31]

The relative improvement in relations between employers and workers was made possible to some extent by the reduction in tensions in the workplace. The first phase of industrialisation had been a profoundly disturbing experience for many workers, who found their skills and livelihoods undermined by technological change. The classic example has been the handloom weaver, but other occupations in the skilled sector were faced with specialisation and encroachments from unskilled workers. The millwrights' trade was broken down into specialised operations; the shipwright was displaced by the change from wood to iron shipbuilding; and building craftsmen saw multi-handed trades such as painter/glazier/plumber divided into separate crafts. All skilled workers faced increased hours of labour and tighter industrial discipline as employers intensified the process of formal subordination of labour to capital.

Although technological change is a continuous process, it would appear that the decades of the 1850s through to the 1880s were less dynamic than had been the case beforehand. Cotton was perhaps most affected with the introduction of the self-acting spinning mule, which was gradually appropriated by women spinners. However, in most trades changes were mainly to be found in the reorganisation of production, which increased firm and product specialisation and intensified the division of labour. In coalmining there were labour saving devices introduced in the 1860s, such as winding machines and endless chains and ropes. There was steam-powered underground haulage engines which replaced men and horses. However, none of the innovations made serious encroachments into the skills of the collier. The most important change in the position of the collier was the introduction of a new contract system in the 1850s which made agreements terminable on a day's notice. In 1866 no notice was required at all, which allowed employers to regulate output more closely with demand, but, at the same time, allowed colliers to leave a badly paid contract for a more lucrative one.[32] In engineering firms began to specialise in particular product lines, such as locomotives or textile machinery, which demanded specialised engineering skills. The change from wood to iron shipbuilding marginalised the shipwright but introduced a highly skilled class of metal workers, whose job it was to shape, bend and join hot iron plates. The technical improvements were not labour displacing, but allowed for a greater accuracy of work and enhanced the quality of the product. The element of "craft mystery" was still in many trades a tangible factor giving the worker a measure of control over the planning and execution of his work. The dependency on the skill of their workers and the reluctance to alter the capital/labour ratio due to recurring problems in world markets, led Scottish employers to experiment with a range of strategies for raising productivity.

As employers redirected their energies away from production into marketing the question of the wage/effort bargain began to assume enormous importance in industry. Each firm developed its own particular set of solutions to this issue, but most forms of individual incentives and supervision involved ceding control of some part of the labour process to the workers. Internal subcontracting of work to a craftsman or groups of workers offered the employer ready made substitutes for inadequate managerial and cost accounting resources. At the same time, it provided avenues of mobility for key workers and, through piece work, ensured individual and group self-discipline. Among Monklands ironstone workers subcontractors were chosen by the employers on the basis of "loyalty and experience" and were left to recruit and organise team workers.[33] In the iron works themselves puddlers paid their underhands, as did the shinglers their assistants.[34] In coalmining and shipbuilding similar arrangements existed between skilled workers and their labourers.[35] Indeed, in occupations where work was dispersed over a wide or inaccessible area and close supervision impossible, internal subcontracting was favoured by employers. But while it provided clear advantages to the employers, it also meant that key workers were effectively setting the intensity of the work rhythm, delimiting the areas of skill and, hence, reward.

In industries where work was more confined, as in workshops and factories, close supervision by foremen was favoured as means of imposing discipline and pushing the workforce to more effort. The foreman performed most of the major tasks of management; he was an organiser, responsible for hiring and firing, as well as the production process; and he was also a quality controller in the absence of such a workplace specialist.[36] The foreman was an authority figure too, embodying the social and economic power of capital. His power is well-illustrated in a letter to a building trade journal, which claimed that

> In nine out of ten establishments, one man – the foreman – has supreme control, and can employ or discharge whomsoever he thinks fit ... By the present working system, a foreman who has supreme control over 50 or 60 men can add to his salary by receiving weekly pay from inferior hands, who are always ready to tender the bribe in return for being kept in constant work.[37]

It would appear that the locus of authority in a number of occupations was not homogeneous. Authority was dispersed within the complexity of occupational structures and this, as Joyce points out, created within the worker "an indistinct notion of the capitalist employer ... as a class, let alone the major class enemy".[38] The social and economic antagonisms of the worker could be spread over a range of authority figures including the employer, foreman, piece master, subcontractor and the ganger, rather than focused on an individual. Therefore, not only were the workplace relations enmeshed in a complex web of group and personal loyalties, but the easing of the rate of technological advance, combined with changes in work organisation, and the division of labour, meant that employers did not exercise total autonomy in the workplace. Moreover, the dependence of capital on the skills of their workers heightened and made real the notion of worker independence and pride.

Independence was derived from a number of interlocking factors which included traditionally inherited ideas of skill as a definition of one's property and status, craft customs and the ownership of tools. As Hobsbawm points out, the latter not only advertised the "relative independence of the artisan from management, but, even more clearly, his monopoly of skilled work".[39] In the building trade, bricklayers' labourers were not allowed to use the trowel; Edinburgh stonemasons let their hammers fall without striking if time was called as a symbolic assertion of their right to control their own pace of work.[40] Even in the newer trades of boilermaking and engineering workers developed a complex system of rituals and ceremonies to impress upon members the importance of craft pride and solidarity. The customs of the trade were maintained through the operation of a process of socialisation based on kinship networks. The practice of sons following fathers into a trade as their "birthright" ensured the transmission of certain customary practices regarding such important issues as workloads and differentials.[41]

Working Class Culture

These socio-economic factors and the values which they engendered in workers had important implications for lifestyle and political and trade union consciousness. They were an essential part of what Fraser has called the mid-Victorian labour movement's "search for respectability".[42]

Respectability was based on a series of social and economic supports including regular earnings and employment, sobriety and thrift. While the fluctuating fortunes of the Scottish economy could not always guarantee the former, there seems clear evidence that many workers and their families subscribed to some negotiated form of the latter. The mid-Victorian labour movement in Scotland, unlike in England, introduced the practice of holding meetings in coffee shops rather than public houses.[43] This also applied to the loosely federated trades councils which emerged in the post-1850 period. The

Edinburgh Trades Council (ETC) met in a coffee house from its inception until 1867 and then for the next twenty years in a temperance hotel.[44] Teetotalism, although with a large subscribing middle class membership, was still largely based on skilled workers and their families.[45] The Independent Order of Good Templars (1869) and the Independent Order of Rechabites were the largest temperance societies in Scotland, with the former's Airdrie branch being the biggest temperance lodge in the world.[46]

The growth of temperance societies and the involvement of artisans in them underscored a cultural shift from the concerns of work to the concerns of the family and home life. Shorter hours of work, particularly from the 1870s, allowed workers more time to spend with their families; a development encouraged by bargaining around the concept of the "family wage". Leisure pursuits such as the day excursion, membership of bowling and golf clubs, mechanics' institutes, volunteer societies, and so on, became more common for workers, and constituted, as Gray notes, a rejection of "certain aspects of the older popular culture, especially drinking customs".[47] Moreover, some of the societies were set up or directly sponsored by the employers, particularly the mutual improvement societies and the mechanics' institutes. Volunteer companies tended to reinforce the authority relations of the workplace. In the integrated coal and iron companies of Lanarkshire, Volunteer Companies were set up in which the managers were the officers, the foremen the non-commissioned officers, and the colliers the privates.[48] Regardless of origin, leisure pursuits had to be afforded and this necessitated commitment to the virtues of thrift. The mid-Victorian decades witnessed the growth of savings banks and co-operative societies as institutions of working class self-help. Savings banks had a preponderance of stonemasons, joiners and engineers among their depositors.[49] Similarly, those workers involved in the co-operative movement in the late 1850s and early 1860s were mainly of the artisan or skilled class.[50]

Although these values were hallmarks of a bourgeois lifestyle, they were sufficiently ambiguous to be open to a variety of interpretations. As Gray points out, "these values and norms were reinterpreted within the upper working class' social world; their meaning might change as they became embroidered in distinctive manual working class institutions".[51]

The meaning the skilled workers attached to the "values and norms" derived from their social and economic concerns and fears. Temperance made sense in as much as marginal income and working time spent in drinking endangered the position of the family as a viable unit and possibly one's life chances. Thrift was necessary for a number of reasons; firstly, to survive periods of distress and illness in a pre-welfare society; secondly, to set aside for the buying and replacement of lost or worn out tools; and, thirdly, to pay the yearly or half-yearly collection of rents.

Although functional in some respects, respectability was a divisive cultural force among workers and made for an understanding between workers and higher social classes. Temperance was based, as we have seen, on an alliance between the petty bourgeoisie and the skilled working class. Its basic premise was that working class poverty was the result of drink, rather than the inadequacies of the free market economy. Such assumptions were shared, at a later date, by socialists such as Keir Hardie; however, in this period it made poverty an individual problem and encouraged ideas of self-help.

Religion also made for all sorts of understandings between the various social classes of Scottish society. Although the majority of workers were not church-going, Brown has convincingly demonstrated that skilled workers figured highly in the congregations of the non-established churches.[52] The United Presbyterians and the Free Church increasingly drew their ministry from the ranks of the petty bourgeoisie and skilled workers.[53] Freemasonry also performed a similar function. By 1879 the Masonic Order in Scotland was estimated to have just over 69,000 members in lodges affiliated to the Grand Lodge and over a thousand in dormant lodges. With its distinguished patrons, including members of the royal family, and high entry fees and annual subscriptions, the Order had a strong artisan and middle class membership.[54] However, even for those workers who did not attend church on a regular basis, or joined the eminently respectable Masonic Order, religion played an important part in the vital moments in their lives through baptism, marriage and death.

The message of religion was brotherly love, the rich helping the poor, the weak the strong, and other homilies which strengthened existing social relationships. These were further enhanced by the all-pervasive sectarianism of Scottish society and its virulent anti-Catholicism. Helen Crawfurd, daughter of a small bakery owner, and, later, a suffragette and member of the Independent Labour Party, recalled in her autobiography that she looked "upon the Fenian and Catholic Irish as sub-human".[55] David Kirkwood, of later "Red Clydeside" fame, said that when growing up in Glasgow he felt "that it would be untrue to say we were one people. Religion and race ... kept us apart".[56]

Such views had a long history; however, although Catholicism had long been held in antipathy by Scottish presbyterianism, sectarianism did not become institutionalised in labour markets until after the Irish famine of 1845. From the 1790s there had been a steady stream of migrant labourers from Ireland to the mainland, particularly at harvest time. However, their object was not to form permanent communities, but to earn money to supplement household income in Ireland. The Famine changed all this with large numbers of Irish workers coming to Scotland in search of work and accommodation. The better off used Scotland as a staging post between the mainland and the United States; therefore, it was the poorer Irish peasant who settled and swelled the already growing numbers of impoverished rural migrants, particularly in the west of Scotland. Slaven puts half the increase in the populations of Glasgow and Lanarkshire between 1801 and 1861 down to immigration.[57] In 1841 the percentage of Irish born in Glasgow was 16 per cent of total population, or 44,000 out of 274,000, and this momentum was sustained until the 1860s when it began to slow.

Although slowing over the time, immigration became based more on Protestants than Catholics. In 1831 it was estimated that in Glasgow out of a total Irish born population of 35,534, the Catholic Irish numbered 26,965. However, in the years 1876–81 by far the greater number of migrants were from Ulster. Out of a total of 42,297 migrants from Ireland 83.2 per cent, or 35,194, were from nine Ulster counties, with 58.7 per cent coming from the four most Prostestant counties, that is, Antrim, Armagh, Down and Tyrone.[58]

Most of the Catholic immigrants found their way into unskilled occupations in spinning factories, coal mines, iron works and numerous casual labouring jobs. In 1851 in Greenock 52 per cent of the unskilled workers were of Irish origin; over fifty years later the proportion was virtually the same.[59]

Coming from a subsistence culture, these immigrants were prepared to work for less than the going rate and this created tensions between them and the indigenous working population. As some were used as strikebreakers relations in some communities, particularly mining, were embittered. Campbell, in his study of the Lanarkshire coalfields, argues that sectarian incidents were most frequent in the years 1850 to 1875, the period of the highest Irish immigration into the industry.[60] Airdrie miners went on strike in 1854 "until all the Roman Catholics should be expelled".[61] During the 1850s the Free Collier Movement, which had emerged in response to the failure of mining unionism, alienated Irish Catholics as it adopted an aggressive Protestant stance. The rituals and symbols were based on the Masonic Order, most of the lodges had chaplains, and there was evidence of Orange influence.[62]

The incoming numbers of Protestant Irish, mainly into the skilled trades, also saw the beginning of the links between sections of the labour movement and the Orange Order in Scotland. The Boilermakers' society in Airdrie met in the Orange Hall, as did the Bakers. The Coatbridge Orange Hall was used as a meeting place by the Amalgamated Society of Engineers (ASE) between 1877 and 1931, and did not have a single Catholic member until the 1930s.[63] In the skilled metal trades of the Clyde Irish Catholics were confined to lowly labouring tasks, while the Protestant Scots monopolised the skilled work through the workings of patronage and the foreman's right to hire and fire. Employers generally colluded in this practice or adopted a position of benign neglect. However, some did adopt an openly hostile position to Irish Catholics. The iron and coal magnate, William Baird, closed his Gartsherrie works in Lanarkshire on Sundays to allow workers to attend church and encouraged strong Orange sympathies among them. The response of the Irish was to withdraw into their community which centred on the church and the reactionary priesthood. As Walker points out "the Catholic Church created an entire way of life based upon the parish church, school and church hall".[64]

Religion was also instrumental in creating an ideological construct in which the subordinate role of women in Scottish society and the workplace could be justified. It was part of the Victorian idea of domesticity in which home and work were viewed as separate spheres. Woman's role was seen as increasingly home-centred and this allowed male workers to bargain around the idea of the family wage. Waged work for married women became rare outside the domestic or sweated trades by 1850. Out of a total workforce in Scottish textiles of 59,314 in 1839 40,868 were female, and of these 43 per cent were under eighteen.[65] Much of women's work was an extension of domestic roles with 90 per cent of them in 1841 employed in domestic service, agriculture, clothing and textiles. The low level of skill and the predominantly young and single nature of those in employment justified employers paying less than a man. Where women were able to make inroads into skilled employment such as compositing exclusionist practices among the male unionised workers prevented them from making a living. Sex like religion was used to police the boundaries of skill. But workplace patriarchy and the masculine culture of the skilled worker also, as Joyce points out, created the basis for "all sorts of understanding with employers (a 'boss' in his sphere as was the worker in his home and work functions)".[66] Although the role of patriarchy has not been fully explored in the context of Scottish workplace relations, its existence points to an important source of working class fragmentation.

The development of the mid-Victorian labour movement in Scotland has to be seen in the context of a restructuring of working class employment and lifestyle, as well as values. It should not be assumed that the working class had become embourgeoisified as what was internalised from the dominant ideology was subject to a filtering process which fitted the realities of working lives. The question which arises from these observations on occupation, skill and values is how did they alter relations between social classes in the terrain of economic and political activity?

Mid-Victorian Trade Unionism

Trade unions and class conflict existed in the first half of the nineteenth century, particularly in the heavily capitalised coal and cotton industries, but they exhibited a dual character. Pre-industrial forms of behaviour during labour disputes included the use of violence, ceremonies, signs and symbols of a mystical kind. When a young collier achieved the status of "full man" he was made a "brother" at a ceremony in which he was asked to swear an oath of secrecy on the bible. In return, he was initiated into the mysteries of the collier's trade, including passwords, signs and grips.[67] During industrial disputes ear-cropping was a popular method of disciplining blacklegs in the mining industry; and in the cotton industry the throwing of vitriol, industrial sabotage and violence, including murder, were used on occasion.

However, accompanying these pre-industrial acts of protest, were recognisably modern forms of worker organisation and activity. Trade societies had visible leaders, an administrative structure of membership cards and dues, meeting places and regular conferences. These elements of modern trade unionism triumphed during the mid-Victorian period. An immediate boost to the latter form of organisation was provided by the failure of the cotton spinners strike of 1837 which discredited violence and inflicted a crushing blow on Scottish trade unionism. The defeat of the spinners encouraged Scottish workers to seek a more acceptable and respectable form of conduct and organisation. This was reflected in the decline of the practice of holding union meetings in public houses.

This shift in attitudes and behaviour on labour's part has allowed the third quarter of the nineteenth century to be seen by virtue of the Webbs monumental history of trade unionism – *The History of Trade Unionism* (1920 ed.) – as the period of "new model" unionism. The archetypal examples of this form of unionism were the ASE and the Amalgamated Society of Carpenters and Joiners. In contrast to the aggressive trade unionism of the 1830s and 40s these new unions were seen by the Webbs as models of pacific, bourgeois-minded behaviour, eschewing the strike weapon and seeking to conciliate rather than confront employers. This change of outlook was accompanied by the centralisation of organisation, the creation of sound financial structures and the payment of friendly society benefits rather than strike pay. These unions were almost wholly the creation of skilled workers thought to be indifferent to the problems of organising the unskilled.

The Webbs' construct of "new model" unionism has been effectively rejected by leading English labour historians, who have demonstrated that the mode of organisation and the concentration on day-to-day issues at the expense of wider socio-political concerns existed among craft workers even during the Chartist era.[68] The Scottish experience would also tend to contradict the views of the Webbs. Far from being models of centralised institutions Scottish unions were highly localised and fiercely independent organisations. Although we have no reliable figures for union membership in the mid-Victorian period, R.H. Campbell, drawing on the work of the Webbs, estimates that of 147,000 trade unionists in 1892 two-thirds were organised in exclusively Scottish unions.[69]

On the Clyde alone it was estimated that there were a hundred unions active in the early years of the twentieth century. Only 21 of them could claim 500 or more members locally; 37 claimed less than 100.[70] Even the archetypal "model" unions such as the ASE exercised little control over the activities of their branches. In the case of the latter this is hardly surprising as it was not until 1892 that the executive of the ASE was elected on a district basis. Previous to this it was composed of representatives of the Society's London members. Scottish trade unionism was thus based on local associations exercising wide powers of autonomy on questions of pay and conditions in sharp contrast to the bureaucratic centralised model put forward by the Webbs.

The bureaucratic approach of the Webbs also fails to recognise that it was the immediate work group rather than the union branch which was the primary unit of organisation in industry during this period. Price has calculated that about 50 per cent of restrictions imposed at the workplace in the engineering industry in the 1860s emerged out of "informal workgroup decisions rather than from shop steward or union policies". In the building industry when employers spoke of "conspiracies" they were often, claims Price, referring to workgroup action rather than trade unionism.[71] Informal trade unionism was perhaps a more appropriate method of organisation given the volatility of the Scottish economy. The boom and bust cycle of nineteenth-century economic development made continuity of organisation problematical. Unionisation was so completely smashed in the coalfields in the 1860s that the miners formed the quasi-mystical Free Collier Movement. Organisation was also fragile in other trades. After the failure of the nine hour strike on the Clyde in 1866 union membership collapsed and two years later the Boilermakers' society was reduced to 156 members in Scotland concentrated in nine branches, the largest being Glasgow No 2 branch with 41 members, and the smallest Paisley with only two members. The weakness of the Boilermakers' society meant that 90 per cent of shipyard workers on the Clyde were unorganised.[72] Unskilled workers understandably found the establishment of viable institutions more difficult to sustain, as did women who were doubly disadvantaged as low paid workers and as wives and mothers reduced to a dependent status. Labourers' unions affiliated to the Glasgow Trades Council (GTC) in the 1860s and 1870s but were wiped out in periods of depression.[73]

Continuity of organisation, therefore, proved difficult even for skilled workers and this enhanced informal workgroup organisation. However, did union weakness encourage a more conciliationist approach to industrial relations by workers and their organisations in mid-Victorian Scotland?

On the face of it there does seem to be strong evidence to suggest that craft and mining unions were actively conciliationist. Presidents of the branches of the Boilermakers' society informed new recruits that "We are not united to set class against class but to teach one another that men are all brothers. Our greatest desire being to cultivate a close and lasting relationship between all those with whom we have to do with in undertaking our daily work".[74]

Moreover, the rule book of the Society allowed members who became small employers, publicans, or members of the managerial staff to remain in the union as honorary members.[75] Miners in the west of Scotland saw strikes as a last resort and the union rule book "emphasised that strikes tended to fail and that collaboration was to be preferred".[76] Midlothian miners shared this view and the United Association of Colliers urged other miners to adopt the "rules and regulations enforced by the Duke of Buccleugh at Dalkeith Colliery".[77]

The degree of craft pacifism was somewhat exaggerated by trade union leaders. Strikes took place in most trades, although more frequently in mining than in any others. Drawing on the work of Wilson on the west of Scotland mining industry, it would appear that major strikes took place on average every four or five years between 1850 and 1874. The longest strike took place in 1856 and involved twelve districts and 15,000 workers for fourteen weeks. However, there were 24 stoppages of a short duration between 1855 and 1874. The cause of these strikes was almost always reductions in pay.[78] Similarly, in shipbuilding prolonged strikes, outside of the 1866 nine hours' strike, occurred during downturns in trade in 1874, 1876 and 1878. In the construction industry, wage demands were the major cause of strikes between 1850 and 1880, although the issue of the labour supply was also important.[79]

Thus conflict was still written into the relationship between capital and labour, but it had undergone a transformation. From issues concerned with the control of the labour process, unions increasingly concerned themselves with the price of labour and the regulation of the supply of it. Market principles were recognised as determining the wage rate rather than custom or morality. The sliding-scale in the mining industry agreed to by miners' leaders is a good example of these changing attitudes. Making the best of the wage/effort bargain, also signalled labour's recognition of the permanency of the industrial order. Moreover, since much of the industrial conflict, whether conducted by the organised or unorganised, was sectional or, at the very best, occupationally-based, and involved only a minority of workers, class interests were subordinated to the concerns of the locality and the immediate workgroup. Care has to be exercised by historians in reading too much into acts of labour protest. While the frequency of protest demonstrates the existence of an oppositional workplace culture, the economism of its demands, that is, better pay and working conditions, can be accommodated within the prevailing set of social relations. On the other hand, class consciousness transforms immediate demands into a wider political struggle for control of the state and the establishment of a new socio-economic order. There is little evidence to show that Scottish workers saw a connection between the economic and the political struggle, or that industrial relations were subject to increasing politicisation in this period. Among the organised workers the belief in self-help made it unlikely; among the unorganised dependency and weakness individualised protest and made organisation inevitably *ad hoc*.

Faced with sectional and sectarian divisions within the working class, and confronted by a self-confident industrial bourgeoisie, the unions of this period were, not surprisingly, weak and fragmented. Indeed, it is clear that many workers, particularly women, saw them as irrelevant to their social situation. The high subscriptions in a low wage economy also made them seem exclusive to the best paid workers, with even those in skilled trades not always able to afford union dues. Membership of the Boilermakers' society was held back by this factor in the late 1860s as shipyard workers on 17s.-24s. per week found it difficult to pay 4s. a month in subscriptions.[80] Furthermore, those workers occupying tied accommodation were often too dependent on their employer to risk joining an organisation proscribed by an employer who was also their landlord. Thus as late as 1892 trade union membership in Scotland amounted to only 3.7 per cent of the total population, compared to 4.9 per cent for England and Wales. Even in the capital goods sector, where union density was higher, it was rarely more than 25 per cent of the workforce.[81]

Workers and Politics in Mid-Victorian Scotland

The absence of a strong trade union movement made the emergence of an independent working class party unlikely in this period. Experience shows that without the members and the financial assistance provided by the trade unions, working class parties rarely succeed in attracting mass support or sustaining their organisation. In our period the problem of class representation was further complicated as it was not until 1867 that the urban male working class was enfranchised. Exclusion from the system of parliamentary politics made it difficult to conceptualise independent working class representation. Even the language in which the demand for the vote was articulated was drawn from the dominant ideology. And after 1867 those workers who gained the vote thought in terms of Gladstonian Liberalism rather than some variant of popular radicalism or socialism.

Chartism had failed to deliver the vote to the workers in spite of repeated petitioning and demonstration. The struggle for democracy continued after Chartism collapsed as a national movement in 1848. However, it was the "moral" rather than the "physical" aspect of Chartism's political practice which dominated the language and strategy of the democratic struggle. Labour argued that the denial of the vote was wrong because it disregarded "the growing virtue and intelligence of the working class".[82] It also allowed parliament to be dominated by class interests which led to the passing of "unjust and tyrannical piece[s] of modern class legislation", such as the Master and Servant Laws.[83] These were the arguments used in the GTC's *Address to the Working Men of the United Kingdom* in 1861. Spokesmen for the workers, therefore, articulated their demands within prevailing notions of respectability. The demand for household suffrage excluded the slum dwellers and other undesirable elements of the working class. What the articulate among the workers wanted was to be part of the major institutions of British society, in spite of the fact that they had no hand in shaping them. Once enfranchised their political moderation was emphasised in their support of the Liberal Party.

This should not be interpreted as simple incorporation with all the connotations of conspiracy, or sell out by the leaders, that such a concept conveys. The politics of the working class were the outcome of their own experiences in the workplace and wider society. They were not simply attempts to imitate the middle classes. If anything they can best be described as independent and hostile to any attempts by the middle class to patronise them. This independence was born out of the place of the worker in the system of production and in the occupational hierarchy. The emphasis on individual effort through the payments systems, the transferability of his skills, his ownership of tools, as well as the authority exercised over other workers, created a strong sense of independence among skilled workers. These feelings transferred themselves to the field of politics. Workers in Glasgow set up the Glasgow Liberal Workingmen's Electoral Union (GLWEU) because of the GTC's distrust of middle class Liberal politics in the city. When the latter formed the Glasgow Liberal Association in 1878 the GLWEU refused to participate in it as it saw the organisation as a front for middle class domination of the Liberal Party in Glasgow. Another source of tension was the failure of the Liberals to appoint working class candidates at election times, which led to Keir Hardie contesting the Mid-Lanark by-election in 1888.

Independence also permeated working class notions regarding the role of the state. The interventionist state was not something to be welcomed in working class circles. As most workers only had experience of the repressive side of the state through the police or the poor laws, extension of state powers was opposed even by the unskilled and lumpen poor. The organised workers were also afraid that interference in the economy might erode free collective bargaining. Henry Tait, secretary of the Amalgamated Society of Railway Servants, captured the fears of the unions of such a prospect, when he argued that state intervention was unnecessary to solve the problem of overwork on the railways, arguing that "self-action is best suited for the case".[84] The manifest faith workers had in free trade as the best guarantee of rising living standards strengthened such convictions.

What motivated the worker politically was the desire to have equal rights with capital. Once enfranchised the state showed a willingness to deal with working class grievances in this respect. Not only was the vote granted in

1867, but the major impediments to the legal status of trade unions were formally abolished under the Trade Union Act of 1871, the repeal of the Criminal Law Amendment Act and the Master and Servant Laws in 1875. Moreover, the Disraeli government introduced a number of important social reforms, not the least being the Cross Act of 1875 which empowered local authorities to acquire and clear whole districts of slum housing, and to provide new housing for slum dwellers. Although these reforms did not encourage workers to vote Tory in Scotland, it proved to them that the political system was responsive to their needs. Resolution of conflict could be achieved within a plural democratic framework in which the state could maintain the appearance of being class neutral.

Conclusion

It was the Liberal Party under Gladstone which, with its emphasis on free trade, self-help and respectability, resonated most with working class aspirations and interests in the period. The utopias of Owenite associations of free producers, the various experiments in guild socialism and other mutualist enterprises crumbled under the weight of rising living standards and occupational change. Respectability was within the grasp of the skilled workers at least, and leisure patterns reflected this. Industrial capitalism acquired a permanency which was recognised by the Scottish workers, many of whom owed their livelihood to the new industries created by it. In recognition of this acceptance the state enfranchised the workers and showed itself, through various social reforms, to be responsive to their needs. Although disenchantment with Liberalism was to grow later in the century and, especially after the First World War, the labour movement in Scotland accepted democratic pluralism as a permanent part of its ideological baggage. The seeds of a reformist Labour Party were sown in this period of transition in working class life.

Notes

I would like to thank Alan MacKinlay and Chris Whatley, as well as the editors, for reading and commenting on my essay. They, of course, bear no responsibility for any errors or misinterpretations on the author's part.

1. R.Q. Gray, *The Labour Aristocracy in Victorian Edinburgh* (Oxford, 1976); J. Foster, *Class Struggle and the Industrial Revolution* (London, 1974); E.J. Hobsbawm, *Labouring Men* (London, 1968).

2. R.Q. Gray, *The Labour Aristocracy in Nineteenth Century Britain* (London, 1981).
3. A. Wilson, *The Chartist Movement In Scotland* (Manchester, 1970), 103; T. Clarke, "Early Chartism in Scotland: a Moral Force Movement?", in T.M. Devine (ed.), *Conflict and Stability in Scottish Society, 1700–1850* (Edinburgh, 1990), 10–20.
4. N. Murray, *The Scottish Handloom Weavers* (Edinburgh, 1978), 232.
5. T.C. Smout, *A Century of the Scottish People, 1832–1950* (London, 1986), ch.10.
6. T. Clarke and T. Dickson, "Class and Class Consciousness in Early Industrial Capitalism: Paisley, 1770–1850", in T. Dickson (ed.), *Capital and Class in Scotland* (Edinburgh, 1982), 14; W.H. Fraser, "The Glasgow Cotton Spinners, 1837", in J. Butt and J.T. Ward (ed.), *Scottish Themes* (Edinburgh, 1976), 81–2; J. Butt, "The Scottish Cotton Industry during the Industrial Revolution, 1780–1840", in L.M. Cullen and T.C. Smout (ed.), *Comparative Aspects of Scottish and Irish Economic and Social History* (Edinburgh, 1977), 123.
7. S. and O. Checkland, *Industry and Ethos: Scotland, 1832–1914* (London, 1984), 19.
8. E. Knox, "The Petty Bourgeoisie in Victorian Edinburgh", (Unpublished PhD, University of Edinburgh, 1986), 28.
9. Checklands, *Industry and Ethos*, 22; A. Slaven, *The Development of the West of Scotland, 1750–1960* (London, 1975), 178.
10. A.B. Campbell, *The Lanarkshire Miners: a Social History of their Trade Unions, 1775–1884* (Edinburgh, 1979), 101–2; Checklands, *Industry and Ethos*, 24–5.
11. *Ibid.*, 25; Slaven, *Development*, 120–1.
12. *Ibid.*, 21.
13. Gray, *Labour Aristocracy Edinburgh*, 38–9.
14. R. Rodger, "Concentration and Fragmentation: Capital, Labour and the Structure of mid-Victorian Scottish Industry", *Journal of Urban History*, 14 (1988), 186–7, 207.
15. J.H. Treble, "The Occupied Male Labour Force", in W.H. Fraser and R.J. Morris (ed.), *People and Society in Scotland, Vol. 2, 1830–1914* (Edinburgh, 1990), 195–8.
16. Checklands, *Industry and Ethos*, 28–9.
17. Campbell, *Lanarkshire Miners*, 109–13.
18. K. Burgess, "Workshop of the World: Client Capitalism at its Zenith, 1830–1870", in T. Dickson (ed.), *Scottish Capitalism: Class, State and Nation from before the Union to the Present* (London, 1980), 223.
19. I. Levitt and T.C. Smout, *The State of the Scottish Working Class in 1843* (Edinburgh, 1979), 115–7.
20. Burgess, "Workshop of the World", 196.
21. Return of Wages, PPLXXXIX, 1887, 145.
22. Burgess, "Workshop of the World", 223.
23. Return of Wages, 384–5.
24. *Ibid.*, 31.
25. *Ibid.*, 218–9.
26. *Ibid.*, 284, 299.
27. Checklands, *Industry and Ethos*, 22.
28. M. Anderson and D.J. Morse, "The People", in Fraser and Morris (ed.), *People and Society*, 15.
29. P. Joyce, *Work, Society and Politics: the Culture of the Factory in later Victorian England* (London, 1980).
30. J.A. Hassan, "The Landed Estate, Paternalism and the Coal Industry in Midlothian", *Scottish Historical Review*, 59 (1980), 86–7.
31. D. Weir, *The Coats' Story*, (4 vols., unpublished bound typescript, Coats Vyella, Glasgow, 1964) i, 73.
32. Campbell, *Lanarkshire Miners*, 105–9.

33. R. Duncan, *Conflict and Crisis: Monklands Miners and General Strike 1842* (Glasgow, 1982), 6–7.
34. Campbell, *Lanarkshire Miners*, 155–6.
35. *Ibid.*, 34; P.L. Robertson, "Demarcation Disputes in British Shipbuilding before 1914", *International Review of Social History*, 20 (1975), 225–6; J. Lynch, "Skilled and Unskilled Labour in the Shipbuilding Trade", *Report of the Proceedings of the Industrial Renumeration Conference* (London, 1885), 114–5.
36. K. Burgess, "Authority Relations and the Division of Labour in British Industry, with special reference to Clydeside", *Social History*, 11 (1986), 215.
37. *Builder*, 10 October 1870, 789.
38. P. Joyce, "Labour, Capital and Compromise: a response to Richard Price", *Social History*, 9 (1984), 71–2.
39. E.J. Hobsbawm, "Artisan or Labour Aristocrat?", *Economic History Review*, 37 (1984), 365–6.
40. R.J. Morris, "Skilled Work and the Politics of the 'Red Clyde' ", *Journal of the Scottish Labour Society*, 18 (1983), 8.
41. W.W. Knox, "British Apprenticeship, 1800–1914" (Unpublished PhD, University of Edinburgh, 1980), 176–94.
42. W.H. Fraser, "Cotton Spinners", 97.
43. J.D. Young, *The Rousing of the Scottish Working Class* (London, 1979), 144.
44. I. MacDougall, "Introduction", *The Minutes of the Edinburgh Trades Council, 1859–1893* (Edinburgh, 1968), vi.
45. D.C. Paton, "Drink and the Temperance Movement in Nineteenth Century Scotland" (Unpublished PhD, University of Edinburgh, 1977), 394.
46. E. King, *Scotland, Sober and Free: the Temperance Movement, 1829–1979* (Glasgow, 1979), 16.
47. Gray, *Labour Aristocracy Edinburgh*, 100.
48. Campbell, *Lanarkshire Miners*, 224.
49. R.Q. Gray, "Thrift and Class Mobility in Victorian Edinburgh", in A.A. MacLaren (ed.), *Social Class in Scotland: Past and Present* (Edinburgh, 1976), 130–1.
50. J. Kinloch and J. Butt, *The History of the Scottish Co-operative Wholesale Society Limited* (Manchester, 1981), 121.
51. Gray, "Thrift", 138.
52. C.G. Brown, *The Social History of Religion in Scotland since 1730* (London, 1987), 165.
53. A.L. Drummond and J. Bulloch, *The Church in Late Victorian Scotland, 1874–1900* (Edinburgh, 1978), 145.
54. E. McFarland, *Protestants First: Orangeism in 19th Century Scotland* (Edinburgh, 1990), 111.
55. H. Crawfurd, *Unpublished Autobiography* (Marx Memorial Library, London, n.d.), 13.
56. D. Kirkwood, *My Life of Revolt* (London, 1935), 60.
57. Slaven, *Development*, 141.
58. McFarland, *Protestants First*, 104.
59. Brown, *History of Religion*, 163–4.
60. Campbell, *Lanarkshire Miners*, 184–5.
61. G.M. Wilson, "The Strike Policy of the Miners of the West of Scotland", in I. MacDougall (ed.), *Essays in Scottish Labour History* (Edinburgh, 1979), 35.
62. Campbell, *Lanarkshire Miners*, 281–3.
63. McFarland, *Protestants First*, 86.
64. W.M. Walker, *Jutetopolis: Dundee and its Textile Workers, 1885–1923* (Edinburgh, 1979), 55–6.
65. E. Gordon, "Women's Spheres", in Fraser and Morris (ed.), *People and Society*, 207.

66. Joyce, "Labour, Capital and Compromise", 75.
67. Campbell, *Lanarkshire Miners*, 41–2.
68. A.E. Musson, *British Trade Unions, 1800–1875* (London, 1972), 50–1; Gray, *Labour Aristocracy Edinburgh*, 45–6.
69. R.H. Campbell, *Scotland since 1707* (Oxford, 1965), 313–5.
70. D.C. Unger, "The Roots of Red Clydeside: Economic and Social Relations and Working Class Politics in the West of Scotland" (Unpublished PhD, University of Edinburgh, 1979), 257–8.
71. R. Price, *Masters, Unions and Men* (Cambridge, 1980), 62.
72. J.E. Mortimer, *History of the Boilermakers' Society, vol. i, 1834–1906* (London, 1973), 68.
73. W.H. Fraser, "Trades Councils in the Labour Movement in Nineteenth Century Scotland", in MacDougall (ed.), *Essays in Labour History*, 6–7.
74. Mortimer, *Boilermakers*, Appendix 1, 200.
75. A. Reid, "The Division of Labour in the British Shipbuilding Industry, 1880–1920: with special reference to Clydeside" (Unpublished PhD, University of Cambridge, 1980), 205.
76. Wilson, *Chartism*, 44–5.
77. Hassan, "The Landed Estate", 81–2.
78. Wilson, *Chartism*, 32; R.P. Arnott, *A History of the Scottish Miners from the Earliest Times* (London, 1955), 40–56.
79. Price, *Masters, Unions and Men*, 86.
80. Mortimer, *Boilermakers*, 6.
81. H. Southall, "Unionization", in J. Langton and R.J. Morris (ed.), *Atlas of Industrializing Britain, 1780–1914* (London, 1986), 189–93.
82. Gray, *Labour Aristocracy Edinburgh*, 156–7.
83. Webb Collection of Trade Unions, British Library of Political and Economic Science, London, vol.xi, ff. 271–3.
84. Amalgamated Society of Railway Servants, *Slavery on the Scottish Railways* (Glasgow, 1884), 12.

List of Contributors

DR. STEPHEN BOARDMAN held the Glenfiddich Research Fellowship in Scottish History at St. Andrews from 1989 to 1992. He is now a British Academy Post-Doctoral Fellow in the Department of Scottish History, and is currently completing a book on the reigns of Robert II and Robert III

DR. KEITH BROWN, now a lecturer in History at the University of Stirling, is a former Glenfiddich Research Fellow at St. Andrews where he also held post-doctoral fellowships from the British Academy and the Royal Society of Edinburgh. He is the author of *Bloodfeud in Scotland 1573–1625* (1986) and is currently writing a more general study of 17th century Scottish politics and society.

DR. JANE DAWSON is a former Glenfiddich Research Fellow at St. Andrews, and is now John Laing Lecturer in the History and Theology of the Reformation, New College, University of Edinburgh. She is the author of numerous articles on 16th century Scottish and British history and is currently writing a book on *Gaelic Lordship and British Politics: The Career of the 5th Earl of Argyll (c. 1530–73)*.

DR. WILLIAM KNOX lectures in Scottish History at St. Andrews, specialising in modern social and economic history. He has written extensively on labour history, including a biography of James Maxton. He is currently researching into the Scottish cotton industry in the period 1850–1914.

DR. NORMAN MACDOUGALL is senior lecturer in Scottish History at St. Andrews. His main research interests are late medieval Scottish government and society, and he has published biographies of Kings James III and James IV.

DR. COLIN MARTIN has specialised in shipwreck archaeology since the late 1960s, and with his colleagues discovered the wreck of the *Adelaar* off Barra in 1972. In 1983, together with Christopher Smout and Robert Prescott, he founded the Scottish Institute of Maritime Studies at St. Andrews, where he is a member of the Scottish History department.

DR. ROGER MASON is a former Glenfiddich Research Fellow at St. Andrews where he now lectures in the department of Scottish History. He has published extensively in the field of 16th century Scottish political thought and is currently researching the development of Scottish national consciousness in the late medieval and early modern periods.

DR. C.J.A. ROBERTSON is a lecturer in Economic and Social History at St. Andrews. His main research interest is in 19th century British transport and urban history and he is the author of *The Origins of the Scottish Railway System 1722–1844* (1983).

PROFESSOR DAVID STEVENSON lectured at the University of Aberdeen for 20 years before moving to St. Andrews in 1990. His obsession with early modern Scottish history has resulted in a number of books, including *The Scottish Revolution* (1973), *Revolution and Counter-Revolution in Scotland* (1978), *The Origins of Freemasonry* (1988) and *The First Freemasons* (1988).

DR. CHRISTOPHER A. WHATLEY, who now lectures in the Department of History at Dundee University, is a former member of the Scottish History Department at St. Andrews. He is the author of *The Scottish Salt Industry* (1987) and has edited and contributed to *John Galt 1779–1979* (1979), *The Remaking of "Juteopolis": Dundee 1891–1991* (1992) and (with I.L. Donnachie) *The Manufacture of Scottish History* (1992). His main research interests lie in 18th century Scottish social and economic history and he is currently working on popular protest in Scotland as well as a study of the linen and jute industries in Dundee.